The Untouchables of India

Robert Deliège

Translated from the French by Nora Scott

English edition
First published in 1999 by
Berg
Editorial offices:
150 Cowley Road, Oxford, OX4 1JJ, UK
70 Washington Square South, New York, NY 10012, USA

Originally published by Editions Imago as *Les Intouchables en Inde: Des castes d'exclus.*

Translated by Nora Scott.

Berg is the imprint of Oxford International Publishers Ltd.

Library of Congress Cataloging-in-Publication Data

A catalogue record for this book is available from the Library of Congress.

British Library Cataloguing-in-Publication Data

A catalogue record for this book is available from the British Library.

ISBN 1 85973 209 7 (Cloth)
1 85973 214 3 (Paper)

Printed in the United Kingdom by Biddles Ltd., Guildford.

Contents

Acknowledgements

Between January 1980 and 1982, I lived in India, where I spent one year in a Paraiyar untouchable village in Tamil Nadu. Since then my interest has focused on these most depressed categories of Indian society, and the present volume is, in a way, the outgrowth of this long period of research. It goes without saying that my work received the intellectual, moral or material encouragement of a number of individuals and institutions. The expression of my gratitude is not a mere formality. Although it would be impossible to list everyone who contributed to my intellectual life over this period, I recall with pleasure several Indian acquaintances, in particular, my long-time friend, Mr N. Thanappan. I also received support from numerous institutions, among which special mention must go to the Fonds National de la Recherche Scientifique, the Fondation Universitaire de Belgique, the British Council, the Fondation Émile Maxweiler of the Académie Royale de Belgique and the Banque Nationale de Belgique. Various colleagues and friends kindly read parts of the present work and gave me the benefit of their comments; I am thinking in particular of Lionel Caplan (School of Oriental and African Studies, University of London), Mark Holmström (University of East Anglia), Declan Quigley (Queen's University, Belfast) and Chris Fuller (London School of Economics); it is obvious that they are in no way responsible for any of the views expressed in the text. Finally, I thank Nora Scott for translating the book.

Preface to the English Edition

Although this book is fundamentally about the 150 million people who belong to the numerous untouchable castes of India, it is only marginally concerned with the present situation and struggle of those who are also variously known as Harijans, Scheduled Castes or Dalits. In a way, this book is above all about untouchability as it has been practised in Indian society from time immemorial. We cannot claim that nothing has changed in India and that untouchability exists in the same way as, for instance, in precolonial days. On the contrary, it has become a commonplace to recognize that Indian society is dynamic and changing rapidly. Pace the previous assumptions of Orientalist discourse, we further believe that there have always been changes within Indian society and that it is therefore misleading to think that there was once a kind of golden age, or even a classical age, a time when the whole society worked in a nicely balanced equilibrium or simply reflected what scholars could read in books. The position of Untouchables has changed over time and from region to region. Yet this does not mean that there is not a general problem of untouchability within the Indian social order. As social scientists, it is our aim to try to understand the phenomenon, and the present book is precisely an attempt to tackle some of the general features of untouchability.

I am well aware that such an attempt involves a good deal of simplification, as indeed any generalization does, and I will often try to nuance some of the general points that can be made. In a way, the picture we draw of untouchability resembles what Max Weber called an ideal type, a typified representation, a model that helps us to understand the social reality by emphasizing some of the most characteristic features of a phenomenon. For instance, the presentation of the various discriminations that were imposed on Untouchables for centuries clearly represents an ideal-typical portrait. At the same time, what is now going on in India cannot be understood without reference to the past, even where radical changes have since intervened. To take an example, one can recall the prohibition on entering Hindu temples. This was clearly a very general taboo that affected Untouchables all over India, and it is therefore interesting to present the general features of this prohibition. In a famous proclamation in 1936, the Maharaja of Travancore lifted this ban and threw the temples of his principality open to all classes. Other temples soon followed, and the Indian constitution, by making the public practice of untouchability illegal, put an end to the formal interdiction on entering temples. And indeed many of the Untouchables started going to the temples to worship. Yet it does not follow that Untouchables have thereby become Hindus like any others. They continue to be unwelcome in many local temples where their caste identity cannot be concealed, and they often do not like to go to temples, feeling shy or simply uninterested. Many militant activists claim today that the *dalits*, as they call them, are not Hindus at all and never have been. In other words, the formal prohibition of earlier times continues to account for many features and behaviours that can be observed in today's India; and therefore it seems to me important to conceive of untouchability in a general, let us say an ideal-typical, way. That is probably why I have not avoided the use of the 'ethnographic present', even though I hope that it will not mislead the reader into believing that nothing has changed in contemporary society. In other words, this perspective does not mean that untouchability is a timeless concept in any way; on the contrary, although this is not basically a historical study, I shall try, as far as I can, to review the various changes that Untouchables have undergone during the last century or so. Yet in spite of the many changes that Indian society and the Untouchables have experienced, there are still many people who live in a condition that is not far remote from the general, ideal-typical picture. Furthermore, untouchability is by no means a vestige of the past, a survival that will disappear in the near future. In the first decades following Independence, people could argue that caste and untouchability had had their day. This proved to be wishful thinking, however, and today caste has even become a major political issue.

In an article that came out after the publication of the French edition of this book and must be mentioned here, Simon Charsley[1] has rightly argued that Untouchables do not constitute a homogeneous category. I can only agree with such a statement, and I would even go further and say that this heterogeneity is an essential characteristic of untouchability. Untouchables were – and still are – divided into numerous castes and subcastes that reject any sense of intercaste solidarity. Undoubtedly, this endemic division has exacerbated the plight of the Untouchables, who have been largely unable to unite in order to take advantage of their demographic strength and translate their movements into an efficient socio-political expression. In recent decades, increasing socio-economic differences have largely reinforced this lack of unity: some castes have certainly progressed much more than others, and conversely this differentiation has produced new divergent economic and political interests. This lack of homogeneity does not mean that untouchability does not exist as a sociological problem. The fact that we assemble a great number of people under one heading does not rule out the recognition of some differences (sometimes significant ones). To take a more familiar example, the fact that we speak of 'old age' does not signify that it is easy to define what 'being old' means; still less that old people constitute a purely homogeneous category. Yet for many purposes, in economics, social work, sociology, politics and so forth, it is a very useful social category that allows us to comprehend a certain number of specific phenomena.

Since the initial (French) publication of the book (1995), increasing attention has been paid to '*dalit* activism' and the very name *dalit*, which, in 1981-2 and later in 1990, was totally unknown to the people I had worked with, has now become much more common, particularly among intellectuals and militant activists. As a matter of fact, it is gaining ground as some sort of politically correct way to refer to Untouchables. Meanwhile, the term 'Harijan' (children of God), which was coined by Gandhi, has become somewhat old-fashioned, and some people even claim that it is

1. S. Charsley, ' "Untouchable": What Is in a Name?'. *The Journal of the Royal Anthropological Institute*, 2, 1996, pp. 1-24.

insulting. Yet the people with whom I worked in Tamil Nadu used the term 'Harijan', as indeed do many other untouchable groups. I do not see any reason why it should be completely dropped or why we ought to feel guilty for using it from time to time. To the anthropologist, however, the word 'untouchable', which is hardly used at all by the people themselves, is perhaps the most neutral way to refer to these people. This concept, which is probably not to be taken literally, nevertheless implies a social relationship and is therefore sociologically interesting. I do not think that the word necessarily implies a view of the people as 'passive victims' of their oppression. I hope that it will be clear from the following pages that I just have the opposite conviction, and I have always admired the stubborn and unceasing efforts that these people made – and make – to improve their lot. It is true that there has been a strong tendency to represent Untouchables as helpless,[2] but this has nothing to do with the adoption of such and such a name. As we shall see, the terms used to designate Untouchables have never stopped changing; but this has little influence on the condition of the people and very little on their social status.

The *dalit* ideology, as it is now sometimes called, is more a contemporary political expression than a scientific category. The study of untouchability has always suffered from biases: the first theoreticians of caste studied it only through the sacred literature; somewhat later, the first anthropologists approached them from the high-caste villages in which they resided. As the Untouchables were poor, helpless, dependent and dominated, studying them has always been a problem, and was often undertaken through some intermediary. I fear that there is today a tendency, which to my mind is also a danger, to see the problem only through the eyes of *dalit* organizations. The temptation is great to focus on the latter, who are highly concentrated in urban areas and are led mainly by radical intellectuals who speak some English. To be sure, *dalit* activism is a respectable topic of research; yet one should not forget the millions, indeed the vast majority, who live in the villages. The representivity of the *dalit* organizations is far from being obvious to me, and I wonder whether they always represent the interests of the people. I also have reservations about those who claim to monopolize the right to speak on behalf of the Untouchables. On the whole, dalit organizations are an interesting development in the history of untouchability. Yet what they say and write is sometimes closer to myth than to history, and deserves to be considered as such: that is to say, as a recent political and limited expression of a struggle, not as any kind of final truth. Many of these groups merely represent their own members; and, in any case, the differences between the various groups are as deep as they are numerous, from some brand of Marxism to the worst type of old-fashioned casteism. I must say that I could find little of the *dalit* ideology and strategy among the villagers with whom I lived. Most of them simply wanted to lead a decent life and be normal Indian citizens. They did not see the rest of the society as radically different from themselves, and they were predominantly non-violent, even though they were no longer ready to tolerate the kind of vexations and discriminations that were formerly common.

2. For a criticism of such a view, see R. Deliège, 'In the Skin of an Untouchable?'. *Anthropology Today*, 14 (1998), pp. 14-16.

In the 1990s, a political party emerged in North India, more particularly in Uttar Pradesh. The Bahujan Samaj Party (BSP), led by Kanshi Ram, succeeded in winning more than 10 per cent of the vote in the various state elections that took place between 1989 and 1998. As this is a relatively recent phenomenon, I will say little about it, but I will take this opportunity to mention Mendelsohn and Vicziany's recent book,[3] which devotes a long discussion to the development of this party;[4] these authors consider that the party did not solve the problem of how to mobilize the scheduled castes.[5] Nevertheless, they also recognize that, by heading a government coalition in the State of Uttar Pradesh between 1995 and 1996, with one of its members, Mrs Mayavati, as Chief Minister, the BSP probably had a radicalizing impact upon the wider Scheduled Castes community.[6] It might well be that the BSP will become something more than a mere 'Chamar party'; but it is still too early to tell. The party will probably have to choose between becoming a kind of radical socialist organization recruiting on the basis of class and remaining a purely ethnic movement confined to some castes only, or, even worse, to a single caste. Some steps taken by Kanshi Ram seem to indicate that he wishes to move in the first direction and to attract all those, including Muslims, who wish to oppose 'Brahmin rule'. At the same time, he and Mayavati have consistently played the caste card, sometimes in a rather ruthless way. Moreover their recent alliance with the Hindu nationalists, the Bharatya Janata Party (BJP), renders the broadening of the social basis of the party quite fragile, and it is clear that the Chamars remain its most consistent supporters. Many in North India continue to refer to the BSP as the Chamar party, just as Ambedkar's parties were previously associated with the Mahar caste. Other untouchable castes are much less enthusiastic about it, and resent the Chamar dominance among the Scheduled Castes. In other words, it is not yet possible to say whether the recent developments will allow the party to overcome the traditional ineffectuality of untouchable movements, which have always been unable to unite different castes beyond the scope of some particular limited action, as we shall see later in this book.

The last recent development I would like to mention here is the transformation of Ambedkar into a kind of saintly figure. Whereas, until a few years ago, most Untouchables had hardly heard of him, this is clearly no longer the case today. Statues of Ambedkar are erected just about everywhere, his portrait is painted on thousands of walls all over India, and his writings are quoted in as many speeches. Most political parties include him among the figures of national importance. In parallel, Gandhi, who was for long the champion of the Untouchables' cause, has now become the villain of the piece, some prominent figures going so far as to describe him as 'an enemy of the *dalits*'. This is quite an amazing reversal of history, since, as we shall see, there was considerable bitterness between the two men. Gandhi succeeded in becoming the 'sole spokesman' of the Untouchables, and remained as such for a long time, the word 'Harijan' having become the most common name used to refer to them. Meanwhile,

3. O. Mendelsohn and M. Vicziany, *The Untouchables: Subordination, Poverty and the State in Modern India* (Cambridge: Cambridge University Press, 1998).

4. Ibid., pp. 218-34.

5. Ibid., p. 225.

6. Ibid., p. 225.

Ambedkar was not regarded as a national figure and was almost forgotten. His return as a national hero is quite amazing. It can be argued that Gandhi's waning prestige parallels the diminishing influence of the Congress Party and the recent transformations of the country, in which there seems to be little room for his message of renunciation. I am not sure, however, that Ambedkar's victory is much more than purely symbolic. To a large extent, Ambedkar's image is used as an alibi; and in any case, his ideas are not taken into account any more than they were previously. He is often simply used as a consensual figure who stood on the side of the people.

All this shows that the problem of untouchability is not merely a historical matter, but has become one of the main social and political issues in contemporary Indian. Today's Untouchables are stronger than they have ever been. The progress they have made over the last century is quite remarkable. Many of the discriminations that once affected them have been seriously attenuated. Yet, and perhaps paradoxically, the great majority remain poor, powerless, and indeed without a voice.

Introduction

On 15 April 1991, the American magazine, *Time*, carried the story of a fifteen-year-old Indian girl who had eloped with her lover, Brijendra, a boy of twenty. The events took place in Uttar Pradesh, India's most populous state. This would have been just another love story if Brijendra had belonged to the same caste as Roshini. But she was a Jat, one of the main agricultural upper castes of North India, and he belonged to the untouchable Jatav caste. And, as Anita Pratap, the *Time* journalist, comments, the price the lovers paid for their violation of tradition was a terrible one. The infuriated elders of Meharan, the girl's village, held a council and pronounced the only acceptable verdict: death!

Brijendra, his friend Ram Kishen, who had helped the lovers elope, and some of their male relatives were thrashed with sticks. The two young men were then hung by their feet; and in a frenzy of violence, their lips and genitals were scorched with burning cloth. At dawn, Roshini was dragged from her house and taken, along with the two young men, to a huge banyan tree. Ropes were placed around their necks and the fathers were forced to hoist them up; when the parents were unable to complete the task, bystanders rushed to take their places. When the young people were taken down, Ram Kishen was no longer alive. But, as though the punishment was not already harsh enough, all three bodies were then placed on a pyre and burned.

It is easy for us in the West to see nothing but pure savagery in such revolting violence, and to condemn it accordingly. Yet those who committed these atrocious acts were not professional killers, but no doubt peaceable farmers who were normally no more violent than any of us. No doubt too, they were upstanding men, good husbands and most certainly devoted fathers, who were hard-working and not out to make trouble. Moreover, most of them had probably never had any previous dealings with the law. And if, in this case, they behaved with such cruelty, it was because, from their point of view, they had good reason for doing so. In fact, when the police arrived on the scene, no one sought to avoid responsibility. The villagers openly admitted their deed and were even quite proud of themselves. Mangtu Ram, the leader, gave the police a detailed account of the execution. Convinced they were in the right, he stressed that they had had no choice: 'If we had not been harsh', he added, not without insight, 'our entire community would have been disgraced. No one would have married Jat girls from our village.' Roshini's mother had pleaded with the pitiless censors for mercy: 'Drive us out of the village, or burn down our house, but spare my daughter.' But this favour was not granted, and the only answer she got was: 'She is not *your* daughter, she is *ours*.'

Everyone knows that death is the normal punishment for any young 'Harijan' boy who dares to seduce a high-caste girl. The difficulty we have in understanding such intransigence no doubt increases when we learn that the distance between the boy and the girl is not necessarily an economic one. To be sure, most Untouchables are poor, and even poorer than the rest of the population; but this is not always so, and two young people who fall in love may well belong to similar economic classes. In many cases of 'atrocities against Harijans', as we shall see, the victims may be 'economically advanced', or even better off than their assailants. Many problems arise from certain untouchable demands for rights, privileges or status symbols more befitting their newly acquired economic situation. Which is not to say that untouchability has nothing to do with material poverty. On the contrary, the *nouveaux riches* are a particular source of irritation to the higher castes, precisely because they are no longer in their traditional place.

Untouchability is therefore not a simple matter of economic deprivation. A look at a few statistics shows this: Untouchables represent only some 15 per cent of the Indian population, whereas economists usually estimate that between 40 and 50 per cent of the population lives below the so-called 'poverty line'. However credible these figures may be, it is clear that the problem of poverty goes well beyond that of untouchability. To take just one example, many Brahmins are quite poor, and one anthropologist reports that even the priests of one great South Indian temple lead a fairly precarious existence.[1] A great many 'high' – or 'middle-caste' – people work as labourers, economically scarcely better off than Untouchables; yet they do not suffer from the same kinds of discrimination as the latter. In short, the majority of Untouchables are poor, and their poverty is even part of their social condition. But poverty alone does not account for the phenomenon of untouchability: it is not merely a case of economic exploitation, it goes much further than that.

Nor does untouchability boil down to a problem of ritual pollution. It is true that the term 'Untouchables' designates social groups that, owing to their association with death, organic waste and evil spirits, are 'permanently polluted'; but it must also be remembered that, in India, everyone is, to a greater or lesser degree, unclean. Furthermore, some groups perform highly polluting tasks, from a ritual standpoint, without incurring the same kind of discrimination and exclusion as Untouchables; this is the case, for instance, of the barbers or the washermen, but also of certain types of funeral priests.[2] In the present study, I shall therefore argue that the term 'Untouchables' refers to those sections of Indian society that are economically dependent and exploited, victims of many kinds of discrimination, and ritually polluted in a permanent way. It is the combination of these three elements that characterizes Untouchables and sets them apart from the rest of the population. It may be of further use to remind the reader that Untouchables cannot be distinguished by any particular physical trait.

Coming back to the *Time* story, now, I would like to emphasize that such events are by no means uncommon in contemporary India. Indian newspapers carry stories almost daily of what they term 'atrocities'; but many, and no doubt most, cases go unreported. D. Von Der Weid and G. Poitevin[3] counted some 130 reports of discrimination in the Marathi-language press for 1972 alone. The list includes 18 cases

1. C. Fuller, *Servants of the Goddess: the Priests of a South Indian Temple* (Cambridge: Cambridge University Press, 1984), p. 98.

2. See J. Parry, 'Ghosts, Greed and Sin: The Occupational Identity of the Benares Funeral Priests'. *Man (NS)*, 21 (1980).

3. *Inde: les parias de l'espoir* (Paris: L'Harmattan, 1978), pp. 22-33.

of various types of violence, 16 of injustice on the administrative level, 14 of electoral fraud and dozens of killings and rapes. The same year, the Marathi papers carried ten stories of Harijans being burned alive in Uttar Pradesh, and one of a pregnant woman's being sacrificed to bring rain in Andhra Pradesh; there were also stories of women raped by students in Maharashtra, a girl exposed naked in a public square, children beaten by Congress Party militants, human excrement dumped into an untouchable well, and so forth. Between six and nine thousand incidents of violence against Untouchables were being reported annually in the late 1970s; and this was only the tip of the iceberg.

Such violence seems indeed to be a feature of the Indian rural scene, then, and urbanization has not really resolved the problem. It is therefore not an exaggeration to say that untouchability is still thoroughly alive today. The present study will attempt to shed some light on what remains a major problem of Indian society. We shall try to become better acquainted with these people who are the target of so much hatred and contempt, and to see what they think and how they live.

Untouchability can be said to be an extreme form of social oppression and economic exploitation, and it could therefore be compared to similar problems found throughout the world. Nevertheless, I have chosen to leave this comparative approach to others; without denying the interest of such a study, I think there is something unique about Indian untouchability, and I feel that, as such, it deserves separate treatment. First of all, there is always the temptation of reduction, if not condemnation, when one does not know or understand a group. And secondly, a comparative approach requires a thorough knowledge of all the terms of the comparison. Not only am I incapable of such an undertaking, but, as we shall have occasion to see, the literature on India alone deserves to be treated separately.

In a recent study, R. Needham[4] deplored the fact that we have so many ethnographic data today that we do not know what to do with them all. Admittedly the literature on Untouchables is not entirely satisfying; but there is so much of it at present that some attempt at a synthesis is badly needed, and this is the task I propose to undertake in the following pages. My views on the problem of untouchability have been largely shaped by my own ethnographic work. However, since much of this research has already been published, I shall refer to it only marginally.[5]

The first chapter of the present book provides a general introduction to the Untouchables of India. The next deals with theories of caste and their approaches to the problem of untouchability. Chapters 3 and 4 focus on the Untouchables' own ideology and more particularly on the way they situate themselves in Indian society. An overview of the kinds of discrimination inflicted on Untouchables is presented in Chapter 5. Following a study of the economic aspects of untouchability, in Chapter 6 I address social change, which is dealt with in more detail in the last three chapters of the book: first of all the social-religious movements led by Untouchables over the last century, and then a chapter devoted to Ambedkar, the principal untouchable political figure, while the closing chapter is devoted to the system of positive discrimination, which has recently become the focus of a number of struggles.

4. R. Needham, *Exemplars* (Berkeley, CA: University of California Press, 1985), p. 40.5.
5. See mainly R. Deliège, *Les Paraiyars du Tamil Nadu* (Nettetal: Steyler Verlag, 1988)

-1-

The Untouchables: An Overview

Outline of a Problem

As we have seen, India's Untouchables constitute some 15 per cent of the total population. Interestingly enough, their percentage has increased slightly over the years, from 14.67 per cent in 1961 to 15.75 per cent in the 1981 census. In this census, the Scheduled Castes, the administrative term for Untouchables, numbered some 104,754,623 individuals, a truly mind-numbing figure, the equivalent of the populations of France and Great Britain together; and their relative strength is likely

Table 1. Percentage and number of Scheduled Caste population by state (Census of India, 1971 and 1981)

State	1971		1981	
	%	Figure	%	Figure
Andhra Pradesh	13.27	5,774,548	14.87	7,961,730
Bihar	14.11	7,950,652	14.51	10,142,368
Gujarat	6.84	1,825,432	7.15	2,438,297
Haryana	18.99	1,895,933	19.07	2,464,012
Himachal Pradesh	22.44	769,572	24.62	1,053,958
Jammu & Kashmir	8.26	381,277	8.31	497,363
Karnataka	13.14	3,850,034	15.07	5,595,353
Kerala	8.30	1,772,168	10.02	2,549,382
Madhya Pradesh	13.09	5,453,690	14.10	7,358,533
Maharashtra	6.00	3,025,761	7.14	4,479,763
Orissa	15.09	3,310,854	14.66	3,865,543
Punjab	24.71	3,348,217	26.87	4,511,703
Rajasthan	15.82	4,075,580	17.04	5,838,879
Tamil Nadu	17.76	7,315,595	18.35	8,881,295
Uttar Pradesh	21.00	18,548,916	21.16	23,453,339
West Bengal	19.90	8,816,028	21.99	12,000,768
India	14.82	79,092,841	15.75	104,754,623

to increase, as they are growing faster than the rest of the population. Between 1971 and 1981, the population of the Scheduled Castes increased by 32.4 per cent, or 3.2 per cent per year, while the overall population of India grew by just 2.3 per cent.

These figures and those contained in Table 1 point to a serious challenge that the Indian government will have to face in the coming decades, for an increase in these lowest sections of the population also means an increase in social problems. The untouchable literacy rate, for instance, is significantly lower than that of the rest of the population. And even though literacy has improved considerably in the last decades, rising from 10.2 per cent in 1961 to 14.6 per cent in 1971 and to 21.38 per cent in 1981, the absolute number of illiterate Untouchables has also increased significantly, from 56,000,000 in 1961 to somewhere around 82,650,000 in 1981. The government's educational efforts have thus been parried by the growth of the population, and the same holds true for other social problems as well. The absolute number of 'poor' people is increasing similarly; and with this rise come the familiar diseases linked to poverty.

The 1991 census is expected to show a staggering 140,000,000 Untouchables. But these figures also suggest the tremendous potential political strength of these groups, which seem to be less loyal to the Congress Party than in the past. They are therefore likely to become an important target for the other political parties, and endeavours to woo this community may well increase in the coming decades if the enlistment of Ambedkar among their great Indian nationalists by the disturbing Hindu nationalist Bharatya Janata Party (BJP) is any indication.[1] Untouchables could wield even greater political weight were they to form a homogeneous community; but Harijans are split into hundreds of castes dispersed throughout the country. No single organization can claim to represent Untouchables as a whole, and the local associations that do exist have very little power of mobilization. The only national leader of importance to have emerged from their ranks was not even capable, in spite of his charisma, of unifying the untouchable castes of his own state, and the members of the Mang caste regarded him as a mere Mahar leader.[2]

There is no denying that this fragmentation is one more curse for Untouchables, making it impossible for them to play on their numerical strength to win a significant role in Indian politics. Furthermore, although nearly every village has its Untouchables, they almost never constitute a majority, but tend to be divided into relatively small communities. Such fragmentation is an essential feature of Indian untouchability, as we shall see later. Traditionally, Untouchables even espoused the quarrels and factions of their masters, and therefore practised vertical solidarity rather than the 'horizontal mobilization' they had always lacked.[3] For example when, on 26 April 1899, the low-caste Nadars of Tamil Nadu rose up in defence of their rights, the

1. C. Jaffrelot, *Les Nationalistes hindous: idéologie, implantation et mobilisation des années 1920 aux années 1990* (Paris: Presses de la Fondation Nationale des Sciences Politiques, 1993), pp. 58 and 278.

2. E. Zelliot, 'Gandhi and Ambedkar - A Study in Leadership', in J. M. Mahar (ed.), *The Untouchables in Contemporary India* (Tucson: University of Arizona Press, 1972), p. 51.

3. L. Rudolph and S. Hoeber Rudolph, *The Modernity of Tradition: Political Development in India* (Chicago: University of Chicago Press, 1967), p. 84; or F. Bailey, *Tribe, Caste and Nation* (Manchester: Manchester University Press, 1960), p. 131.

untouchable Pallars joined with the high-caste Maravars in the violent repression of the Nadar movement.[4] And in Uttar Pradesh, older people remember that they used to side with 'their' Thakur masters in quarrels that often ended in bloodshed.[5] This division, as Opler notes,[6] is a constant and almost insurmountable threat to Untouchables. What we need to realize, then, is that, in every region, Untouchables are divided into numerous castes and subcastes that are strongly endogamous and very particular about avoiding contact with each other.

Untouchables are *par excellence* those groups that carry out the various menial tasks that keep the village running. This means that they are rarely numerically dominant in a village. In the North Indian plain, for example, the Chamars are one of the largest castes after the Jat agriculturalists. And yet, out of a sample of 167 villages, they were numerically dominant in only 16.[7] It is likely, moreover, that these villages are fairly recent settlements. An even more typical example is that of another untouchable caste, the Pasis, who are found in practically every village, but in small numbers.[8] More generally, the proportion of Untouchables in a population seems to vary with the environment and agrarian relations.

For Tamil Nadu, Gough[9] has shown a significant correlation between the number of Untouchables, paddy cultivation and the agricultural value of the land: Untouchables are more numerous in regions having the most fertile land, the best irrigation, the most intensive agriculture and the highest crop value per acre. The most arid regions, where agriculture is both less intensive and less productive, have a lower percentage of Untouchables.[10] It is not unreasonable to think that this correlation holds true for the whole of India, with a few exceptions, such as Kerala, which is known for being a 'special case'.[11] Clearly, then, Untouchables provide the bulk of agricultural labour, and agricultural work, in the broad sense, is an essential feature of untouchability.

As we have seen, Untouchables as a group do not coincide perfectly with the class of agricultural labourers, who are recruited from other classes as well. But it is also true that members of higher castes who are obliged to provide agricultural labour regard the work as degrading, almost unnatural, and emphasize that they do it only out of necessity. Manual labour is held in contempt, at least among high-caste Indians. And it is well known that Brahmins, even those who call themselves agriculturalists, are not allowed to work the land themselves. High-caste people like the North Indian

4. R. Hardgrave, *The Nadars of Tamilnad: The Political Culture of a Community in Change* (Bombay: Oxford University Press, 1969), p. 115.

5. B. Cohn, 'Some Notes on Law and Change in North India'. *Economic Development and Cultural Change*, 8 (1959), p. 88.

6. M. Opler, 'North Indian Themes: Caste and Untouchability', in J. M. Mahar (ed.), *The Untouchables in Contemporary India* (Tucson: University of Arizona Press, 1972), p. 5.7. J. Schwartzenberg, 'The Distribution of Selected Castes in the North Indian Plain'. *Geographical Review,* 55 (1965), p. 488.

8. Ibid., p. 494.

9. K. Gough, *Rural Society in Southeast India* (Cambridge: Cambridge University Press, 1981).

10. See also J. Mencher, *Agriculture and Social Structure in Tamil Nadu: Past Origins, Present Transformations and Future Prospects* (Bombay: Allied Publishers, 1978), p. 146.

11. K. C. Alexander, 'Caste Mobilization and Class Consciousness: The Emergence of Agrarian Movements in Kerala and Tamil Nadu', in F. Frankel and M. S. Rao (eds), *Dominance and State Power in Modern India: Decline of a Social Order* (Delhi: Oxford University Press, 1989), p. 363.

Table 2. Sex ratio (females per 1, 000 males) of Scheduled Castes by state *(Census of India*, 1981)

Andhra Pradesh	971
Bihar	966
Gujarat	942
Haryana	864
Himachal Pradesh	959
Jammu & Kashmir	922
Karnataka	968
Kerala	1,022
Madhya Pradesh	932
Maharashtra	948
Orissa	988
Punjab	868
Rajasthan	913
Tamil Nadu	980
Uttar Pradesh	892
West Bengal	926
India	932

Thakurs never take on agricultural work, which they regard as particularly demeaning.[12] And although the women from the village of Mallikundu were working as coolies on the reservoir construction project, a farmer from the Udayar caste, the only caste in the village, told me that it was only because of the drought that they allowed their wives to do this degrading work. Many untouchable castes, however, such as the famous Pallars of Tamil Nadu, have only one occupation, which is agricultural labour.

Here I must press a point that I shall develop later: untouchability cannot be reduced, as Hocart does, to a question of ritual. As we shall see, Dumont, too, tends to regard Untouchables as merely the necessary complement of Brahmins. For Dumont, Untouchables do not form a separate category and therefore are not 'outcastes'; Moffatt, for his part, even qualifies them as 'last among equals', which is tantamount to passing over an essential aspect of untouchability.[13]

The problem of untouchability, as Oommen correctly writes,[14] is above all one of 'cumulative deprivation', and it must be made clear that Untouchables do indeed constitute a distinct group, even if the vernacular has no specific term for them and even though they are highly fragmented, as I have already said. In a study rightly

12. C. Bliss and H. Stern, *Palanpur: the Economy of an Indian Village* (Oxford: Clarendon Press, 1982), p. 94.

13. M. Moffatt, *An Untouchable Community in South India:* Structure and Consensus (Princeton, NJ: Princeton University Press, 1979), pp. 222, 247 and 270.

14. T. K. Oommen, 'Sources of Deprivation and Styles of Protest: The Case of the Dalits in India'. *Contributions to Indian Sociology (NS)*, 18 (1984), p. 46.

15. A. Béteille, *Caste, Class and Power: Changing Patterns of Stratification in a Tanjore Village* (Bombay: Oxford University Press, 1966), p. 3.

Table 3. Literacy rate among Untouchables by state *(Census of India*, 1961 and 1981)

States	1961	1981	Males	Females
Andhra Pradesh	8.47	17.65	24.82	10.26
Bihar	5.96	10.40	18.02	2.51
Gujarat	22.46	39.79	53.14	25.61
Haryana	N.A.	20.15	31.45	7.06
Himachal Pradesh	N.A.	31.50	41.94	20.63
Jammu & Kashmir	4.72	22.44	32.34	11.70
Karnataka	9.06	20.59	29.35	11.55
Kerala	24.44	55.96	62.33	49.73
Madhya Pradesh	7.89	19.0	30.6	6.9
Maharashtra	15.78	35.55	48.85	21.53
Orissa	11.57	22.41	35.26	9.40
Punjab	9.64	23.86	30.96	15.67
Rajasthan	6.44	14.04	24.40	2.69
Tamil Nadu	14.66	29.67	40.65	18.47
Uttar Pradesh	7.14	14.96	24.83	3.90
West Bengal	13.58	24.37	34.36	13.70

regarded as a classic, Béteille[15] argues that the population of Tamil Nadu can be divided into three broad categories: Brahmins, non-Brahmins and Untouchables. He argues that this division is significant from a sociological standpoint. Socio-economic dependence, material poverty, social deprivation and lack of political power combine with ritual pollution to make Untouchables a social category clearly set apart from the rest of society. Yet this is not to say that Untouchables are completely cut off from the rest of society; nor are they marginalized, as gypsies tend to be in Western societies. Unlike gypsies or renouncers, for instance, Untouchables are marginalized only up to a point; while for many aspects of life, they are an integral part of Indian society. Their marginal status is therefore complex and paradoxical; they are, as I shall have occasion to repeat, both outside and inside the system. They are unquestionably set apart by their ritual pollution; but at the same time, they do not constitute a separate society. They reside on the outskirts of villages, but not in the wild. This ambiguity has not always been sufficiently stressed by observers, who have generally emphasized either the one or the other aspect of the Untouchables' position: some underscore their social integration, while others regard them as a totally rejected group with its own culture. I suggest that the two models are not contradictory, but that they work together to give Indian untouchability its original character.

Some statistics support the argument that, while they may be socially rejected, Untouchables are not completely cut off from the rest of society. This is the case, for instance, of the sex ratio, which follows the same trend as that of the overall population.

From Table 2 it is clear that the sex ratio of Untouchables living in the South Indian states is much more balanced than that of the North Indian states, something that is true of the overall Indian population as well. In this matter, which is closely related to specific social and cultural practices, Untouchables reproduce the pattern of Indian society as a whole. Kerala is a significant case, since the higher proportion of women among Untouchables is a feature found in the rest of the population. The same thing could be said about literacy: in states with a literacy rate as high as that of Kerala, Untouchables also are on the whole better educated than elsewhere. The reverse holds true as well, and in the comparatively backward state of Bihar, the proportion of Untouchables able to read and write is particularly low.

Table 3 shows that, with an average literacy rate of 21.38 per cent, Untouchables are far below the national norm (36.2 per cent); but the fluctuations around this figure generally reflect the variations found from state to state. Language is an even better indication of the Untouchables' integration into the surrounding community: Untouchables do not have a language of their own; they speak the local languages and dialects. Although there are a few terms and expressions specific to their group, this is not enough to constitute an original culture. To be sure, marriage rules, eating habits and religious practices sometimes reveal originalities; but once again, this is not enough to be able to speak of a true 'Untouchable culture'. In short, India's Untouchables do not constitute a uniform community with its own culture: they are widely integrated into the local communities and share the basic values of these communities. If untouchability can be said to have one primary characteristic, it is this fragmentation, which binds them inexorably to the very communities that reject them.

Finally it can be said that Untouchables are proportionately more numerous in rural areas, where they constitute 15.97 per cent of the population, while they represent only 8.7 per cent of urban dwellers. Being socially deprived, economically backward and for the most part illiterate, Untouchables are less likely to migrate to the cities, where jobs tend to be more specialized. They are above all a feature of the Indian rural scene, then; but this does not mean that urbanization has resolved the problem of untouchability. Recent studies show that the Scheduled Castes are far from having vanished from the city.[16]

A Name for Untouchables

In this section I would like to discuss the thorny question of what to call Untouchables, how they refer to themselves and how they are referred to or addressed by non-Untouchables. Far from being trivial or futile, as we shall see, this question brings out

16. See, for instance, R. S. Khare, *The Untouchable as Himself: Ideology, Identity and Pragmatism among the Lucknow Chamars* (Cambridge: Cambridge University Press, 1984), or D. Pawar, *Ma vie d'intouchable* (Paris: La Découverte, 1990), and especially, O. Lynch, *The Politics of Untouchability: Social Mobility and Social Change in a City of India* (New York: Columbia University Press, 1969) and S. Molund, *First We Are People ... The Koris of Kanpur between Caste and Class* (Stockholm: Stockholm Studies in Social Anthropology, 1988).

a series of elements, the first among which is a difference between Western anthropologists, who continue to use the term 'Untouchable', and Indian anthropologists and sociologists, who have all but banished the word from their vocabulary.

Generic Terms

Of all the generic terms used to refer to 'Untouchables', none is entirely satisfying. The preceding section stressed the lack of unity of this social category, and this lack is reflected in the lack of a single, universally accepted term to denote its members. This absence entails further complications, because it is not always clear whether or not a given group belongs to the category designated.

For instance, to a certain extent everyone in Indian society is ritually impure and therefore 'untouchable'. A Brahmin in mourning for a close family member or a Benares funeral priest are in a sense untouchable. In fact the very ideas of 'impurity' and 'untouchability' are relative. Reiniche[17] has shown that Pallars or Paraiyars can be considered impure only with respect to certain criteria associated with Indian society; and it is never said of an Untouchable that he pollutes the land he tills. But we have also argued that untouchability cannot be reduced to a matter of relative purity; Untouchables are clearly set apart from the rest of society. However we must also agree with Den Ouden[18] when he argues that untouchability is not defined by rigid or firmly established boundaries. Around the blurred edges of this social group stand various other groups whose status is ill defined. One familiar example may help us see that these two statements are in no way contradictory: in Western society, youth and old age are specific social categories, each with its own characteristics and problems; and yet it is not always easy to say who is young and who is old. The frontiers of these categories are fuzzy. Now the same can be said about untouchability, without taking anything away from its specificity.

The matter is further complicated by the fact that the Indian constitution establishes a system of positive discrimination that provides various advantages for Untouchables and a few other social categories. It is in this way that the official category of 'Scheduled Castes', which officially designates the untouchable groups, came about. We shall elaborate on this later; but for the moment suffice it to say that, by such a provision, the Indian government drew a veritable boundary line around untouchability, whereas in purely sociological terms the concept had been fairly fluid. There are now some classes that are 'Scheduled', and others that are not. In other words, untouchability is now an officially recognized category, and this recognition has had important social consequences. Significantly, in many parts of India, Untouchables are commonly called Scheduled Castes, or S.C., and the registered groups have discovered that they have some characteristics and interests in common.

17. M. L. Reiniche, *Les Dieux et les hommes: étude des cultes d'un village du Tirunelveli (Inde du sud)* (Paris: Mouton, 1979), p. 13.

18. J. Den Ouden, *De Onaanraakbaren van Konkunad: een Onderzoek naar de Positie-verandering van de Scheduled Castes in een Dorp van het District Coimbatore, India* (Wageningen: Madedelingen Landbouwhogeschool, 1975), p. 61.

In many parts of the country, this has led to their forming organizations for the defence of the interests of Scheduled Castes. As Christian Untouchables are not an official Scheduled Caste, they cannot be members of these associations, and are therefore excluded from the Untouchable movement.[19] Positive discrimination, then, has resulted in strengthening Untouchables' unity to a degree, but in so doing, it has perversely also contributed to their stigmatization; and it is for this reason that some authors, like Srinivas, have argued that caste as an institution has been reinforced in modern society.[20]

While Untouchables may have found a community of interest thanks to the recent legislation, it by no means follows that they now form a uniform category. Solidarity remains highly limited, and has not led to a fusion of castes. And while it is true that, over the last century, the subcastes of any one caste have had a tendency to merge, this process has never cut across caste barriers, so that the different untouchable castes continue to be highly divided. The best indication of this is caste endogamy, which has not suffered any serious breach in the past century. On the whole, Untouchables remain split into a myriad of widely dispersed castes having little contact with each other.

Now we are ready to return to the problem of what to call these castes. In the Sanskrit literature, Untouchables are known as *chandala* (Sanskrit: *çandaala*), a term that designates those who were not allowed to dwell in a town or a village but had to live in special quarters outside the village or town limits. In theory, their main task was the carrying and cremation of corpses; but they had other means of earning their livelihood as well. The law books stipulate that *chandalas* must eat their food from broken vessels and avoid any contact with higher castes. High-caste individuals could be reduced to the status of *chandalas* by merely touching the latter.[21] *The Laws of Manu* refer to the *chandalas* as 'the last among men',[22] and they add that they can produce even more degraded beings by marrying women of various low castes, for example: the Andhras and the Meedas, who must live outside the village, the Paandusopaaca, who are bamboo-workers, the Sopaaca or executioners, and the Antyaavasaayiis or funeral attendants, who are looked down on by even the most wretched, and are even lower than the *chandalas* themselves.[23] *Chandalas* must reside outside the village limits, they may not own whole vessels, they must dress in clothes taken from the dead and must eat from broken dishes. They are forbidden contact with other people and must marry among themselves. They eat only table scraps and leftovers, and are not allowed to walk through the village except when on business. They should be easily distinguishable from other people and not conceal their low origins. Lastly, they defile the other classes.

19. See R. Deliège, 'A Comparison between Hindu and Christian Paraiyars of South India'. *Indian Missiological Review,* 12 (1990), p. 58.

20. M. N. Srinivas, *Caste in Modern India and Other Essays* (Bombay: Asia Publishing House, 1962), pp. 15 and 70.

21. A. L. Basham, *The Wonder that Was India: A Survey of the History and Culture of the Indian Sub-Continent before the Coming of the Muslims* (London: Fontana-Collins, 1967), p. 146.

22. X, 12; see A. Loiseleur-Deslongchamps (ed.), *Lois de Manou, comprenant les institutions religieuses et civiles des Indiens* (Paris: De Crapalet, 1833), p. 372.

23. Ibid., p. 377.

The *Code of Manu*, written probably around the third century AD,[24] thus describes a social group that strongly resembles today's Untouchables: *chandalas* are excluded from living in villages, they constitute a servile class, dress in rags, eat scraps and must be kept in a state of abjection, all of which, as Moffatt notes, still characterizes Untouchables some 1,500 years on.[25]

I am not going to review the history of Untouchables here - this is not the place; but it is clear that the phenomenon has existed in India for a very long time. Many later reports confirm the persistence of this condition over the centuries. Duarte Barbosa, Magellan's cousin, who visited India in the sixteenth century, mentions various categories of persons of low station:[26] for Malabar, he lists eleven classes of 'Tivers' (probably today's Iravas,[27] known as Tyyas in North Kerala), who 'gain their livelihood by all kinds of labour', but mainly as serfs of the Nayars. Below them, Barbosa cites the Poleas (or Pulayas), who are described as an 'even lower sect', regarded as excommunicated and 'cursed'. They live in 'swampy fields and places where respectable people cannot go'. They plough and sow the fields and may not speak to the Nayars except from a shouting distance. When they encounter someone on a path, they must step aside. They can be killed without any penalty. They are thieves and very base people. And yet there exists an even lower category: the Pareas or Paraiyars live in uninhabited places and are regarded as so low that a person can be excommunicated merely by looking at them. They live on roots and wild animals. In spite of its historical interest, Barbosa's report contains a number of inaccuracies; but it does point up the important distinction between Iravas and Pulayas. Later, in the twentieth century, the Iravas were to set themselves apart from the other low castes and endeavour to better their condition. On the other hand, Barbosa describes Pulayas and Paraiyars as 'excommunicated' (a highly significant term on the lips of a sixteenth-century European), 'accursed', living in the wilderness, and so on. In other words, what struck this great Portuguese traveller were the various discriminations and the social exclusion.

Barbosa does not mention any generic term in referring to these lower classes. No doubt the term *chandala* was already somewhat obsolete by the sixteenth century, and today it has completely dropped out of everyday language and contemporary literature. And yet it has not really been replaced, since the modern vernaculars have no term that embraces Untouchables as a category. In Tamil, for instance, the word *theendajadhi* ('the castes which defile') is not used in everyday speech (was it ever?), and may perhaps be a recent translation of the English 'untouchable'. Another Tamil word has overtly militant echoes, since *taazhttapattor* means literally 'those who are forced to be low'. This, too, is probably a recent lexical invention. It is commonly used by Untouchable associations, but has not entered the everyday language.

24. A. Macdonnell, *A History of Sanskrit Literature* (Delhi: Motilal Banarsidass, 1971), p. 364.

25. M. Moffatt, *An Untouchable Community*, p. 37.

26. D. Barbosa, *A Description of the Coast of East Africa and Malabar in the Beginning of the 16th Century* (London: Hakluyt Society, 1970), pp. 137ff.

27. I have chosen this phonetic spelling rather than the more common 'Izhava' or sometimes 'Ezhava'.

As Khare[28] and Béteille[29] have pointed out, there are many terms for Untouchables. They are called antyaja ('the last born'), *adi-dravidas* ('first settlers of the Dravidian country'), *adi-andhras or adi-hindus;* in Hindi-speaking regions, the names *achchuuta* or *achut* ('the polluted') are more common, but these designate more a state than any particular social category. On the whole, no one term has become generalized, which may well explain why the diverse administrative terms have met with a certain amount of success: over the years Untouchables have been classified as Depressed Castes, Exterior Castes, Outcastes, Backward Castes and, of course, Scheduled Castes. We have seen that the introduction by the British colonial government of legal measures in favour of the most disadvantaged groups in Indian society endowed these lower classes with a semblance of unity.

Self-representation and Representation

There is, then, no truly satisfactory term for Untouchables in general. And yet, in everyday life, the different social actors, including the Untouchables themselves, are obliged to use certain terms in referring to their social origin. The problem can be broken down into three parts: first we shall look at how Untouchables refer to themselves. We shall then see the expressions used by higher castes to designate them. And finally we shall briefly discuss the terms used by social anthropologists and sociologists.

The first to grasp the importance of caste names among Untouchables was the American anthropologist, H. Isaacs, who devoted part of his interesting study to this revealing issue. He noted that even the 'ex-untouchables'[30] had no solution to the problem: 'Right now', he writes, 'ex-untouchables do not know what to call themselves for they are people trying to cease being what they were and to become something else, though they are not sure what'.[31]

Caste names are generally considered demeaning or even insulting, and Untouchables avoid using them. The term *chamar,* for example, has injurious connotations throughout North India, where it is used in such expressions as 'black as a Chamar' or 'dirty as a Chamar'.[32] If he is asked about his caste, an Untouchable will often hesitate to give his real caste name, which he feels to be disgraceful. Depending on the circumstances, he will use an euphemism such as Harijan or Scheduled Caste, and will give his real caste name only after repeated questioning. This was certainly the case with the Paraiyars in Tamil Nadu, who were annoyed at such insistence. Some even refused to divulge their caste at all, replying 'What does it matter? After all we

28. R. S. Khare, *The Untouchable as Himself,* p. 119.

29. A. Béteille, *Castes: Old and New. Essays in Social Structure and Social Stratification* (Bombay: Asia Publishing House, 1969), p. 87.

30. This is Isaacs' term.

31. H. Isaacs, *India's Ex-Untouchables* (New York: Harper Torchbooks, 1964), p. 34.

32. B. Cohn, 'The Chamars of Senapur: A Study of the Changing Status of a Depressed Caste' (Doctoral Dissertation, Cornell University, 1954), p. 110.

are human beings like you.' This was a fairly common response to our questioning. Some observers have explained this reticence by the fact that Untouchables know that their caste name does not actually matter, since their questioner's attitude will be the same whatever their caste. For a Tamil Brahmin, for instance, Pallars and Paraiyars are both so unclean and structurally distant that the differences between these two Untouchable castes do not have a great deal of importance.

Yet experience and ethnographic studies teach us that this is not always so. In the sixteenth century, as we have seen, observers had already noted the marked differences between Pulayas and Paraiyars in Malayali[33] society. In more recent times, Den Ouden systematically demonstrated that high-caste people's attitudes varied considerably depending on whether they were dealing with Pallars, Sakkiliyars or Kuravars:[34] a carpenter will repair a Pallar's roof but not that of someone from a lower caste,[35] and the local high-caste Kavuntars regard Pallars as 'touchable' and entertain a great many relations with them. At the other end of the subcontinent, Cohn[36] observed that the higher castes did not treat all the groups known as *achuts* in the same way. And we know that, in Hindi-speaking regions, Chamars rank much higher than Bhangis.

Untouchables themselves are most certainly aware of this difference. For instance, in Tamil Nadu, I noted that Paraiyars almost always gave their caste as Harijan when asked. Pallars, on the other hand, were forthcoming about their caste name in the same circumstances. Kapadia's observations[37] substantiate this, emphasizing that Pallars are less ashamed of their caste name than other untouchable groups; she explains this difference by the fact that the Pallars' traditional occupation, agricultural labour, is not considered to be unclean. Moreover, Pallars are always anxious to emphasize the auspicious nature of their work.[38] I would add that the generic terms assimilate Pallars to castes they regard as inferior, and they therefore prefer their own caste name to this degrading amalgamation.

Most untouchable caste names, however, evoke low status. As one Telugu Untouchable explained: 'It was easier to say "I am a Harijan" than "I am a Mala".'[39] The same informant recalls the sad experiences of his childhood in these terms: 'I was in the 6th Standard when the teacher asked me what caste I was. I said: "I am Harijan". The whole class mocked at me when I said that. All the heads turned as though to look at a convict. I felt ashamed, embarrassed and looked down on.'[40]

The quotation is highly significant; it expresses what a Harijan feels when he is obliged to acknowledge his caste in public. And it introduces us to another important aspect of untouchability: whatever their social position and merit, Untouchables are

33. The inhabitants of Kerala are called Malayali, after their language Malayalam.

34. J. Den Ouden, *De Onaanraakbaren van Konkunad* (1975), p. 85.

35. Ibid., p. 134.

36. B. Cohn, 'The Shamars of Senapur', p. 1.

37. K. Kapadia, 'Gender, Caste and Class in Rural South India' (Doctoral Dissertation, London School of Economics, Department of Anthropology, 1990), p. 235.

38. Ibid., p. 241.

39. H. Isaacs, *India's Ex-Untouchables,* p. 42.

40. Ibid., p. 42.

ashamed of their social background and try to conceal it whenever possible. To be forced publicly to acknowledge one's caste is humiliating and insulting. Even people who have made it up the social ladder and hold an enviable job do not boast about their humble origins, as may be the case in the West. In fact it is not uncommon for an Untouchable who lives outside his traditional environment to conceal his identity.[41]

In short, the very question of caste is embarrassing for an Untouchable, and he will generally resort to euphemisms in answering. The most commonly used term in this case was 'Harijan', a word coined by Gandhi in the 1930s to denote Untouchables that has become extremely widespread. It means 'people' or, by extension, 'children' (*jan*) of God (*Hari*). Unlike caste names, this is a fairly neutral term, which was not originally insulting but on the contrary aimed at making these lowly groups into children of God. The Paraiyars of the Tamil Nadu village of Valghira Manickam always give this name when asked their caste. And yet the term 'Harijan' has not won unanimous acceptation.

Following the 1936 Government of India Act, the administrative term Depressed Classes was officially dropped and replaced by Scheduled Classes. At the time, Gandhi and Ambedkar were vying to represent 'Untouchables'; Gandhi's sympathizers adopted the term 'Harijan', while the followers of Ambedkar rejected it in favour of 'Scheduled Castes'. In the same year, the Nagpur session of the All India Depressed Classes Conference voted to mark its 'hatred of the name Harijan'.[42] The two terms continue to be opposed today. For instance, Khare notes that the Chamars of Lucknow see the term 'Harijan' as a ploy used by Gandhi and high-caste Hindus to avoid feelings of guilt.[43] The Jatavs of Agra city, too, stress that the word is fundamentally paternalistic.[44] It is hard to fault them on this point, since, in borrowing this term from the 'great Brahmin saint', Narasinha Mehta, Gandhi wanted to remind people that God is the friend of the downtrodden and protector of the weak.[45] In the Punjab, Chamars rejected the term 'Harijan' for the same reason, namely its paternalistic connotations.[46] It seems that those who reject the use of 'Harijan' generally belong to politically active communities close to Ambedkar, who was a known opponent of Gandhi. It must also be stressed that an originally neutral term can, with time, take on pejorative connotations. In Maharashtra, for example, many Mahars who followed Ambedkar and converted to Buddhism demanded to be called 'Neo-Buddhists'; today, however, this expression has become practically synonymous with Untouchable.

In recent years, militant Untouchables and their intellectual leaders have taken to calling themselves *dalit,* a term that seems to have become popular among certain untouchable groups, particularly in North India. It means 'the downtrodden', and

41. See L. Vincentnathan, 'Harijan Subculture and Self-Esteem Management in a South Indian Community' (Doctoral Dissertation, University of Wisconsin, Madison, 1987), pp. 187-200.

42. E. Zelliot, 'Dr. Ambedkar and the Mahar Movement' (Doctoral Dissertation, University of Pennsylvania, 1969), p. 214.

43. R. S. Khare, *The Untouchable as Himself,* p. 120.

44. O. Lynch, *The Politics of Untouchability*, p. 31.

45. M. Gandhi, *The Removal of Untouchability* (Allahabad: Navajivan Publishing House, 1954), p. 13.

46. M. Juergensmeyer, *Religion as Social Vision: the Movement against Untouchability in 20th Century Punjab* (Berkeley, CA: University of California Press, 1982), p. 14.

comes from a political movement, the Dalit Panthers, which was created in Bombay in 1972 along the lines of the American Black Panthers.[47] The Dalit Panther movement was clearly an intellectual one, with among its members a great number of poets and other writers.[48] Unable to agree on its manifesto, the group eventually disintegrated, but the term *dalit* survived, and is widely used by intellectuals throughout India. It also spawned an important literary movement in Maharashtra, the *Dalit Sahitya* ('literature of the downtrodden'), which has been particularly active.[49] The term *dalit* is interesting for its more aggressive overtones. To be a *dalit* is to be a proud militant, ready to stand up for one's rights: attitudes that contrast with the Untouchables' traditional self-effacement and baseness. Nevertheless, it is only fair to point out, in the first place, that this term is only now beginning to be known to the mass of those concerned, and, in the second place, that higher castes never use it in referring to Untouchables, although in recent years it has become the politically correct term.

We have seen that the expression 'Scheduled Castes' is widely used to designate Untouchables. Some even prefer the abbreviation S.C. As for the term 'Harijan', it is a way of getting around caste names felt to be insulting. As we have explained elsewhere,[50] caste names are important ideological markers, and it is no accident that the first thing a caste does, when undertaking to improve its status, is to change its name. This was the case with the Shanars, now known as Nadars ('Lords of the land')[51] or the Ahirs, who prefer to be called Yadavas.[52] Even the Kanbis of Gujarat, though by no means a low caste, prefer to call themselves Patidars, as a sign of their social aspirations.[53] A number of other untouchable groups have also chosen similar action. The Koris of Kanpur call themselves Koli Rajput[54] and, in Tamil Nadu, Pallars have recently taken to claiming that their true name is Teventira Kula Vellalar, which links them with the local high-caste Vellalars.[55] Nevertheless, Untouchables as a whole have not sought to alter their names, as their social status has not improved to the point of making a name change acceptable, as was the case with the Nadars. Meanwhile they chafe at their old names, which remind them of their abject condition, so that, as Isaacs so judiciously noted, since none of the available solutions is truly satisfactory, they do not in fact know what to call themselves. It is this quandary that explains the hesitations or contradictions we have just seen.

By and large, the higher castes are perfectly aware of the problem and have similar difficulties knowing how to refer to Untouchables. Traditionally, these problems did

47. D. Von der Weid and G. Poitevin, *Inde, les parias de l'espoir* (Paris: L'Harmattan, 1978), p. 61.

48. B. Joshi (ed.), *Untouchables! Voices of the Dalit Liberation Movement* (London: Zed Books, 1986), p. 87.

49. See J. Gokhale-Turner, "Bhakti or Vidroha: Continuity and Change in *Dalit Sahitya*". *Journal of Asian and African Studies,* 15 (1980).

50. R. Deliège, *Les Paraiyars du Tamil Nadu* (Nettetal: Steyler Verlag, 1988), pp. 120-4.

51. R. Hardgrave, *The Nadars of Tamilnad.*

52. M. S. Rao, *Social Movements and Social Transformations: A Study of Two Backward Classes Movements in India* (Delhi: McMillan, 1979), p. 141.

53. D. Pocock, *Kanbi and Patidar: A Study of the Patidar Community of Gujarat* (Oxford: Oxford University Press, 1972), p. 1.

54. S. Molund, *First We Are People*, p. 220.

55. S. Mosse, 'Idioms of Subordination and Styles of Protest among Christian and Hindu Harijan Castes in Tamil Nadu'. *Contributions to Indian Sociology (NS)*, 28 (1994), p. 95.

not arise. They used to be able insult their servants as they saw fit and use caste names without shame. Today things have grown more complicated, and the way high-caste people address or refer to Untouchables depends on context and circumstances. Everyone knows that an Untouchable might become angry and react if called by a rude name or one felt to be insulting. And more enlightened or educated people eager to show their democratic principles refuse to use derogatory names. For all these reasons, many people resort to the various euphemisms we have discussed, the most common of which are 'Harijan' and 'Scheduled Castes' and, more recently, 'Dalits'.

In more private or traditional contexts, however, the former names are far from having disappeared. In Tamil Nadu, it is not uncommon to hear a high-caste person shout 'Parapaiyale', a very rude term indeed, at a Paraiyar. Likewise, the imperatives *wada/poda* ('go/come'), although commonly used in speaking to Untouchables, are highly resented.[56] Djurfeldt and Lindberg[57] tell how a Vellalar called out to a Paraiyar girl 'You Paraiya dog! Look at your face and chin, you ugly monkey!' The Nadars are well aware of the ambiguity of high-caste people's attitudes: no one in Tamil Nadu would now dare call a Nadar 'Shanar' to his face, and the name Nadar has become accepted; but behind their backs, the higher castes still use the name Shanar. Some of my informants maliciously added that it is not possible to use this name in their presence. But the majority of untouchable groups are not as powerful as the Nadars, and for the most part, they still have to let themselves be called by their caste name, even if this practice wounds them. In the Himalayas, high-caste people refer to all Untouchables as 'Dom', the name of one untouchable caste, and the low castes feel humiliated by this.[58] One of Isaac's Malayali informants expresses this well: 'For someone simply to say "You are a Pulayan", was to call a bad name. The upper-caste children used these names to insult us'.[59] In sum, though high-caste people in the presence of outsiders or in public use more neutral terms, in everyday life the traditional insulting expressions have by no means disappeared, especially when a person is addressing his labourers and dependants.

We social scientists, too, must ask ourselves what term we should use in our research. My choice to speak of 'Untouchables' needs a few words of explanation. It is interesting, for example, that most Indian researchers have dropped this name in favour of the more commonly used 'Harijans', 'Scheduled Castes' or 'Dalits'. The Indian constitution formally abolished untouchability and, were they to use the term 'Untouchable', Indian researchers might feel they were approving the practice of untouchability or, at least, that they might seem anti-democratic. Furthermore, the simple fact of being Indian makes them more sensitive to the derogatory or rude tone of certain expressions. A Tamil sociologist friend of mine, on seeing my book, *Les Paraiyar du Tamil Nadu,* expressed his shock at the title; for him, the very word

56. See J. Den Ouden, 'Social Stratification as Expressed through Language: A Case Study of a South Indian Village'. *Contributions to Indian Sociology (NS),* 13 (1979), p. 43.

57. G. Djurfeldt and S. Lindberg, *Behind Poverty: The Social Formation in a Tamil Village* (London: Curzon Press, 1975), p. 219.

58. G. Berreman, *Hindus of the Himalayas: Ethnography and Change* (Berkeley, CA: University of California Press, 1963), p. 216.

59. H. Isaacs, *India's Ex-Untouchables*, p. 43.

Paraiyar was so rude, so 'dirty', that it would have been unthinkable to use it in a book title. Western anthropologists, however, are generally free of such scruples. They simply observe the problems raised by the various generic terms we have enumerated, and find that the term 'Untouchable' has at least a certain sociological content. Even if all Untouchables are not strictly speaking 'untouchable',[60] the term is nevertheless indicative of a special position occupied by this social category in India.

Untouchables Outside India

The controversial question of whether untouchability is a specifically Indian[61] phenomenon is directly related to the more general problem of the Indian caste system itself. Whether or not the institution of caste is regarded as universal depends on the aim of the researcher's work. The first thinkers to address the question often stressed the similarities between Indian castes and other closed-status groups found throughout the world. This is certainly the case of Senart, a Sanskritist who interpreted the caste system as a local expression of an Indo-European institution. From a comparative standpoint, it is indeed interesting to see caste as a general, and perhaps even universal, phenomenon; yet, since Dumont,[62] anthropologists of modern-day India tend to stress the undeniably unique aspects of the caste system.

But tendency is not unanimity, and on this point, Gerald Berreman, an American anthropologist, has strongly argued not only that is caste a universal phenomenon, but that Untouchables can usefully be compared with Black Americans. According to Berreman,[63] cross-cultural comparison is essential to the progress of science. He readily acknowledges that there are differences between Black Americans and Indian Untouchables, but he does not accept that the two phenomena are to some extent different and therefore incomparable: 'Everything is to some extent unique, he writes, but there can be no science of the unique.'[64] For Berreman, then, the concepts of caste, ethnic stratification and race are not basically different;[65] 'race' as a basis of social rank, for example, is always a socially defined category and corresponds only very imperfectly with genetically transmitted traits. Caste, race and stratification are all birth-ascribed systems, and as such are comparable, he argues.

60. See A. Good, *The Female Bridegroom: A Comparative Study of Life-Crisis Rituals in South India and Sri Lanka* (Oxford: Clarendon Press, 1990), p. 14.

61. 'Indian' in this context denotes Indian society or more generally South Asia, since the institution of untouchability is also found in neighbouring Hinduized regions such as Nepal and Sri Lanka.

62. L. Dumont, *Homo Hierarchicus: essai sur le système des castes (*Paris: Gallimard, 1966), p. 271; translated in English as *Homo Hierarchicus. The Caste System and Its Implications,* trans. Mark Sainsbury, Louis Dumont and Basia Gulati (Chicago and London: University of Chicago Press, 1980), complete revised edition; page references are to the French edition.

63. G. Berreman, 'Structure and Function of Caste Systems', in G. De Vos and H. Wagatsuma (eds), *Japan's Invisible Race: Caste in Culture and Personality* (Berkeley, CA: University of California Press, 1967), p. 277.

64. G. Berreman, 'Race, Caste and Other Invidious Distinctions in Social Stratification', *Race,* 13 (1972), p. 395; see also *Caste and Other Inequities: Essays on Inequality* (Meerut: Folklore Institute, 1979), p. 2.

65. G. Berreman,'Race, Caste and Other Invidious Distinctions', p. 392.

Although comparing caste with other systems of social stratification may be of some use in certain circumstances, Berreman fails to convince me that the similarities between Blacks in America and Untouchables in India go deeper than a few very general or even superficial observations. Nor does he avoid the pitfall, pointed out by Marcus and Fisher,[66] of comparing sophisticated information gathered in another society with clichés on his own: while his analysis of India is based on an intensive study, what he has to say about Black Americans boils down to a few commonplace remarks of little scientific value. Black Americans certainly suffer from all manner of discrimination, but I wonder if the similarities with India do not stop there. At any rate, Black Americans are not divided into hundreds of endogamous groups, the United States has no ideological system that underpins and rationalizes racial discrimination, Blacks are not confined to ritually unclean occupations, the black/white dichotomy has no equivalent in India, where hierarchy is highly complex, Untouchables are not physically distinguishable from the rest of the population, and so on.

A jumbo jet and a bee have some features in common, but I wonder what would be gained by placing them in the same category. Most anthropologists of India would probably agree with the sentiments L. Dumont expressed in his famous article, 'Caste, racisme et "stratification"':

"The oneness of the human species, however, does not demand the arbitrary reduction of diversity to unity, it only demands that it should be possible to pass from one particularity to another, and that no effort should be spared in order to elaborate a common language in which each particularity can be adequately described. The first step to that end consists in recognizing differences.[67]"

If the comparison between untouchability in India, and racial discrimination in America or apartheid in South Africa is not particularly convincing, it should be recognized that, as Passin[68] suggests, the untouchability encountered in other Asiatic societies bears a much closer resemblance to the Indian case. This is no doubt because certain Indian values, like Buddhism, have made their way across the Far East. Countries as different as Tibet, Korea and Japan have social categories that share many features with India's Untouchables. The Ragyappa of Tibet, who numbered a scant thousand in the 1950s, live in separate quarters outside the walls of Lhasa's inner sanctum. They perform various services connected with dirt, death and blood: they act as scavengers, butchers, street sweepers, and so forth. Other people find their neighbourhood filthy and even terrifying. Similarly, Korea's Paekchong work as butchers, tanners, slaughterers; they are looked on as both unclean and dangerous. They are subjected to a number of discriminatory practices: their dead must be buried apart, they are not listed with human beings on official registers, they may not wear silk , and so on.[69]

66. G. Marcus and M. Fisher, *Anthropology as Cultural Critique: An Experimental Moment in the Human Sciences* (Chicago: University of Chicago Press, 1986), p. 140.

67. L. Dumont, *Homo Hierarchicus*, p. 377. On Berreman, the reader may also consult U. Sharma, 'Berreman Revisited. Caste and the Comparative Method', in M. Searle-Chatterjee and U. Sharma (eds), *Contextualizing Caste: Post-Dumontian Approaches* (Oxford: Blackwell, 1994).

68. H. Passin, 'Untouchability in the Far East'. *Monumenta Nipponica*, 2, 1955.

69. Ibid., p. 36.

One of the most striking examples, however, is Japan, which Berreman and his Berkeley colleagues have studied at length.[70] The Eta of Japan number about one million and constitute some 2 per cent of the Japanese population.[71] In Japan, the very word *Eta* is considered a serious insult, and one can be fined for using it.[72] The Chinese character for Eta means 'defilement abundant', and in common Japanese speech it has many of the same connotations as the American 'nigger'. It is for this reason that, as in India, a number of other terms are used, so that the Japanese speak of *Burakumin*,[73] or *Shin-Heinin*, 'the new common people',[74] a euphemism reminiscent of modern-day Indian usage. But such circumlocutions soon take on the derogatory overtones of the original words.

Burakumins live in separate quarters, outside the town or village; they work as butchers, tanners, slaughterers, weavers, basket- and mat-makers, and so forth. The Buddhist prohibition on killing animals may well have combined with the Shinto stress on cleanliness to 'ostracize' the Etas.[75] They used to be held in contempt and regarded as non-human: in 1859, an Eta was killed by a Japanese, and the leaders of the community brought the matter before the Civil Court. When all the arguments had been heard, Ikeda Harima No-Kami, the local judge, rendered a verdict that caused quite a stir: in so far as an Eta was worth only one-seventh of a human being, if the guilty party were to be sentenced for murder, he should be allowed to kill six more Etas.[76] Even today, a frequent insult consists of waggling four fingers at an Eta, to signify that he is four-legged like an animal. The Burakumins have remained strongly endogamous, even though more and more marry non-Etas. Economically they are poor, and their wages are always lower than those of other groups.[77] The attitudes of ordinary Japanese towards Etas can be summed up by the word 'disgust';[78] Japanese avoid having anything to do with them and even consider them to be dangerous; general opinion regards them as thieves, gangsters and likely to be infected with syphilis, tuberculosis and leprosy. They always trigger a 'gut' reaction, and they are felt to have about them something like a disgusting body odour that is repulsive to the ordinary citizen.[79]

In an important study, Passin identified a number of points common to all the Asiatic examples of untouchability, and these similarities cannot be discounted:

70. G. De Vos and H. Wagatsuma (eds), *Japan's Invisible Race: Caste in Culture and Personality* (Berkeley, CA: University of California Press, 1967).

71. H. Wagatsuma and G. De Vos, 'The Ecology of Special Buraku', in G. De Vos and H. Wagatsuma, *Japan's Invisible Race*, p. 118.

72. H. Wagatsuma, 'Postwar Political Militance', in G. De Vos and H. Wagatsuma, *Japan's Invisible Race*, p. 81.

73. G. Totten and H. Wagatsuma, 'Emancipation: Growth and Transformation of a Political Movement', in G. De Vos and H. Wagatsuma, *Japan's Invisible Race*, p. 35.

74. H. Passin, 'Untouchability in the Far East', p. 29.

75. J. Price, 'A History of the Outcastes: Untouchability in Japan', in G. De Vos and H. Wagatsuma, *Japan's Invisible Race*, p. 17.

76. H. Passin, 'Untouchability in the Far East', p. 35.

77. G. De Vos and H. Wagatsuma, 'Minority Status and Attitudes towards Authority', in G. De Vos and H. Wagatsuma, *Japan's Invisible Race*, p. 259.

78. J. Donoghue, 'The Social Persistence of an Outcaste Group', in G. De Vos and H. Wagatsuma, *Japan's Invisible Race*, p. 137.

79. G. De Vos and H. Wagatsuma, 'Socialization, Self-Perception and Burakumin Status', in G. De Vos and H. Wagatsuma, *Japan's Invisible Race*, p. 237.

1. The segregation to which 'untouchables' are subjected is often attributed to their supposed foreign origin.

2. They are considered inferior and unclean; in extreme cases they are even thought non-human.

3. They are forced to live apart, and this segregation reflects their 'outcaste' status.

4. Contact with them must be reduced to a minimum, and intermarriage with them is strictly forbidden.

5. They are subjected to many kinds of discrimination.

6. Their professional occupations are associated with waste, filth, blood and death. They perform menial tasks for the community.

7. In principle they are not allowed to own land.

All the above cases occur in societies that have ranked, hereditary groups; these groups are based on the ideology that social ranking is inherent in the construction of the universe and that ritual pollution is incurred through contact with organic waste and death.[80] As the same features also characterize Indian untouchability, it is not unreasonable to think that the various Asiatic cases may be 'offshoots' of the Indian system, perhaps spread by the expansion of Buddhism.[81] Yet it may also legitimately be argued, with Dumont, that the simple presence of Untouchables does not mean that the entire society is divided into castes.[82]

In the first place, several features remain peculiar to India. Unlike the Etas of Japan, Indian Untouchables have had practically no privileges as such; whereas in Japan, Etas had the monopoly on trade in armour, saddlery and other military goods, which garnered them a certain consideration that they turned to their advantage.[83] The Korean Paekchongs, too, controlled certain areas of economic activity, which ensured them a degree of independence.[84] Untouchables have never enjoyed such advantages, or at least have never been able to obtain any consideration, material or other, from the activities assigned to them. Do as they might, they have been condemned to dependency and exploitation.

In the second place, untouchability in India has never been a secondary phenomenon reserved for a peripheral section of the population. Untouchables are found in every part of India, even in the smallest towns and villages; untouchability is an inherent feature of Indian life.

Lastly, from a sociological standpoint, Untouchables in no way constitute a homogeneous community. They are divided into hundreds of castes, as we shall see, and these often take great pains to avoid each other. This fragmentation is an essential feature of untouchability in India, and entails a number of important consequences for the community. Among Japan's Burakumins, social solidarity seems much more

80. See H. Passin, 'Untouchability in the Far East', pp. 40-2.

81. H. Gould, 'Castes, Outcastes and the Sociology of Stratification'. *International Journal of Comparative Sociology,* 1 (1960), p. 232.

82. L. Dumont, *Homo Hierarchicus,* p. 262.

83. J. Price, 'A History of the Outcastes', p. 21.

84. H. Passin, 'Untouchability in the Far East', p. 36.

85. G. De Vos and H. Wagatsuma, 'Group Solidarity and Individual Mobility', in G. De Vos and H. Wagatsuma, *Japan's Invisible Race*, p. 242.

pronounced:[85] they discourage infighting,[86] and have developed a hostile attitude towards the greater part of society. This no doubt explains their failure to develop a political movement or to elect representatives to the Diet.[87] Conversely, we have already seen that lack of unity is one of the major obstacles to the Untouchable movement.

Continuing in a comparative perspective, it should be stressed that Max Weber's concept of a 'Pariah people' does not fit the Indian case. It seems that Weber had European Jewry in mind when he coined the phrase: in effect, he defined the 'Pariah people' as living in diaspora, and forming an 'often privileged' political community.[88] He went on to conclude that the Jews constitute 'the most superb historical example' of a 'Pariah people'.[89] In other places, Weber spoke of a 'guest people', who, like gypsies, are more or less nomadic and entertain certain relations with the main community; but when a 'guest people' is ritually impure, it becomes a 'Pariah people', with whom commensality and marriage are formally prohibited.[90] According to Sigrist, though, Weber defined the 'Pariah people' in a number of ways, so that the concept seems to lack consistency.[91] Weber betrayed his own misconceptions about untouchability in India when, for instance, he claimed that Paraiyars were not Untouchables. Ultimately, I am left wondering whether a comparison between Jews and Untouchables is of any interest at all.

In any event, the present study makes no claims to being comparative. To be sure, Indian untouchability is a particular form of man's exploitation by man, but this is so obvious as to be self-evident. What can be said is that there is no reason to equate institutions that bear no more than a vague superficial resemblance to each other.

Various Untouchable Castes

I have argued that one of the essential features of untouchability in India is the extreme fragmentation of its constituent units. In other words, as I have said a number of times, Untouchables by no means form a uniform community. They are, on the contrary, divided into hundreds of castes and subcastes dispersed over the entire subcontinent. Some castes contain a scant few hundred individuals, while the major, best-known groups – like the Chamars, Bhangis, Paraiyars and Mahars – count hundreds of thousands and even millions of members. Some castes are highly localized, while others, like the Chamars, are dispersed over vast areas that cut across state boundaries.

86. G. De Vos and H. Wagatsuma, 'Group Solidarity and Individual Mobility', p. 245.

87. H. Wagatsuma, 'Postwar Political Militance', p. 69.

88. C. Sigrist, 'The Problem of Pariahs', in O. Stammer (ed.), *Max Weber and Sociology Today* (New York: Harper & Row, 1971), p. 240.

89. W. Muhlmann, 'Max Weber and the Concept of Pariah-Communities', in O. Stammer (ed.), *Max Weber and Sociology Today*, p. 252.

90. M. Weber, *The Religion of India: The Sociology of Hinduism and Buddhism* (New York: The Free Press, 1958), pp. 11-12.

91. C. Sigrist, 'The Problem of Pariahs', p. 241.

Table 4. Untouchable castes by state

State			Number	%
Andhra Pradesh	(1)	5,774,548		
	(2)	60		
	(3)	Adi Andhra	616,319	10.6
		Madiga	2,514,848	43.5
		Mala	2,113,393	36.5
Bihar	(1)	7,950,652		
	(2)	23		
	(3)	Chamar/Mochi	2,382,440	29.9
		Dusadh/Dhari	2,105,413	26.4
		Musahar	1,168,447	14.6
Gujrat	(1)	1,825,432		
	(2)	42		
	(3)	Bhambi	321,868	17.6
		Bhangi	181,601	9.9
		Mahyavanshi	510,256	27.9
		Vankhar/Dedh	239,917	13.1
Haryana	(1)	1,895,933		
	(2)	37		
	(3)	Balmiki/Bhangi	374,960	19.7
		Chamar	1,004,413	52.9
		Dhanak	206,783	10.9
Himachal Pradesh	(1)	769,572		
	(2)	60		
	(3)	Charmar	224,574	29.1
		Koli/Kori	237,614	30.8
Jammu & Kashmir	(1)	381,277		
	(2)	13		
	(3)	Chamar	93,997	24.6
		Doon	78,430	20.5
		Megh	152,886	40.0
Kerala	(1)	1,772,168		
	(2)	69		
	(3)	Cheruman	259,966	14.6
		Kuravan	178,060	10.0
		Pulayan	586,988	33.1
Madhya Pradesh	(1)	5,453,690		
	(2)	69		
	(3)	Chamarv (various)	3,018,208	55.3
Maharashtra	(1)	3,025,761		
	(2)	69		
	(3)	Bhambi	439,503	14.5
		Mahar (various)	1,071,087	353
		Mang (various)	915,518	30.2

Table 4. continued from page 23

State			Number	%
Mysore	(1)	3,850,034		
	(2)	100		
	(3)	Adi-Dravida	429,601	11.1
		Adi-Karnataka	1,404,946	36.4
		Holeya (various)	374,270	9.7
Orissa	(1)	3,310,854		
	(2)	91		
	(3)	Bauri	303,460	9.1
		Dhoba	322,216	9.7
		Dom	370,236	11.1
		Ganda	325,053	9.8
		Pan	672,67	20.3
Punjab	(1)	3,348,217		
	(2)	37		
	(3)	Ad Dharmi	439,632	13.1
		Balmik/Bhangi	401,960	12.0
		Chamar	981,471	29.3
		Mazhabi	962,546	28.7
Rajasthan	(1)	4,075,580		
	(2)	81		
	(3)	Balai		
		Chamarv (various)	1,580,858	38.7
		Megh	599,644	14.7
Tamil Nadu	(1)	7,315,595		
	(2)	75		
		Adi-Dravida	2,547,166	34.8
		Chakkiliyan	864,842	11.8
		Pallar	1,326,745	18.1
		Paraiyar	1,533,482	20.9
Uttar Pradesh	(1)	18,548,916		
	(2)	66		
	(3)	Chamar	10,121,421	54.5
		Pasi/Tarmali	2,572,563	13.8
West Bengal	(1)	8,816,028		
	(2)	63		
	(3)	Bagdi/Duley	1,291,127	14.6
		Namasudra	980,524	11.1
		Pod	975,352	11.0
		Rajbanshi	1,35,919	15.3

(1) Total number of Untouchables
(2) Number of Scheduled Castes
(3) Names of principal castes in the state

The larger 'castes' are no doubt more confederations than castes properly speaking, being divided into countless endogamous 'subcastes', which in turn sometimes have their own hierarchy. A. Mayer[92] has shown that the relevance of the notions of 'caste' and 'subcaste' depends on context: in intercaste relations, a man represents his caste, but within his own caste, he acts as a member of his subcaste. This general principle holds for Untouchables as well.

Within a linguistic region, the various untouchable castes are usually associated with a traditional occupation, which may also be a ritual task: in Tamil Nadu, Pallars were for the most part agricultural workers, Paraiyars played the drums (*parai*) for inauspicious ceremonies, and Sakkiliyars were cobblers and scavengers. In Hindi-speaking regions, Chamars were tanners and cobblers, Bhangis sweepers, Koris weavers, and so on. In Maharashtra, Chambhars were leather-workers and the famous Mahars were messengers and watchmen, while their Mang rivals were rope-makers.[93] In Andhra Pradesh, Madigas were leather-workers, and Malas 'village servants'. Many occupations were associated with untouchability in this way.[94] As a rule, however, untouchable occupations have some tie with organic waste, filth, ritual pollution, death, evil spirits or various menial tasks. For instance, the Doms of Benares are funeral attendants, while the Paraiyars of Tamil Nadu play drums at funerals to keep away evil spirits. Throughout India, the sweepers, knackers, night-soil removers and scavengers are invariably Untouchables, as are the tanners and cobblers. Basket- and mat-making, too, are generally associated with untouchability. But the most frequent occupation of Untouchables is no doubt agricultural labour, together with the various menial tasks that keep the village running smoothly.

A typical Indian village often has more than one untouchable caste. The village of Endavur, studied by Moffatt,[95] for instance, has a whole list of untouchable castes: Valluvar Pandarams are the Harijan temple priests, Paraiyars are the most numerous caste, Vannans do the Untouchables' washing, Sakkiliyars are the tanners and Kuravars are known for catching and eating crows. Many other villages, however, have only one untouchable caste, which must then perform most of the tasks for the local community normally done by Untouchables: thus, as Srinivas aptly notes,[96] although Chamars generally regard themselves as superior to Bhangis, who are sweepers and scavengers, in the many villages where only Chamars are to be found, the latter perform all the work normally done by the Bhangis. This probably explains the very loose relationship between Untouchables and their traditional occupation:[97] very few Paraiyars actually play the *parai* drums, and in the 1930s, Blunt estimated

92. A. Mayer, *Caste and Kinship in Central India: A Village and Its Region* (Berkeley, CA: University of California Press, 1960), p. 160.

93. I. Karve, *Maharashtra Land and Its People* (Bombay: Maharashtra State Gazetteers General Series, 1968), p. 92.

94. See S. Fuchs, *At the Bottom of Indian Society: The Harijan and Other Low Castes* (Delhi: Munshiram Manoharlal, 1980).

95. M. Moffatt, *An Untouchable Community in South India*.

96. M. N. Srinivas, 'Some Reflections on the Nature of Caste Hierarchy'. *Contributions to Indian Sociology (NS)*, 18 (1984), p. 165.

97. K. Gough, 'Harijans in Thanjavur', in K. Gough and H. Sharma (eds), *Imperialism and Revolution in South Asia* (New York: Monthly Review Press, 1973), p. 223.

that only 4.8 per cent of Chamars worked leather.[98]

To gain a clearer and more concrete idea of the fragmentation of untouchable castes, it may be helpful to look at the principal states of India and the untouchable castes found there. Table 4 is based on the 1971 census. Item (1) indicates the total number of Untouchables in the state at the time of the census; (2) indicates the number of untouchable castes recorded in the same state; and (3) gives the castes comprising more than 10 per cent of the state's untouchable population.

This table gives us an idea of the diversity of castes in India. In the state of Orissa, for example, there are some 91 Scheduled Castes. Most of these are numerically insignificant, however. In addition, census categories are not always precise or appropriate. For example, in Tamil Nadu, the largest untouchable caste is the Adi-Dravidas, but we have also seen that *adi-dravida* is one of the generic terms used to refer to Untouchables in general, so that, in all likelihood, those listed as Adi-Dravida are actually Pallars or Paraiyars.[99] And similar problems must arise in other states: in North India, certain subcastes are sometimes lumped together with Chamars and sometimes listed separately. This is the case of such groups as the Jatavs, Mochis, Ramdasias, and so on.

Most Untouchables in any one state therefore belong to a handful of castes (see Table 4, no. 3). In Andhra Pradesh, for instance, Malas and Madigas alone account for some 80 per cent of the state's untouchable population. In Haryana, 53 per cent of Untouchables are Chamars, who also make up 55 per cent of the Scheduled Castes of Madhya Pradesh. The principal castes are also often concentrated in certain regions. In Tamil Nadu, although the three main castes are found throughout the state, Sakkiliyars constitute a clear majority in the Coimbatore region, Paraiyars in the eastern part of the state, and Pallars in the south.[100]

The size of these groups should not, however, be allowed to overshadow the fact that these huge castes are, as we have said, more like confederations, and do not constitute homogeneous blocs. Chamars are divided into a great many endogamous groups with no overarching institutions. The members of one of these large castes often entertain relations with only a very few of their fellow caste-members, and in Valghira Manickam, for example, Paraiyars intermarry with only some 15 villages, all located within a radius of a few kilometres.[101]

The purpose of this introductory chapter has been to familiarize the reader with this important category of the Indian population, the untouchable groups. Until now we have taken untouchability to be an established fact. In the following chapters, I will attempt to explain why such a large portion of the population has been reduced to subhuman status; and how the system works to keep them there.

98. E. Blunt, *The Caste System of Northern India with Special Reference to the United Provinces of Agra and Oudh* (Delhi: S. Chand and Co., 1969), p. 242.

99. See M. Moffatt, *An Untouchable Community in South India,* p. 112.

100. Ibid., p. 60.

101. R. Deliège, *Les Paraiyars du Tamil Nadu*, p. 200.

-2-

Untouchability: Theories of Caste

The importance of the problem of untouchability is widely recognized, if only by the enormous population concerned by this incredibly sophisticated system of social exclusion. And yet Untouchables cannot be said to have pride of place in sociological theories of social stratification. Few sociologists venture to discuss what is nevertheless an important sociological problem, and admittedly we Indianists are readily exasperated by any layman who dares set foot in our territory, and we poke fun at the commonplaces sometimes written by non-specialists. No doubt this, but also the highly complex nature of our object of study, explain the fact that the sociology and ethnology of India are still largely the preserve of specialists, and that the heated discussions within these subdisciplines rarely raise a response from the general fields of ethnology and sociology. The discussion of Nayar marriage is one notorious exception to the rule.

It is therefore hardly surprising that untouchability has sparked little in the way of theoretical enthusiasm on the part of the sociological community at large; more surprising, though, is the fact that Untouchables have not always received the attention they deserve from the theoreticians of caste themselves. This chapter will therefore endeavour to analyse how the principal theories of caste have approached the problem of untouchability, and will conclude with a list of the main features characterizing the Untouchables' position within the caste system.

Theories of Caste and Untouchability

Those writing on caste generally agree on the 'importance' of the question of untouchability; but paradoxically, this does not always translate into a probing discussion of the position occupied by Untouchables within the caste system itself. Several reasons combine to explain this paradox.

A number of caste theories, in particular the earliest ones, are based largely on 'textual' sources, often in Sanskrit, that show little interest in the lowest levels of society. Several Sanskrit specialists have tried their hand at constructing a true theory of caste, basing their reasoning for the most part on their knowledge of the sacred literature. Senart, Renou and Biardeau are the most eminent examples of this tendency. A few, theoretically more empirical, sociologists have gone down the same road; I am thinking of researchers like Max Weber, Celestin Bouglé, to a lesser extent Arthur Maurice Hocart, and, more recently, Claude Meillassoux or Jean Baechler, all of whom have written general works or articles on caste without firsthand knowledge of Indian society.

To be sure, all used appreciable empirical material; but it should still be stressed that, until the 1960s, Untouchables had practically never been studied from the inside, and what was known about them came, in most cases, from studies conducted in high-caste villages. Now, to take a more homely example, we know that it is hard to find out what a worker really thinks about on-the-job conditions if he is questioned in the presence of his boss. Likewise, it is very difficult to grasp what goes on in an untouchable hamlet when one approaches it through the dominant high-caste groups. Even as brilliant an observer as Srinivas[1] acknowledged these difficulties; deploring his relative unfamiliarity with the Harijans of Rampura village, he concluded: 'I would have obtained a new angle on the village if I had spent more time in their areas'.[2] It took Cohn some time to win the trust of the Chamars of Senapur, in Uttar Pradesh, and only then did they tell him 'Nothing but tales of the abuses and chicanery of the Thakurs'.[3] Fuchs[4] was probably the first to devote a monograph to an untouchable caste, and even then, in spite of its length, the work is hardly satisfying; somewhat later, Bernard Cohn submitted a dissertation at Cornell University;[5] but it was never published *in extenso*; however it can be considered a groundbreaking work, since it was not until Isaacs[6] and Lynch[7] that a new, insider approach to the question of untouchability was attempted.

In sum, for a long time the sources concerning these groups were disappointing, and in elaborating his interpretation of the ideology of untouchability, Max Weber made use of almost no documents stemming directly from untouchable communities. In fact, it has not been all that long since scholars claimed to know what Untouchables were thinking without taking the trouble to ask them! Even as experienced an anthropologist as Edmund Leach did not avoid this pitfall. Until very recently, theories of caste devoted little space to Untouchables. It is therefore not surprising to see that, in the last few decades, researchers have been paying increasing attention to these groups in their criticism of earlier theories and their new interpretations of the caste system: this is characteristic of the approaches taken by Berreman, Mencher, Kolenda, Bailey, and so on.

1. M. N. Srinivas, *The Remembered Village* (Berkeley, CA: University of California Press, 1976), pp. -.
2. Ibid., p. 49.
3. B. Cohn, 'The Chamars of Senapur', p. 5.
4. S. Fuchs, *The Children of Hari: A Study of the Nimar Balahis in the Central Provinces of India* (Vienna: Verlag Herold, 1950).
5. B. Cohn, 'The Chamars of Senapur'.
6. H. Isaacs, *India's Ex-Untouchables*.
7. O. Lynch, *The Politics of Untouchability*.

There are a number of ways of classifying theories of caste. Louis Dumont listed a few in his book *Homo Hierarchicus*, but his typology does not work very well. Alternatively, Moffatt's[8] is not only clearer, but also has the immense advantage of classifying these theories according to their approach to the problem of untouchability. We will therefore adopt these categories, with a few simplifications.

Moffatt distinguishes three types of approach to untouchability, which he calls 'models': outcaste models, models of diversity and models of unity. The first two emphasize separation, 'disjunction', between Untouchables and the rest of society, while the third, to which Moffatt largely subscribes, places the stress on 'conjunction', on the consensus that unites Untouchables with Indian society at large. The difference between the defenders of the 'outcaste' models and those of the models of diversity is slight in Moffatt's estimation: the first stress Untouchables' lack of a separate culture and their exclusion from the dominant culture, while the second, on the contrary, regard Untouchables as bearers of an 'alternative culture'.

The two models are not really contradictory, though, and Moffatt presents Kathleen Gough's approach as exemplifying both. Of chief importance is the fact that, ultimately in both cases, Untouchables appear as largely separate from the dominant culture; the emphasis is on separation, exclusion and even opposition. In this case, Untouchables can be described as 'out-castes', living outside the society from which they are very noticeably set apart. Kolenda, for instance, was among the first to show that fundamental concepts of Hinduism like *dharma* and *karma* do not operate among Untouchables,[9] while R. Miller shows that Mahars have developed a social and political culture of their own.

Moffatt observes that these tendencies are typical of those researchers who, as of the 1950s, began attempting to fill in the gaps we have indicated in the earlier ethnographic material by means of studies on the untouchable groups themselves. Most of these anthropologists were biased in favour of Untouchables,[10] which partly explains their point of view; moreover, as a rule anthropologists prefer discovering something new to confirming what everyone already knows. These arguments are not lacking in good sense, but it must also be pointed out that, if these anthropologists felt drawn to untouchable groups, it was also because they had shared a brief moment of their lives and suffering, which also enabled them to expose the inadequacies of earlier theories. Nevertheless, though it may be more gratifying to underscore the originality of one's data, this does not mean that these researchers fabricated what they affirm; to a great extent their interpretation coincides with reality. In any case, the first two models can be combined into a single category that I will call 'models of separation', and that I shall oppose to the 'models of unity'.

When Moffatt published his study in 1979, his intention was to refute these recent studies and to support, with his own findings, Dumont's theory, which had received some harsh treatment at the hands of the authors we have just discussed. Moffatt saw Dumont's theory as the archetypal 'model of unity', according to which the ideology

8. M. Moffatt, *An Untouchable Community in South India.*

9. P. Kolenda, 'Religious Anxiety and Hindu Fate', in E. Harper (ed.), *Religion in South Asia* (Berkeley, CA: University of California Press, 1964).

10. M. Moffatt, *An Untouchable Community in South India*, p. 9.

of caste was all-encompassing and imposed itself at all levels of the population. From this standpoint, there was consensus, interdependence and continuity between Untouchables and the rest of the population; the superiority of the Brahmin was structurally inseparable from the debased status of the Untouchable, and this interdependence at the level of societal organization reflected the opposition between pure and impure that was the foundation of the caste system.

I shall argue throughout the present book that these two apparently contradictory aspects - interdependence and exclusion - are in fact characteristic of untouchability, and that the two models are therefore not opposed, whatever Moffatt may say. Untouchables are not a marginal population with a veritable counterculture; quite the contrary: they are an integral part of Indian society. Nevertheless, the position assigned them within this society is indeed separate, and the discrimination from which they suffer attests this singularity.

Now we are ready to take a brief look at the different theories of caste; I shall show that the majority have passed over this articulation of apparently contradictory aspects and instead stressed one of the two models discussed. Louis Dumont's book, *Homo Hierarchicus*, is the most important of these. It is also a pivotal work, a key work and even a milestone in the history of Indian sociology, and will therefore be given pride of place in this overview, which will also serve as an introduction to the foundations of the caste system in general.

Models of Unity

One of the primary features of the early theories of caste was no doubt their emphasis on the integrated aspect of the system, on its harmonious nature. A good number of these authors based their work largely on the sacred literature, which obviously presented a picture of caste society as fairly stably balanced. Senart[11] himself recognizes that his sources led to certain deformations, owing to their tendency to exaggerate the privileges and the importance of Brahmins.[12] He argues that there is nothing odd about the caste system, which is simply the Indian version of a general Indo-European institution, a variant of the Roman *gens* or the Germanic tribe. Exogamy forces the traditional family to establish relations with other families, but at the same time it needs to avoid the corrupting influence of these outsiders. This is the role of the endogamy, the commensality and the rules of ritual purity that are found in the European civilizations of antiquity; but they have been systematized in India as nowhere else. Purity went on to become a fundamental Indian preoccupation, and that is why high-caste people must avoid any contact with the lower castes. Senart had little to say about Untouchables, and scarcely goes beyond these few generalities.

Max Weber, on the other hand, gives them ample space. The great German

11. The first edition of *Les Castes de l'Inde: les faits et le système* was published in 1894, but I have used the 1975 Indian edition: *Caste in India: The Facts and the System* (Delhi: ESS, 1975).

12. E. Senart, *Caste in India*, p. x.

sociologist maintains that Indian social organization is a veritable masterpiece of legislation, and astounding above all for its eminently coherent, rational and integrating character. He stresses the close link between religious beliefs and social structure, writing that the religious concepts of *samsara* (transmigration of souls) and the related notion of *karma* (the doctrine of rewards) constitute the 'veritable doctrine' of the caste system. He emphasizes that the doctrine of *karma* stipulates that every act has an inevitable effect on the fate of the actor. All a person's good actions and all his bad actions are 'totted up', as it were, and the result determines the person's fate in society. Sickness, handicaps, poverty, for instance, are the result of previous failings; but even more striking is the notion that a person's social rank, too, is determined by actions in a previous life. There is no such thing as an accident of birth, for a person determines what he becomes by his actions. A low-caste person, Weber goes on to say, thinks he must expiate numerous 'sins' committed in a past life, and that leading an exemplary life will earn him a better fate the next time round. The doctrine of *karma* transforms the Hindu's world into a strictly rational, ethically determined cosmos, and as such it represents the 'most consistent theodicy every produced by history'.[13] The lower castes therefore have everything to gain by strict compliance with ritual demands. What characterizes Untouchables, for Weber, is the fact that they have literally 'internalized' the Hindu order, which legitimizes their economic and social position. They adhere totally to Hindu rules and norms, and do not set themselves apart. One of the most surprising aspects of Weber's theory, however, is that he claims to reveal what Untouchables think without ever having gone to the trouble of asking them. — Important criticism

At the other end of the scale, Blunt, the superintendent of the 1911 All-India Census, excels in first-hand knowledge of Indian society; and the study he published in 1931 teems with statistics. In contrast with Weber, Blunt leaves hierarchy and status to one side, and instead stresses the exclusive nature of castes, with their concern for ritual purity. But, like Weber, he views Untouchables as particularly docile agents of the caste system. In effect, Blunt underscores the internal divisions and numerous subcastes found within untouchable groups. He points out that, among the Chamars, Johalas consider themselves superior and claim to be weavers, Rajarags are bricklayers, Sombattas are rope-makers, and so on. Confident of the prestige of their position, the Chamars who serve in European households have formed their own endogamous subcaste, the Gharuks, which goes to show, Blunt remarks, that untouchability is such a deeply ingrained practice that it is respected by Untouchables themselves: an Agarya regards a Dom as untouchable, while the latter considers Dhobis impure; at the very bottom of the social ladder are the Chamars.[14] Like Weber, Blunt argues that the system is legitimized by the adoption of its basic principles at every level of society. In other words, Blunt points out the continuity, the consensus that binds untouchable groups to the rest of society; Untouchables reproduce among their own ranks the various forms of exclusion and discrimination that are inflicted on them from above.

13. M. Weber, *The Relion of India*, p. 121.
14. E. Blunt, *The Caste System of Northern India*, p. 107.

Oddly enough, Untouchables are practically absent from Celestin Bouglé's study of the caste system. This is probably because the French sociologist has nothing original to say about them. His book, an otherwise penetrating study, puts Untouchables at the far end of the social scale from Brahmins, at the very bottom of the ladder; but this is all he has to say about their position. He attributes Brahmins' supremacy to their role as sacrificial priests, a theme taken up and systematized by Hocart, as we shall see. The importance of sacrifice in Indian society enables sacrificial priests to partake of the world of the gods, thus endowing them with a 'sacred' character that they are anxious to protect by dint of rules and taboos. According to Bouglé, Brahmin domination is the very model of the Indian social hierarchy, and it is not hard to guess that the Untouchable is therefore merely the opposite of the Brahmin, whose purity he ensures by performing the degrading tasks in society. This idea, as I have said, will be taken up by Hocart, who sees the caste system as a particularly brilliant illustration of the connection between ritual and social organization, the leitmotiv of his entire work.

According to Hocart, it is not economic reasons that bring men together, for the pursuit of profit tends to divide rather than to unite.[15] Alternatively, mankind the world over has always aspired to conquer nature, and to do this he needs the help of 'outside forces', namely the gods and demons.[16] Humans therefore organized their societies around this ritual necessity of obtaining the gods' favour; and the caste system in particular can be seen as an organization whose essence is primarily sacrificial. Or to put it another way, it was the organization of sacrifice that dictated the articulation of the different social classes, and 'every occupation was a priesthood', whereby each occupation fulfilled a priestly function. What distinguishes the barber, the washerman or the drummer is not their economic function, then, but the position they occupy in the ritual. Of course, over the centuries these tasks have also become specializations; but specialization is the consequence of differentiation, and not the other way around. In other words, if the blacksmith specialized in ironworking, it is because he was originally set apart from the other social categories, and this was for essentially ritual reasons.[17] Society has no inherent need of a caste of woodworkers to make ploughs or a caste of fishermen to catch fish.[18] Furthermore, the different farming castes are not the only ones who work the land.[19]

Therefore, according to Hocart, society has been divided into groups, each of which plays a specific role in the ritual. Each sacrifice reaffirms the gods' might and their victory over darkness. Kings and priests are associated in the ritual and form an inseparable pair. The cultivators are responsible for preparing and bringing the food used in the ritual. The auspicious life ritual must not be contaminated by inauspicious death ritual, and therefore a hereditary group is necessary to deal with all matters having to do with death. The drummer thereby becomes first and foremost the priest of the demons, and it is in this role that he beats the drum. Relegated to the bottom of

15. A. Hocart, *Kings and Councillors: An Essay in the Comparative Anatomy of Human Society* (Chicago: University of Chicago Press, 1970), p. 35.

16. Ibid., pp. 27 and 41.

17. Ibid., p. 39.

18. A. Hocart, *Les Castes* (Paris: Librairie orientaliste Paul Geuthner, 1938), p. 170.

19.Ibid., p. 197.

the hierarchy, he performs only at funerals and blood sacrifices. Likewise, washermen and barbers do much more than simply washing and shaving; they play an indispensable role in every ritual. The barber builds the funeral pyre, for instance; but more generally, each caste fulfils a ritual function: the carpenters make the wheels of religious carts, the goldsmiths fashion various religious ornaments, and so forth. This is why Hocart concludes that, in India, 'every caste is a priesthood'. Such a conception of course underscores the interdependence of castes, the integrated character of society, wherein each member fulfils a function that is essential if the whole is to run smoothly. Without the participation of each of its members, society cannot achieve the prosperity essential to its survival. It is in this context that the Untouchables' position must be understood.

Hocart was one of the first to reject the term 'outcaste', which was in wide use at the time, because, in his view, all castes, whatever their position, entered into the overall harmonious composition of society. In fact he did not even distinguish Shudras from Untouchables. He argued that the latter only appeared to be excluded, for the success of the sacrifice actually depended on being able to control the lower infernal powers - demons and evil spirits - as well as to propitiate the superior heavenly powers.[20] Society does not need untouchable castes to carry out the various economic tasks usually performed by them. But the demons, or *asura*, must absolutely be controlled by categories set apart from society; therefore without the untouchable castes, he argues, society would be unable to function. Exclusion, discrimination, poverty are all missing from Hocart's picture, which is one of the most developed examples of the consensual approach.

Among the most recent analyses of the caste system, Quigley's lively and polemical book has updated Hocart's theses in the light of the latest ethnography. Untouchables are not given pride of place in Quigley's approach, which further argues that the opposition between Brahmins and Untouchables is not an essential feature of the system.[21] One of the guiding ideas of this work is the refusal to consider that the Brahmin priest occupies a 'supreme' or even elevated position in Indian society. Basing his argument on work by Parry, Fuller and Raheja, Quigley also maintains that Brahmins, particularly when they act as priests, can even 'be untouchable'.[22] After having rejected Dumont's disjunction between status and power, Quigley himself seems to fall prey to a somewhat idealistic view of caste societies, in that he restricts his view of Untouchables to their ritual function. But, while they may sometimes be the object of scorn, Brahmins are never reduced to the rank of Untouchable; while they can be *achut* (impure), they can never become untouchable, any more, for that matter, than a woman who is menstruating or a chief mourner. Later, however, Quigley emphasizes the Untouchables' position as intermediary between society and the world of demons;[23] but he seems to have no inclination to consider the economic and social aspects of untouchability, and, as in Hocart's case, the deprivations imposed on the lower levels of Indian society do not really engage his attention.

20. Ibid., p. 27.
21. D. Quigley, *The Interpretation of Caste* (Oxford: Clarendon Press, 1993), p. 160.
22. Ibid., p. 16.
23. Ibid., p. 156.

One of the most influential books on the caste system was no doubt Hutton's *Caste in India*; Hutton, like Blunt, also directed a census before going on to become a Cambridge don. First published in 1946, *Caste in India* remained the chief reference work until the appearance of *Homo Hierarchicus*, exactly 20 years later. Hutton paints an integrated and harmonious picture of the system. He argues that caste is a useful institution because it provides people with a secure and reassuring social environment; it takes care of arranging marriages and serves as both a trade union and an orphanage. It replaces life insurance and ensures that everyone has a profession. Caste has also enabled a pluralistic society to hold together, and therefore is a basic factor of stability for both the individual and society. Unlike his predecessors, Hutton does not regard Untouchables as an essential category, but, on the contrary, contends that their existence is the most repugnant aspect of this society, a sort of diseased growth of which society would do well to rid itself. Hutton was one of the first authors to devote an entire chapter to what he calls 'exterior castes', which he identifies by means of the various taboos and disabilities imposed on them. Nevertheless, he is more communicative about the recent changes than about the structural position of Untouchables, of which he has little to say.

Hutton stresses separation between the castes and maintains that harmony would be achievable were it not for untouchability; he considers that the system has no religious basis and that, this being the case, Untouchables are an altogether unnecessary evil. The same idea can be found in Gandhi's writings. Although his conceptions evolved over time, the slogan 'separate but equal' seems to sum up his views on caste. Until the 1920s, Gandhi argued in favour of the caste system, even to the extent of regarding the prohibitions on intermarriage and commensality as an essential stage in the soul's progress; later, however, he toned down his enthusiasm and restricted his message to *varna shrama dharma*, or a four-part division of society, which he regarded as fundamental to Hinduism.[24] He drew a distinction between caste, *jati,* of which India must rid itself (he wrote a pamphlet entitled *Caste Must Go*), and *varna,* which remains highly desirable. According to Gandhi, there is no reason to regard a Shudra as inferior to a Brahmin, but every man is duty-bound to follow the traditions and occupation of his forebears. To do so is simply to follow the law of nature, which decrees that we are born with the same features as our parents.[25] It is therefore not desirable for a Brahmin to become a sweeper or for a Shudra to train for an intellectual profession: a Shudra who wants to become a lawyer simply wants to make money,[26] and this is not a desirable inclination.

It was in Sri Lanka that the famous English anthropologist, Edmund Leach, conducted one of his principal field studies. In 1960, a work devoted to the caste system was published under his direction, and he supplied a substantial introduction that pretty well summed up the 'models of unity' we have encountered to this point. This was the heyday of structuralism, and the Cambridge don was among those who helped popularize French structuralist ideas on the other side of the Channel. Leach's

24. D. Dalton, 'The Gandhian View of Caste and Caste after Gandhi', in P. Mason (ed.), *India and Ceylon: Unity and Diversity* (Oxford: Oxford University Press, 1967), p. 172.
25. M. Gandhi, *The Removal of Untouchability* (Allahabad : Narajivan Publishing House, 1954), p. 33.
26. Ibid., p. 48.

conception of caste fits in with this perspective. He argues that the phenomenon of caste cannot be understood outside a system, and he stresses the interdependence of castes, which are thus united in a system of organic solidarity, in the Durkheimian sense of the term. Each caste fulfils a well-defined function. He deplores the fact that anthropologists tend to emphasize endogamy, exclusiveness and separation between castes, whereas in fact the fundamental characteristic of the system is interdependence: all castes are bound up in a network of reciprocal ties of an economic, political and ritual nature. The accent on the harmony of the system could not be more explicit, and Leach continues with this almost idyllic vision, stressing that, in a caste society, unlike those based on class, the labouring classes constitute a numerical minority, are guaranteed a certain degree of economic security and, above all, enjoy certain privileges. They therefore do not see themselves as being rejected by the system, but, on the contrary, as having the privilege of performing a task denied all other groups.[27] The caste system therefore rests on a sort of consensus in which everyone is ultimately content with his lot and all share the same values. Cooperation is inherent to the caste system; and when castes come into competition, they cease to be castes. Competition may exist within the caste, between individuals in the group, since they are of the same nature; but different castes, by their very essence, cannot compete with each other. According to Leach, the present-day demands being made by Untouchables tell us nothing about the nature of the caste system. They are protesting against their economic deprivation, but not against their place in the system.

Untouchables suffer not because they are low-caste, but because their position has degenerated in the wake of changes introduced by capitalism. To a certain extent, Leach shares the views of Hutton and Gandhi on the integrated and harmonious character of the caste system. But unlike these two authors, he does not consider untouchability an anomaly; he regards Untouchables as an integral part of the system, and even stresses that they are all but perfectly content with their condition. It must be noted, however, that Leach's generalizations are not underpinned by a single interview with low-caste people; this overall satisfaction is deduced from their position in a system presented as being basically harmonious and therefore supposed to satisfy everyone. Leach's theory breathes new life into the myth of a Golden Age before British colonial rule. It stems no doubt from the idealized accounts of the village community, that 'veritable small republic', given by certain nineteenth-century observers like Munro, Elphinstone or Maine, who, as Dumont stressed, refused to see the caste system for what it was.[28]

Among others who have emphasized the village community and 'vertical solidarity' is the great Indian anthropologist, M. N. Srinivas, whose two monographs, *Religion and Society among the Coorgs and The Remembered Village*, are both 'classics'. This student and even disciple of Radcliffe-Brown was one of the first to study an Indian plains village in accordance with the canons of participant observation. As a consequence, he emphasizes the 'social structure' of these villages, happily showing

27. E. R. Leach, 'What Should We Mean by Caste?', in E. Leach (ed.), *Aspects of Caste in South India, Ceylon and North Western Pakistan,* (Cambridge: Cambridge University Press, 1960), p. 6.

28. L. Dumont, *La Civilisation indienne et nous* (Paris: A. Colin, 1975), p. 138.

their solidarity and overall smooth functioning. He sees caste society as being marked by two characteristics: separation and dependence, or hierarchy and interdependence.[29] Professional specialization creates caste interdependence, while hierarchy stresses endogamy and restrictions on commensality, and therefore separation. A caste-based society thus combines these centrifugal and centripetal tendencies, and hierarchy and interdependence are but two aspects of a single system.[30]

Dumont, as we shall see, believes that interdependence is always subordinated to hierarchy; but not Srinivas, who, on the contrary, underlines the existence of a veritable village community. Whenever there is a festival or a catastrophe, all castes of a village overcome their differences and act together, and there exists a veritable 'village patriotism'.[31] Untouchables are indeed ritually impure categories, *pole* in the Coorg region; but they are an integral part of the village community, and have close ties with their masters. In fact, in Karnataka, Harijans are called *halemaga*, meaning 'old sons',[32] and servants must be treated well. For instance, Harijans tell their employers: 'You can strike me on the back, but don't strike me on the belly.' Villagers enjoy telling about people who have grown rich at the expense of their servants only to have all manner of misfortune befall them. In other words, there are 'mystical' sanctions for mistreating the poor. The position of Untouchables cannot therefore be thought of in terms of exploitation, for there are rules that ensure that the worker will be treated fairly.[33] This brilliant anthropologist is unmoved by the deprivations inflicted on Untouchables, or at least he has little to say about them. Rather he argues that the ritual marginality of this category is very definitely compensated by a certain degree of protection and material security.

In sum, most of the theories of caste before *Homo Hierarchicus* emphasized the inherently balanced character of the system and the interdependence of the castes. Ghurye, whom we will discuss later, is an exception, since in the 1930s he suggested that separation between the castes and caste endogamy were the essential features of this institution. As Moffatt pointed out in his book, Dumont's theory resembles the models of unity, but it cannot be reduced to them, for his theory is far more subtle and complex than any of the preceding approaches, and its importance deserves a longer development.

Homo Hierarchicus

Homo Hierarchicus is no doubt Louis Dumont's principal work, the one that has had the greatest impact; it is truly a classic of sociology in the broad sense of the term. The book is both a masterly synthesis of what is known about caste and a vigorous

29. M. N. Srinivas, *The Remembered Village,* p. 166.
30. Ibid., p. 185.
31. M. N. Srinivas, 'The Social Structure of a Mysore Village', in M. N. Srinivas (ed.), *India's Villages* (London: Asia Publishing House, 1955), pp. 32-3.
32. M. N. Srinivas, *The Remembered Village,* p. 199.
33. M. N. Srinivas, 'Some Reflections on the Nature of Caste Hierarchy'. *Contributions to Indian Sociology (NS),* 18 (1984), pp. 151-67, p. 166.

theoretical analysis of the principle of hierarchy, which is the basis of the system. The author invites us to reflect and draw comparisons, and this is a good part of what has made the book such a success. Although Dumont has not managed to resolve all the questions that arise in the analysis of Indian society, he seems to have at least addressed them all, and among these, the issue of untouchability, which occupies both an essential and a limited place in this work: essential because Untouchables are perceived as the indispensable complement to Brahmins; and limited because they receive relatively little space. Nevertheless, the book has had an enormous influence, and everything subsequently written on caste has been in one way or another a reaction to *Homo Hierarchicus*. We shall return to this point.

Dumont's work is at once a synthesis and a thesis. It rests on the compilation of a huge bibliography, while presenting an original view of Indian society. Ultimately, his goal is to show that the caste system is the creation, at the level of the social organization, of a veritable mode of thought that is radically different from our own and that is characterized first and foremost by the principle of hierarchy. Dumont's approach is anthropological, in the full sense of the term, and his intellectual journey leads him eventually to distinguish traditional, 'holistic' societies, among which he places India, from modern societies, in which 'individualism' prevails.

According to the principles of structuralism that Dumont espouses, reality is the creation of mental categories; and, consequently, he views the caste system as an ideology, that is to say, as a system of values and ideas that is both rational and intelligible. Ideology here is understood as the 'fundamental ideology of a society', in other words, the set of ideas and values shared by all members of a society, in the same way, for example, as the national language. The anthropologist's role, according to Dumont, is to reconstruct this ideology from what peoples themselves believe and think.[34] In passing we should note a fairly basic difference between Dumont's structuralism and that of Lévi-Strauss, who was not afraid to say that 'the conscious awareness of the actors appears as the hidden enemy of the sciences of Man'.[35] For Dumont, on the contrary, understanding a society implies making an effort to put oneself into the skin of the natives, which helps avoid one's ethnocentric tendencies. But when it comes to studying India, this is a particularly arduous method, for the underlying ideology of the society is summed up in the notion of hierarchy, which goes against our Western principles of liberty and equality, and even against the very notion of the individual.

Traditional societies have the specific characteristic that they do not think of Man as an individual, but rather as a member of a collectivity. Such societies stress collective man, and their ideal is not equality and individual liberty but order; the overall order of society is the supreme value. This 'holism' is expressed strikingly in the organization of Indian society, which takes the form of a hierarchy. To create a hierarchy is to create an order, a 'ladder of command', and this hierarchy can be defined as 'the principle by which the elements of a whole are ranked in relation to the whole'.[36] In India, hierarchy is the means by which traditional societies achieve

34. L. Dumont, *Homo Hierarchicus: essai sur le système des castes* (Paris: Gallimard, 1966), p. 56.
35. C. Lévi-Strauss, *Anthropologie structurale deux* (Paris: Plon, 1973), p. 344.
36. L. Dumont, *Homo Hierarchicus,* p. 92.

'holism'. The caste system can therefore be regarded as a hierarchical ranking, and hierarchy as the Indian counterpart of the notion of equality. This is the principle around which the whole society is articulated. In the case of India, however, hierarchy is not simply a linear ranking in which each caste stands above one and below another. In this instance, the hierarchy of castes is organized as a structure, as a system of oppositions.[37] Dumont is fairly vague about what he means by structure, but it is clear that the opposition between pure and impure forms the basis of the system and serves as the fundamental criterion of rank. To use Dumont's terminology, it can be said that the whole system rests on the 'necessary and hierarchical co-existence of the two opposites'.[38] It is this opposition that accounts for all the social relationships found in Indian society. It is 'by implicit reference to this opposition that the society of castes appears consistent and rational to those who live in it'.[39]

The opposition between pure and impure is first and foremost of a religious nature. Of course these notions are found in most of the world's religions, but they provide the actual foundation of the religious and social system of the Hindus. Maintaining a certain degree of purity is a constant concern for Indians, and division into endogamous castes is one way of preserving the relative purity of a group. The primary source of defilement is contact with death and organic wastes, primarily those from the human body (faeces, saliva, urine, perspiration, hair, menstrual blood, etc.). Every area of social life is pervaded by this dichotomy: the type of food eaten, for instance, can be ranked, and the strictly vegetarian diet associated with Brahmins and a few other high castes is considered the most pure; next come diets that allow eggs; then fish, chicken, mutton and, right at the bottom, pork and beef. Similarly, certain materials are ascribed a ritual value: silk is more pure than cotton, gold more than silver, brass more than copper. So pervasive is the opposition between pure and impure that we could go on to enumerate many more applications .

Impurity, unlike purity, is contagious. An entire family can be contaminated, as in the case of pollution stemming from contact with death, a particularly powerful pollutant: when someone dies, the deceased's entire family is polluted, and it is not until the ritual bath and various purifying rites, performed at the end of the mourning period, that the pollution is lifted. Birth pollutes only the mother and the child, while menstruation pollutes only the woman herself, providing she is careful to avoid contact with other people and with their food. Shaving and cutting the hair also entail a degree of pollution, which can be remedied by simply taking a bath. Bathing in running water, especially in the Ganges, is a particularly effective means of purification. In addition to water, other purifying agents exist, among which, and in pride of place, are the five products of the cow: urine, dung, *ghee* (clarified butter), milk and yogurt.

This highly simplified and very incomplete picture leads us to make two observations, both of which are equally general, but closely connected with the subject at hand: in the first place, pollution is temporary, which means that it is more or less easy to eliminate. Nevertheless we shall see that there is also a permanent kind of

37. Ibid., p. 59.
38. Ibid., p. 65.
39. Ibid., p. 66.

pollution that it is impossible to rid oneself of, however hard one tries. In other words, there is a category of persons who can never achieve ritual purity. These 'categories' are of course 'castes', since the second point we must now underscore is obviously the fact that this hierarchy based on the distinction between pure and impure is reproduced in the social order by the presence of 'closed' status groups that are anxious to protect their purity. In effect, a society that attaches so much importance to purity tends to produce closed social groups, in other words to protect the members of a group. Castes therefore are these endogamous groups, more or less associated with an occupation, each of which is ranked as higher or lower with respect to every other. At the summit of the hierarchy are the Brahmins, and at the base, the different untouchable castes, who form a sort of antithesis to Brahminic purity, and who are in a permanent state of impurity because of their association with death and the various forms of organic waste.

Thus the position of the Untouchables in Dumont's theory is of the essence. We have seen, in effect, that he understands hierarchy as a structure, a system of oppositions, and that the opposition Brahmin/Untouchable sums up or reflects, at the level of social organization, the dichotomy between pure and impure. This is such a basic opposition that Dumont is not afraid to come straight out and say that untouchability cannot disappear so long as Brahmins continue to exist. There is a clear difference here between Dumont and authors like Hutton or Gandhi, who, on the contrary, consider untouchability to be a cancerous sore eating away at Hinduism that must be cut out. Dumont also signals his difference from the earlier 'models of unity' when he stresses the 'hierarchical' integration of society. For instance, he criticizes authors like Wiser - of whom more later - for emphasizing 'reciprocity' within the system; any 'reciprocity' there may be, Dumont points out, is altogether hierarchical.[40] On a more general level, though, Dumont can indeed be associated with these 'models of unity', since for him the ideology of pure and impure is the 'fundamental ideology of the society', in the sense that it is shared by all members of the society. Untouchables thus share the values of this society, and an American anthropologist, Michel Moffatt, has applied himself to demonstrating this consensus.[41] We will discuss his work at length in a later chapter; but for the moment we will stay with Dumont, who points out that Untouchables even practise untouchability among themselves: the Doms, Chamars and Dhobis mutually regard each other as untouchable.[42]

The Indian obsession with purity culminates in untouchability. The relegation of Untouchables to the bottom of the social ladder is therefore religious in nature,[43] and stems from their association with impure tasks. Here we touch on an aspect of Dumont's study that has caused much ink to flow: the dissociation of status and power. For Dumont, caste ranking is essentially a ritual matter, stemming from the notions of purity and impurity, and not from the possession of power. One of the specificities of the Indian system is the fact that a spiritual authority is never at the same time a temporal power: 'the supremacy of the spiritual was never expressed politically'.[44] The

40. Ibid., p. 134
41. M. Moffatt, *An Untouchable Community in South India.*
42. Dumont, *Homo Hierarchicus*, p. 174.
43. Ibid., p. 70.
44. L. Dumont, *Homo Hierarchicus*, p. 100; see also p. 273.

explanation of the Untouchables' debased status must be sought in religion, and not in the political or the economic spheres: the execution of the impure tasks by one group is necessary to maintaining the purity of the others.[45] The impurity of the Untouchable is conceptually inseparable from the purity of the Brahmin.[46] Untouchables are therefore the social categories whose task it is to clean up society, to remove its organic wastes and to keep away all sorts of inauspicious influences. The cow, which, as we know, is the object of religious veneration, indicates the religious basis of the Untouchables' position: in effect it is always the task of untouchable castes to dispose of dead cattle; they do the leatherworking, the drumming and the shoemaking. Their members are also street-sweepers and night-soil removers.

The segregation of Untouchables in separate hamlets is the spatial expression of their specialization in impure tasks.[47] This last reference shows that Dumont does indeed occasionally mention the discriminations and disabilities from which Untouchables suffer.[48] But far from emphasizing this exclusion, he tends to minimize it; it is inaccurate, he says, to see them as being outside religious society: the two poles of society, representing the pure and the impure, are 'equally necessary, although unequal';[49] 'social reality is a totality made up of two equal but complementary halves'. Which eventually leads him to write that, in sum, the caste system should appear as rather less exploitative than democratic society.[50] This conclusion, highly personal it must be said, infuriated a good number of those researchers who later studied the life of Untouchables; therefore the question of untouchability occupies a decisive place in the assessment of *Homo Hierarchicus*.

Models of Separation

Dumont's book rapidly became the ultimate reference for the study of the caste system and Indian society. The intelligence of his observations, the sophistication of his argumentation, the abundance of his sources and his great erudition have made this an 'indispensable' work. And more than twenty-five years after its publication, we are obliged to say that it remains largely unequalled. But whereas there is unanimous agreement as to the importance of this study, some of its content has given rise to very serious criticisms,[51] and all those who have subsequently written on caste have positioned themselves in relation to Dumont's theses. However, again this is not intended to be a history of caste theories in general. My aim is to focus on theories dealing with untouchability. And it is precisely Dumont's views on this subject that are the target of the attacks.

45. Ibid., p. 78.
46. Ibid., p. 77.
47. Ibid., p. 173.
48. See also e.g. Ibid., p. 112.
49. Ibid., p. 78.
50. Ibid., p. 139.
51. See in particular, D. Quigley, 'Le Brahmane pur et le prêtre impur'. *Recherches sociologiques*, 23 (1992).

The earliest theories of caste, as we have seen, stressed the integrated character of the system. Ghurye, the father of Indian sociology, was also the first to underscore the exclusion of Untouchables. Furthermore, Ghurye was not only a sociologist, but an Indian nationalist as well. He wrote in the 1930s, with the liberation movement in full swing, and the influence of secular Congress Party ideals can be felt throughout his work. For instance, he was to rise in violent opposition to Verrier Elwin's proposal to create reservations as a means of protecting India's tribal peoples from alien influences.[52] In his book on caste, first published in 1932, Ghurye stresses endogamy as the essential feature of caste, or even the 'essence of caste'.[53] Ghurye was also the first to take a close interest in the changes occurring at the time in the caste system: the British Raj had a number of fairly perverse effects on the system, which tended to reinforce the divisions between castes. Singling out non-Brahmins to receive a number of privileges had the effect of consolidating the notion of caste, notably by the creation of caste associations. Ghurye is truly the pioneer of the study of social change in India. Whereas Western analysts have always tended to regard Indian society as immutable and timeless, he showed the importance of the link between caste and politics, and analysed social movements and ongoing transformations in the system.

After this brief excursus to point out the contribution made by this pioneer, we can turn back to the critics of *Homo Hierarchicus,* among whom Berreman stands out in particular relief. I have already spoken, in Chapter 1, of the contribution made by his theories, which assimilate the Indian caste system to racial segregation in America. This comparison clearly shows the importance of Untouchables in this author's mind, since, after a fashion, he identifies them with Black Americans. In an article entitled 'The Brahmanical View of Caste',[54] Berreman criticizes Dumont for having given a partial (in both senses of the term) picture of the caste system. He recounts that, when he exposed Dumont's views to one untouchable informant, the latter laughed and replied: 'You must have been talking to Brahmins.'[55] In reality, Berreman goes on, Dumont's theory is typically Brahminic, stereotypical and idealized at the same time: Dumont describes the high-caste ideal or rather the system as high-caste people would like it to be, and not as it really is and as it is experienced by millions of Indians. The voices of those oppressed by the system are not heard in Dumont's work. He postulates that the ideology he has reconstructed is universal and accepted by all. Berreman argues that the Indian caste system is not a harmonious, balanced and unanimously accepted structure. The separation Dumont makes between status and power is similarly disputable. The two are in fact inseparable, and it is impossible for a group to improve its status if it does not at the same time increase its power. The Gond groups that control a territory are called Raj-Gond, and are not included among the ranks of the Untouchables, unlike the rest of the Gonds. In short, for Berreman and for many other authors, the religious sphere cannot be dissociated from the political-economic sphere: status is not separable from power.

52. G. S. Ghurye, *The Scheduled Tribes* (Bombay: Popular Prakashan, 1963), 165ff.

53. G. S. Ghurye, *Caste and Race in India* (Bombay: Popular Prakashan, 1969), p. 182.

54. Reprinted with a number of other articles in G. Berreman, *Caste and Other Inequities: Essays on Inequality* (Meerut: Folklore Institute, 1979).

55. Ibid., p. 163.

We have seen that, of all contemporary social anthropologists, Berreman is without doubt the one who insists most heavily on caste as a system of stratification. He argues that, in order to understand the phenomenon of caste, it is useful to compare it with similar systems in other parts of the world, contending that there is a caste system wherever groups are birth-ascribed, ranked and 'culturally distinct'.[56] This definition allows him to see caste wherever hierarchy is institutionalized.[57] We will not dwell on this viewpoint, which is worthy of respect even though one may not share it; but we can note that, according to Berreman again, castes are 'culturally distinct' entities, and that they do not share a common culture. Or to put it another way, Untouchables do not share the values of the rest of society or the Brahminic foundations of the system as they are set out by Dumont. Anyone who has gone to the trouble to talk with low-caste Indians knows pertinently that they in no way accept their debased condition.

Berreman's views seem to have grown more radical over time; for in his monograph *Hindus of the Himalayas*, published in 1963, and his article 'Caste in India and the United States',[58] his treatment of the contrasts between low and high castes was more nuanced. Indeed, in his early publications he made a distinction between the attitude of low-caste people, and Untouchables in particular, to the system as such and the attitude of the same people to their own place within the system. The difference may be subtle, but it is important, for Berreman notes that low-caste people are usually dissatisfied with their condition within the system, but at the same time do not question the system as such.[59] Without getting ahead of ourselves, let us note that this idea sums up my analysis of the ideology of Untouchables and their origin myths, as we shall see in the course of in the present book. Berreman saw clearly that low-caste people are always prompt to rationalize their caste status, but also their own position. It would be psychologically untenable, he says, for a low-caste person to regard himself as a scoundrel condemned to expiate faults committed in a previous life.[60] But in this case, then, it is not India's caste society as such that is being contested, but the person's status within the system. In these publications, he holds this up as an essential difference between India and the United States, since, in American society, Black Americans do not so much want to improve their position within the system as to put an end to the whole system of segregation.

Berreman seems to have divested himself of these nuances when he considers, particularly in his later publications, that the Untouchables in the Himalayan regions where he has worked form a distinct and relatively homogeneous social category, given that the caste system can be reduced to the opposition between twice-born[61] and Untouchables, in other words between Khas and Doms. In reducing the system to this simple opposition, Berreman obliterates the large differences between Rajputs and

56. See G. Berreman, *Hindus of the Himalayas Ethnography and Change* (Berkeley, CA: University of California Press, 1963), p. 98; 'Caste: The Concept of Caste', in E. Sills (ed.), *International Encyclopedia of the Social Sciences* (New York: Macmillan Free Press, 1968), II, p. 334; 'Race, Caste and Other Invidious Distinctions in Social Stratification'. *Race,* 13 (1972), pp. 378-414, p. 401; and *Caste and Other Inequities*, p. 2.

57. G. Berreman, *Caste and Other Inequities*, p. 159.

58. Published in 1960, but quoted here from Berreman, *Caste and Other Inequities*, 1979.

59. G. Berreman, *Caste and Other Inequities*, p. 9.

60. G. Berreman, *Hindus of the Himalayas*, p. 223.

61. High-caste people, who go through a ritual of rebirth.

Brahmins, or those between Bajgis (drummers) and metalworkers. There is no need to elaborate in the case of the Brahmins and the Rajputs; but we can note that, in Berreman's region, metalworkers refuse the name Dom, which is what they call barbers and Bajgis. The latter also reject the name, claiming that only shoemakers are Doms. The taboos and differences separating these castes are far from negligible, and it therefore becomes difficult to reduce the Indian caste system to a simple bipolar opposition. Moreover, in *Hindus of the Himalayas*, Berreman admitted that 'All castes are so imbued with the value of hierarchy that none wants to associate with those it considers inferior.'[62] Here we are no longer so far from Dumont! Untouchables therefore do not oppose the values of the system as much as Berreman has claimed in others of his writings.

Yet the idea that Untouchables do not subscribe to the prevailing values of the system was gathering support. It was expressed, in particular by Joan Mencher, an American anthropologist, who launched a direct attack on Dumont's views. The very title of her famous article, 'The Caste System Upside Down or the Not-So-Mysterious East', is evocative and foreshadows its contents. Mencher argues that viewing India from the low-caste standpoint sheds a new light on the system. The caste system appears as the particular application of a feature that is common to all stratified societies, namely the fact that some people are able to live a life of relative luxury while others, often the majority, are exploited, obliged to live in destitution in order to satisfy the needs of those at the top. The notion of *dharma* has been interpreted by some anthropologists as the main idea that accounts for the harmony of the system and the cooperation among its members. Yet such a conception, Mencher contends, does nothing more than reflect the official view of society as it is formulated by the traditional elite. Defenders of the system maintain that it guaranteed the most deprived material security, even in case of famine; but that (Mencher continues) is a legend. It is true that low-caste people were assured of finding work; but that is not the same thing as saying that this work ensured an adequate 'income', or that people were content with their lot. Far from promoting social harmony, the notion of *dharm*a was a tool of repression and served to preserve inequality. For Mencher, it is not this religious concept of 'duty', but rather the economic superiority and the political power of the high castes that keep the low castes low. The caste system can be therefore interpreted above all as 'a system of economic exploitation'.[63] Caste has worked to keep Untouchables from improving their living conditions.

This point of view brings out conceptions among Untouchables that are radically different from those of the upper castes. The lower castes feel no need to rationalize the inequalities of the system, and display an attitude that is at once materialistic and realistic: 'If we refuse to do our work, we will starve to death', they say. There is also much less emphasis on purity among low-caste people. When pressed, all admit to eating beef; so their values are radically different from those of the upper castes.

Untouchables occupy a key position in such a conception, since they are the epitome of the exploited castes. The fact that Untouchables are divided into many subcastes has

62. G. Berreman, *Hindus of the Himalayas*, p. 224.

63. J. Mencher, 'The Caste System Upside Down, or the Not-So-Mysterious East'. *Current Anthropology*, 15 (1974), p. 478.

blinded observers to the way the system functions to maintain a distance between individuals and to prevent them acquiring land, in other words the principal means of production. All the early testimonies concur in emphasizing the extreme poverty of the untouchable groups. In the eighteenth century, they used to be sold in the district of Chingleput (Tamil Nadu). Many researchers have wondered why Untouchables have never risen up against such crushing oppression. Weber, as we have seen, considered that the Untouchables' internalization of the religious concepts had paved the way for legitimizing this oppression by the promise of a better future. Mencher strongly contests this view. She points out that, as Untouchables have always been illiterate, we have no written evidence of their grievances, nor do we have any idea of how many uprisings may have occurred over the centuries, since there was no one to give voice to their demands. In addition, she recognizes that their internal divisions prevented them uniting in the face of the oppressor. Even so, the repression and the strength of political power have been seriously underestimated by observers. Furthermore, many precolonial uprisings took the form of religious movements.

Mencher has a slight tendency to confuse the caste system with the functions it ensures, and to reduce it to an opposition between labourers and landowners. The system is far more fragmented and complex than she suggests. Nevertheless, her criticism is not unuseful. For one thing, it shows clearly that the system has a political-economic dimension. Whereas Berreman tends to regard the differences as primarily of an 'ethnic' or even 'racial' nature, Mencher stresses the economic basis of the Untouchables' plight. This idea is shared by authors like Frederick G. Bailey, another of Dumont's critics,[64] who esteems that Untouchables are primarily those social categories that are deprived of access to land and are therefore politically and economically dependent on the higher castes.[65] Once Untouchables manage to acquire land, their status improves; which is the case, for example, with the Boad distillers he studied in Orissa - this group originally made its fortune selling alcohol in the nineteenth century, and has gone on to achieve an enviable economic position.[66]

The authors last cited hold views that are closely akin to those of Marx. Yet Marxism has shown itself remarkably discreet about analysing Indian society, no doubt because the latter did not fit nicely into the 'ready-made' categories of this theory. Might Indian society be an exception to the universality of Marxist theory? But the most militant researchers are not easily discouraged, and one French Africa specialist, Claude Meillassoux, tried to resolve the problem once and for all by tackling the caste system: as might be expected, he was not the least disoriented by his foray into South Asia.

In his work in Africa, Meillassoux had come across social divisions that fit the definition of the Indian caste system, and he was loath to consider the Indian phenomenon unique. On the contrary, it seemed to him nothing more than a mere 'ideological veneer' invented by the dominant classes to disguise the true class relations. For Meillassoux, castes are never anything but an illusory reality, a 'repressive ideological arsenal' or, elsewhere, an 'ideological veneer' that veils the

64. See F. Bailey, 'For a Sociology of India?'. *Contributions to Indian Sociology,* 2 (1959).
65. F. Bailey, *Tribe, Caste and Nation* (Manchester: Manchester University Press, 1960), p. 133.
66. F. Bailey, *Caste and the Economic Frontier* (Manchester: Manchester University Press, 1957), p. 198.

underlying reality of the relations of production.[67] For, he reminds us, we must distinguish between the representations of social relations and the social relations themselves. Studying a society through its own representations can never be anything more than a preliminary approach; these representations must then be compared with an analysis of the real social relations. But, according to Meillassoux again, structuralism feeds on idealism: it stems from a conservative ideology, and does not aim at revealing social reality. At best, analyses like that of Dumont manage to seize semblances of knowledge, whereas the discovery of the 'real' (Meillassoux again) cleavages that divide society eludes him completely. It is therefore urgent to discover the production relations that underpin Indian society as a whole. And we shall see that the point around which the different Indian social classes are articulated is ultimately landownership.

The author's attention is drawn primarily to the *varna*, at the expense of the *jati*. According to Meillassoux, the *varna* structure is quite similar to the reality of class divisions, which brings us back to the opposition between *dvijal and shudra*: between the twice-born and the labouring classes. Meillassoux does not take the trouble to distinguish between Shudras and Untouchables, lumping them together into 'dominated classes', which he successively calls 'the people', 'producing groups' and 'exploited classes'. He too is guilty of 'ideological veneering' when he indiscriminately applies concepts spawned by the industrial revolution to a traditional agricultural society. There is no need to expound here on the many patent discrepancies in this analysis; I shall summarize my criticisms in the pages that follow. But I shall also refer to other, much more sophisticated, studies[68] that show that an analysis of Indian society in terms of class, while a legitimate approach, cannot allow itself to take these short cuts. It should also be said that, while the theory of exploitation accounts for certain aspects of the relationship between dominant castes and Untouchables, it is entirely incapable of explaining the nature of the caste system as a whole, which is far more complex than this one opposition.[69]

We shall come back to this problem; but first we must note that, in the ethnographic effervescence of the last few years, many researchers have taken an interest in Untouchables, and most of them favour the 'models of separation' we have been discussing. In 1972, J. M. Mahar published a collective volume devoted to Untouchables, which emphasized the different forms of emancipation found among them. As Moffatt rightly notes, most of the anthropologists who have worked on untouchability have tended to stress the segregation and destitution of Harijans, and many have reported the Untouchables' efforts to end the oppression they endure. These movements will be studied in a later chapter; but we can already enumerate a few of the most significant or best-known cases.

Agra's Jatavs, studied by Lynch,[70] worship Ambedkar as though he were a god, and

67. C. Meillassoux, 'Y a-t-il des castes aux Indes?'. *Cahiers internationaux de sociologie*, 44 (1973), p. 27.

68. Cf. e.g. A. Béteille, *Studies in Agrarian Social Structure* (Delhi: Oxford University Press, 1974) or *Essays in Comparative Sociology* (Delhi: Oxford University Press, 1987), p. 52.

69. See, on this subject, S. Barnett, L. Fruzzetti and A. Ostor, 'A Hierarchy Purified: Notes on Dumont and His Critics'. *Journal of Asian Studies*, 35 (1976), pp. 627-50, p. 636.

70. O. Lynch, *The Politics of Untouchability*.

are definitely not resigned to their fate; nor are the Koris of Kanpur, who, Molund tells us, are in the majority Communist,[71] nor the Chamars of Punjab, whose Ad-Darm movement was analysed by Juergensmeyer.[72] The religious leader Ravi Das has also had an ideological influence on the Chamars of Lucknow.[73] Various studies on Tamil Nadu reinforce this view of Untouchables as militants. Gough is certainly in this category, underscoring the Pallars' 'fanatical emphasis on equality',[74] or the 'social and religious gulf' between Untouchables and the rest of the population.[75] This rejection of Brahminic ideology and submission is also visible in their ignorance of the basic concepts of Hinduism,[76] or in the songs hummed by farm labourers.[77] In 1966, R. Miller argued that Untouchables had a traditional culture of their own which was separate from the Brahminic culture.[78] One of his students went on to develop the theme in a doctoral dissertation that argues in favour of an untouchable subculture in which she even finds elements of a counter-culture.[79]

We shall return to these authors in the course of this work. Suffice it here to note that the majority of contemporary anthropologists have shown a tendency to emphasize the discontinuity between Untouchables and the rest of Indian society. But it must also be said that these studies have often focused on fairly atypical communities: choosing to study the sects in the Punjab, or the workers of Kanpur or the Buddhists of Agra, strongly inclines one to a dynamic, militant view of untouchability; whereas the majority of Untouchables in rural areas of Indian are neither Buddhists nor Communists, and many have never heard of Ambedkar and are still largely dependent on the higher castes. That is why, in breaking with the near unanimity, Moffatt's study has the merit of attempting to seize the essence of the relationship between Untouchables and the higher castes, leaving aside the recent changes in society. No doubt that is why various authors[80] in recent years have tried to introduce some nuances by showing that Untouchables are neither on the brink of revolution nor completely satisfied with their position in society and always prepared to legitimize the oppression they endure.

71. S. Molund, *First We Are People ... The Koris of Kanpur between Caste and Class* (Stockholm: Stockholm Studies in Social Anthropology, 1988), p. 95.

72. M. Juergensmeyer, *Religion as Social Vision: The Movement against Untouchability in 20th Century Punjab* (Berkeley, CA: University of California Press, 1982).

73. R. S. Khare, *The Untouchable as Himself: Ideology, Identity and Pragmatism among the Lucknow Chamars* (Cambridge: Cambridge University Press, 1984).

74. K. Gough, '*Caste in a Tanjore Village*', in E. Leach (ed.), *Aspects of Caste in South India, Ceylon and North-West Pakistan,* (Cambridge: Cambridge University Press, 1960), p. 44.

75. K. Gough, '*Harijans in Thanjavur*', in K. Gough and H. Sharma (eds), *Imperialism and Revolution in South Asia* (New York: Monthly Review Press, 1973, pp. 222-45), p. 223.

76. C. Maloney, 'Religious Beliefs and Social Hierarchy in Tamil Nadu, India'. *American Ethnologist*, 2 (1975).

77. M. Trawick, 'Spirits and Voices in Tamil Songs'. *American Ethnologist*, 14 (1987).

78. R. Miller, 'Button, Button ... Great Tradition, Little Tradition, Whose Tradition?'. *Anthropological Quarterly,* 39 (1966), p. 41.

79. L. Vincentnathan, 'Harijan Subcultures and Self-Esteem Management in a South Indian Community'. (Doctoral dissertation, University of Wisconsin, Madison, 1987).

80. For example: D. Mosse, 'Caste, Christianity and Hinduism: A Study of Social Organization and Religion in Rural Ramnad', unpublished D. Phil thesis (Oxford University, Institute of Social Anthropology, 1985); R. Deliège, *Les Paraiyars du Tamil Nadu* (Nettetal: Steyler Verlag, 1988); or K. Kapadia, 'Gender, Caste and Class in Rural South India'. Doctoral dissertation, London School of Economics, Department of Anthropology, 1990.

Complementary Models

I find each of the points of view I have just exposed at once convincing and irritating. On the one hand, it is hard to see how one can deny the importance of the opposition between pure and impure as an ideological foundation of Indian society. But on the other hand, it is equally hard to believe that there can be people who are content with the poverty they endure.

The Indian sociologist, André Béteille, is, together with M. N. Srinivas, the leading exponent of the Indian social sciences, and he will be able to help us grasp the complementarity of these two conceptions of untouchability. While the two men have at times co-signed articles, their sociology differs appreciably, and Béteille does not have the same tendency to idealize the social harmony that results from the caste system. Like Srinivas, Béteille has a long list of publications to his name; but he has written only one monograph,[81] the rest of his work being composed primarily of a multitude of articles that have often been gathered into collections.[82] The dispersion of these publications makes any attempt at synthesis fairly arduous; but we can nevertheless pick out a few general features that seem to emerge from the work of this Marxist-leaning, rather than truly Marxist, intellectual.

As an Indian sociologist, Béteille is clearly interested in the contemporary changes affecting Indian society, and he observes that Dumont's ideas do not provide an adequate explanation. Anthropologists analysing Indian society have focused almost entirely on the phenomenon of caste, and have left aside the other aspects of the social structure. This has led them to give too much importance to ritual pollution and status hierarchy, and to neglect the other systems of social inequality, in particular the differences in power and wealth. One of the guiding ideas of Béteille's work is that, alongside caste hierarchy, there also exists another division of society in terms of property and yet a third, in terms of power. In his study of Sripuram, a village in Tanjore district, he notes that Indian society is in the process of becoming a society in which the various forms of ranking no longer correspond across the board. However, traditionally, Béteille explains, there is no dissociation between status and power:[83] the highest castes also control the land and wield the political power.

But if he constantly repeats that Indian society must be studied in terms of class, Béteille also stresses the many difficulties that beset this type of analysis. For instance, the distinction between 'small landowner' and 'landless' is not always clear, and it is further complicated by the concept of 'tenant', a status that is not always very well defined, or that of the 'small peasant', who does not have enough land to feed his

81. A. Béteille, *Caste, Class and Power: Changing Patterns of Stratification in a Tanjore Village* (Bombay: Oxford University Press, 1966).

82. Cf. e.g. A. Béteille, *Castes: Old and New. Essays in Social Structure and Social Stratification* (Bombay: Asia Publishing House, 1969); or his 'The Concept of Tribe with Special Reference to India'. *Archives européennes de sociologie*, 27 (1986).

83. A. Béteille, *Castes: Old and New*, p. 22..

family, and who must also sell his labour to make ends meet. These difficulties mean that the notion of 'class' is not strong enough in rural India to rally people with a view to political action:[84] for instance, high-caste Hindus who work as agricultural labourers in Tanjore district refuse to combine forces with their Untouchable colleagues[85] because the two classes do not form a community[86] - there is no such thing as class consciousness in rural Indian society. Marxist simplifications based on concepts created for the study of Western society turn out to be highly inadequate, and artificially imposing categories such as 'landowners', 'tenants', 'semi-feudal aristocracy', and so forth does as much to confuse matters as it does to clarify them.[87] While Sripuram's Brahmins are different from the rest of the population, they can hardly be compared with a Western-style 'gentry'; and in general many 'peasant' castes, such as Okkaligas, Vellalars or Marathas, do not work the land, yet this does not make them 'absentee landlords'.[88]

Today, then, caste, political power and economic domination no longer coincide. In Tamil Nadu, for example, political life is no longer based primarily on caste,[89] and new factors have emerged that have contributed to changing the traditional order: new, 'caste-free' occupations, land-as-commodity, generalized education, monetarization of the economy, democratization of political life.[90]

Traditionally, then, according to Béteille, Untouchables were not only those social categories held to be ritually impure, but also those that were at the same time deprived of political power and excluded from owning the means of production. It can therefore be said that any acceptable vision of untouchability should take into account all these aspects, which are by no means mutually contradictory. Furthermore, most of the criticisms made of Dumont in no way contradict his analysis proper; they simply stress that his is a limited viewpoint (for example, Berreman and Mencher), or a false consciousness (Meillassoux). Berreman and Mencher are right in stressing in that the ideology of pure and impure produces an idealized vision of Indian society. And Dumont is not saying anything else when he states that 'ideology is not everything',[91] or when he writes further on: 'I do not claim that the opposition between pure and impure is the "foundation" of society except in the intellectual sense of the term: it is by implicit reference to this opposition that the society of castes appears consistent and rational to those living in it. In my opinion this fact is central, in and of itself.'[92]

Advocates of the models of separation are nevertheless wrong in wanting to reduce this ideology to a purely Brahminic theory that they claim is wholly alien to the lower castes, and particularly to Untouchables. The latter espouse this theory up to a certain point, reproducing it within their own group; and they have certainly not developed any true counter-culture. The ideology of caste extends well beyond the upper castes.

84. A. Béteille, *Studies in Agrarian Social Structure*, p. 136

85. Ibid., p. 166.

86. A. Béteille, *Caste, Class and Power*, p. 4.

87. A. Béteille, *Studies in Agrarian Social Structure*, p. 47.

88. A. Béteille, *Essays in Comparative Sociology* (Delhi: Oxford University Press, 1987), pp. 52 and 54.

89. A. Béteille, 'Caste and Political Group Formation in Tamil Nad', in R. Kothari (ed.), *Caste in Indian Politics* (Poona: Orient and Longman, 1970), p. 260.

90. A. Béteille, 'Closed and Open Social Stratification'. *Archives européennes de sociologie*, 7 (1966), p. 226.

91. L. Dumont, *Homo hierarchicus*, p. 56.

92. Ibid., p. 66; in English translation, p. 44.

But this relative acceptation of the system, or at least this relative inability to set up 'alternative' values, does not mean, as the 'models of unity' would have us admit, that Untouchables are content with their lot, that they enjoy a number of privileges and that, all in all, theirs is a rather enviable status. No human being would willingly put up with the sometimes inhuman conditions that are imposed on Untouchables - how could they? Untouchables resent their socio-economic condition, and ask nothing better than to improve it. They do not feel it is fair to be reduced to this condition, which they nevertheless judge appropriate for the castes below them. And therein lies the ambiguity of their attitude.

Coming back to Béteille, he does indeed point out that the problem of untouchability is above all a problem of economic and social deprivation.[93] This is a crucial point, which is lacking in theories like that of Hocart. For, if the term 'sacrifice' describes the untouchable specialization in areas associated with death and demons,[94] it does not explain why these 'specialists' should be kept in a state of such profound abjection, nor why their women should not be able to dress decently, nor why they should not use a parasol. Hocart says there is no need of a peasant caste to work the land; but I could add that nothing obliges society to show such contempt for those who deal with demons, and nothing except certain political and economic considerations forces Indians to reduce those who perform such important ritual functions to subhuman status.

In other words, the ideology of purity accounts for Untouchables' occupations and especially their ritual specializations; but it does not explain why they are stripped of every attribute and symbol normally attaching to human beings. In the traditional system, 'Untouchables' are not only those groups that are ritually impure, they are also those that are not allowed to own land and that must perform the lowliest tasks for the rest of the population; they have no right to political expression, nor to any power whatsoever; in sum, they have no right to human dignity, and their every attitude must show their baseness. Is there some ritual rule that obliges Untouchables to refer to their children as 'calves' when speaking to a high-caste person?[95] Is there something in the ritual that explains why, in Kerala, Pulayas could be bought and sold?[96] Why must an Untouchable use the term 'Lord' when addressing a peasant who may be a brute or a prodigious eater of meat? Why do Thakurs more or less have the right to bed any Chamar woman?

Ritual pollution does not explain everything. When their work requires it, Untouchables may use village streets that are normally closed to them. Good also notes that, while people say that physical contact with an Untouchable is polluting, he never met any one who actually purified himself after such a contact, and accidental contact is not taken seriously.[97] Cohn, too, noted that the 'Untouchables' of Senapur,

93. A. Béteille, Castes: *Old and New*, p. 6.

94. See also S. Randeria, 'Carrion and Corpses: Conflict in Categorizing Untouchability in Gujarat'. *Archives européenes de sociologie*, 30 (1989).

95. A. K. Iyer, *The Tribes and Castes of Cochin* (New Delhi: Cosmos, 1981), 3 vols.; Vol. I, p. 87.

96. K. Saradamoni, *Emergence of a Slave Caste*: *Pulayas of Kerala* (Delhi: People's Publishing House, 1980), p. 55.

97. A. Good, *The Female Bridegroom: A Comparative Study of Life-Crisis Rituals in South India and Sri Lanka* (Oxford: Clarendon Press, 1990), pp. 14-15.

in Uttar Pradesh, did not defile Thakurs by touching them.[98] This by no means signifies that rules of purity are a simple 'ideological veneer' - without them it is impossible to understand why Untouchables themselves are divided into so many castes that carefully avoid each other; but these rules alone do not explain everything about the Untouchables' position.

Untouchability, as Oommen so well defined it, is a system of 'cumulative domination'. Their deprivation is threefold: Untouchables have low ritual status, they live in wretched economic conditions, and they have no political power.[99] This conjunction of three factors reminds us that Béteille stresses that poverty, too, is a characteristic of untouchable groups.[100] To this we can add that Untouchables are refused a whole series of status symbols that might make them like the rest of society. For, and this is essential, Untouchables are truly a category apart. We know that in the Indian social system everyone is to some extent impure, and that impurity is a relative concept. But the impurity of Untouchables is peculiar to them, in that it is indelible and irreversible. Theoretically an Untouchable can be a medical doctor, a vegetarian and particularly clean about his person; yet he pollutes as much as a night-soil remover. A good many Untouchables do not perform ritually impure tasks; but that in no way alters their status. Harper tells the following story: One day he was walking with a Havik Brahmin when they saw a Holeru Untouchable working in a nearby field. The Brahmin explained that Holerus are an impure, debased caste, because they eat beef. Harper objected that he thought Holerus were not beef-eaters. Sure of himself, the Brahmin asked the Untouchable, who replied that they had stopped eating beef over thirty years ago. Triumphantly the Brahmin turned to Harper and said: 'There, I told you they ate beef.'[101]

The 'stigmata' of untouchability are not merely ritual. South Indian barbers and washermen perform ritually impure tasks, and also help dispose of wastes associated with death, which is the strongest pollutant.[102] But these castes are not untouchable, like for example Pallars and, even more, Paraiyars or Sakkiliyars. The latter are not only impure, they are also forced to perform all the socially debasing tasks, and a variety of means are employed to keep them in this state of inferiority and abjection. It is this deprivation that defines the Untouchables' specificity, and that will retain our attention in the next chapter.

98. B. Cohn, 'The Chamars of Senapur', p. 120.

99. T. K. Oommen, 'Sources of Deprivation and Styles of Protest: The Case of the Dalits in India'. *Contributions to Indian Sociology* (NS), 18 (1984), pp. 45-61, p. 46.

100. A. Béteille,'Pollution and Poverty', in J. M. Mahar (ed.), *The Untouchables in Contemporary India* (Tucson: University of Arizona Press, 1972), p. 412.

101. E. Harper, 'Social Consequences of an Unsuccessful Low Caste Movement', in J. Silverberg (ed.), *Social Mobility in the Caste System* (The Hague: Mouton, 1968), p. 36.

102. S. Randeria, 'Carrion and Corpses'.

-3-

The Ambiguity of Untouchables[1]

What do Untouchables themselves think of untouchability? This is a question that has not ceased to preoccupy anthropologists, and it will be the focus of the present chapter. Let us recall that, according to the eminent German sociologist, Max Weber, Untouchables have never rebelled against the system that oppresses them for the good reason that they have internalized its values. Such a conception contains a good dose of idealism and naïveté, but it still prevails in certain popular works, ever ready to point to the 'fatalism' supposedly inherent in Hinduism. This is notoriously the case of the winner of the Nobel prize for economics, Gunnar Myrdal, who does not hesitate to describe 'religious beliefs' as irrational or a 'hindrance to economic development', without ever bothering to adduce proof of these claims, which often verge on the fantastic.[2] Anthropologists on the whole have been much more circumspect, even though, as we have seen, many theoreticians of caste consider that Untouchables themselves practise untouchability. Those most familiar with Untouchables subsequently tend to reject this symbiosis and to stress the particularities of untouchability and even Untouchables' opposition to the system. But it was not until 1979 that an anthropologist, the American, Michael Moffatt, devoted a book to this important issue; since this work generally opposes the prevailing tendencies, it will serve as the basis of the analysis presented in this chapter.

It has now been twenty years since Moffatt published his vigorous analysis of Untouchables within the caste system. This important study has had a considerable impact on Indian anthropology and rapidly came to be regarded as an essential contribution to our knowledge of India's lowest castes. Yet Moffatt's views on Untouchables are rather one-sided, and as such, do not fully satisfy – to say the least – those who have done fieldwork among them. My own work among Paraiyars and Pallars, two major untouchable castes of Tamil Nadu, has also led me to feel that, although Moffatt's views are not to be rejected in their entirety, they are in need of serious reassessment.

Moffatt's ethnographic study is based on his fieldwork in a village in Chingleput district that he calls Endavur, but his ultimate ambition goes well beyond this limited context: he aims to provide a general interpretation of the position of Untouchables

1. This chapter is a slightly modified version of an article published in *Man (NS)*, 27 (1992), pp. 155-73.
2. G. Myrdal, *Asian Drama: An Inquiry into the Poverty of Nations* (New York: Pantheon, 1968), 3 vols; I, pp. 104-12.

within Indian society as a whole. This is clearly the primary intent of his book, and so is the reason for our devoting an entire chapter to it.

Moffatt's Study

Before proceeding with a critical assessment of Moffatt's study, it might be useful to summarize his main arguments. The aim of Moffatt's study is to see whether, in the last analysis, Untouchables have a culture of their own, or on the contrary, share the values and the beliefs of the majority of Indian people. In other words, do Untouchables possess distinctive social and cultural forms as a result of their position in the system? Is there such a thing as a Harijan 'subculture'? Moffatt gives us his answer on page 3:

"They do not possess a separate subculture. They are not detached or alienated from the 'rationalizations' of the system; Untouchables possess and act upon a thickly textured culture whose fundamental definitions and values are identical to those of more global Indian village culture. The 'view from the bottom' is based on the same principles and evaluations as 'the view from the middle' or 'the view from the top'. The cultural system of Indian Untouchables does not distinctively question or revalue the dominant social order. Rather, it continuously recreates among Untouchables a microcosm of the larger system".[3]

The crucial idea that emerges here is that Untouchables live in consensus with Indian culture as a whole. It is important to note that, according to Moffatt, Untouchables are both excluded from and included in Indian social life, and that the consensus is visible in both cases. When Untouchables are included within a set of social relations, they *complement*, that is they play the appropriately low roles necessary to maintaining the divine and the human orders. This complementarity, which consists in playing the subordinate role assigned to them, can be interpreted as an indicator of cultural consensus; but it is a weak indicator,[4] for they can always be said to be playing this role because they are forced to do so by the higher castes and not because they have strongly internalized the postulates of the system. They behave in this way because they have to. But Untouchables are also excluded from certain relations with high-caste people because of their extreme ritual impurity; and when Untouchables are excluded, they *replicate*.

"The Untouchables of Endavur replicate among themselves, to the best of their materially limited abilities, almost every relationship from which they have been excluded by the *uur* castes. And this replicatory order is constructed in the same cultural code that marks highness and lowness, purity and impurity, superordination and subordination among the higher castes. It thus implies among the lower castes of Endavur a deep cultural consensus on the cognitive and evaluative assumptions of the system as a whole".[5]

3. M. Moffatt, *An Untouchable Community in South India: Structure and Consensus*. (Princeton, NJ: Princeton University Press, 1979), p. 3.

4. Ibid., p. 4.

5. Ibid., pp. 5 and 89.

'Replication', a key concept of Moffatt's analysis, is thus a stronger indicator of cultural consensus than complementarity, since it operates within the untouchable subset of castes, where the power of the higher castes does not. In other words, Moffatt argues that the reproduction or the 'replication' by Untouchables of the institutions from which they have been excluded is the strongest evidence of their acceptance of the values and institutions of the wider society to which they belong. This is so true, Moffatt goes on, that, 'if we found a situation where the untouchable population was sufficient for replication, and none occurred ... we would have strong structural evidence for cultural disjunction at the bottom of society'.[6] 'However', he concludes, 'no such case is known to this ethnographer.' In summary, the Untouchables' response to exclusion is replication, and the latter is, according to Moffatt, the strongest evidence for cultural consensus.[7] Thus the division of Harijans into different grades 'indicates in a most forceful manner the degree to which the Harijans are in consensus with a system that defines them as fundamentally low'.[8]

Moffatt is clearly directing this analysis against what he calls the 'disjunctive models of untouchability', in other words those that were analysed in Chapter 2, and that stress the contrast between Untouchables and the higher castes. Moffatt's views are based on Dumont's structural model of Indian society[9] and uphold the latter's assumption of cultural homogeneity throughout the caste order.

Before continuing with the analysis, I would like to mention that Moffatt begins his book with an excellent preface entitled: 'On Doing Fieldwork with Untouchables'. In these courageous and honest pages, he relates the failure of his first attempt at fieldwork, his tribulations and the various problems he encountered in the course of his research. These pages should be read by all students of anthropology, as they show how a field study can depart from Malinowski's model (as I suppose most of our studies do) and yet produce valuable results.

After this brief digression, let us now see how Moffatt sets about demonstrating his thesis. The village of Endavur, where he conducted his study, is located some 80 kilometres from Madras. Untouchables constitute 32 per cent of the village population, which is dominated by the peasant caste of Reddiyars. The untouchable colony (*ceeri*) is separated from the main settlement (*uur*) by a vacant plot of land. Among Endavur's Untouchables, 43 per cent own land, compared with 28 per cent for the whole district. Economically, then, Endavur Harijans tend to be better off than average for the region; nevertheless they are still controlled by the dominant caste, for whom they work as agricultural labourers. 'This means that the Reddiyars retain ultimate control of the local Untouchables' behavior', as Moffatt aptly remarks.[10]

The Harijan principle of 'replication' can be seen in three areas: first, the Untouchables are divided into different castes that replicate the main caste order. Secondly, the Paraiyars, the main untouchable caste in Endavur, are themselves divided into ranked grades. And third, Harijan religion largely replicates the cult of Hindu deities found among the higher castes. We will now look at these points.

6. Ibid., p. 298.
7. Ibid., p. 148.
8. Ibid., p. 215.
9. Ibid., p. 24.
10. Ibid., pp. 81-2.

• The Untouchables of Endavur are divided into several communities, which call themselves 'castes' (*jati*), are hierarchically disposed, and behave towards each other exactly as the higher castes do. These castes are:

1. The Vallavur Pandarams: at the top of this hierarchy stand the Vallavur Pandarams, who act as priests for the lower castes, and are sometimes called the 'Brahmins of Harijans'; they are *purohit*, or household priests, which means that they officiate at life-cycle rituals of Untouchables (marriage, first menstruation, etc.). They avoid eating beef and are even vegetarian for four months of the year. They are regarded as distinctly more pure than other Harijans, and are themselves quite emphatic about this distinction.

2. The Harijan caste: Paraiyars are numerically the dominant untouchable caste, but I fail to understand why Moffatt calls them 'the Harijan caste', since all the groups referred to here are Harijans. The Paraiyars control most of the resources of the *ceeri,* thereby replicating within their hamlet the Reddiyar domination over the village as a whole. Their origin myths express their foolishness, naïveté, or stupidity, thus replicating the way they are regarded by the higher castes.[11]

3. The Harijan Vannan caste: as those who wash for the higher castes refuse to wash the Untouchables' clothes, this tiny subcaste replicates their *tozhil* (duty, function) within the untouchable community. They are considered to be very polluted and are not allowed to enter Paraiyar houses. They also perform various ritual tasks such as washing clothes at first menstruation, decorating the marriage booth, and arranging the funeral bier. They also act as ritual barbers. Vannans are endogamous.

4. The Sakkiliyars: this major untouchable caste of Tamil Nadu is represented in Endavur by a mere three families. They are leather-workers, and their association with dead cattle explains their very low status. Even Paraiyars avoid entering their street for fear of being polluted.

5. The Kurivikaran caste: this caste of bird-catchers is considered to be the lowest of all because they eat crows. They replicate the role played by Untouchables in the village as a whole: they are the poor who are willing to be fed. They are also beggars and fortune-tellers.

This brief survey of untouchable castes in Endavur, Moffatt explains, indicates that the response of Harijans to their exclusion from caste society is to 'replicate'. And, he goes on, this is crucial evidence of cultural consensus. Like any other Indians, Untouchables are concerned about their position in the hierarchy.[12]

Furthermore, replication does not only occur between the untouchable castes, it also characterizes the internal structure of the main Harijan caste, the Paraiyars, which accounts for 98 of the 110 untouchable families. The Endavur Paraiyars belong to the endogamous Sanger subcaste. This subcaste is itself divided into three *vagaiyara* (divisions): Talaiyaris, Pannaikkars and Vettiyans.

Talaiyari means 'head person', and ten families belong to this highest grade. It is so named because it provides the *talaiyari*, the assistant of the *munsif* (village policeman). The Talaiyaris also provide the two untouchable members of the *panchayat* or local council. They claim to avoid eating beef and are emphatic about

11. Ibid., p. 129.
12. Ibid., p. 147.

their superiority over other Harijans. In a sample of 21 marriages, 13 were endogamous, while 8 were with persons of the Panaikkar grade. Speaking of marriage with the latter, Talaiyaris claim that they take women from Pannaikkars, but that they never give them their daughters; but this claim is contradicted by the facts.

With 48 households, the Pannaikkars are the largest group; they avoid all contact with Vettiyars, whom they regard as lower, and boast of their unions with Talaiyaris. One Pannaikkar lineage fulfils the function of village announcer (*varayan*), which is considered to be a degrading task because it is associated with death (the *varayan* usually carries news of a death). This specialization is the source of some embarrassment for the Pannaikkars and of contempt on the part of Vettiyans, who use it to challenge the Pannaikkars' superiority. The latter point out that only one of their lineages performs this task, whereas all Vettiyans do degrading jobs. Others claim that Pannaikkars are divided into 'dirty' and 'clean'. Of the 28 marriages analysed, only one had been made 'upwards', with a Talaiyari, 12 had been made within the Pannaikkar grade and 11 with Vettiyans.

According to Moffatt, Vettiyans are at the bottom of this internal scale and perform the most degrading *tozhil*. They are also called *tootti*, to emphasize their role as 'grave-diggers': they remove dead animals from the village (*uur)* and work as cremation-ground attendants. Lastly, Vettiyans play the famous *parai* drum, which keeps the demons (*pey*) away, at funerals. The *parai* drum is an inauspicious instrument and cannot be played at auspicious ceremonies, like marriages, when it is the barber (*ambattan*) who takes on the role of musician. Ambattans obviously refuse to play for Untouchables, who must therefore replicate this role for themselves by distinguishing between a 'good' beat and a 'bad' beat. Out of 73 Vettiyan marriages, 36 took place within the grade, 19 with Talaiyaris (13 women given and 6 taken) and the rest with Pannaikkars.

The internal division of the Paraiyars, Moffatt concludes,[13] clearly indicates in a radical way that Untouchables are in consensus with the system, even though it defines them as fundamentally low; it is, he writes, 'a very strong socio-cultural indicator of the Harijans' own hierarchical values'.[14] And, he concludes: 'All Harijans thus agree on the criteria by which their own lowness is defined in the system as a whole.'[15]

• The last chapter of Moffatt's study is devoted to the Harijans' religious practices. Here, too, Untouchables waver between 'complementarity' and 'replication'. In other words, they either participate in the village cult when they have a role to play, or they are excluded from the cult and therefore replicate it for themselves. There is 'homology' or 'analogy' between the divine and the social orders, both of which are governed by the same principles: opposition between purity and impurity, or between control and subordination. And yet it would be wrong to think that, because they are relegated to the bottom of the human hierarchy, Untouchables take a greater interest in the bottom of the divine hierarchy; with the exception of the Brahmins' Sanskrit formulas and the barber's auspicious drumming, 'there is nothing in the total religious

13. Ibid., p. 215.
14. Ibid., p. 217.
15. Ibid., p. 216.

system as it is defined and enacted by the higher castes of Endavur from which the Harijans are cut off for reasons of their lowness'.[16] Whether they participate or replicate, Harijans are just as much Hindus as any other villagers. Their *kula devam*, or lineage gods, are generally lesser deities; but so are those of the higher castes.[17] Likewise the Hindu doctrine of *karma* is particularly weak among Untouchables; but Moffatt emphasizes that it is just as weak among the higher castes of the village.[18]

The Harijan colony is under the protection of the goddess Mariyamman, whose cult is a replication of the uur cult of the goddess Selliyamman. Mariyamman, a fallen and ambiguous form of Parvati, is said to be Selliyamman's younger sister; but some say the two are one and the same. In either case, the Hindu orthodoxy of the Harijans is in no doubt, and they express it in particular by their enthusiastic participation in the village festival of the goddess Selliyamman.[19] On this occasion, they act as intermediaries between human beings and the bloodthirsty demons drawn by the blood sacrifices made to the goddesses.

In all these instances, Moffatt concludes, Untouchables accept the ideology of caste as completely as any of the castes above them. They 'participate willingly in what might be called their own oppression',[20] in other words in a system that defines them as fundamentally inferior.

After this short presentation of Moffatt's work, it is now time to turn our attention to the main points of his theory. Our discussion will be articulated around two basic concepts central to his thesis: *replication* and *consensus*. I question the necessity of a link between the two: in fact I would argue that 'replication' does not necessarily mean 'consensus'. We shall also see that Untouchables do not merely replicate; they also have their own values, which are not those of caste orthodoxy. Finally, and perhaps above all, Moffatt fails to consider that, even though Untouchables may use caste ideology to explain the inferiority of the castes below them, it does not necessarily follow that they 'accept' the debased situation of their own caste. On the contrary, as much ethnographic evidence indicates: they seldom consider themselves as inherently impure, and their own degradation seems to them entirely unfounded.

Replication

Moffatt's concept of *replication* is particularly interesting, and has been used in different contexts by a number of ethnologists.[21] It should be noted from the outset that the very idea of replication implies some 'exteriority'. A 'replica' is a reproduction of someone else's values, institutions or accomplishments, and implies their removal to a different context. Moffatt himself, as I have already pointed out, stresses that

16. Ibid., pp. 223-4.
17. Ibid., p. 230.
18. Ibid., pp. 268, 294 and 296.
19. Ibid., p. 272.
20. Ibid., p. 303.
21. See, e.g., R. Hirschon, *Heirs of the Greek Catastrophe: The Social Life of Asia Minor Refugees in Piraeus* (Oxford: Clarendon Press, 1989), pp. 13, 31.

Harijans replicate whenever they are excluded. Endavur Harijans, in particular, replicate at three main levels: in their own caste order, in the internal structure of the Paraiyar caste and, lastly, in the cult of the village goddess. Again I would like to insist on the idea of exteriority: clearly, to replicate, one has to be in a different situation. The very concept therefore implies that there is something intrinsically different about Untouchables. If this were not so, the concept would be useless; whereas on the contrary, I find it useful, precisely because it expresses the ambiguity of the Untouchables' position, at the same time like and unlike, inside and outside society. But do Untouchables really 'replicate' as much as Moffatt suggests? We shall examine the three cases of replication he has cited.

• The untouchable caste order discovered by Moffatt seems almost too good to be true; but we have no reason to doubt his ethnography. Moffatt has put his finger on a remarkable case of 'replication'. But such a case is relatively rare, for the simple reason that one needs a numerically large Untouchable community for such a level of segmentation to be reached. It is not often that one finds, in the same village, Vallavur Pandarams, Paraiyars, Vannans, Sakkiliyars and Kurivikarans. The names as such are unimportant, though; what really matters is that such castes exist and that they are more or less hierarchically disposed. In other words, Harijans do not form a homogeneous community: they are divided into several distinct castes, which are ranked according to the criterion of purity/pollution and may even sometimes, but not always, perform some ritual tasks for the 'dominant' untouchable caste. I do not see how this could be denied - not even by the militant literature, which prefers to ignore rather than to deny it.

Ethnographic reports from all over India confirm the existence of internal segmentation. In 1806, Abbé Dubois had already stressed that 'Pallers' (*sic*) considered themselves better than 'Pariahs' because they did not eat the flesh of the cow; but the latter contested this claim, recalling that they belong to the 'right-hand faction', whereas Pallars belong to the 'left hand'. He also pointed out that there was a caste among the Pariahs that dominated all the others; these were the Vallavurs, who are often mockingly called 'Brahmans of the Pariahs'.[22] Much later, Blunt stressed the internal divisions in the Chamar and the Dom castes,[23] while Briggs reported that the Chamars of North India are divided into many sections that refuse to eat together.[24] According to his report, these restrictions can be so strict that a Satnami Chamar can be excommunicated simply for being touched by a sweeper.[25] The Doms, too, are divided into several ranked sections.[26] For Andhra Pradesh, the Madigas are divided into six subcastes, each of which has a different function in the community: the Nulka Sandayyas are the descendants of Jamananta, the mythological founder of the caste; the Baindlas act as priests for Madiga marriages; the Sindus are minstrels, and the Mashyos acrobats, whereas the Dakkals, the lowest of all, refuse to take food from all

22. J. Dubois, *Hindu Manners, Customs and Ceremonies* (Oxford: Oxford University Press, 1906), pp. 60-1.

23. E. Blunt, *The Caste System of Northern India with Special Reference to the United Provinces of Agra and Oudh* (Delhi: S. Chand & Co., 1969), p. 107.

24. G. Briggs, *The Chamars* (Delhi: B.R. Publishing Corporation, 1920), p. 46.

25. Ibid., p. 223.

26. G. Briggs, *The Doms and Their Near Relations* (Mysore: Wesley Press, 1953), p. 81.

non-Madigas, including Brahmins.[27] Coming back to North India, Bhatt observes that the Chamars of Lucknow keep a rigorous distance from the Bhangis;[28] while in Dehradun two Chamar segments, the Jatyas and the Raidasas, each claim to be higher than the other. Patwardhan was probably the first to speak of 'replication', when he wrote of the situation in Maharashtra: 'There is a sub-system of the Harijans which is to a lesser extent a replica or miniature of the wider caste system.'[29]

There are many other examples; but the above should be enough to convince us that Untouchables all over India are divided into castes and subcastes, and that the differences between these groups are expressed in the same language as that used by the higher castes; it establishes a scale running from high to low, based on association with death, on certain dietary rules and on degrading social practices. In Tamil Nadu, for instance, there are profound differences between the three main untouchable castes: Pallars, Paraiyars and Sakkiliyars.

But the concept of replication is itself somewhat ambiguous. For example, it suggests that the division of Untouchables reproduces almost perfectly the overall social hierarchy, including a high degree of interdependence between the different groups. Yet this is far from exact and, as I have stressed, Endavur is not really representative. My own research leads me to think instead that, although there may be strongly marked differences between various Untouchable castes, these do not correspond to a real hierarchical order.

Valghira Manickam, the village I studied in 1981-2, was inhabited by Untouchables only, who were divided into three communities: Hindu Pallars, Hindu Paraiyars and Catholic Paraiyars, who alone made up a little over half the population. The three communities were clearly distinct, if only because they were endogamous; but there was a clear separation between Pallars and Paraiyars. There was little interaction between the two castes, almost no friendship, and some tension, stemming from various incidents, among them the construction of a road leading to the village that the Pallars wanted to divert to their own advantage. Pallars are generally said to be 'superior' to Paraiyars; but in Valghira Manickam, they had little opportunity to express this superiority, which was in any case contested by the Paraiyars. There were practically no relations of dependence between Pallars and Paraiyars. Some Pallars claimed, for example, that they did not accept water from Paraiyars; but I regularly observed scenes that contradicted these claims; one day I even came upon a Pallar woman drinking a glass of water in a Paraiyar house, whereas a little earlier she had claimed that she never accepted water from them. The same is true about food: some Pallars claimed that they never accepted food from Paraiyars, but they were somewhat embarrassed when I pointed out that they willingly let their children eat food cooked by Paraiyars at the village nursery school (*balwadi*). Some Paraiyars drew their water from the Pallar pump, and both castes bathed in the same spot at the village reservoir (*kanmai*). In other words, though both castes were clearly separated, it is hard to speak of true inequality, and I would not venture to say that they were 'hierarchized'.

27. S. Dube, *Indian Village* (London: Routledge and Kegan Paul, 1955), pp. 41-2.

28. G. S. Bhatt, 'The Chamars of Lucknow'. *The Eastern Anthropologist*, 8 (1954), pp. 27-42.

29. S. Patwardhan, *Change among India's Harijans: Maharashtra - A Case Study* (New Delhi: Orient Longman, 1973), p. 7.

Relations between Hindu and Catholic Paraiyars were even less hierarchical; the two communities considered each other as brothers and sisters, and used kinship terms to address each other. Friendships were common, and there was even evidence of love affairs between Catholics and Hindus. Whereas the Pallars lived in a separate hamlet from the Paraiyars, Hindus and Catholics lived in the same streets; their children played together, and the two communities were indistinguishable in everyday life. Paraiyars, on the other hand, rarely went to the Pallar hamlet. Nothing actually forbade them going there; they simply had no reason to do so.

In sum, the material from Valghira Manickam tells us three things: First, separation does not necessarily mean hierarchy. Second, a clear distinction needs to be made between what people say about their status and their actual behaviour: when interviewed, a Pallar is anxious to express his dignity by claiming to be higher than a Paraiyar, but in his daily life, he rarely worries about his alleged superiority. Third, there are no caste rules or sanctions connected with these matters. A few individuals might be concerned about ritual purity, but the majority are not.[30] Generally speaking, it seems to me that the divisions between the various untouchable castes are particularly strong (even militant Untouchables admit that doing away with endogamy is unthinkable), but that we cannot conclude that they 'exactly' replicate the model of the wider society; for instance, there is often an absence of interdependence between the untouchable communities and no real hierarchy. Nor does any one untouchable caste monopolize the means of production as a 'dominant caste' may do. Later we shall see that this is a crucial point: untouchable communities never dominate economically; they are *panniyals* or unfree laborers *par excellence*.[31] There is little economic difference, and therefore the various castes are more separate than hierarchized.

If we define hierarchy as a way of ranking in relation to the whole,[32] then it is difficult to speak of a hierarchy among untouchable castes, as they do not form a whole. In his detailed study of Harijans in Coimbatore district, Den Ouden[33] saw a certain status inequality (*status-ongelijkheid*) between Pallars and Sakkiliyars, but he also observed many friendly relations between the two castes; as for relations between the other untouchable castes (Kuravars and Paraiyars), these are ill defined (*status-onzekerheid*), and on the whole members of the various untouchable castes have little contact ('they meet as the fathers of public-school boys'). Finally it can be noted that Valghira Manickam has no specialized untouchable castes (such as priests, washermen, etc.), as is also the case in the village of Alangkulam, which I studied in 1989.

There is no doubt, then, that there is a clear-cut separation between the untouchable castes of a region, and we are grateful to Moffatt for having reasserted the importance of caste among Untouchables. Moreover, the differences between these groups are

30. For a fuller account, see R. Deliège, *The World of the Untouchables: Paraiyars of Tamil Nadu,* (Oxford: Oxford University Press, 1998).

31. See e.g., J. Mencher, 'The Caste System Upside Down, or the Not-so-Mysterious East'. *Current Anthropology,* 15 (1974), pp. 469-93, p. 473.

32. L. Dumont, *Homo Hierarchicus: essai sur le système des castes* (Paris : Gallimard, 1966), p. 92.

33. J. Den Ouden, *De Onaanraakbaren van Konkunad* (Wageningen: Mededelingen Landbouwhogeschool, 1975), p. 74.

expressed in the language of caste hierarchy (diet, purity, occupation). Yet it is difficult to speak of a true hierarchy, since there is little interaction and even less interdependence between the different subcastes. Though untouchable service castes are not actually rare, they are not found everywhere, and therefore cannot be considered indispensable to Untouchables.

• The second form of 'replication' found in Endavur concerns the internal organization of the Paraiyars. Here I find Moffatt's evidence much less convincing. He argues that hierarchy and the notions of purity and pollution also characterize the internal organization of Endavur's main untouchable caste, the Paraiyars. If this is 'replication', it seems extremely loose to me. First of all, the *vagaiyaras* (internal subdivisions) are not at all endogamous. Secondly, marriage between the different *vagaiyaras* is not even hypergamous, as one would expect, for these groups exchange women. And in India, the exchange of women clearly signifies equality. I wonder whether a Vettiyar woman married into a Panaikkar family would consider her father and brothers inferior to her husband's family. Surely not, and the practice of bilateral cross-cousin marriage clearly rules out such ranking between the different lineages.[34] Moffatt's informants themselves do not seem convinced of this hierarchy; and indeed they do not fail to contest it.

It therefore would seem difficult to consider the internal structure of the Paraiyar caste as a true hierarchy. References to other ethnographic contexts may help us to see that the internal divisions, which are far from universal, are usually loose and cannot be associated with a clear-cut hierarchical order. On this point, Untouchables are not much different from most castes in Tamil Nadu, which are often not divided into ranked sections. Such subdivisions, when they do occur, are more often territorial than hierarchical. In Alapuram, a village in Ramnad district, Mosse found among the Paraiyars an internal division into exogamous *kilai* (lineages). Some of his informants claimed that these lineages were ranked, but the nature of this ranking seemed at best obscure,[35] and hardly credible. Among the same Paraiyars, but this time in South Arcot district, Vincentnathan found a division into grades that resembles the one described by Moffatt; but she notes that members of the different grades do not hesitate to perform each others' duties,[36] and she stresses that they all, including the *pusari* (priests), recognize the equality of all members of the caste.[37]

This is precisely what one can observe in Valghira Manickam and Alangkulam, where neither Pallars nor Paraiyars are divided into hierarchized grades. Catholic Paraiyars vaguely called themselves Nesavukara Paraiyars, or 'weaving Paraiyars', and they claimed to know of two other 'subcastes' - Kannatu Paraiyars and Tootti Paraiyars; but these two groups lived in other regions and had no contact with the people of Valghira Manickam. The latter had a strong preference for cross-cousin

34. R. Deliège, 'Patrilateral Cross-Cousin Marriage among the Paraiyars of South India'. *Journal of the Anthropological Society of Oxford* 18 (1987), p. 228.

35. D. Mosse, 'Caste, Christianity and Hinduism. A Study of Social Organization and Religion in Rural Ramnad'. (D.Phil. Thesis, Oxford University, Institute of Social Anthropology, 1985), p. 222.

36. L. Vincentnathan, 'Harijan Subculture and Self-Esteem Management in a South Indian Community'. (Doctoral dissertation, The University of Wisconsin, Madison, 1987), p. 287.

37. Ibid., p. 291.

marriage, and 82 per cent of all marriages took place among only four villages.[38] Contact with other Paraiyars was extremely limited; but the villagers claimed that there was theoretically nothing to stop them marrying a Paraiyar from any part of Tamil Nadu. They also emphasized the equality of all Paraiyars. For a number of reasons, they preferred to marry close relatives, or at least someone they knew; but when circumstances warranted it, for instance in the event of 'some problem' or when a wealthy, educated partner was sought, they did not hesitate to venture further afield to locate a suitable spouse.

Vagaiyaras could also be found among the Catholic Paraiyars in Valghira Manickam, but these were by no means 'hierarchized grades'. *Vagaiyaras* here are what could be called 'family nicknames': not really 'names', because they were neither official nor permanent; they were often funny, but not necessarily used by everyone. The members of one family who had spent some years in Colombo (Sri Lanka) were called 'Colombars'; the relatives of a man who had a curious navel were called 'Topulans' (navels), and so forth. But generally speaking, little reference was made to these *vagaiyaras,* and they had no real importance.

Hindu Paraiyars had even fewer sociological distinctions, and knew of no internal subdivisions. They sought brides even further afield, and they too considered that all Paraiyars were basically equal. Pallars, on the other hand, maintained that their caste was divided into five subcastes and that they belonged to the Ayya Pallar division, because they called their fathers *ayya*, whereas Appa and Agna Pallars called their fathers, *appa and agna* respectively. They also said that there were two more divisions, Amma and Atta Pallars, so named for the way they address their mothers; but they were not sure about these two divisions, while others claimed that there were really only two Pallar subcastes: Atta Pallars and Amma Pallars. And they added that Ayya and Atta Pallars were one and the same. These ambiguities are worth reporting, for they indicate the sociological insignificance of the subdivisions, which are usually territorial, with practically no relations between them. In any event, they are not hierarchized.

In Alangkulam, near Manamadurai, the Pallars claimed to be Amma Pallars, and said they knew of only two subdivisions, Amma and Atta Pallars. They told me that all the local Pallars were Amma Pallars, and that they were normally endogamous. But they were prompt to add that all Pallars are equal; and some even claimed they did not take women from Atta Pallars because they regarded the latter as *pankalis*, or brothers and sisters. It is becoming clear that these subdivisions do not matter. They are probably left over from a time when contacts were limited to a very few members of one's own caste, and will probably disappear as these relations become more diversified. In any case, people pay little attention to these subdivisions, which are not ranked into any sort of grades. The same absence of 'internal structural replication' is reported by McGilvray, who worked among the Paraiyars of Sri Lanka.[39]

Moffatt's data on this 'internal structure' were already none too persuasive in themselves, and the ethnographic evidence we have just been discussing makes it even

38. R. Deliège, *Les Paraiyars du Tamil Nadu*, p. 198.

39. D. McGilvray, 'Paraiyar Drummers of Sri Lanka: Consensus and Constraint in an Untouchable Caste'. *American Ethnologist*, 10 (1983), p. 112.

clearer that the Untouchable castes of Tamil Nadu are far from always being divided into ranked grades. It therefore follows that hierarchy cannot be considered to encompass all the social relations of Untouchables, who are also familiar with egalitarian values. I would not go as far as Gough and claim that they place a 'fanatical emphasis on equality',[40] for the group I studied had not developed any egalitarian ideology. Yet the endogamous units were in no hierarchy, and people even went to considerable lengths to prevent inequality from arising within their own ranks: jealousy, constant disputes, unceasing accusations of theft and total absence of leadership were some of the many symptoms of this deep-rooted internal equality.[41] In any case, the structure of these castes did not attest to a consensus with the ideology of caste.

• We have no objection to considering Untouchables as Hindus. Their religious practices must be understood within the overall framework of Hinduism. However, to speak of 'religious Hindu orthodoxy', as Moffatt does, seems somewhat exaggerated.[42] Harijans call themselves Hindus, and this is confirmed by their practices and their deities. And yet one must not confuse religion and ritual; religion includes beliefs, world-views and values as well. When these are taken into account, it becomes clear that different social actors do not necessarily attribute the same meaning to formal ritual practices.[43] Once again, what I am questioning is the passage from replication to consensus; and it is to the latter concept that I shall now turn my attention.

Consensus

The ultimate goal of Moffatt's study is to show that India's Harijans do not have a separate culture, but that they live in consensus with Indian culture as a whole. The idea of consensus is therefore crucial for Moffatt. The notion of 'structural replication' analysed above is only one stage of the evidence adduced to sustain the consensus hypothesis; and as we have already seen, absence of replication does not necessarily mean absence of consensus.

1. The first problem we must point out is the passage from a 'structural' concept (replication) to a 'cultural' one (consensus). To be sure, it would be hard to deny that there is general agreement between the high castes and Harijans about the foundations of the caste system; but it does not necessarily follow that this agreement is as all-encompassing or as general as the idea of 'consensus' suggests.

First, an Untouchable will refer to caste ideology for the purpose of explaining the degradation of the castes below him, but he will never use these values to explain his own status or to legitimize the position of his caste. In other words, Harijans may use

40. K. Gough, 'Caste in a Tanjore Village' in E. Leach (ed.), *Aspects of Caste in South India, Ceylon and North-West Pakistan* (Cambridge : Cambridge University Press, 1960, pp. 1960), p. 44.

41. See R. Deliège, *Les Paraiyars du Tamil Nadu*, pp. 31-45 and 'Caste Without a System: A Study of South Indian Harijans', in M. Searle-Chatterjee and U. Sharma (eds), *Contextualising Caste: Post-Dumontian Approaches* (Oxford: Blackwell, 1994).

42. M. Moffatt, *An Untouchable Community*, p. 268.

43. L. Vincentnathan, 'Harijan Subculture and Self-Esteem Management', p. 69.

the criteria of purity and pollution to lower other castes, but this does not mean that they see themselves as inherently polluted or impure. Furthermore, replication, even when it clearly occurs, cannot be considered the sole and ultimate proof of consensus. It is true that Untouchables are both Indian and Hindu. They speak the language of the majority, eat the same food whenever they can, and follow the same customs when they are allowed to. They are divided into castes, worship Hindu deities ('Only Hindu gods are available', one of Moffatt's informants commented symptomatically).[44] They therefore have little choice but to submit to the 'dominant' culture, the term being particularly apposite in this case. Furthermore, they are obliged to take into account the fact that Indian society in general, and the untouchable population in particular, is divided into hundreds of groups, which obviously does nothing to promote collective action or group solidarity. Untouchables, then, do not form a homogeneous category capable of opposing the system, still less of endangering it; they have to put up with it, and so their resentment is not directed against the system as such, but rather against their own position within it.[45] They therefore do not try so much to eliminate the system as to improve their place within it.[46] Because they are destitute, illiterate and divided, Untouchables have been unable to develop either a counter-ideology or a counter-culture. But this does not mean that they consider themselves impure. Berreman rightly emphasizes that he has never personally met an Untouchable who would say 'I am of low status because I and my family are impure.'[47] Such a statement, he comments, would be psychologically untenable. Harijans are well aware of caste ideology, but they subscribe to it only up to a point, and certainly not in order to legitimize their own economic deprivation, as Weber said.[48]

Recent analysis of Untouchable origin myths shows that, contrary to Moffatt's interpretation, Untouchables attribute their own debased position to a mistake, some sort of trickery, or accident, and therefore consider it undeserved.[49] In fact, Untouchables call themselves *tazhttapattor*, 'those who are forced to be low', and they do not accept the idea that their caste is inherently low. The model of caste hierarchy held by Harijans is that of a humanly instituted order in which they find themselves in an undeservedly low position as a consequence of misfortune, historical accident or trickery. Although in broad agreement with Moffatt, Randeria recognizes that the Untouchables' discourse on their position within the caste system differs markedly from high-caste views,[50] while Kapadia is even more emphatic that Untouchables have

44. M. Moffatt, *An Untouchable Community*, p. 268.

45. G. Berreman, *Caste and Other Inequities Essays on Inequality* (Meerut: Folklore Institute, 1979), p. 10.

46. G. Berreman, 'Concomitants of Caste Organization', in G. De Vos and H. Wagatsuma (eds), *Japan's Invisible Race: Caste in Culture and Personality* (Berkeley, CA: University of California Press, 1967), p. 313.

47. G. Berreman, *Hindus of the Himalayas Ethnography and Change* (Berkeley, CA: University of California Press, 1963), p. 242.

48. M. Weber, *The Religion of India: The Sociology of Hinduism and Buddhism* (New York: The Free Press, 1958), p. 21.

49. See this volume, Chapter 4 or R. Deliège, 'Les Mythes d'origine chez les Paraiyar'. *L'Homme*, 109 (1989), pp. 107-16.

50. S. Randeria, 'Carrion and Corpses: Conflict in Categorizing Untouchability in Gujarat'. *Archives européennes de sociologie*, 30 (1989), pp. 171-91, p. 188.

never accepted the image that the upper castes have of them.[51] Their relationship with the dominant communities is determined by the forced obligation to perform a series of services, many of which are considered to be particularly degrading. Mosse[52] maintains that Untouchables explain their position in the system with reference to a secular model, and perceive their lowness in terms of poverty and servitude, and never as any kind of ritual pollution. Nobody refers to ritual occupations to explain his caste status. On the contrary, Kapadia goes on,[53] Pallars see themselves as 'providers of agricultural bounty', and they are very proud of their agricultural skills. They often quote a saying that highlights the auspicious nature of their caste: 'A farm will not prosper unless there is a Pallar to till it.'

In second place, although Untouchables may use the categories of purity and pollution, it does not follow that their ideology is a mere replica of high-caste values. They know full well that they must speak the language of pure/impure if they want to be understood, and above all respected. For instance, it is rare to find a Harijan who admits to eating beef, and most claim they have never eaten it. Yet Harijans do eat beef. But to recognize this explicitly in India is tantamount to saying 'we are dirty fellows'. The fact that they do eat beef and at the same time deny it is highly significant: they want to show their respectability, but at the same time do not attach much importance to the dominant values. If they go on eating beef, it is because they are not really convinced of the devastating effects of such a diet. They thus resort to notions of purity to prove their honourability and to show that they are just as respectable as any other social category.[54] Similarly, asking a Paraiyar whether or not he accepts food or water from a Sakkiliyar is another way of asking him whether or not he is more respectable than a Sakkiliyar. Of course he will affirm his superiority, even though, as we have seen, his behavior may often contradict his claims. Hierarchy tends to be more obvious in the Harijans' formal and ritual practices than in their values and beliefs. Molund[55] writes that the Koris of Kanpur live very differently from the higher castes, emphasizing the pleasures of the 'here and now', especially those that are immediate and sensuous, such as hot foods, drugs, sex and gambling.

Epistemologically, Moffatt does not always distinguish between the norm and the act, between the ideal and reality, between the rule and actual practice. In spite of its undeniable overall quality, his ethnography seems based chiefly on what people told him, and little reference is made to actual behaviour or concrete examples.[56] As Mosse points out, one of the problems with Moffatt's structural approach is that he assumes that practice is generated by an implicit ideology in a direct, unmediated way.[57]

Which brings us naturally to the third point I should like to consider. Structuralists build up their models from the 'raw materials' of empirical reality. By definition, these

51. K. Kapadia, 'Gender, Caste and Class, *in Rural South India'*. (Doctoral dissertation, London School of Economics, Department of Anthropology, 1990), p. 232.

52. D. Mosse, *'Caste, Christianity and Hinduism'*, p. 256.

53. K. Kapadia, 'Gender, Caste and Class', p. 118.

54. L. Vincentnathan, 'Harijan Subculture and Self-Esteem Management', pp. 69, 113 and 437.

55. S. Molund, *First We Are People ... The Koris of Kanpur between Caste and Class* (Stockholm: Stockholm Studies in Social Anthropology, 1988), p. 88.

56. See R. Deliège, *Les Paraiyars du Tamil Nadu*, p. 112.

57. D. Mosse, 'Caste, Christianity and Hinduism', p. 261.

models are 'secondary elaborations', abstractions that should not be confused with empirical reality itself. Structuralists rarely miss an opportunity to remind their critics of this. But it also happens that they completely forget this basic principle and take their models for the empirical reality. This is precisely the trap Moffatt stumbles into when he states that Untouchables create among themselves 'the *entire* set of institutions' or '*virtually every* relation' from which they have been excluded. Reading Moffatt, it would seem that all untouchable institutions and relations were characterized by the concepts of purity and pollution. Even Dumont, Moffatt's mentor, showed more caution when he wrote: 'I do not claim that the opposition between pure and impure is the "foundation" of society except in the intellectual sense of the term: it is by implicit reference to this opposition that the society of castes appears consistent and rational to those living in it. In my opinion this fact is central, in and of itself.'[58]

'In and of itself' means here that the pure/impure dichotomy does not explain everything; and this is particularly true for Harijans. Vincentnathan is right to say that, contrary to Moffatt's interpretation, Dumont's analysis does not necessarily imply the existence of a single ideology.[59] Moreover, one does not adhere to such an ideology as one belongs to a Church, a football team, a political party - that is, fairly exclusively. The existence of a dominant ideology does not rule out the development of other ideologies.

2. Above and beyond the issue of untouchability, another aspect of Indian culture has recently been called into question, and that is its homogeneity. For instance, in a series of articles, Fuller has pointed up the distinction between Sanskritic religion and village religions.[60] Furthermore, the basic values of Indian civilization are not necessarily shared by all: for the fishermen of Andhra, for example, vegetarian food is no good; a meal without meat or even fish 'is a wretched thing to swallow'.[61] Maloney[62] has shown that the meaning given to religious concepts is not the same in higher and lower castes: whereas Tamil Brahmins refer to the concepts of reincarnation (*samsara*), *karma* and *dharma*, the lower castes are fairly suspicious about these key concepts of Hinduism.[63] We will see in the next chapter how the Untouchables' origin myths give a slightly different interpretation of the wider ideology; and this is even more true of the songs sung by Untouchables in Tamil Nadu, which express their resentment and bitterness, and even their revolt at the unfairness of their condition.[64] In Benares, Searle-Chatterjee tells us, the Harijan pattern of life is

58. L. Dumont, *Homo hierarchicus*, p. 66.

59. L. Vincentnathan, 'Harijan Subculture and Self-Esteem Management', p. 116.

60. See e.g., C. Fuller, 'Sacrifice (Bali) in the South Indian Temple', in V. Sudarsen, G. Reddy and M. Suryanarayana (eds), *Religion and Society in South India: A Volume in Honour of Prof. N. Subba Reddy* (Delhi: B.R. Publishing Corporation, 1987), or 'The Hindu Pantheon and the Legitimation of Hierarchy'. *Man (NS)*, 23 (1988).

61. O. Herrenschmidt, *Les Meilleurs Dieux sont hindous* (Lausanne: L'Age d'Homme, 1989), p. 33.

62. C. Maloney, 'Religious Beliefs and Social Hierarchy in Tamil Nadu, India'. *American Ethnologist*, 2 (1975), pp. 169-92.

63. See also K. Gough, 'Harijans in Thanjavur', in K. Gough and H. Sharma (eds), *Imperialism and Revolution in South Asia* (New York: Monthly Review Press, 1973), p. 234 or P. Kolenda, 'Religious Anxiety and Hindu Fate', in E. Harper (ed.), *Religion in South Asia* (Berkeley, CA: University of California Press, 1964), p. 197.

64. M. Trawick, 'Spirits and Voices in Tamil Songs'. *American Ethnologist*, 14 (1987), pp. 193-215, p. 197.

much more democratic than that of the higher castes, and the social differences based on age or sex, too, are much less striking than among the high castes. She even speaks of a 'culture of poverty', in the sense that Lewis gives to that term. One may recall here that according to Lewis himself poor people are aware of middle-class values, are able to discuss them, and are even able to take over some of them for their own purposes.[65]

In Valghira Manickam one sees a greater emphasis on equality and the freedom of women, a lack of concern about ritual purity and formal practices, a certain toleration of marrying for love, the absence of dowry, and the remarriage of widows, all practices that run counter to high-caste ideals.[66] This untouchable 'subculture' is not necessarily a 'counter-culture', but it may, in certain instances, take the form of an open opposition to the oppressive system. This kind of movement has probably always existed; but it has assumed more importance in the last century.

3. One final problem with Moffatt's approach is its ahistorical character. Moffatt seems to consider that the ideology of the people of Endavur has been untouched by contemporary changes. Yet his own data suggest that Harijans are not simply consenting victims, but that they have effectively taken steps to improve their condition. Serious disputes arose between Endavur Harijans and the Reddiyars as early as 1940; more recently, a Harijan did not hesitate to insult a Mudaliyar in front of other Mudaliyars; Harijans also fought to get three representatives in the *panchayat*,[67] and dared to vote against the most powerful person in the village in some important elections. For more than a century now, Untouchables all over India have been increasingly involved in emancipation movements, which have taken three general forms: religious, socio-political and cultural. The *Satnami* movement among the Chamars,[68] the Ad-Dharm movement in the Punjab,[69] and the massive conversion to Buddhism of Mahars in Maharashtra[70] are but a few examples of the movements that will be further discussed in a later chapter.

These movements have been analysed in detail by a great number of researchers, and cannot be ignored in any discussion of the untouchable world-view. It would certainly be wrong, though, to consider them as evidence of some revolutionary bent. Untouchables, too, are ambivalent about their social position. There are and have been few true revolutionaries among India's lower castes. Nevertheless, these social movements show that Harijans are not resigned to their fate; nor are they waiting for

65. O. Lewis, 'The Culture of Poverty'. *Scientific American*, 215 (1966), p. 23.

66. R. Deliège, *Les Paraiyars du Tamil Nadu*, p. 287.

67. M. Moffatt, *An Untouchable Community*, pp. 83-4.

68. S. Fuchs, *Rebellious Prophets: A Study of Messianic Movements in Indian Religions* (Bombay: Asia Publishing House, 1965), p. 98.

69. M. Juergensmeyer, *Religion as Social Vision: The Movement against Untouchability in 20th Century Punjab* (Berkeley, CA: University of California Press, 1982).

70. E. Zelliot, 'Gandhi and Ambedkar - A Study in Leadership', in J. M. Mahar (ed.), *The Untouchables in Contemporary India* (Tucson: University of Arizona Press, 1972), or O. Lynch, *The Politics of Untouchability: Social Mobility and Social Change in a City of India* (New York: Columbia University Press, 1969). Cf. Also accounts of Harijan involvement in the *Dalit Sahitya* literary movement: M. Bhoite and A. Bhoite, 'The Dalit Sahitya Movement in Maharashtra: A Sociological Analysis'. *Sociological Bulletin*, 26(1977) and J. Gokhale-Turner, 'Bhakti or Vidroha: Continuity and Change in *Dalit Sahitya'. Journal of Asian and African Studies,* 15 (1980), pp. 29-42.

better conditions in some hypothetical life to come, as Weber naively thought. Like any other social group, Untouchables are not content with being poor and oppressed.

Excluded and Dependent

McGilvray[71] rightly remarked that Moffatt's study is polemical: it is directed against anthropologists such as Gough, Berreman or Mencher, who, generally speaking, argue that there is something different about Untouchables and that indeed they explicitly reject the system. Moffatt, on the other hand, defends Dumont's idea that, in India, hierarchy is an encompassing and universal ideology. He strives to show that the values that govern Indian society as a whole also operate among Harijans.

One consequence of this 'integrative' approach is that the very notion of 'outcaste', which had long been the official concept used to denote Untouchables, has vanished from the literature and has become practically obsolete or at least very old-fashioned. Yet this disappearance is unfortunate. To be sure, we have emphasized that Untouchables are part of Indian society as a whole; but at the same time we have seen that the idea of ritual pollution alone does not account for their position. Ritual impurity cannot be separated from servitude or powerlessness. As Mosse says: 'There is no evidence that the Harijans' status is more clearly defined by their religious role as funeral servants, than by their economic role as labourers.'[72] In fact, both aspects are of equal importance. Harijans not only perform certain ritual tasks, they also have to toil for the higher castes, and are held in contempt and constantly kept down. Moffatt's characterization of Untouchables as 'last among equals'[73] is totally unacceptable. Untouchables are indeed an integral part of Indian society, as their essential economic and ritual roles show; but they are, also and at the same time, excluded from this society, and their marginal position is constantly underscored through various taboos and discriminations. They live both inside and outside the main society; they participate in village life, but they are also rejected in some circumstances, and their spatial isolation reflects this relative ostracism. The prohibitions on entering temples, on drawing water from the village wells, on wearing decent clothes are just a few of the many examples cited in the preceding chapter, further signs of the stigma attached to them.

One cannot say, therefore, that during the mourning period a man becomes untouchable, or that a menstruating woman is temporarily reduced to the state of a *Chandala* as, for instance, Eichinger Ferro-Luzzi claims.[74] During menstruation, a woman is secluded rather than excluded from society, and this seclusion is meant to protect her from hostile powers and demons, which are always attracted by her state.[75]

71. D. McGilvray, 'Paraiyar Drummers of Sri Lanka', p. 97.
72. D. Mosse, 'Caste, Christianity and Hinduism', p. 247.
73. M. Moffatt, *An Untouchable Community*, pp. 222, 247 and 270.
74. G. Eichinger Ferro-Luzzi, 'Women's Pollution Periods in Tamilnad (India)'. *Anthropos,* 69 (1974), p. 113.
75. N. Yalman, 'On the Purity of Women in the Castes of Ceylon and Malabar'. *Journal of the Royal Institute of Great Britain and Ireland,* 93 (1963), p. 29.

Conversely, Untouchables, although extremely polluted, do not really fear these hostile influences; their impurity does not particularly attract evil spirits; if it did, these impure beings would be constantly possessed. Nor can it be said that their impurity repels demons and evil spirits; for if it did, Untouchables would never be possessed, or at least very seldom. But Untouchables are possessed as often as any other caste. Impurity is a relative matter, after all; everyone is impure with respect to someone. The problem of untouchability therefore does not come down to a question of permanent impurity. A woman who is menstruating or has just given birth is highly polluted, but she is not enslaved, insulted, held in contempt or belittled. One can say with Reiniche[76] that Untouchables and women have something in common; but untouchability cannot be reduced to a problem of ritual pollution; it is *also* a problem of social exclusion. Untouchables are not simply ritually impure, they are also rejected from society, despised and exploited. They are denied access to culture, worship, human dignity and material well-being. They are kept out of the mainstream of social life, in which their participation is restricted to specific ritual and economic roles.

The position of Untouchables in society is ambiguous. They live on the fringes of society, as intermediaries between the human world and the surrounding 'forests'. Among Tamils, for instance, there is a strong opposition between the inhabited world, the *uur* (village) and the rather terrifying world outside it. The ideal of every Tamil is to live inside his *uur*, that is, in the place that is compatible with his own substance. Other inauspicious substances surround the *uur*; these signify incompatibility, disorder, chaos and danger.[77] Untouchables, as we have seen, do not really live outside society; but neither are they fully part of it. They reside in *ceeri* (untouchable hamlets), which are clearly distinguished from the *uur*. They must be kept apart, at the periphery of civilization. They are 'fools of the jungle'.[78] One of the hallmarks of South-Indian culture is its antiprimitivism, the conviction that life in the state of nature is horrible and full of suffering. Hills, deserts, jungles, forests and the wilderness are imagined to be full of evil powers that disorganize human society and make people unlucky, enraged, impoverished and chaotic. Symptomatically, Untouchables are described as people of 'disorder' (*toosam*), black, always shouting or making noise, with their hair sticking out in all directions.[79] 'They live like dogs', one high-caste woman explained;[80] and Pawar, an Untouchable writer, remembers that, as a boy, he was disgusted by the girls of his own caste, with their hair dirty and sticking out in all directions, like demons.[81]

Furthermore, such social exclusion has an economic dimension: Untouchables are also denied access to the means of production. Economic dependence and material

76. M. L. Reiniche, 'La Maison du Tirunelveli (Inde du Sud)'. *Bulletin de l'École Française d'Extrême-Orient,* 70 (1981), p. 28.

77. See V. Daniel, *Fluid Signs: Being a Person the Tamil Way* (Berkeley, CA: University of California Press, 1984), p. 77.

78. B. Pfaffenberger, 'Social Communication in Dravidian Ritual'. *Journal of Anthropological Research,* 36 (1980), pp. 207 and 213.

79. Ibid., pp. 209-10.

80. L. Vincentnathan, 'Harijan Subculture and Self-Esteem Management', p. 161.

81. D. Pawar, *Ma Vie d'intouchable* (Paris: La Découverte, 1990), p. 79.

poverty are inherent in their condition.[82] Until recently they were not allowed to own land, but they provided the bulk of the agricultural labour force. Indian society places a premium on intellectual work, and looks down on manual labour. It is not uncommon to meet Indian agriculturalists who never touch the land. All over India, Untouchables provide an inexhaustible source of agricultural labour. This rural proletariat has only its labour power to earn a livelihood, and as a consequence it struggles along in a permanent state of economic dependence on landowners. This dependence is an essential aspect of untouchability, although it tends sometimes to be forgotten. It is true that an explanation of the caste system in terms of economic exploitation often amounts to condemning the system without first trying to understand it;[83] but one should also remember that Dumont himself criticized Wiser for having idealized the reciprocity of economic exchanges within the '*jajmani* system', thereby missing the fundamentally hierarchical, and therefore inegalitarian, nature of the system.[84] For Dumont, the fundamental principle of caste is hierarchy;[85] complementarity is only one aspect of the system. The emphasis on inequality differentiates Dumont's approach from that of Hocart, who, on the contrary, considers that caste complementarity is necessary for the realization of the sacrifice on which the system is based.[86]

Moffatt[87] himself recognizes the paradoxical, ambiguous marginality of Untouchables, when he writes that they are at times 'excluded' and at times 'included'. So why should the 'models of unity' be considered to be totally irreconcilable with the 'outcaste models'? Parry[88] regretted that the emphasis on the 'encompassing' ideology of ritual pollution, though extremely useful, had fostered a 'rather cavalier neglect of those "encompassed" aspects of the ideology which might tone down the contrast'. And what Caplan writes about the Protestants of Madras could apply to Untouchables: 'Even if we find a strong commitment to caste within non-Hindu communities, that does not rule out an equal if not greater commitment to a set of values which are distinctively Christian.'[89] And he concludes that 'the majority of Protestants, in as much as they behave as devoted Christians and at the same time adhere to caste practices, subscribe, in various measures, to two quite distinct and opposed sets of values.'[90] Untouchables, too, are both the victims and the agents of the caste system, its defenders and its enemies.[91]

We are wrong to assume that humans are always rational, consistent, unambiguous beings who subscribe exclusively to one ideology. Instead, the world is made up of

82. T. K. Oommen, 'Sources of Deprivation and Styles of Protest: The Case of the Dalits in India'. *Contributions to Indian Sociology (NS)*, 18 (1984), pp. 45-62, p. 46.

83. S. Barnett, 'Identity Choice and Caste Ideology in Contemporary South India', in K. David (ed.), *The New Wind: Changing Identities in South Asia* (Paris and The Hague: Mouton, 1976), p. 637.

84. L. Dumont, *Homo Hierarchicus*, p. 134.

85. L. Dumont, *Homo Hierarchicus*, p. 14.

86. A. Hocart, *Les Castes* (Paris: Librairie orientaliste Paul Geuthner, 1938), p. 27.

87. M. Moffatt, *An Untouchable Community*, pp. 4-5.

88. J. Parry, 'Egalitarian Values in a Hierarchical Society'. *South Asian Review,* 7 (1974), p. 119.

89. L. Caplan, 'Caste and Castelessness among South Indian Christians'. *Contributions to Indian Sociology (NS)*, 14 (1980), p. 216.

90. Ibid., p. 239.

91. R. Deliège, *Les Paraiyars du Tamil Nadu,* p. 117.

beings who are complex and sometimes contradictory. For instance, one can find people who are at the same time Christian *and* Communist, democrat *and* elitist, pacifist *and* violent. The only Communist in the village of Alangkulam is also the *pusari* (priest) of the Muni temple and a member of a particularly brutal high caste. Theoretically these various traits seem incompatible; but this does not bother Kandaswami, who, like the rest of us, assumes his contradictions. The same is true of a social group like the Untouchables, who are pulled between two different, if not opposed, ideologies: they are 'those who are forced to be low' (*tazhttappattor*), or even militant *dalits*; but at the same time they also reproduce the system by looking with contempt on those who are below them.

-4-

Untouchable Myths of Origin[1]

The ambiguity of the position occupied by Untouchables in Indian society can be seen in their world-view and the way they think about their caste. This was the lesson of Chapter 3. The present chapter is going to show that the origin myths of this important segment of the Indian population reveal an underlying ambiguity. Before going into this analysis, though, it is important to note that different versions of what can be regarded as a single origin myth can be found in all parts of India. Behind these variants, however, lies a structure common to all. Because of the great diversity of castes, languages and regions, transmission of this myth is highly unlikely: indeed, it is hard to see how the myth told by Paraiyars in Tamil Nadu could have been transmitted to the Uttar Pradesh Chamars living thousands of kilometres away, since the two castes are separated by a number of states and have never had any contact with each other. It is therefore legitimate to think that, if these two castes, along with many others, report myths with highly similar structures, it is because these express and reflect the ways these castes think. And this is obviously why they are of interest to us.

In a famous study already mentioned, Max Weber argued that India's oppressed classes readily accepted their lot because they believed that, by doing so, their condition would be improved in the next life.[2] Low classes, Weber claimed, 'perfectly internalized' the Brahminic concepts of *samsara* (rebirth), *karma and dharma;* they are 'tamed' by Brahmanical theory,[3] so that they do not revolt against their state of servitude.

Anthropologists today are more cautious about the significance of Sanskritic concepts in Hindus' daily life. It is often reported, for example, that basic Hindu concepts such as *karma* are rarely used in the lower castes, and that many people have never even heard of them.[4] Although Weber argues that the Hindu explanation of the afterlife and their theodicy is one of 'most consistent … ever produced by history', this

1. This chapter is a slightly modified version of an article published in *Man (NS)*, 28 (1993), pp. 533-49.

2. M. Weber, T*he Religion of India: The Sociology of Hinduism and Buddhism* (New York: The Free Press, 1958), p. 122.

3. Ibid., p. 130.

4. P. Kolenda, 'Religious Anxiety and Hindu Fate', in E. Harper (ed.), *Religion in South Asia* (Berkeley, CA: University of California Press, 1964), p. 80.

remarkable clarity is not substantiated by reality, and the lower castes usually claim that they have no idea of what happens after death; my persistent questions on the subject were invariably answered by, 'How could we know?'[5] Gough ran into similar scepticism among the Untouchables of Tanjore district:

"One day, sitting in the Adi-Dravida street, I tackled a group of older Pallars on the subject of death, duty, destiny and rebirth of the soul. In my inadequate Tamil, I asked them where they thought the soul went after death. The group collapsed in merriment - perhaps as much at my speech as at the question. Wiping his eyes, the old man replied, 'Mother, we don't know! Do you know? Have you been there?' I said, 'No, but Brahmans say that if people do their duty well in this life, their souls will be born next time in a higher caste.' 'Brahmans say!' scoffed another elder. 'Brahmans say anything. Their heads go round and round!'"[6]

For over a century, untouchable emancipation movements of various sorts have been undermining Weber's generalizations. Untouchables today certainly do not believe their condition results from misconduct in a former life, nor are they willing to bear oppression in this world in the hope of being reborn in the 'womb of a queen and Brahman's daughter'.[7] But it might be argued that these views have been affected by the democratization that has been going on in Indian society for a number of decades. In the past, before British colonization, was their world-view perhaps closer to Hindu orthodoxy as presented by Weber?

It is obviously impossible to interview Untouchables who lived two hundred years ago, and there is practically no historical evidence from this period that might help us resolve the problem. The oral tradition handed down by Untouchables is therefore the only evidence that might provide access to their traditional modes of thought. This is particularly true of their origin myths. The myths collected by contemporary anthropologists were already reported in the nineteenth-century literature, so that they may be assumed to have a fairly long history behind them. Moreover, as such myths are related by Untouchables throughout India, we are led to believe that they say something about how Untouchables view themselves and their place in society, and therefore express a commonly held world-view. It is for this reason that they will occupy our attention in this chapter. Even when the content of the different versions varies slightly, they seem to share a 'common structure'. Moreover, these myths are radically different from those of the higher castes.

In an already published article devoted to the Paraiyar myth of origin, I emphasized the disagreement between the myth and the Hindu theodicy.[8] My analysis questioned Dumont's view that the ideology of hierarchy pervades Hindu social life.[9] Although I do not entirely abjure my earlier analysis, it seems to me that a few nuances could be added that bring us closer to Dumont. I still argue that, through their myths,

5. R. Deliège, 'Souffrance et échange: quelques croyances religieuses des intouchables catholiques de l'Inde du sud'. *Anthropos,* 82 (1987), p. 422; see also A. Good, *The Female Bridegroom: A Comparative Study of Life-Crisis Rituals in South India and Sri Lanka* (Oxford: Clarendon Press, 1990), p. 154.

6. K. Gough, 'Harijans in Thanjavur', in K. Gough and H. Sharma (eds), *Imperialism and Revolution in South Asia* (New York: Monthly Review Press, 1973), p. 234.

7. M. Weber, *The Religion of India*, p. 122.

8. R. Deliège, 'Les Mythes d'origine chez les Paraiyar'. *L'Homme*, 109 (1989), pp. 107-16.

9. See, e.g. L. Dumont, *Homo Hierarchicus. essai sur le système des castes* (Paris: Gallimard, 1966), p. 268

Untouchables contest their position in Indian society; but at the same time, it must be said that they do not question the ideological foundations of the system, nor the system itself, which they present as almost natural. Through their myths, then, Untouchables legitimize the fact that those who deal with impure matter are irrevocably relegated to the bottom of the social ladder. Once again, this ambiguity is typical of the Untouchables' position in Indian society. They question the position of their own caste within the system, but continue to legitimize the system as a whole.

In this chapter, I shall compare untouchable myths from various parts of India and show that they share a similar underlying structure. I shall begin with the Paraiyar myth of origin, in part because I myself collected several versions, but also because this myth has been the object of some spirited discussion among anthropologists, of whom Michael Moffatt is a prominent example.

The Paraiyar Myth

I shall begin with the myths I collected in the southern Tamil Nadu village of Valghira Manickam. But I would like first to make one or two remarks concerning the relative importance of these myths for the people in the village. Our interest, however legitimate, could suggest that they are central to the villagers' everyday concerns. But this is not the case. Some Paraiyars had never heard of them; others remembered only bits and pieces, or even simply the basic message. My harvest was therefore the result of a certain stubbornness on my part. Nevertheless, people regularly referred to these myths to illustrate the way they saw their condition, and I think or at least hope that they would recognize themselves in the analysis I propose.

One version of the myth collected in Valghira Manickam had already been recorded by Thurston.[10] It would therefore be legitimate to think that this is a very old myth that probably predates the British colonization of India. The same myth has also been reported by anthropologists working in other parts of Tamil Nadu, and even in Sri Lanka, where Paraiyars are also found. The following is one of the most typical versions I collected:

> "*Myth 1, version 1:* In the beginning, there were two brothers who were poor. Then they went together to pray to God. God asked them to remove the carcass of a dead cow. The elder brother answered: *Een thambi pappaan* ('My younger brother will do it'), but God understood: *Een thambi paappaan* ('My younger brother is a Brahmin'), and that very day, the younger brother became a Brahmin *(paappaan)*, and the elder brother became a Paraiyar. All castes originate from these two brothers."

This version of the myth contains all the essential elements. However, the fact that God plays a role is not determinant; in many other versions, it is a king or a father that talks with the brothers. In the above version, God does not decide anything - all he does is to sanction the elder brother's statement; moreover, my Paraiyar informants, to

10. E. Thurston, *Castes and Tribes of Southern India* (Madras: Government Press, 1909), 7 vols.; vol. VI, p. 84.

whom we shall return, were quick to play down God's role in this business, as they did in the establishment of the caste system in general. Two points are crucial, however: first, the fact that the two men were brothers, and, second, the misunderstanding that resulted in the debasement of the elder.

The Tamil language does not have a single term for 'brother', but distinguishes between the elder brother *(annan)* and the younger *(thambi)*. This is an important distinction because, in the Tamil family structure, the elder brother is considered superior to the younger brother, and is associated with the father, whom he will succeed as head of the family. It could therefore be argued that, in a sense, the myth stresses the Paraiyar's original superiority over the Brahmin. This interpretation is confirmed by Iyer,[11] who reminds us that, in Kerala, the Paraiyar is called the 'elder Brahmin', and by Aiyappan, who writes that, in the same region, the very low Nayadis are called 'old sons' *(halle makkalu)* and that they, too, are mythologically related to the Brahmins.[12] The villagers of Valghira Manickam say that the local Brahmins themselves acknowledge this connection by giving the Paraiyars small wedding gifts called *annan varisai,* 'the gift to the elder brother', composed of betel nuts, flowers and fruit. The neighbouring Pallars, in spite of their constant readiness to denigrate the Paraiyars at every occasion, also stressed that the Paraiyar and the Brahmin were originally brothers. In other words, in the beginning, the Paraiyar was not at all inferior. How then did he lose his prestige? Had he done something basically reprehensible, or did he have an inherent, almost natural defect?

This brings us to the second essential point of the myth, the misunderstanding that led to the elder brother's loss of status. This misunderstanding is present in all versions of the untouchable myth, and can therefore be considered crucial to its message. If Untouchables have lost their original relative superiority, it is not because they did something wrong, and even less because of some inherent defect: it was because of a mix-up, a pun, a misunderstanding or even an error, or because of the younger brother's cunning. In many of the versions, the elder brother acts in an exemplary way: he is brave, obedient and respectful; his fall is therefore unjust and undeserved. At worst, the elder brother may considered rather naive; but this in no way justifies his subsequent downfall. Things might well have gone the other way.

In a more 'Sanskritized' version of the myth, God even thanks the elder brother for his efficiency:

> "*Myth 1, version 2:* Two brothers went to a temple to conduct a prayer ceremony (*jabbam*). On their way, the found the remains of a dead cow. As the younger brother was weak and small, the elder proposed to remove the carcass himself. The people present told him that he should conduct the prayer session instead, but he answered: *Een thambi pappaan.* The people understood that his younger brother was a Brahmin, *paappaan.* To thank the elder brother for his work, God blessed him and made him a Paraiyar, whereas the younger brother became a Brahmin."

Version 2 of Myth 1 presents being a Paraiyar as an honour, almost a privilege

11. A. K. Iyer, *The Tribes and Castes of Cochin* (New Delhi: Cosmos, 1981), 3 vols); p. 69.

12. A. Aiyappan, *Social and Physical Anthropology of the Nayadis of Malabar* (Madras: Bulletin of the Madras Government Museum, 1937), pp. 131-5.

granted by God to thank the elder son. Everyone there recognizes him as a priest, which shows that nothing in his nature predestined him to become a Paraiyar. In other versions, a king or a father figures:

> "*Myth 1, version 3:* A man had five sons. He always asked the eldest to work for him, to fetch water, and so forth. But the eldest always refused and said: *Een thambi pappaan.* The father understood that his younger son was a Brahmin, and the eldest became the Paraiyar."

There are many more versions of this myth, but there is no need to detail them here. All the versions are clearly organized around a common structure: in each, the ancestor starts in an elevated situation, one of equality or even relative superiority (as elder brother), and is associated with positive values (piety, honesty, devotion, willingness, diligence, dutifulness, etc.). The younger brother is shown as passive, perhaps even rather dull. Only in some versions does he actually intervene (see below), where he is depicted as wicked, falsely accusing his elder brother of theft.

Untouchable myths always contain an element that reverses the initial situation: this 'reversible factor' is invariably a pun, a misunderstanding or a trick. It completely reverses the initial situation, and the superior suddenly finds himself the inferior. Nothing inherent in the elder brother's nature makes his loss of status inevitable. If the Paraiyar is poor and must work hard, it is not because of some congenital defect, but because of a mix-up, due to some error. Consequently, it would seem that the low status of the Paraiyar is largely undeserved.

Paraiyars do not believe that they could be reborn as Brahmins or as members of another caste. Caste *(jati)* is understood here as a species, and it is neither possible nor desirable to change one's caste. For this reason among others, intercaste marriages, including those into higher castes, are not looked upon with favour. Paraiyars do not consider it a curse to be a Paraiyar. If they did, it would be pointless to strive to better their lot; and, in contradiction with a strict reading of the law of *karma*, Paraiyars are engaged in a number of struggles to assert their rights and to improve their lives.

Diverging Interpretations

This interpretation of the untouchable myth of origin is supported by most of the anthropologists who have reported similar myths. Kolenda was probably the first to stress the discrepancy between the philosophical concepts of Hinduism and the beliefs of Untouchables. For instance, she tells that the sweepers of Khalapur, in Uttar Pradesh, do not believe that the position of their caste reflects punishment for deeds in a past life, but that it is just 'a terrible historical accident'.[13] R. Miller, too, stresses the place of Untouchables outside the Brahminic religious and social traditions.[14] Berreman similarly suggests that Untouchables do not consider themselves a 'degraded social category', but rationalize their low status as the result of bad luck or

14. R. Miller, 'Button, Button ... Great Tradition, Little Tradition, Whose Tradition?' *Anthropological Quarterly,* 39 (1966), pp. 26-42, p. 29.

13. P. Kolenda, 'Religious Anxiety and Hindu Fate', p. 75.

misfortune.[15]

"No informants were found who said in effect, 'I was a scoundrel in a previous life and now I am getting my just deserts.' Neither was any caste found whose members said in effect: 'We have always done defiling work. This was what we were created to do and we do it. Therefore we are untouchable.' These (and particularly the first) seem to be psychologically untenable positions for individuals to accept."[16]

Mosse collected a version of the Paraiyar myth from the Totti Paraiyars in Alapuram village (Ramnad district); his interpretation is quite close to our own:

"*Myth 3:* There were two Brahmin brothers *(annan and tampi)*. Annan went to the temple every day to conduct *puja.* A cow came from *intira lokam* (heaven) and after cooking the ponkal rice and other offerings, Annan would take one drop of blood from the cow to worship (*irattapali,* blood sacrifice). The cow would then go away. Daily he went to the temple and brought back *ponkal* rice for his wife and younger brother. One day a rumor was spread and the villagers told Tampi: 'Every day your brother is eating meat in the temple and only bringing you rice *piracaatam.'* Tampi told his brother's pregnant wife and asked her to tell his brother to bring her a little beef next time. When her husband returned, she told him: 'You were eating beef, yet I am pregnant and you are only bringing *piracaatam* to me. If you don't give me any beef, I will kill myself.' Annan, who had in fact never eaten any beef, was worried, thinking a woman's word must be obliged. He therefore went to the temple and cut a piece of flesh from the cow. The cow died. Tampi, seeing what had happened, hid and refused to eat the beef. Villagers held a *panchayat* and said to Annan: 'Since you killed the cow, you must take it away and eat it. You are untouchable, you beefeater *(niintintaamai niimaatvvettipayal)*. Go away from the village.' When leaving the village, Annan met a man who said to him: 'Where are you going *swami*?' 'It is my bad time, I am going', Annan replied. 'If you go, who will look after the temple?' Annan replied with the pun: '*Koiyl velai tampi paappaan*' ('Tampi will see to the temple work' or 'Tampi is a Brahmin'. Annan and his wife arrived in another village. The people gave them a hut and told them to collect cooked rice daily for their food. Then they held a *panchayat* and gave Annan the job of 'village watchman' and calling people for meetings. To make his work easier, he took some skin from a dead calf and made a *tappu* (or *parai*) drum. From this came the title *paraiyan.* At first people brought him their dead animals, but later they made him go and collect dead cows, and they avoided him because of his work."[17]

This remarkable version of our myth includes all the essential ingredients: an unfounded rumour brings about the downfall of the elder son. The younger son has a more active role in this reversal, but he is cast as first an envious and then a cowardly figure. The initial higher status of the elder son also features prominently: he is the

15. G. Berreman, *Hindus of the Himalayas: Ethnography and Change* (Berkeley, CA: University of California Press, 1963), p. 243.

16. Ibid., p. 223.

17. D. Mosse, 'Caste, Christianity and Hinduism. A Study of Social Organization and Religion in Rural Ramnad'. (D. Phil. Thesis, Oxford University, Institute of Social Anthropology, 1985), pp. 242-4.

temple priest, particularly pious, and conducts the rites in accordance with tradition. People call him *swami,* a title used in addressing the gods or important people. Eating beef never crossed his mind; it was his younger brother, the future Brahmin, who had this desire. Lastly, this myth illustrates the secular nature of decisions having to do with caste; the decisions are taken by the villagers in the course of a meeting (*panchayat*). The elder brother's original jobs did not entail ritual pollution, it was only little by little that he came to be excluded. Mosse remarks that this version illustrates the fall of Untouchables from prosperity and high-caste status to a position of servitude. He supports his judgement by the views of the people themselves: 'High castes, explained one youth leader, obtained land by fraudulent means, and through the generosity of the Pallars who allowed these people to settle in the village.'[18]

We shall return to this theme of untouchable generosity later; but it should be noted here in passing that it is a common form of self-representation, and, in particular, that it contrasts with an image of permanent impurity. Mosse emphasizes that this loss of status was unintentional, and that it was brought about by men rather than desired by the gods.[19] The servitude and poverty of lower castes were instituted by men, and are not understood as inherent attributes of caste.[20] Thus far, Mosse confirms all our interpretations of the myth; but he also adds an essential element neglected by other scholars: the Totti Paraiyars, he points out, assert through their myths that they do not deserve to be low and that their inferiority is the result of bad luck (*viiti*), trickery by high castes or historical accident. At the same time, however, their myths accept that cattle scavenging, funeral service, drumming and beef-eating are indeed despicable and even disgusting activities. They refuse to consider these tasks as an inherent characteristic of their caste; but at the same time, they recognize that those who do perform them are contemptible.[21]

This critical shading suggests that untouchable myths do not reject the caste system as such, but do on the contrary legitimize its ideological foundations. In fact, generally speaking, Untouchables have never challenged caste values and the behaviour they engender. What they do contest is their own position in the system. They legitimize untouchability, but refuse to accept that their own caste is polluting and degraded. Mosse's remarks are clearly crucial to our understanding of the untouchable myth, and I can only agree with him. In fact, they explain the general ambiguity of the Untouchables' own position.

As one might guess, Michael Moffatt was intrigued by this myth, and proposed an analysis that challenged earlier interpretations. Moffatt collected several myths among the Paraiyars of Endavur, and it is useful to quote one of his versions:

> "*Myth 4:* At the origin, there was nothing in the world. There was no life. There was nothing except one woman, Aadi ('origin'). She was all alone and wanted a husband. She made a sacrificial fire and finally a handsome man emerged from the fire. He married her. He was none other than Iswaran (Siva) himself. The couple lived happily.
>
> After some time four children were born to Aadi. The gods were satisfied that

18. Ibid., p. 238.
19. Ibid., p. 246.
20. Ibid., p. 237.
21. Ibid., p. 246.

everything was complete except for the creation of the castes. So they planned it. According to their plan, the four children, who had become adults, were made to cook beef one day. The eldest son offered to do the cooking. While he was cooking, the other three brothers sat around him, watching him cook. While the meat was boiling, one piece fell from the pot. The eldest son saw it fall to the ground and thought it would bring a bad name to his cooking. So, meaning well, he hid it under a heap of ash. Immediately the others accused him of theft and scolded him for stealing a big piece of meat for himself. They shouted at him: '*Paraiyaa maraiyaade!*' ('Paraiyan, do not hide [that]'). Hence the name 'Paraiyan'. Eventually the elder brother was forced to live separately, and was called 'Paraiyan'."[22]

Very similar versions of this myth are found in other parts of India.[23] Although it differs in many ways from the myth we have been analysing, its 'structure' remains the same: in both cases, a reversal from a relatively favourable to a fallen situation is brought about by a misunderstanding. Moffatt recognizes that 'the central incident of the myth is important structurally, for it represents an inversion'.[24] He also agrees with Kolenda that the myth fulfils a psychological function in offering the Harijans a 'prideful claim to former precedence, despite the present low status'.[25] Nevertheless, on the whole, Moffatt's interpretation is altogether different from those that went before, particularly because he refuses to regard the fall as an accident. For Moffatt, the 'Gods had planned for it',[26] they had set it up. This is a crucial point, for it implies that caste hierarchy is divinely ordained and that the gods themselves wanted the Paraiyars to be inferior because of their nature.

We have seen, however, that God is not always present in these myths. Even in the version presented by Moffatt, he intervenes only at a preliminary stage; admittedly he wants to establish the caste system, but in no way does he decree that the elder brother should be inferior. In fact, he withdraws and lets the brothers work it out. This early episode adds little to the core of the myth. It is worth remembering here that the people of Valghira Manickam always insisted that the caste system was not divinely instituted, that certain men, often Brahmins, made it in order to dominate society.[27] This insistence on the secular nature of the caste system is widely confirmed by numerous ethnographic contexts: Molund, for instance, reports that the Koris of Kanpur have no doubt on the matter, as one informant told him: 'The caste system is a human thing. If a man gets blind it is because of God (Bhagwan), if he is born into a low caste it is because man has created a society of castes … God has not made it impossible for us to try to improve our situation.'[28]

The Untouchables that Kapadia met in Tamil Nadu regarded their 'impurity' as an

22. M. Moffatt, *An Untouchable Community in South India: Structure and Consensus* (Princeton, NJ: Princeton University Press, 1979), pp. 120-1.

23. See, for example, G. Briggs, *The Doms and their Near Relations* (Mysore: Wesley Press, 1953), p. 51.

24. M. Moffatt, *An Untouchable Community*, p. 123.

25. Ibid., p. 123.

26. Ibid., p. 122.

27. R. Deliège, 'Les Mythes d'origine', p. 109.

28. S. Molund, *First We Are People ... The Koris of Kanpur between Caste and Class* (Stockholm: Stockholm Studies in Social Anthropology, 1988), pp. 156-7.

'unfair ascription imposed on them by the upper castes',[29] and the Paraiyars of Alapuram also regarded caste as 'a humanly instituted order'.[30] Similarly, the Pallars of Alangkulam often told me that it was not God but the Brahmins who invented the caste system to protect their own interests. Finally, as I have already said, the key concepts of Hinduism, such as *karma* and *dharma*, often mean little to the lower castes.[31] Therefore the fact that god is present in some versions may not be crucial, since he always leaves people to decide for themselves. He merely acknowledges their decision, and many versions do not even mention him.

Moffatt also introduces a second element which he sees as fundamental to his interpretation of the myth and which differs from what we have been saying; according to him, the 'central incident' is due to the inherent stupidity of the Paraiyar. What the myth is saying, Moffatt argues from the commentaries of his informants, is that Untouchables are indeed foolish, stupid and unable to see a task through. He cites one old man as saying: 'Even now the same situation continues. We are generally innocent, without any idea of theft and cheating.'[32] Moffatt further argues that Paraiyars often describe themselves as foolish and naive, 'images in accord with those in the myths'.[33] This foolishness, he continues, 'results from a curse of the god'. In other words, if the gods reduced the Untouchables to their present status, it is because of some intrinsic characteristic in them. Moffatt thus rejects the accidental character of the fall and refuses to regard the story as the unfortunate consequence of a mistake or misunderstanding.[34]

Moffatt's position is not always consistent; on the one hand, as I have said, he agrees with Kolenda that the myth fulfils a psychological function in providing Untouchables with a claim to former precedence; but he also maintains that the myth justifies their low status because of their stupidity and gullibility.[35] The two elements seem somewhat contradictory: can Untouchables be proud of being foolish? In contrast to Moffatt's interpretation, the elder brother's attitude can be read as being socially positive: he is hardworking, generous, obliging, helpful, responsible, devout, strong, well-meaning. Admittedly there is some degree of naïveté in his behaviour; but this can be interpreted as a morally positive element, as something inherently good in a pitiless world.

To be 'naive' is not the same thing as to be 'foolish'. On the contrary, the recent studies I have cited show that Untouchables have a positive image of themselves,

29. K. Kapadia, 'Gender, Caste and Class in Rural South India'. (Doctoral dissertation, London School of Economics, Department of Anthropology, 1990), p. 249.

30. D. Mosse, 'Caste, Christianity and Hinduism', p. 256.

31. P. Kolenda, 'Religious Anxiety and Hindu Fate', p. 72; M. Jurgensmeyer, Religion as Social Vision. The Movement against Untouchability in 20th Century Punjab (Berkeley, CA: University of California Press, 1982), p. 99; C. Maloney, 'Religious Beliefs and Social Hierarchy in Tamil Nadu, India'. *American Ethnologist*, (1975), pp. 169-92, pp. 74-5; J. Freeman, *Untouchable: An Indian Life History* (Stanford, CA: Stanford University Press, 1979), p. 52.

32. M. Moffatt, *An Untouchable Community*, p. 121.

33. Ibid., 128.

34. Ibid., p. 122.

35. Ibid., p. 128.

36. O. Herrenschmidt, *Les Meilleurs Dieux sont hindous* (Lausanne: L'Age d'Homme, 1989), pp. 31-6; see also O. Lynch, *The Politics of Untouchability. Social Mobility and Social Change in a City of India* (New York: Columbia University Press, 1969), p. 163.

whereas they often depict the higher castes in negative terms. In Andhra Pradesh, for instance, the low-caste representation of the Brahmins is one of greediness, avarice, impotency and ridiculousness.[36] In Tamil Nadu, the Pallars view themselves as 'auspicious providers of agricultural bounty', and they say that a farm cannot prosper unless tilled by a Pallar.[37] Harijans often consider members of other castes as 'greedy, proud and lazy', whereas they see themselves as generous and hardworking.[38] This last characteristic is certainly present in several versions of the myth, and the elder brother is sometimes thanked for his willingness to work. In the former district of Ramnad, Untouchables depict the locally dominant Kallars as oppressive, violent, rough and authoritarian.

In sum, the Untouchables' self-representation is, on the whole, far from negative. Of course they sometimes stress the difficulties of improving their position, but this recognition is based on experience rather than being a mark of 'fatalism'; it is objectively very difficult for a Harijan to climb the social ladder, and no one could contradict them on this point.

Surprisingly enough, Moffatt fails to point out how the myth legitimizes the social hierarchy on the basis of the notion of ritual pollution. The myth does not criticize the system; it simply contests the position of the members of one caste within it. It accepts the idea that breaking the rules of pollution justifies low status and that ritually impure tasks are also socially degrading. The cow and its carcass are central to most of the versions, which suggests that the untouchable myth also legitimizes untouchability. At no time is this ideology challenged. Untouchables accept that those below them are untouchable, by which they justify the ideological foundations of untouchability, even if the myth is meant to signify that their own caste is respectable.

While Moffatt's views imperfectly reflect the ideology of Untouchables, they do account for the way the high castes see them. Whereas Untouchables consider themselves naive, the higher castes emphasize their stupidity. I have come across other examples of 'double readings': for instance, according to a Marathi proverb: 'In Maharasthra no village is without its Mahar quarter (Maharwada).' The Mahars are proud of this saying; and interpret it as emphasizing the widespread presence of the Mahars and their importance in the region. But high-caste people read it differently and interpret it to mean much the same as the English proverb, 'Every flock has its black sheep.'[39] In the next section we will see that the high-caste view is expressed particularly clearly in certain myths.

Sanskritization and Other Myths

Before examining untouchable myths from other parts of India, I shall show how the myths analysed above are typical of low castes that recognize their inferiority. When a low caste wants to improve its status, it often begins by adopting a new myth of

37. K. Kapadia, 'Gender, Caste and Class', p. 118.

38. G. Djurfeldt and S. Lindberg, *Behind Poverty. The Social Formation in a Tamil Village* (London: Curzon Press, 1975), p. 219.

39. E. Zelliot, 'Dr. Ambedkar and the Mahar Movement'. (Doctoral dissertation, University of Pennsylvania, 1969), p. 17.

origin consistent with its new ambitions. This is part of a process of Sanskritization through which a low caste changes its customs, ideology, ritual and way of life in keeping with high-caste norms and practice.[40]

As early as the nineteenth century, the Nadars, a low caste of Tamil Nadu, launched a movement of social emancipation and popularized myths that portrayed them as the descendants of seven brothers who were born of a celestial virgin and brought up by the goddess Bhadrakali; after the river Vagai flooded, the brothers refused to obey a royal order to build a dam by carrying baskets of earth on their heads. The king beheaded two of the brothers for their disobedience, but their heads floated away shouting: 'I shall not carry baskets.' Frightened by this miracle, the king released the five remaining brothers, who gave birth to the Nadars, who to this day refuse to carry baskets on their heads.[41] This story provides the Nadars with a divine ancestry, but at the same time it legitimizes their refusal to perform menial and degrading tasks. Its nature is radically different from the Paraiyar myth. It is no longer a question here of degradation; on the contrary, the myth substantiates the Nadars' dignity, whether from their heavenly birth, their heroic resistance to the king, the miracle that occurred, or their refusal to perform low tasks associated with the labouring classes from whom they wanted to dissociate themselves as clearly as possible.

More recently, in the 1980s, the Pallars of Tamil Nadu also launched an emancipation movement; and they, too, popularized a myth celebrating the former glory of the caste:

> "*Myth 5*: The original inhabitants of a fertile river valley, who therefore held the title of Vellalas, were an ancient cultivator and warrior people called Mallars. They worshipped Intiran or Teventiran, and were called Teventira Kullar Vellalars. As heads of the village councils, or *kutumpus,* they were also known as Teventira Kutumpan. They were the first to till the land and build the cities of the ancient Tamil civilization. At that time, ancestors of Kallars, Maravars, Akamutayars, etc. were tribal inhabitants of the Palai dry land. Mallars (i.e. Pallars), enjoyed all the rights and honors of royalty. They were the Pandara warriors and were responsible for the Harappa civilization.
>
> However they were conquered by Muslim and Telugu invaders, in the seventeenth century, who raised up the jungle tribes, such as the Kallars and Maravars and the Palaiyakkars (Poliyars), seeking to overthrow the original rulers of the land. The Mallars were deprived of their land and reduced to the state of serfs. They were weakened by being scattered, and their name was changed into Pallars, meaning low and despicable."[42]

Myth 5 differs radically from the Paraiyar myths in its thinly veiled intentions and pseudo-historical character. Not only are the Pallars described as kings, but currently dominant castes are reduced to the status of 'jungle tribes' and owe their present social situation to the foreign invaders, which makes them in a sense 'collaborators'. This

40. M. N. Srinivas, *Social Change in Modern India* (Berkeley, CA: University of California Press, 1971), p. 6.

41. R. Hardgrave, *The Nadars of Tamilnad. The Political Culture of a Community in Change* (Bombay: Oxford University Press, 1969), pp. 19-21.

42. D. Mosse, 'Caste, Christianity and Hinduism', p. 356.

tribal, savage origin also explains why these castes are presently seen as rough and violent. Pallars, in contrast, are depicted as the founders of the remarkable Indus civilization.

It is clear that castes that want to express their greatness and Sanskritize their way of life adopt new origin myths. The old myths are not consistent with their new social aspirations. In contrast, the Paraiyar myth acknowledges the present situation, and does not attempt to alter it. As such, it cannot be used to support claims to a higher status.

In the village of Kuliyanur (Muthuramalinga Thevar district), the Koonars are the dominant caste: they own the land, control village institutions such as the *panchayat,* and represent the majority of the population. Traditionally the status of these goatherds was fairly low; but, in the last fifty years, they have considerably improved their position and Sanskritized their way of life.[43] The myth that I collected in Kuliyanur also expresses this mobility, and is a reversal of the Paraiyar myth:

> "*Myth 6:* The Koonars were the last of all people. At that time, they were even worse than Pallars. They were kept aside. No one would drink water or eat food from them. One day, Lord Krishna thought: 'Since these people are kept aside, someone should give them importance.' Therefore he went inside the house of a Koonar and took some buttermilk and butter. This was witnessed by all people, and then all castes, including Brahmins, started to be friendly and drink buttermilk and water from Koonars."

The myth does not end here, however, but goes on to tell how Siva and Parvati gave powers to the caste, which has been blessed by the gods ever since. What is interesting about this myth is that it shows how a previously inferior status is transformed into a much higher one as a result of the blessing of the gods. These Nadar, Pallar and Koonar myths differ greatly from each other; I have presented them here only to show how the myths of socially mobile castes differ from untouchable myths.

In the Koonar myth, God's blessing is the crucial factor of the transformation and is what permits the Sanskritization of the caste. God's blessing often features in South Indian mythology; it is therefore not surprising that it is a central element of a myth that I collected among the Valaiyars in the village of Aangkulam, not far from Kuliyanur. Although the Valaiyar are not a Scheduled Caste, they are very low indeed, and their myth clearly expresses their degraded status. It thus seems useful to present it here. While the Valaiyars work as coolies and agricultural labourers, they are primarily hunters, and they catch small game with their nets, *valai*, whence their caste name.

> "*Myth 7:* Lord Iswaran was giving his blessing (*aaseervatham*) to all people and distributed sacred ashes (*thiruneeru*). The Koonars came up with a big pot and thus a lot of ashes fell into the pot; they were very blessed and that is why today many people among them are well off. Other people came with their hands and they were also blessed; today they are also well off.
>
> The Valaiyars were foolish enough to come with a *valai* (net), and thus when Iswaran gave the ashes most of them fell on the ground. Only a few particles

43. See M. S. Rao, *Social Movements and Social Transformations. A Study of Two Backward Classes Movements in India* (Delhi: Macmillan, 1979).

remained on the knots of the valai, and the Valaiyars were little blessed."

Those who told me the myth interpreted it in a way that partly supports Moffatt's analysis. They stressed that it explains why the Valaiyars have always remained poor: because they were unable to use God's blessing. However, they add that it was not Siva who made them poor, but because they were stupid enough to try to collect ashes with a net. God wished them well, but they were too stupid to take advantage of his blessing. In this light it is interesting that Djurfeldt and Lindberg report that the Paraiyars in a village 35 kilometres south of Madras city have a myth that strangely resembles that of the Valaiyars.

"*Myth 8*: Once upon a time, a group of people belonging to different castes were out fishing in a tank. Among them was a Harijan. While they were fishing, Iswaran (*i.e.* Siva) suddenly appeared before them. He promised each of them a gift. But before they would get it, they were all asked to put on a sacred thread. So they did.

Our Harijan was fishing with an *ottu* that day. An *ottu* is a cone-shaped basket, open at both ends … When they had put on the thread, God asked them all to line up and receive the gift. They all got their gifts and wrapped them up in pieces of cloth and carried them safely away, except our foolish Paraiya, who held out his *ottu*, forgetting that it was open at both ends.

When he got home he looked in his *ottu* for the gift God had given him; but to his grief he found it empty. He felt very sad and brooded over his bad luck.

That is how our Paraiyar lost his gift from God. And even today the saying has it that: *ottuvile vanginadu, suttal vittam, i.e.* an *ottu* is like a human body, mouth at one end and anus at the other. Our Paraiya received his gift from God through the mouth of the ottu and lost it through the bottom of it."[44]

This myth is clearly a variant of the Valaiyar myth cited above; it depicts Untouchables as stupid, and the man who gave this version to the ethnographer stressed the 'badness' of Untouchables.[45] Yet, at the same time, the myth also corresponds to what Moffatt calls an *uur* or high-caste version of untouchable status. The high-caste myths reported by Moffatt systematically emphasize the stupidity of the untouchable ancestor and give God a prominent place in the story.[46] These versions are sometimes reported by Untouchables themselves, especially when they live in a high-caste village and know of no other myth; but they do not seem to reflect their own ideology. Djurfeldt and Lindberg themselves pointed out that Untouchables have a positive image of themselves.[47] Whereas high-caste people systematically describe them as foolish, dirty, stupid, savage, lazy, unsophisticated and irreligious, it is uncommon for Untouchables to have such a negative self-image. On the contrary, it is the Brahmins whom they see as crooked and lazy, and Moffatt himself describes their delight in telling stories of high-caste beef-eating. Untouchables also value physical strength, and when Moffatt remarks that physical strength is not highly prized in 'Tamil culture',[48] he should have specified in 'Tamil *Brahmanical culture*'. There is

44. G. Djurfeldt and S. Lindberg, *Behind Poverty*, pp. 222-3.
45. Ibid., p. 224.
46. M. Moffatt, *An Untouchable Community*, pp. 126-7.
47. G. Djurfeldt and S. Lindberg, *Behind Poverty*, p. 219.

thus some degree of discordance between untouchable and high-caste cultures, and the myths of origin illustrate this discrepancy.

Myths from Other Regions

As we have seen, the Paraiyar myth is but one local version of what more generally can be called the untouchable myth. Indeed it is striking that closely similar versions of the myth are found thousands of kilometres from Tamil Nadu, where people speak radically different languages. It is highly unlikely that this myth could have passed between these different illiterate castes who had neither the right nor the means to travel. If these castes so geographically distant tell very similar stories, it must be because the myth expresses their point of view on their position in the class system. Chamars are one of the largest and best-known untouchable castes of North India, and their origin myth is very similar to that of the Paraiyars.

> "*Myth 9:* In the beginning, there was one family of men and they were all of the highest caste. They worked in the fields. In this family, there were four brothers. It happened that a cow died one day and the body lay in the garden until evening. Since no one could be found to remove the carcass, the three older brothers agreed, that their younger brother should carry away the body from the yard and that they would all take a bath on the same footing of equality. To this the younger brother agreed and he dragged the carcass into the jungle. After the bath, the brothers compelled him to remain at a distance. They told him that henceforth he would do the work of a Chamar and that they would take care of him for his services. Thus the Chamar caste arose."[49]

The similarity between this and the Paraiyar myth is striking. The main difference is that the hero of this myth is the younger brother: the relative superiority is less pronounced, but the initial equality of all the brothers is clearly asserted. Most of the other ingredients of the Paraiyar myth are also present: the original group of brothers, the dead cow, the collective decision, the trickery. Here the elder brothers are more active and treacherous than the younger brother of the Paraiyar myth, who had a passive role. The Chamars' ancestor is deliberately cheated and reduced to an inferior position.

The Bhangis, sweepers of North India, stress the trickery of the brothers in an even more explicit way:

> "*Myth 10:* When the Pandus were starting out for the Himalayas, after the great war, one of their cows died and they did not know how to dispose of the carcass, as it was a sin to touch it. The four brothers conspired against Nakula and asked him to remove it: 'Good lad, remove the carcass and we promise not to excommunicate you.' He hid the carcass under some leaves near a tree. But on his return, his brothers refused to receive him unless he brought mango wood for the performance of the *hom* or fire sacrifice. While he was away fetching the wood,

48. M. Moffatt, *An Untouchable Community*, p. 119.
49. G. Briggs, *The Chamars* (Delhi: B. R. Published Corporation, 1920), pp. 15-16.

they deserted him. Afterwards he returned to the cow and wept. When Po! by the grace of the Almighty, the cow was returned to life. Nakula grew up on the milk of the cow. Later the cow died and while he was lamenting a voice from heaven said: 'Do not grieve! You Balmik are destined to be the progenitors of those who make fans and sieves from the hides of the cow. These you will sell and you will teach the world the art of grinding and sifting flour for bread.' Nakula became an ascetic and taught the art of making bread."[50]

In this myth, God consoles the mythic ancestor and makes him humanity's 'bread-giver'. The ancestor even becomes an ascetic, which, in untouchable ideology, represents the 'hope for egalitarian idealism'.[51] At the same time, the events occur when it is already a 'sin' to handle dead animals, particularly the cow. As in Myth 9, caste ideology antedates the appearance of the caste system. In contrast, other myths relate the origin of this taboo, as in this version from the Mahars of Maharashtra:

"*Myth 11:* Before beef had become a prohibited food, Mahamuni was left to watch a pot of meat cooking. None other than the divine cow Tripad Gayatri was in the stew. When a piece of flesh fell out, Mahamuni, rather than return it to the pot, ate it. Discovered in his delinquency by the gods, he was penalized by being required, along with his descendants, to eat the flesh of dead cows."[52]

Unlike many other versions, here God plays a more explicit role. But here, too, the hero has been implicitly cheated: if the meat was cooking, it was no doubt to be eaten! Yet when Mahamuni eats a morsel, he is immediately treated as a 'delinquent' and punished accordingly. The prohibition on eating beef seems to have been deliberately created in order to harm Untouchables.

More generally, many versions of this myth feature several brothers and a dead cow. A similar story is told by the Doms of the Punjab,[53] and the Chamars of Senapur relate a myth very similar to Myth 10:

"*Myth 12:* Once four Brahmin brothers were going to a fair. On their way, they had to cross a river, but as they came to the river, they saw a cow stuck in the mud by the bank. One by one, they tried to extricate the cow from the mud. As the younger brother was pulling on the tail of the cow trying to get it out, the cow died. As the younger brother was touching the cow when it died, his other brothers considered him to be unclean and had nothing to do with him from then on. The present-day Camars [*sic*] are descendants of this outcasted Brahmin."[54]

Each version differs to some extent, but all share certain elements: the fall of the Untouchables is the consequence of a misunderstanding or a trick; the beginning of time is characterized by social equality, and the destitution of one caste is not due to any inherent defect. At the same time, however, the myth legitimizes a hierarchy based on ritual pollution, even if its primary purpose is to contest the justice of degrading the

50. G. Briggs, *The Doms and Their Near Relations*, p. 64.

51. R. S. Khare, *The Untouchable as Himself: Ideology, Identity and Pragmatism among the Lucknow Chamars* (Cambridge: Cambridge University Press, 1987), p. 27.

52. G. Briggs, *The Doms and Their Near Relations*, p. 61.

53. Ibid., p. 53.

54. B. Cohn, 'The Chamars of Senapur. A Study of the Changing Status of a Depressed Caste'. (Doctoral dissertation, Cornell University, 1954), p. 113.

hero's caste. This ambiguity in untouchable ideology was pointed out by Cohn:

"It should be realized that, although the Camars attack the superior social position of the Thakurs and are actively trying to raise their own status, they are not consciously trying to eliminate the caste system. No one in the village is interested in destroying the caste system. The Camars are solely interested in raising their status in the system."[55]

The myths I have described clearly reflect this ambiguity. To be sure, Untouchables have not absorbed all the values of the caste system, and their world-view does not reproduce the dominant culture in its entirety.[56] Nevertheless, they have not developed a 'counter-culture', but have generally tried simply to improve their position within the system rather than to replace it altogether. The myths discussed here therefore do not provide 'models for action', nor even challenge untouchability, for they support its foundations. However, they do make social mobility ideologically possible and ethically acceptable. Even the most traditional Untouchables do not consider their position to be God-given, even less that it would be a sin to try to change it. On the contrary, by depicting their ancestor as generous, pious, hard-working and honest, they reinforce the idea that any attempt to improve their status is justified. This conclusion is largely supported by the comments of the contemporary Untouchables we interviewed, and fits well with the many movements for emancipation and untouchable rights that will be discussed in later chapters.

A Legitimization of the Caste System

While the myths discussed above show a certain degree of consistency in the untouchable ideology, they also reflect the ambiguity of the untouchable position. There is no complete disjunction between the untouchable ideology and higher-caste views. Generally speaking, the lower castes offer no alternative to the caste system; in fact their myths take caste for granted. Though they stress their brotherhood with Brahmins, they acknowledge the superiority of the latter. They also believe that all members of a caste share the selfsame substance, and that the behaviour of one individual affects the whole caste. Yet Untouchables do not think that their own degraded position is the will of God, and therefore immutable. The myth makes it clear that social change is possible, if not desirable.

At the beginning of this chapter, we saw that the importance of these myths should not be overestimated, and that many Untouchables were even unaware of their existence. The Pallars of Alangkulam, for instance, knew no myths about their caste origins, nor had the Helas of Allahabad any mythological explanation for their low position in society.[57] Even when a myth is known, its value is primarily historical. In the absence of textual sources on untouchable ideology, myths and other oral traditions

55. Ibid., p. 262.

56. L. Vincentnathan, 'Harijan Subculture and Self-Esteem Management in a South Indian Community' (Doctoral dissertation, University of Wisconsin, Madison, 1987), p. 69.

57. W. Houska, 'Religious Belief and Practice in an Urban Scheduled Caste Community' (Doctoral dissertation, Syracuse University, 1981), p. 83.

can be taken as evidence about the past,[58] or, in this case, about what Untouchables thought in the past. Other forms of oral expression seem to support the idea that Untouchables do not believe their social position is deserved.[59]

If origin myths are less frequently told today, it is not only because people are now more interested in popular film music than in their own tradition, as Houska suggests,[60] but also because these myths have lost much of their significance. Untouchables today hold strong views about the unfairness of their position, and wish to improve it. They are more concerned with bettering their concrete living conditions than with questions of ritual purity. In fact, in many parts of India, Untouchables have long given up performing demeaning tasks for the higher castes. This change does not mean that untouchability has now disappeared, or even that it has sharply declined in contemporary India. The gulf between Untouchables and the rest of the population is as great as ever, and the privileges granted to Untouchables by the Indian constitution have even helped to stigmatize them. However, while untouchability persists, it is no longer expressed in terms of ritual purity. It is much too naive to reduce untouchability to a mere problem of ritual purity, as Dumont tends to do. Of course the impurity of the Untouchable is conceptually derived from the purity of the Brahmin; but, in practice, untouchability is little affected by the relative devaluation of Brahmin purity, as Dumont believed.[61] In Tamil Nadu and elsewhere, for instance, anti-Brahmin movements have considerably weakened the status of Brahmins, but without improving that of Untouchables.

Untouchables themselves are perfectly aware of this, and no longer see the question of ritual purity as critical. Parry[62] and Mines[63] have illustrated this switch from traditional values to more political and economic concerns: among the Koli of North India, for instance, the younger generation opposed the status claims of their elders in order to be officially recognized as 'Backward Castes' and thereby benefit from the government programme of positive discrimination. But the Koli example is not an exception, and it can be said that, while caste and untouchability are still very much alive in contemporary India, the question of ritual status has become increasingly irrelevant. That is probably why the myths discussed here are less popular today than they once were: they are concerned with rather out-dated issues, and fail to promote the type of change that Untouchables now desire.

The contemporary Pallar myth (Myth 5) exemplifies the more aggressive and militant attitudes of those who call themselves *Dalits* (the 'downtrodden'). Yet these more recent myths share something with the traditional untouchable myths: they do not question the foundations of the caste system. The Pallar myth does not deny the reality of caste; on the contrary, by glorifying the caste's own past and denigrating that of the other castes, it contributes to the reification of the system. In both types of myth, the inability of Untouchables to overcome caste ideology is striking. And this is no

58. J. Vansina, *Oral Tradition as History* (London: James Currey, 1985).

59. Cf. e.g., M. Trawick, 'Spirits and Voices in Tamil Songs'. *American Ethnologist*, 14 (1987), pp. 193-215.

60. Houska, 'Religions Belief and Practice'.

61. L. Dumont, *Homo Hierarchicus*, p. 77.

62. J. Parry, 'The Koli Dilemma'. *Contributions to Indian Sociology (NS)*, 4 (1970), pp. 84-104.

63. M. Mines, *The Warrior Merchants: Textiles, Trade and Territory in South India* (Cambridge: Cambridge University Press, 1984).

doubt yet another curse that haunts Untouchables: they are unable to contest the barriers of caste. The only great leader they have produced, the former Law Minister, B. R. Ambedkar, was himself unable to win the vote of Untouchables who did not belong to his own caste![64] And Untouchables today remain hopelessly divided along caste lines.

While untouchable myths contest the basic concepts of Hinduism, they nevertheless also uphold caste as an institution. Such ambiguity is certainly a striking example of the insidiousness of caste ideology, even among the most obvious victims of the system.

-5-

Discrimination, Disabilities and Segregation

The Specificity of Untouchables

The ideology of pure and impure, Louis Dumont writes, helps make Indian society appear consistent to those who live in it. It also accounts for the Untouchables' position at the bottom of the hierarchy; but it does not suffice to characterize them. While a woman who has just given birth, a Brahmin who has just lost his father or a girl who is menstruating are all ritually impure and, in a way, placed outside society, they are never truly untouchable. They are still respected members of society and are not to be belittled or humiliated. Untouchables, on the other hand, are a separate category of Indian society.

Of course, their marginality has its limits. They live outside the village, but not in the jungle. They are forbidden to wander around the village, but they may work there. They do not take part in worship proper, but they keep evil spirits away. In reality they are more inferior than marginal: they do not have a true culture of their own, they are not proud of their origins, and whenever possible, they conceal their own particular practices. For although they are segregated, they are also dependent.

In this, they contrast with the various 'gypsy' or 'tribal' groups found throughout India, who advertise their specificity: with their distinctive colourful clothing and flashy jewellery, they are recognizable on sight. At religious festivals they can be seen catching crows in broad daylight, unafraid to show their taste for this bird, regarded by the rest of society as particularly repugnant.

Untouchables have none of these behaviours; if they eat meat, they do it in secret; it is well known that they drink, but they are never seen with a glass of alcohol. Whenever possible they try to go unnoticed, *incognito,* and they are prompt to deny their caste whenever they can. They do not have a counter-culture, but imitate or replicate the dominant culture. Their marginality is therefore entirely relative. But, as they have no culture of their own, no language of their own, no distinctive physical characteristics, society sees to it that they are saddled with certain taboos, certain restrictions and discriminations that constantly remind them of their lowness. It is these disabilities that set them apart from the rest of society and that will be the subject of this chapter.

Not all these disabilities are religious in nature - some are secular marks of lowness and deprivation; but it is not always easy to tell the two apart. Furthermore, the social actors are sometimes entirely unaware of the ritual origin of certain discriminations. At all events, however, both kinds are meant to segregate and lower Untouchables, and to set them apart from the rest of society.

While some of these disabilities are specific to a region or a caste, the principal ones are found practically throughout India, and were used by the government to identify the Untouchable groups. Hutton considers the decisive criterion for whether or not a caste fits the officially recognized category of 'outcastes' to be the prohibition on using public facilities (schools, roads, streets, wells), followed by various religious and social prohibitions. Almost everywhere in India, Untouchables can be recognized by the ban on their taking water from the main village wells and on entering high-caste temples. And throughout the country various other prohibitions also reinforce the Untouchables' segregation. These taboos vary with the locality, but some, like having to adopt submissive attitudes, are so common as to be almost universal.

Lastly, the untouchable castes are those from whom no one will accept cooked food or water. This prohibition is relative, though, since theoretically no caste will accept water or certain kinds of foods from any caste below it; ideally, then, the Brahmins are the only ones who can give food and water to all the rest of society. In practice, however, many castes are fairly negligent about these rules, and do not hesitate to eat food cooked by a caste slightly below theirs. Most people, though, refuse all cooked foods from castes officially classed as untouchable.[1] In other words, although there is a certain separation between all castes, the gulf separating Untouchables from the rest of the population is clearly marked and structurally much more significant than the differences between 'touchable' castes.

The categories I have drawn up for the various disabilities and discriminations imposed on Untouchables are not empirical entities that can be isolated; they are more like 'ideal-types', in Weber's sense of the word, in other words analytical constructions that transcend regional and historical differences. This means that no one caste is the victim of all of the discriminations listed below; these vary with the region or social group concerned. Some of the discriminations, as we shall see at the end of this chapter, have been greatly attenuated of late, and others have even disappeared altogether. Nevertheless, the list is far from arbitrary, and it enumerates disabilities that are, if not universal, at least so common as to be almost general. Furthermore, the fact that one prohibition or another has vanished has in no way altered the nature of untouchability. Since the late 1930s, for instance, Untouchables have increasingly been allowed to enter the large temples; but this has not radically changed their life. Although untouchability does not always have the same intensity or take the same form in every part of India, it is nevertheless a feature of Indian social life in general; and it is this that justifies our synthesis.

1. A. Mayer, *Caste and Kinship in Central India*, p. 46 or J. Parry, *Caste and Kinship in Kangra* (London: Routledge and Kegan Paul, 1979), pp. 73 and 94.

Religious Taboos

As a direct consequence of their ritual impurity, Untouchables incur a series of religious disabilities, the most common being that they are forbidden to enter temples and religious edifices. Untouchables are supposed rid society of its various organic wastes: they are sweepers, renderers, night-soil collectors and scavengers; but they are also, some of them above all else, in charge of certain very specific religious functions. As Hocart points out, the auspicious ritual of life must not be contaminated by the inauspicious ritual of death, and the drummer is first and foremost the demons' priest. Relegated to the bottom of the hierarchy, he officiates in specific circumstances, mainly as a funeral priest. The Paraiyar *parai* drum is used only in inauspicious rituals, whenever demons must be driven away. At weddings, another band, from a 'touchable' caste, is engaged. Randeria stresses that 'death' is the most potent source of pollution, and that the main characteristic of Untouchables is their association with death, whether as those who scavenge animal carcasses or those who prepare human cremation sites.[2] The Brahmin funeral priests who officiate at the *ghats* of Benares are themselves considered impure and are sometimes called *achut*.[3] Demons and evil spirits are also associated with death, which they often cause and sometimes personify. Their ritual is considered inauspicious, and they must be kept away from the world of the gods and auspicious rituals. By doing this, Untouchables play an important role in the cult.

The auspicious life ritual and the cult of the pure gods must therefore be protected from the inauspicious influence of death, organic waste and malevolent spirits. This is why, with the exception of the specific activities mentioned above, Untouchables used to be kept away from the auspicious ritual and were absolutely forbidden to enter temples, for their presence would profane the temple and no doubt also anger the gods who live there, with the terrible consequences that can be imagined. This exclusion from temples is a highly symbolic form of disability.

In reality, Untouchables do not particularly worship the major Sanskrit gods, who are more concerned with seeing that the universe runs smoothly than with the problems that beset our day-to-day lives;[4] but in a country where religion plays an important role, this taboo was keenly resented, and it was one of the first demands presented by the untouchable emancipation movement, which will be discussed later. In 1924, the struggle known as the 'Vaikom satyagraha' was the first time Untouchables attempted to enter a temple; and it ended in partial victory, since the Maharani of Travancore relaxed restrictions on the use of the roads around the temple, but continued to reserve temple access exclusively for 'high-caste Hindus'.[5] It was

2. S. Randeria, 'Carrion and Corpses', p. 172.
3. J. Parry, 'Ghosts, Greed and Sin', p. 93.
4. C. Fuller, *The Camphor Flame: Popular Hinduism and Society in India* (Princeton, NJ: Princeton University Press, 1992), p. 36.
5. M. S. Rao, *Social Movements and Social Transformations*, p. 66.

another ten years before a radical change occurred: in 1936, the Maharaja of Travancore decided to open the temples to Untouchables; this was a veritable revolution, and became a historic date, not only for the Iravas of Kerala, but for Untouchables throughout India. From this moment on, temple entry would be one of their basic demands.[6]

Today the temples are theoretically open to Untouchables, though they do not necessarily want to use them;[7] but the former prohibition on access to temples was a symbol of their oppression. The importance of the temple-entry battle attests to Untouchables' attachment to the Hindu religion, even though they are excluded from part of the ritual. In spite of solicitations from all sides, the mass of Harijans has nevertheless remained faithful to Hinduism, and their struggle to be allowed to enter temples clearly reflects their deep attachment to this religion.

But Untouchables were not only denied access to the temples; they had to stay at a certain distance, and were even formally forbidden to use the streets leading to the temple. These streets were often the home of the Brahmins, as in Madurai; more generally the Brahmin quarters, called *agraharam* in Tamil Nadu, were formally closed to Untouchables. In some cases, Untouchables were allowed as far as the outer court of the temple, but not into the temple itself.[8] And in no case could they make offerings to the principal gods, for these could not accept food from such impure people.[9] In 1956, the orthodox Brahmins of Benares even built a new Kashi Viswanâtha temple at Mîr Ghât because the old temple had been defiled by the presence of Untouchables.[10] In Karnataka, I was told that one day a group of Untouchables decided to enter a temple; they were stopped at the gate by a priest, who told them to purify themselves at the pool next to the temple before entering. When they went to wash in the pool, they were sucked into the water and drowned. Such is the wrath of the gods.[11] It is also important to note that distinctions were sometimes made among the different untouchable castes themselves: for instance, in the Orissa village of Kapilesway, Hadis (sweepers) were entirely excluded from the temple, whereas Bauris were allowed into the outer court.[12] Several hundred kilometres away, in Coimbatore district (Tamil Nadu), Pallars could enter the Mariyamman temple, but Paraiyars, Sakkiliyars and Kuravars were strictly forbidden to do so,[13] which shows that here, too, Untouchables do not form a homogeneous category and are not seen as one.

In South India the Untouchables who converted to Catholicism hardly improved their situation by doing so, and they now find themselves marginalized within the Church. Not so long ago Untouchables were still made to sit on the floor, or stand outside. In Tamil Nadu, there were even 'trouser churches', that is churches with two

6. R. Jeffrey, 'Temple-Entry Movements in Travancore, 1860-1940'. *Social Scientist*, 4 (1976), p. 4.

7. M. L. Reiniche, *Les Dieux et les hommes*, p. 88.

8. L. Babb, *The Divine Hierarchy: Popular Hinduism in Central India* (New York: Columbia University Press, 1975), p. 189.

9. Ibid., p. 180.

10. D. Eck, *Banaras: City of Light* (London: Routledge and Kegan Paul, 1983), p. 135.

11. E. Harper, 'Ritual Pollution as Integrator of Caste and Religion'. *Journal of Asian Studies*, 23 (1964), pp. 179-80.

12. J. Freeman, *Scarcity and Opportunity in an Indian Village* (Menlo Park, CA: Cummings, 1977), p. 38.

13. J. Den Ouden, *De Onaanraakbaren van Konkunad* (1975), p. 98.

naves: in Vadakkankulam, a six-metre-high brick wall had been built down the middle of the church to separate the Nadars from the Vellalars.[14] And only recently people were still fighting in Trichy to prevent Untouchables from being buried in the same cemetery as the high castes. On the whole, Catholics have reproduced all the Hindu discriminations, and, although the official discourse of the Church has grown more liberal, Untouchables still encounter a clear sentiment of rejection, even among the clergy.[15] In Kerala, the Syrian Catholic Church has fiercely maintained its separation from the Roman Church, mainly because all the latter's members are very lowcaste.[16] The Mar Thomas Church is the only Syrian congregation to have recruited Pulayas, but they were so marginalized in this Church that many left to form new Protestant denominations.[17] As a rule, Catholic Untouchables are entitled to the services of a priest;[18] but many complain, often bitterly, of the way the clergy treat them.[19] In Hinduism, the devotional movements (*bhakti*), which some have presented as opposed to the caste mentality, nevertheless continue to exclude Untouchables, who find themselves, for example, forbidden to enter the temples of Ramanadi and Swaminarayan.[20]

Although banned from the temples, Untouchables were nevertheless not completely excluded from religious life. As we have seen, they even played an indispensable role. When it comes to religion, as Moffatt observed, Untouchables are at once excluded and included.[21] In the village of Endavur, for instance, they are totally excluded from the cult of Mariyamman, the goddess of the *uur*, that is the village with the exception of the untouchable hamlet (*cheri*); on the other hand, they take part in the festival of the goddess Selliyamman, protectress of the entire territory and its inhabitants.[22] But even here, the Untouchables play a subordinate role, and people are constantly reminding them of their inferiority. They are not allowed to approach the goddess as closely as the other castes. The cart bearing the goddess does not enter the *cheri*, and the Untouchables must content themselves with acting as intermediaries between this world and that of the demons.[23] The festival of Holi, in North India, is well known for its inversion of structures; but this does not extend to the Untouchables, who even then are kept at a distance.[24]

Even when they are not expressly forbidden to attend a festival, Untouchables do not like to mingle with high-caste festivities. The people of Valghira Manickam told me, for example, that they would go to the festival of the Sunamurthi Iswaran temple,

14. S. Bayly, *Saints Goddesses and Kings: Muslims and Christians in South Indian Society, 1700-1900* (Cambridge: Cambridge University Press, 1989), p. 438.

15. On this issue, see R. Deliège, *Les Paraiyars du Tamil Nadu*, pp. 244-6.

16. R. Deliège, 'Les Chrétiens de Saint Thomas du Kerala (Inde du Sud)'. *Dictionnaire d'Histoire et de Géographie religieuses* (Paris: Letouzey & Ané, 1994).

17. K. C. Alexander, 'The Neo-Christians of Kerala', in J. M. Mahar (ed.), *The Untouchables in Contemporary India* (Tucson: University of Arizona Press, 1972).

18. D. Mosse, 'Caste, Christianity and Hinduism', p. 187.

19. R. Deliège, *Les Paraiyars du Tamil Nadu*, pp. 248-9.

20. C. Fuller, *The Camphor Flame*, pp. 168 and 173.

21. M. Moffatt, *An Untouchable Community*, p. 222.

22. Ibid., p. 247.

23. Ibid., p. 270.

24. L. Babb, *The Divine Hierarchy*, p. 171 or B. Cohn, 'The Chamars of Senapur', p. 203 and C. Fuller, *The Camphor Flame*, p. 129.

in nearby Kanda Devi village; but on the day, I was surprised not to see anyone from Valghira Manickam in the vicinity of the Kanda Devi temple. On my way home, I was again surprised to see all the Paraiyars massed at the entrance to the village, watching the Kallar festivities from afar. Cohn reports that low-caste people easily feel insulted or humiliated when they venture into a religious festival, and therefore prefer to stay away when they have no specific business there.[25] Vincentnathan has shown that these tactics are a common strategy that enables Untouchables to avoid harassment and blows to their self-esteem.[26]

The relative exclusion of Untouchables from high-caste worship means that they have a very limited knowledge of their religion. Even the Valghira Manickam Catholics had only a very elementary notion of the basic principles of Christianity and Church dogma.[27] As for the Hindus, who have neither a structured clergy, nor dogma nor Church, their knowledge of religion is just as rudimentary. Furthermore, Untouchables were formerly not allowed to study the sacred texts - a fairly redundant prohibition, as most of them were illiterate anyway. In general, however, they often do not know the myths and legends concerning the major Hindu gods and goddesses, whom they were not permitted to approach. Even today, the fundamental concepts of Hinduism are often totally unfamiliar, as is the case of reincarnation[28] and the associated idea of *karma.*[29]

Finally, no Brahmin will perform a religious ceremony for an Untouchable. Properly speaking, the presence of a Brahmin is not necessary to Hindu religious and social life; one may marry and die without a Brahmin. But the presence of Brahmins considerably enhances the prestige of a ceremony[30] and gives it a more elaborate religious dimension. Brahmins officiate primarily for the major divinities, and have very little to do with local and territorial cults. And it is in these that the Untouchables participate the most. There is a great distance between Brahmins and Untouchables, then, and their religious worlds are clearly separated.

Prohibitions on the Use of Public Facilities

The temple-entry ban was not the only taboo imposed on Untouchables. As we will see later, Untouchables were required to live outside the village proper and might enter its streets only for specific reasons, principally to work. People would not tolerate a group of Untouchables taking an evening stroll through the village for no apparent reason. Their presence would not be regarded as exactly 'polluting'; but it could easily earn them a thrashing.

25. B. Cohn, 'The Chamars of Senapur', p. 204.

26. L. Vincentnathan, 'Harijan Subculture and Self-Esteem Management', p. 210.

27. See R. Deliège, 'Souffrance et échange', p. 415.

28. C. Maloney, 'Religious Beliefs and Social Hierarchy', p. 172.

29. See also L. Vincentnathan, 'Harijan Subculture and Self-Esteem Management', p. 419; K. Gough, 'Harijans in Thanjavur', p. 234; R. S. Khare, *The Untouchable as Himself*, pp. 45-6; W. Houska, 'Religious Belief and Practice', p. 86, etc.

30. L. Babb, *The Divine Hierarchy*, p. 181 or A. Good, 'The Actor and the Act: Categories of Prestation in South India'. *Man (NS)*, 17 (1982), p. 29.

After the various religious prohibitions, the ban on taking water from the village well is another important test of untouchability. Normally Untouchables did not have their own well; their women had to wait near the village well until some high-caste person deigned to draw some water and pour it into their bucket. Elsewhere, Untouchables were not even allowed near the well.[31] Furthermore, their material (bucket and rope) could not be lowered into a high-caste well, not even by a high-caste person.[32] Today the ban on taking water from wells is still widespread; but in many villages, the Untouchables now have their own well, although it is often not nearly as deep as the main well, where they do not have the right to draw water. Although not universal, the prohibition on using village wells is nevertheless still extremely common, and is often just as strictly enforced as in the past.[33] Were they to use high-caste wells, so the feeling goes, Untouchables would dangerously contaminate the water, and with it, all the communities in the village. Any Untouchable who ventured to violate this rule would risk a thrashing, as Mahar reports concerning a jungle well.[34] In the last few years, Untouchables have become more conscious of their rights, and D. B. Miller tells of an incident in 1964 in which an educated Chamar, Bana Ram, made a great show of taking water from the village well without waiting for a higher-caste person to help him. A Banya woman, enraged, threw Bana Ram's water pot to the ground, and he complained to the police of this violation of the Untouchability Offences Acts. A compromise was reached; but rather than allow Chamars to use the main well, the village decided to dig them a well of their own.[35] Today Untouchables tend to have their own standpipes, and well-ownership is officially recognized, since the *panchayats* regularly decide to deepen the well of one caste or another.[36] As a corollary to the well ban, Untouchables may not bathe wherever they want in the village reservoir. Often there is a corner reserved for them, on the opposite side from the high-caste bathing area.

We have seen that the streets leading to religious buildings and the Brahmin quarters that often surround the temples were strictly off-limits to Untouchables. In reality, the latter were allowed to use the roads and paths only if no one else was in sight. As soon as they saw a high-caste person coming, they would have to step off the path and let him or her pass. In Uttar Pradesh, high-caste people would warn the Bhangis of their approach by shouting.[37] In Kerala, Pulayas had to call out every four or five steps when using a path, to make their presence known; and, when they heard someone answer in a higher voice, they would have to step down into the ditch.[38] Iyer likens them to hares who dash away as soon as someone comes along.[39] It is said that in some parts of

31. J. Hutton, *Caste in India: Its Nature, Functions, and Origins* (Delhi: Oxford University Press, 1973), p. 196.

32. J. Den Ouden, *De Onaanraakbaren van Konkunad* (1975), p. 85.

33. S. Epstein, *South India Yesterday, Today and Tomorrow* (London: MacMillan, 1973), p. 214.

34. J. M. Mahar, 'Agents of Dharma in a North Indian Village', in J. M. Mahar (ed.), *The Untouchables in Contemporary India* (Tucson: University of Arizona Press, 1972), p. 22.

35. D. B. Miller, *From Hierarchy to Stratification: Changing Patterns of Social Inequality in a North Indian Village* (Delhi: Oxford University Press, 1979), p. 146.

36. J. Den Ouden, *De Onaanraakbaren van Konkunad* (1975), p. 85.

37. W. Wiser and C. Wiser, *Behind Mud Walls: 1930-1960* (Berkeley, CA: University of California Press, 1969), p. 47.

38. K. Saradamoni, *Emergence of a Slave* Caste, p. 61.

39. A. K. Iyer, *The Tribes and Castes of Cochin*, p. 121.

Maharashtra, Mahars had to drag a thorny bush behind them wherever they went, in order to erase their footprints so that they would not pollute the path. In Poona, Untouchables were allowed inside the city walls only between 9a.m. and 3p.m., because during these hours their shadow would be short enough not to pollute passers-by.[40] The Balahis of Central India wore a little pot around their neck because they were forbidden to spit on the ground.[41] But the Nayadis of Kerala, who will be discussed later, are no doubt the most extreme case: they were also 'unseeable', and had to hide whenever they met someone from a higher caste. Yet their case is perhaps not as isolated as all that, since the Valghira Manickam Paraiyars still remember when the Brahmins who skirted their village would cover their heads with a towel in order not to see the Paraiyars.

This ostracism also applied to the marketplace. In Kerala, when Pulayas wanted to sell the items they had made, such as palm-leaf umbrellas, they would place the objects on a mat beside the road and then retire to a distance from which they could negotiate with passers-by. When they wanted to buy something, on the other hand, they would leave a coin on a stone, withdraw and call out what they wanted to buy.[42] In places where pollution rules were less strict, Untouchables might not hand a coin to someone directly, but had to lay it down for the other person to pick up. Sometimes they even had to place the coin in water to cleanse it.

Clearly, Kerala holds the record for keeping Untouchables at a distance. In this state, all castes had to respect a certain distance from the Nambudiri Brahmins: a Nayar could come within seven feet, an Irava had to keep a distance of thirty-two feet, a Pulaya, sixty-four feet, and a Nayadi between seventy-four and a hundred and twenty feet.[43] As no one walked around with a measuring tape, these distances were relative, and referred primarily to parts of the house. Traditionally a house had a verandah, and various thresholds, gates and inner courts, which had a sociological function.[44] While elsewhere the prohibitions were not always as strict as in Kerala, Untouchables were nevertheless always obliged to keep a certain distance from their superiors and to act in a humble manner. We shall return to this question later.

Tea-shops occupy an important place in Indian society. Although tea was introduced relatively late (the first plantations date from the 1830s),[45] it has become a veritable institution, and tea-shops are so much a part of the Indian landscape that it is hard to imagine it was ever otherwise. They are a very important meeting-place, and men like to sip a glass of tea at the end of a day's work. The relatively recent appearance of tea-shops has not prevented untouchability from establishing itself there as well. Traditionally, Harijans may not enter a tea-shop as they like. Obviously, they may not sit on the same bench as high-caste customers, and above all their tea is served in

40. S. Patwardhan, *Change Among India's Harijans*, p. 34.

41. S. Fuchs, *The Children of Hari*, p. 59.

42. K. Saradamoni, *Emergence of a Slave Caste*, p. 62 and A. K. Iyer, *The Tribes and Castes of Cochin*, pp. 95 and 121.

43. A. Aiyappan, *Social and Physical Anthropology of the Nayadis*, p. 19; C. Fuller, *The Nayars Today* (Cambridge: Cambridge University Press, 1976), p. 35 and many others with a few variants.

44. M. L. Reiniche, 'La Maison du Tirunelveli', p. 29.

45. R. Dutt, *The Economic History of India in the Victorian Age* (London: Kegan Paul, Trench, Trubner & Co., 1903), p. 143.

different receptacles from that of the higher castes. Whereas tea is normally served in a glass, Untouchables must make do with a coconut shell and must go outside to drink.[46] Given the importance of tea-shops in daily life, this discrimination is keenly felt by Untouchables. They know that it is not in their interest to enter certain tea-shops, as they would promptly be thrown out. After eating at a restaurant, known as a *hotel,* Untouchables must themselves dispose of the banana leaf that served as their plate.[47] They also keep their distance from public meeting-places; they listen in on village gossip, but never mix in the conversation.[48]

In the past, education was a right that was automatically refused the lower classes. But the degradation of Untouchables was such that the right to education was not even one of their basic demands, and nearly the whole Indian population was illiterate, with the exception of the Brahmins. Even the great Akbar himself was illiterate! Today Harijans still do not have a shining school attendance record, and many continue to feel that they are not cut out for that and that it no use 'putting on airs'.[49] They therefore have a very high rate of absenteeism. One Paraiyar grandfather recalls that, after only a few days of class, a goat chewed up his textbook, which put an end to his schooling. In the same village, parents told me that their son got a migraine at the very sight of the school, and so he did not know how to read or write. Muli, the hero of Freeman's book, had not brought his teacher a coconut for the festival of the goddess Saraswati; the schoolmaster therefore gave him a thrashing, and Muli stopped going to school.[50]

Increasingly Untouchables are rejecting this defeatist attitude, however. Many rebel at the idea that 'all they are good for is to run behind a cow'. When the British opened up new socio-economic perspectives for Untouchables, they also gave them the idea of getting an education, and, as of the nineteenth century, a good many Untouchables decided to go to school. This required courage, and they were obliged to face a new series of mortifications. In a society where the division between intellectual work and manual labour is so marked, where the Brahmin is said to have come from the head of Manu, the first man, while the Shudras come from his feet, the Untouchables' 'proper' place was certainly not among the intellectual elite.

Given these circumstances, the missionaries saw school as a means of attracting the lower castes. Ambedkar's father, who did know how to read, had taken another path, namely the British Army, which saw to it that its soldiers received an education. When, in 1900, Ambedkar attended the English school in Satara, many Mahars already knew how to read and write, and Ambedkar was the second Mahar to enrol at the university of Bombay, in 1907. Yet this was the tree that hid the forest. The few untouchable children attending school were made to sit apart, which was also true for Ambedkar.[51] In Bhubaneswar, the Bauris had to sit on the verandah, outside the classroom,[52] and the

46. D. Mosse, 'Caste, Christianity and Hinduism', p. 186 or J. Den Ouden, *De Onaanraakbaren van Konkunad* (1975), p. 114.

47. J. Den Ouden, *De Onaanraakbaren van Konkunad* (1975), p. 114.

48. Ibid., p. 79.

49. See for example D. Pawar, *Ma vie d'intouchable*, p. 59.

50. J. Freeman, *Untouchable: An Indian Life History*, p. 68.

51. E. Zelliot, 'Dr. Ambedkar and the Mahar Movement', p. 84.

schoolmaster refused to touch them except to cane them. High-class farmers know full well that every child in school is one less agricultural labourer.[53]

Residential Segregation

We have seen the high-caste groups' constant concern with keeping Harijans at a distance. However, the same discrimination is found in all social relations, in every instance of daily life; it is therefore not surprising to see that this segregation applies to the Untouchable settlement. Here, too, Untouchables are clearly separated from the rest of the population. Of course, each of the castes has a tendency to group together, to live together in one and the same quarter; but their segregation is not total, and intermingling is not uncommon. By contrast, not only do Untouchables live together, but their quarter is ideally situated at some distance from the other castes, and the line separating the two settlements is often clearly drawn. Of the high castes, only the Brahmins live in a quarter marked off from the others; but even in this case the boundary between the Brahmin streets and the rest of the village is not as rigid as the one dividing the village from the untouchable hamlet. In some places a river bed serves as a demarcation line; in other places the untouchable houses are clustered on the other side of the paddy fields.[54] In mountain villages, the higher castes tend to live further up the mountain than the low castes.[55]

Tamil Nadu has at least three names for the various quarters. The Brahmins live in the *agraharam*, to which access is severely restricted and that Untouchables are absolutely forbidden to enter. The village proper is known as the *uur*, and many castes reside there. In Tanjore, non-Brahmins live in a quarter called the *kudania*.[56] The term *uur* has important affective connotations, as Daniel has nicely shown.[57] But Untouchables do not live in the *uur*, they reside in the *cheri*, the untouchable hamlet or quarter, situated ideally in a separate place. In principle, high-caste people never enter the *cheri*, which remains a largely unfamiliar world to them. In Ramkheri, Central India, high-caste people do not enter the untouchable quarter unless they have specific business there, and it is even said that they must wash their feet afterwards;[58] while in Irupatur, Tamil Nadu, high-caste people shout from a distance or send a servant when they need the services of an Untouchable.[59] Such hamlets are found in most parts of India, even if they are not always clearly segregated from the rest of the village. In Uttar Pradesh, the Chamars live in separate areas called c*hamarauti*, a term that has acquired highly pejorative connotations and is associated with filth and

52. J. Freeman, *Untouchable: An Indian Life History,* p. 67.

53. Sachchidananda, *Social Change in Village India* (Delhi: Concept, 1988), p. 16.

54. K. Gough, 'The Social Structure of a Tanjore Village', in McKim Marriott (ed.), *Village India: Studies in the Little Community* (Chicago: University of Chicago Press, 1955), p. 41.

55. J. Parry, *Caste and Kinship in Kangra*, p. 20.

56. A. Béteille, *Caste, Class and Power*, p. 25.

57. V. Daniel, *Fluid Signs.*

58. A. Mayer, *Caste and Kinship in Central India*, p. 57.

59. J. Den Ouden, *De Onaanraakbaren van Konkunad* (1975), p. 74.

stench.[60] And in Maharashtra, people say that every village has its *maharwada*, or Mahar quarter.[61]

Untouchables also tend to cluster together in towns and cities; but that is generally true of most castes. This concentration of castes is not always possible in large urban centres, but certain urban studies show that there is nevertheless a tendency for the Untouchables to cling together.[62] In Benares, the inhabitants of a quarter are bound together by kinship ties.[63] D'Souza even argues that, as the population grows more dense, the houses in each quarter are built closer and closer together, which intensifies segregation.[64]

Residential segregation is highly symptomatic of the Untouchables' position within Indian society. But even when they are confined to places clearly set apart from the village, they still do not live in the jungle or the 'forest' (*kadu* in Tamil). While the temple and the Brahmin quarters are located at the centre of the village space, the Untouchables live on the periphery, as far as possible from the residence of the principal gods. Thus, although their quarter occupies an ambiguous position, it does not lie outside society. At certain festivals, the god's procession even stops at the entrance to their quarter to receive offerings from the Untouchables, as part of the community. However, the procession does not enter the hamlet. The Untouchables' space is thus situated on the border between human society and nature, between the civilized world and the uncivilized world.

Their quarter is described as being filthy, repugnant and stinking, in other words as slightly inhuman, at the extreme limit of humanness. Pallars, for example, are said to be always shouting, to have hair sticking out all over and frighteningly black skin.[65] By segregating them, the high castes feel they are protecting the village from this primitiveness.[66] When a Vellalar falls ill, he says he is disordered (*toosam*), like a Pallar.[67] The centre of the village is reserved for the pure, benevolent divinities; the further out one goes, the more one risks encountering the *tusta teevatai*, frightening evil divinities.[68] Demons always come from outside.[69] The village itself is protected, but the outskirts are more vulnerable. People say that, at night, certain divinities, like Karuppaya, patrol the edges of the village to protect them from unwanted visits by demons.[70] Untouchables thus do not live quite among the demons.

Sometimes Untouchables take part in the collection of funds for the village festival; but sometimes, too, they are excluded.[71] The patron goddess, on the other hand, reigns

60. B. Cohn, 'The Chamars of Senapur', p. 106.

61. S. Patwardhan, *Change among India's Harijans*, p. 29.

62. S. Molund, *First We Are People*, or O. Lynch, *The Politics of Untouchability.*

63. M. Searle-Chatterjee, 'Kinship in an Urban Low-Caste Locality'. *The Eastern Anthropologist*, 27 (1974), p. 340.

64. V. D'Souza, 'Does Urbanism Desegregate Scheduled Castes? Evidence from a District in Punjab'. *Contributions to Indian Sociology* (NS), 11 (1977), p. 226.

65. B. P. Pfaffenberger, 'Social Communication in Dravidian Ritual', p. 210.

66. Ibid., p. 214.

67. Ibid., p. 215.

68. M. L. Reiniche, 'Les "Démons" et leur culte dans la structure du panthéon d'un village du Tirunelveli'. *Purusârtha,* 2 (1975), p. 184.

69. Ibid., p. 193.

70. V. Daniel, *Fluid Signs*, p. 77.

over the entire village and protects all the inhabited spots,[72] and the various *jajmani* relations testify amply to untouchable participation in village life. When they are asked where they come from, Untouchables unfailingly give the name of the village proper, and not that of their hamlet. Even though, from a certain point of view, the Chamars of Senapur are not part of that community, they are still attached to the village and regard it as home.[73] This is a particularly clear example of the ambiguity of the Untouchables' status.

Village land used to belong, in principle, to the dominant castes. For the Tamils, the inhabitants of a village and its land are united by what might be called a form of consubstantiation.[74] Similarly, the Gujars say that where the soil is sweet, men too are kindhearted, and where the soil is sour, men are quarrelsome.[75] Although traditionally all village land belonged to the dominant castes, other castes had real rights in it. In Uttar Pradesh, for example, there were different types of landholding, several of which conferred permanent rights.[76] The Untouchables, however, were not allowed to own land permanently, and were allocated plots for limited periods, with rights that were similarly limited. There was, then, a hierarchy of land tenure that corresponded to the social hierarchy.[77]

Today this right to village land still exists: the dominant castes continue to regard the village land as their own property, even though they have no official documents to prove it. In Valghira Manickam, it is generally said that the land belongs to the Kanda Devi Kallars. The lands worked by the Paraiyars are for the most part rented from Kallars on the *varam* system (*i.e.* for a price set in grain). Sometimes a Kallar may sell a plot of land to a Paraiyar without transferring the title papers, probably because he does not have them. Yet it never for a moment enters the Paraiyars' minds to contest the Kallars' right to the land, for they know the violent repression to which they would be exposing themselves were they to attempt anything of the kind. In addition, although renting land from the Kallars reinforces the Paraiyars' dependency on this caste, tilling the soil brings prestige, and the Paraiyars are willing to supply labour in exchange for this privilege.

Refusal to Provide Professional Services

Various specialist castes refuse to work for certain social categories. This is especially true of those that perform traditional services, in other words that occupy a privileged position in the '*jajmani* system'. In this system, village specialists do not work for daily wages, but are supposed to provide services to the other castes in exchange for

71. M. L. Reiniche, *Les Dieux et les hommes,* p. 154.
72. Ibid., p. 182.
73. B. Cohn, 'The Chamars of Senapur', p. 109.
74. V. Daniel, *Fluid Signs,* p. 67.
75. G. Raheja, *The Poison in the Gift: Ritual, Prestation and the Dominant Caste in a North Indian Village* (Chicago: University of Chicago Press, 1988), p. 268.
76. B. Cohn, 'The Chamars of Senapur', p. 57.
77. M. L. Reiniche, 'Statut, fonction et droit: relations agraires au Tamilnad'. *L'Homme*, 18 (1978), p. 158.

which they receive a traditional fee, often paid in kind at harvest time. The barber, the washerman, the carpenter, or the blacksmith thus serve a certain number of families and receive a fixed amount of grain when the fields are cut. Characteristically, all these castes refuse to work for Untouchables.

When occupations become modernized and monetarized, they become more accessible to the lower segments of the population, since everyone knows that money has no odour. But high-caste specialists do not always yield without protest, and we have already seen the precautions a Harijan must take when making a purchase. Money must not be handed directly to another person, and often must even pass through water. Pocock reports that, in Gujarat, Patidar tailors are willing to sew for Untouchables on the condition that they take their own measurements.[78]

Refusal of service, then, is a good gauge of a caste's untouchability. Alangkulam village, where I worked, is inhabited by two fairly equally distributed communities: the Pallars, who are 'untouchable' and a Scheduled Caste, and the Valaiyars, who are not, although they are very low. The village also has two families of washermen, who accept doing the Valaiyars' washing, but in no case that of the Pallars. It is interesting to note that, in economic terms, the Valaiyars are no richer than the Pallars, among whom even figure some of the most well-to-do families in the village.

One of the most striking, and no doubt most symptomatic, facts is that these castes began to accept working for Harijans once payment was made in money. The services the Alangkulam washers perform for Valaiyars are primarily of a ritual nature, washing clothing that has become ritually impure after first menstruation, a birth or a death. Moreover, the Valaiyars are incapable of keeping one or two families of washers the year round. As a consequence, the village washermen have a number of other clients who pay them in money. In principle, they do not refuse to work for Harijans under these conditions, and they have some low-caste clients; in fact, they do not always know their clients' caste, as these often come from the nearby village of Manamadurai. By contrast, it would be unthinkable to entertain traditional relations with the Pallars from the village.

In Ramkheri, a village in Madhya Pradesh, the same phenomenon can be observed: for instance, the potters sell Untouchables their pottery, but will not perform the traditional services for them,[79] for traditional clientele relations create important personal bonds, and the *kamin* is in a relation of inferiority with the *jajman*. It is therefore unthinkable for an artisan to entertain this kind of relationship with people from so low a caste, for it would mean that they were even lower than the latter. Outside the traditional ritual framework, however, inferiority disappears, and a barber does not really object to cutting the hair of untouchable clients who come to his shop.

The lower castes react in different ways to this refusal. The first solution, adopted for example in Valghira Manickam, is simply to do without these specialists, and for each to perform the various tasks himself. It is true that it is possible to get along without a caste of washers or barbers. A second solution is to ask a family or a lineage to specialize in a given task. These 'specialists' are not distinguishable from the rest

78. D. Pocock, *Kanbi and Patidar*, p. 37.
79. A. Mayer, *Caste and Kinship in Central India,* p. 65.

of the community and are not regarded as lower; they marry women from the group, and do not form a caste within a caste. The third solution, which has aroused much excitement among sociologists, is not the most common, but it is the most spectacular: in a certain number of cases, there are, among the Untouchables, castes that have specialized in one service or another, thereby reproducing the dominant system within the untouchable group.

The most familiar example of such 'replication' has been described by Michael Moffatt, in a village in Chingleput district, Tamil Nadu: Paraiyars are a 'dominant' caste among the Untouchables of Endavur. The Valluvar Pandarams are described as the 'the Brahmins of the Untouchables', and act as priests for these low castes. The 'Vannan Harijans' wash for them, and the Sakkiliyars perform the most degrading tasks. Similar subcastes or castes can be found in other parts of India. The Pallars, for example, also have a subcaste of washermen.[80] It seems that the Madigas of Andhra Pradesh are split into six subcastes, each of which performs a different function for the community,[81] and these few examples are far from exhausting the list.

Nevertheless, the phenomenon of subcastes is far from universal or indispensable, and such subdivsions are not necessarily linked to specific functions: for example, the many Chamar subcastes[82] do not have any specific role within the community. The authors who look to the existence of various specialized groups to support their argument that Untouchables replicate the entire caste system within their own group are being perhaps a bit hasty, even though the fact remains that Untouchables themselves do practise untouchability.

Commensality Taboos

One of the most common expressions of the caste system is the ranking of food and drink that may or may not be accepted. Or at any rate, this is what a good number of sociological studies say. Ideally the most punctilious Brahmins accept cooked food and drink only from other Brahmins, and some even observe further restrictions and refuse to touch food cooked by one or another Brahmin subcaste. The caste immediately beneath the Brahmins accepts food from the latter, but from no other group, and so on down the ladder.

I am a bit sceptical as to the existence of perfect congruity between social hierarchy and rules of commensality. Many relatively 'low' castes, for example, mark their orthodoxy by refusing all food cooked by high-caste cooks, including Brahmins. By contrast, many castes often behave in a manner that contradicts their affirmations, and in practice do not worry much about the caste of the cook. I myself have observed such inconsistencies. Furthermore, such scales tend to make us think that caste 'ranking' is linear and unanimously agreed on, something like military rank, whereas this is not so.

Nevertheless, three things are certain: First, there is definitely a general tendency to

80. D. Mosse, 'Caste, Christianity and Hinduism', p. 204.
81. S. Dube, *Indian Village,* p. 41.
82. See, for example, C. Briggs, *The Chamars*, pp. 21-6.

take food and water from higher castes and to refuse them from castes that are much lower. Second, Brahmins are certainly the most orthodox, and today the strictest castes are bent on imitating the Brahmins. Third, food and water offered by untouchable castes are unanimously rejected. In Tamil Nadu there are hardly any restrictions among non-Brahmin castes, and at wedding feasts numerous castes may be seen mingling and eating together without any problem: in the region of Manamadurai, for instance, a few families of Valaiyars, a very low but not untouchable caste, have specialized in the cooking of wedding meals without this seeming to pose a problem for anyone. But no one would accept Untouchables' doing likewise, for, generally speaking, there is a barrier between Untouchables and all other castes. The acceptation of food and water is therefore a decisive criterion of untouchability. For instance, while Den Ouden shows that the restrictions and taboos are not the same for the different untouchable castes, he stresses that no caste accepts food and water from the region's four Scheduled Castes, and that, from this standpoint, they do indeed form a separate category.[83]

The distinctions made in North India between *pakka* ('perfect') and *kakka* ('imperfect') foods do not concern Untouchables, from whom the other castes refuse to take any kind of food whatsoever. The same holds for water. It is interesting that, in Tamil Nadu, if an Untouchable wants to offer a high-caste person something to drink, he can buy him a bottle of lemonade, but he cannot offer him water. Kandaswami, the only Maravar in Alangkulam, even claims that he does not accept water from Pallars; yet his family take their water from the same pump as the Pallars. On the other hand, uncooked food can be accepted from anyone; the contrary would be somewhat awkward, since Untouchables often do most of the agricultural work, including harvesting and threshing! It is therefore the status of the cook and the preparation of the food, in particular as regards the purity of the utensils, that constitute the essential criteria. And that is why Untouchables must absolutely be kept away from the kitchen, which is generally located at the back of the house. It is not uninteresting to observe here that untouchable houses, often simple huts, are not built on the model of the high-caste house. Untouchable houses often have a single room; the fireplace and grindstone, in other words the kitchen proper, are usually located in front of the house, and sometimes practically on the street. Any passer-by can therefore watch the food being prepared and cooked; this violates all rules of ritual, so that the ritual taboos concerning the house and kitchen are here reduced to a minimum.[84]

Eating together symbolizes equality. One of the most common rituals of the wedding ceremony has the newly-weds share food from the same plate. To accept food from an Untouchable, then, would be tantamount to considering him an equal, and such an attitude would defile the whole caste; therefore excommunication is the punishment usually prescribed for anyone who might commit such an error.[85] Not only can one not accept food cooked by an Untouchable; one cannot share a meal either, whatever the status of the cook. Even when they pause from their work in the field,

83. J. Den Ouden, *De Onaanraakbaren van Konkunad* (1975), p. 137.

84. See R. Deliège, *Les Paraiyars du Tamil Nadu*, p. 23.

85. M. N. Srinivas, *Religion and Society among the Coorgs of South India* (Bombay: Asia Publishing House, 1965), p. 27.

Sakkiliyars take their meals to one side.[86] Ideally, the lower castes should even place themselves on a physically lower level than the others, for example by sitting on the ground. At 'festive' meals, the different castes in Kangra are arranged in a set order or separated into different 'lines'.[87]

The discussion of food leads us naturally to the observation that the caste hierarchy is also a dietary hierarchy. Barring a few exceptions, Brahmins are strictly vegetarian, and, at least theoretically, the further down the social ladder one goes, the more lower kinds of food are accepted. For food, too, is ranked: vegetarianism is distinctly the highest; then come eggs, fish, chicken, mutton, pork, beef and, last of all, carrion. The untouchable castes are those that eat beef, and even worse, carrion. Eating beef is, in any case, a shameful and degrading practice. There are a few other types of food that are not included in this hierarchy: for instance, many castes eat crows, monkeys or rats; but they tend to be situated outside society, and are therefore 'out of the running', so to speak, because they often do not play an integral role in socio-economic life.

Unlike these special castes, Untouchables do not have any specific culinary practices; they do not have a culture that might distinguish them from the rest of the population or of which they might boast. In reality, their extremely dependent situation is fragmented here as well. They would willingly eat like the rest of the population, but they have neither the right nor the possibility; they possess nothing, and they eat what society condescends to leave them or whatever it does not want. The Untouchables, then, are those who, on the one hand, eat table scraps and leftovers and, on the other hand, must beg for their food. The idea of eating someone's leavings is particularly repugnant to any Indian, for in India no one eats from another's plate, and, ideally, cooked food that has been touched by a person should be eaten by that person. Untouchables are an exception to this rule, because they do not turn up their noses at table scraps or leftovers. In fact, they often receive the leavings from ritual meals. Carcasses, which society does not want, which it must get rid of, also belong to Untouchables. Sometimes, too, Harijans are practically forced to beg for their food or their wages. They must adopt a humble, submissive attitude when asking for what they are owed.[88] Pawar tells how high-caste people paid the wages for traditional tasks (*balute*), saying, 'Now get away from here, you Mahar'[89] - and they would go on pouring out insults.

Some castes were even reduced to outright begging. This was the case of the Nayadis of Kerala, on whom Aiyappan has written a monographic study.[90] During festivals and at various other times of the year, the Nayadis go from house to house, calling out for alms.

86. J. Den Ouden, *De Onaanraakbaren van Konkunad* (1975), p. 149.

87. J. Parry, *Caste and Kinship in Kangra*, p. 96.

88. W. Wiser, *The Hindu Jajmani System: A Socio-Economic System Interrelating Members of a Hindu Village Community in Services* (Lucknow: Lucknow Publishing House, 1936), p. 35.

89. D. Pawar, *Ma vie d'intouchable*, p. 64.

90. A. Aiyappan, *Social and Physical Anthropology of the Nayadis.*

Languages and Attitudes

This submissive attitude is not reserved for the payment of wages; it is a basic feature of untouchability, and can be observed in different forms throughout India. We have seen, for example, that an Untouchable who met a high-caste person coming along a path had imperatively to step out of the way. He was obliged to step aside, or, even better, down, from the path, for an Untouchable was supposed, in so far as it was possible, to occupy a lower position, even physically, than the higher castes. In the same vein, an Untouchable was not allowed to sit beside someone from a higher caste. If the latter was seated on a *cot*,[91] the Untouchable would sit on the floor. Even in the *panchayat* councils, one of India's democratic organs, it is still not unusual to see Untouchables 'sitting' in such a low position.

But this is not the only sign of submission and humility that Untouchables must manifest. When they meet a high-caste person, they must stop and wait for permission to go on. An Untouchable riding a bicycle will stop and get off when he meets an important person, and will not get back on until further down the road. And there are many other attitudes that mark their inferiority. In some regions, Untouchables would place their hands in front of their mouths when speaking to someone from a high caste.[92] Elsewhere they used to cross their arms on their chest as a sign of humility.[93] They also used to keep their eyes and their voices lowered. It is still not unusual to see an Untouchable greet a high-caste person by touching his feet. When a high-caste person passes, it is fitting to rise; and it is always recommended to adopt a respectful attitude. Such signs of inferiority mark the day-to-day life of Untouchables, and constantly remind them of their true place in society.

This 'respectful' attitude is so deeply ingrained that Untouchables have difficulty overcoming it, and it often becomes a sometimes irritating obsequiousness. Even when invited to do so, an Untouchable finds it hard to sit on the same level as a higher guest. When they must ask for something, they often act as though they were begging, or humiliating themselves. When they enter a public place, they do it discreetly, and then stay on the sidelines. They never show self-confidence, and even less arrogance. It is for this reason that they do not feel at ease with people of higher condition.

This 'humility' is also reflected in their way of speaking. When addressing a high-caste person, Untouchables use terms meaning 'lord' or 'master', whatever the person's function. In Tamil Nadu, for example, the term *swami*, which usually refers to God, is used by Untouchables for all higher castes,[94] and the Sakkiliyars carry orthodoxy so far as to use the term with a Pallar. In Kerala, a high-caste person is addressed as *tampuran,* or 'lord'. This term of address must be used even with children. Conversely, high-caste people address Untouchables as inferiors, and they have a variety of ways of showing their contempt. The Untouchable is often treated

91. A type of bed often used to receive visitors

92. A. Aiyappan, *Social and Physical Anthropology of the Nayadis,* p. 23.

93. R. Deliège, *Les Paraiyars du Tamil Nadu,* p. 163.

94. J. Den Ouden, 'Social Stratification as Expressed through Language', p. 51.

like a child, even if the high-caste person is younger than the Untouchable. Insults are just as common: in Kerala, high-caste people call an Untouchable *karuppan*, and his wife *karuppi*, meaning 'black man' and 'black woman'. In Orissa, people hail them with terms meaning 'savage' or 'madman'.[95] In Maharashtra, it was not unusual for astrologers to give untouchable babies derogatory names like 'idiot' or 'trash'.[96] The same practice can be observed in Uttar Pradesh, where astrologers used to take caste into consideration when making their calculations for giving a name, which is how some Koris came to be called *Magan* (humble), *Buddhu* (stupid) or *Sure* (blind).[97]

When a high-caste man hails an Untouchable, he can simply use his caste name, which, as we know, carries extremely pejorative connotations. When a Paraiyar hears himself called 'Parapayale', he feels humiliated. In Tamil Nadu, there are several forms of address, which Den Ouden breaks down into three categories: respectful, neutral and contemptuous. For instance, *poo* ('go') and *vaa* ('come') are neutral forms; adding the suffix *-nkoo (poonkoo* and *vaankoo*) makes them respectful. But when someone addresses an Untouchable, they use *potaa* and *vataa*, and these forms are clearly disrespectful.[98] In Kerala, the Pulayas and other low castes once had to use contemptuous forms when referring to themselves: they would say for instance, 'my old ear' or 'my old eye', when speaking of these body parts. They called their own children 'my calves' or 'my monkeys', and their rice, 'my straw'. When speaking to a superior, they were not allowed to say 'I', but spoke of *adiyen* ('the slave'): 'Your slave would like to ask you …'[99]

Although Untouchables do not speak a true dialect, certain linguistic quirks do identify them. These are the expressions I have just discussed. Their vocabulary also contains a few distinctive items: in Tamil Nadu, the suffix *-tchi* is fairly typical of Harijan speech, which also shortens some words.[100] Most of these terms are popular usages, in the broad sense, rather than specifically Harijan; yet people often claim to be able to tell Untouchables by their way of speaking, and in particular by their accent.[101] A more systematic study, by Gumperz, has shown that the Chamars of Uttar Pradesh indeed had a characteristic way of pronouncing certain vowels, and that people identified this pronunciation as 'Chamar speech'. These usages are usually regarded as out-dated or even quite vulgar and unsophisticated.[102] What is astonishing, on the other hand, is that Bhangis, who are considered to be much lower than Chamars, speak a Hindi that is much closer to the cultivated speech.[103]

95. J. Freeman, *Untouchable: an Indian Life History*, p. 51.
96. D. Pawar, *Ma vie d'intouchable,* p. 17.
97. S. Molund, *First We Are People,* p. 142.
98. J. Den Ouden, *De Onaanraakbaren van Konkunad* (1975), p. 43; see also R. Deliège, *Les Paraiyars du Tamil Nadu,* p. 152.
99. A. K. Iyer, *The Tribes and Castes of Cochin,* p. 87 and R. Yesudas, *A People's Revolt in Travancore: A Backward Class Movement for Social Freedom* (Trivandrum: Kerala Historical Society, 1975), p. 39.
100. R. Deliège, *Les Paraiyars du Tamil Nadu,* p. 163.
101. S. Fuchs, *The Children of Hari,* p. 8.
102. J. Gumperz, 'Dialect Differences and Social Stratification in a North Indian Village'. *American Anthropologist,* 60 (1958), p. 673.
103. Ibid., p. 675.

Dress, Adornments and Status Symbols

Physical anthropologists have shown that Untouchables do not have any distinctive physical traits; this means that they cannot be recognized by some particular physical characteristic. It is true that high-caste people often claim to be able to pick out a Harijan on sight; in the South, for instance, people invariably say they are darker than the rest of the population. In reality, the observable differences are essentially of a cultural nature, and have nothing to do with a physical 'type'. Furthermore, we have just seen that speech is a fairly unreliable criterion for distinguishing Untouchables.

In sum, if society wanted to distinguish Untouchables from the rest of the population, it had to impose cultural taboos. Sociologists sometimes tend to underrate these; and yet they are a key element in the practice of untouchability, and were the objects of the first emancipation movements. Even today, failure to respect these taboos can spark violent repression, and it is not uncommon for newspapers to report Harijans' being burned alive for such apparently trivial reasons as riding a horse in a wedding procession, and high-caste people can be heard to complain of Harijans' being so bold as to want to wear shirts and sandals.[104]

Indian clothing is not complicated. In rural South India, a white shirt and a *chomin* or *dhoti*, a white loincloth, is the most traditional male garb, while in the North, the more common *kurta* and *pyjama* show the Muslim influence.[105] A cloth worn over the shoulder can be used to staunch perspiration or be worn as a turban. The women cover their breasts with a short coloured blouse or a breast cloth, and wrap the famous *sari* around their waist. Nevertheless, this relatively simple wardrobe has not prevented the imposition of numerous clothing restrictions on Untouchables.

In Tamil Nadu, for instance, an untouchable man could not wear a turban or cover his chest. His loincloth could not reach below his knees. They more commonly wore brightly coloured materials whereas high-caste Hindus go out dressed all in white, or at least in very pale colours.[106] Low-caste people were not allowed to carry a parasol or an umbrella, or to wear sunglasses or shoes. Even today it is not unusual for Harijans to be obliged to remove their shoes before entering the village. Umbrellas, sunglasses and shoes are not essential items, but they are the signs of a certain social standing.[107] Such prescriptions applied to women as well: they were not allowed to cover their breasts, and their *sari* was not supposed to reach down to the ankle. They were forbidden any concession to fashion, and neither they nor the men, whatever their financial means, were allowed to wear gold jewellery. Precious cloth, such as silk, was not allowed; in Kerala, Harijan women were even made to wear loincloths made from aquatic plants.[108] Traditionally, Untouchables received their clothing from

104. J. Mencher, *Agriculture and Social Structure in Tamil Nadu*, p. 153.

105. J. Dupuis, *L'Inde et ses populations* (Brussels: Éditions Complexe, 1982), p. 126.

106. L. Dumont, *Une sous-caste de l'Inde du Sud: organisation sociale et religieuse des Pramalai Kallar* (Paris: Mouton, 1957), p. 69.

107. Ibid., p. 35.

their *jajman* at festival time, and they would wear each item until it fell to pieces. All of this, plus the difficulties they had in finding water, made them dirty, foul-smelling and generally repulsive. Their outward appearance thus reflected their social condition, which is why it is not surprising to see today's young people quite fashion-conscious.

In fact the right to wear a breast cloth was the object of one of the first campaigns conducted by the low castes of South India, no doubt influenced by the missionaries. This was admittedly a question of principle, though, for in the countryside even high-caste women did not cover their breasts. This was true, for example, of the Kallars, whom Dumont studied in the late 1950s,[109] or of the Nayar women in Kerala, photographed by Prince Peter of Greece in the 1930s and 1940s, who went about bare-breasted.[110] But clothing has considerable ceremonial and symbolic value; items of clothing are given or exchanged on all important occasions. Being forbidden to wear the same clothing as other people was therefore felt to be particularly humiliating. And for a man to bear his chest is a sign of humility and inferiority. In the past, many temples made it a rule for men to remove their shirts before entering, and this holds true in certain places today, like the Suchindram temple, near Nagercoil. Being allowed to cover one's chest, then, was felt to be a mark of dignity, of respectability; which is why, in the nineteenth century, the Shanars of Tamil Nadu led a fight, which came to be known as the 'breast-cloth controversy', for the right for their women to wear tops.

As early as 1812, Colonel Munro, the British Resident in Travancore (South Kerala), decreed that Christian women should be allowed to cover their breasts.[111] Nayar reaction was swift: in the 1820s, the Nayars instigated a number of incidents targeted at the Shanars (or Nadars) and, in 1829, the Travancore government issued a 'royal proclamation', declaring that Shanar women were not allowed to cover their breasts. That did not discourage the Shanars, and those who had remained Hindu soon began imitating the Christians. In 1859, violent clashes broke out between Shanars and the high castes in the Madras Presidency. But we will not dwell on the Shanars, who enjoyed much higher status than the Untouchables, and who were seeking to transform recently acquired material wealth into status and dignity.[112] What is most interesting is to see that the low castes were ready to die for such rights, which shows just how important these symbols were.

An eighteenth-century document bears eloquent testimony to this determination. Damaji, a local petty king, had built a small fort in Dawali, a village some 50 kilometres from Poona, in Maharashtra. But the building fell down, and it was decided to rebuild the entire edifice; in order to make the building more solid, a couple was to be immured alive. Davaji asked Kalu Raut, a villager from the Mang caste, to sacrifice his newly married son and his wife to this noble cause. Kalu replied that he would prefer to sacrifice himself, but in exchange he demanded a list of privileges for the

108. A. S. Menon, *Social and Cultural History of Kerala* (Delhi: Sterling Publishers, 1979), p. 117.
109. L. Dumont, *Une sous-caste de l'Inde du Sud,* p. 69.
110. Peter of Greece and Denmark, *A Study of Polyandry* (The Hague: Mouton, 1963).
111. R. Hardgrave, *The Nadars of Tamilnad,* p. 59.
112. R. Jeffrey, 'Temple-Entry Movements in Travancore', p. 3.

Mangs. Among these were the right to go on horseback and to play the drums at weddings. The Mangs also asked that the villagers protect them during weddings, because their untouchable rivals, the famous Mahars, would inevitably be extremely jealous of these prerogatives. The other Mang requests also concerned 'privileges'. The agreement was signed on 7 May 1752. A procession conducted Kalu to the site, where he repeated his demands and then told the masons to go ahead and wall him in. Today, it is still the custom for the Mangs of Davadj to lead the bridegroom about on a horse.[113]

Human sacrifice was not unknown in nineteenth-century India, where it was widely believed that this would give life to a construction. In 1923, there was an uprising on a tea plantation sparked by a rumour that some children had been abducted for the purpose of strengthening the construction of a bridge, and the following year some taxi drivers were killed in Calcutta because they were suspected of having kidnapped children for the construction of the docks at Kidderpore.[114] More generally, human sacrifices are supposed to ensure prosperity. The practice is found throughout India, for example in Mysore[115] and in the mountains of Orissa.[116] There is nothing shameful about human sacrifice, Herrenschmidt's informants told him,[117] and if it has fallen out of practice, it is mainly for lack of volunteers. And so the sacrifice of animals is substituted: 'Behind every ram stands a man.'[118]

Untouchables seem to have been the ideal victims for human sacrifice. It is reported, for example, that, like the Mangs, the Mahars won a list of 52 rights in exchange for having sacrificed a young couple in the foundations of the fort at Purandhar.[119] And a legend tells how a Mahar hero, responsible for escorting the queen on a long journey, had himself castrated in order to be sure of not succumbing to temptation. He placed his genitals in a coffer, which he delivered to the king, who expressed his gratitude by granting the Mahars 52 rights. It is perhaps not so surprising that the tradition has endured and that a Marathi newspaper, dated August 1972, reported that the inhabitants of Erangao, a village in Nagpur district, sacrificed a Mahar in order to stop a cholera epidemic.[120]

We can now close this parenthesis on sacrifice and return to the importance of the status symbols at the centre of the bloody struggles. Hutton reports the 1930 conflict between Kallars and Adi-Dravidas in Ramnad district: the Kallars recalled the eight prohibitions that were supposed to be strictly observed by Untouchables:

1. Adi-Dravidas are not allowed to wear gold or silver jewellery;
2. the men may not wear clothing below the knees or above the hips;
3. the men are not allowed to wear cloaks, shirts or *banyans*;[121]
4. they may not wear their hair short;

113. S. R. Kulkarni, 'Human Sacrifice and its Caste Context in Eighteenth-Centruy Maharashtra: A Case Study' (Poona: Gokhale Institute of Politics and Economics, mimeo, 1976).
114. J. Hutton, *Caste in India,* pp. 249-50.
115. J. Dubois, *Hindu Manners, Customs and Ceremonies,* p. 646.
116. F. Bailey, *Caste and the Economic Frontier,* pp. 139-40.
117. O. Herrenschmidt, *Les Meilleurs Dieux sont hindous,* p. 152.
118. Ibid., p. 153; see also C. Fuller, *The Camphor Flame,* p. 84.
119. D. Pawar, *Ma vie d'intouchable,* p. 63.
120. D. Von Der Weid and G. Poitevin, *Inde: les parias de l'espoir,* p. 28.
121. An undershirt.

5. they are not allowed to use anything but earthenware vessels in their houses;
6. their women are not allowed to cover the upper part of their body;
7. their women are not allowed to wear flowers in their hair or to use saffron powder;
8. the men may not carry parasols or umbrellas and may not wear sandals.

As these prohibitions were not obeyed to their satisfaction, the Kallars met again, in June 1931, and drew up another, more stringent, list of eleven prohibitions. Among these were the bans on learning to read and write and on tilling the land, the establishment of a minimum salary, the prohibition on playing music at weddings and other ceremonies, on using horses or any kind of sedan chair in weddings, and so forth. The Kallars burned shacks, destroyed grain stores and killed people.[122] For every violation is followed by violent repression - of this the Untouchables were well aware; and even today they run the same sad risk.

And Today?

The question now is whether the picture I have just painted is still valid today, or if it is only a relic of the past. Before looking at a few specific points, we can already outline some general features. It must be said that not only has untouchability not disappeared, but most of the discriminatory measures discussed above are still in force, even though sometimes in an attenuated form. But the persistence of these taboos does not mean that the Untouchables' situation has not improved at all over the last few decades. Quite the contrary.

For over a century now, Untouchables have been engaged in a struggle for social progress, and they have won a number of battles. Most young children now attend school, for example, if only for a few years. An elite has emerged from the untouchable ranks, composed of politicians, doctors, engineers and so forth, and their numbers are far from negligible. To be sure, the members of this elite are not spared all humiliations and mortifications; but they no longer have to put up with the same living conditions as their ancestors did. Many types of discrimination persist in the villages; but there, too, things are visibly changing. In short, I would say that the Indian practice of untouchability has generally withstood the onslaught of time and the democratization of society; but today, Untouchables no longer form an economically undifferentiated mass; a certain degree of upward mobility exists.

This persistence can be illustrated by a few examples. In the first place, untouchability is now illegal and unconstitutional. This official abolition is not without crucial consequences, since any official, declared practice of untouchability is now forbidden. Throughout India, Untouchables now have the right to board a train, to sit down on a bus and to enter a restaurant or any other public place. They can apply for important posts, run for election and buy anything they desire if they have the means. Not only are these rights established in law, but also Untouchables do not fail to use

122. J. Hutton, *Caste in India,* pp. 205-6.

them. Wherever they are able to blend in with the crowd or to avoid traditional social contexts, Untouchables contrive to escape notice.

Mental attitudes, however, have changed far less than the laws. In the villages, the Harijans' condition is still a hard one, especially where they are economically dependent. Nevertheless, even in the most precarious situations, their condition has improved, and the prohibitions are not as strict as they used to be. Nayadis are no longer obliged to live in virtual hiding, and their women now habitually cover their breasts. In most villages, Untouchables have their own pump or well, and no longer have to beg for water beside high-caste wells. Yet discrimination has not completely disappeared; sometimes it has merely shifted ground; sometimes it has become more insidious. For example, when it comes to clothing, Untouchables are still required to dress with a certain humility. The young people in Valghira Manickam like to tell how furious it makes high-caste people to see them dressed in fashion; and this stylishness can spark reactions running from sarcasm to blows.

The taboos on water and food seem still to be largely respected, and in general, Untouchables still tend to be segregated from social life. All the elite Untouchables interviewed by Sachchidananda claimed still to experience discrimination. One deputy tells that he was once invited to eat at the home of a high-caste friend. When his meal came on a silver plate, he protested mildly that a simple man like himself did not deserve such an honour. But he later learned that his hosts had chosen this plate because they considered that silver was the only material that would not be polluted by contact with an Untouchable.[123] One government minister says that he used to be seated to one side at certain election rallies; another tells that his host's servants refused to wash the dishes from which he had eaten. All elite Untouchables complain that attitudes change as soon as their caste becomes known: expulsion, purification of the chair they have used, changing train compartments, or straightforward boycotting are the most common reactions.

There is no scarcity of villages that fit the picture we have drawn in this chapter. One thing, in fact, seems to have changed very little, and that is the repulsion, sometimes verging on hatred, that high castes feel for Untouchables. In the present circumstances, marriage with an Untouchable is quite simply unthinkable, and we have heard several people say that death was the only possible punishment when a girl eloped with a young Harijan. Furthermore, Den Ouden noticed that young people from high castes were far more strict in their practice of untouchability than older persons.[124]

While high-caste feelings have evolved very little, it is certain that there are hardly any Untouchables today who find their condition justified. Resentment of discrimination is general, and everyone would like, if not to put an end to it, at least no longer to be a victim. It is obviously the discrepancy between the opposing points of view that explains the many 'atrocities' that appear almost daily in the newspapers. Yet, as I have just suggested, while Untouchables consider the discrimination they endure to be unjustified and even unjust, they have not really developed an egalitarian ideology, and have shown themselves incapable of opposing the system as such. Their

123. Sachchidananda, *The Harijan Elite: A Study of the Status, Networks, Mobility and Role in Social Transformation* (Delhi: Thomson Press, 1976), p. 46.

124. J. Den Ouden, *De Onaanraakbaren van Konkunad* (1975), p. 153.

protest is aimed more at the place assigned to their own caste within the system than at the system itself. They reject the discriminations inflicted on them, while legitimizing those imposed on the other untouchable castes. Because of this, they are clearly incapable of understanding the foundations of a system they help to maintain. The many emancipation movements of the last hundred or more years have only rarely involved more than one caste, and for this reason have not presented a challenge to the caste system as a whole, which continues to thrive.

In the following chapters, we shall see that the system of positive discrimination, which guarantees Untouchables certain privileges and advantages, has had its perverse effects as well, not the least of which has been to exacerbate the difference between caste Hindus and Untouchables. The latter are grouped into official lists of 'Scheduled Castes', which has in a way contributed to stigmatizing them, to fuelling the jealousy of those castes that do not enjoy such advantages, and finally to reinforcing the quarantine in which Untouchables have been kept for so many centuries.

From Stigmatization to Exploitation

The reader unfamiliar with Indian reality cannot help being struck by the above picture. My insistence on the long list of discriminations might give the impression that I accept the models of separation we discussed earlier. Therefore I repeat my overall adhesion to Dumont's theory, which holds the opposition between pure and impure to be the ideological basis of the caste system. Without reference to this opposition, it is impossible to understand either the caste system or untouchability. But I would also like to show that this ideology alone cannot account for all aspects of the phenomenon of untouchability, which is the subject that interests us in this work. This cannot be grasped without emphasis on the rejection, social exclusion, contempt and disgust that surround Untouchables. And this rejection cannot always be explained by the notion of impurity.

To be sure, many discriminatory measures are driven by this ideology: I am thinking particularly of the prohibition on taking water from wells, on entering temples or on cooking food for higher castes. Many of these prohibitions have a ritual explanation. But there is no ritual reason that can explain why high-caste men can have sexual intercourse with untouchable women without being polluted: in Irupatur, the many Kavuntars who have sexual relations with Pallar women do not even feel the need to wash afterwards.[125] There is no ritual motive that prevents an Untouchable riding a horse at his wedding or wearing sunglasses, no more than there is a ritual explanation forbidding a good haircut. No religious cause can be found for banning clothing above the waist or below the knees. All these are measures designed to mark Untouchables as low or even debased; their origin is purely sociological. In fact the pollution rules themselves have a sociological component, and, as Reiniche notes, the purity or impurity of Pallars or Paraiyars exists only with respect to the criteria of organized

125. Ibid., p. 175.

village society,[126] and, as she goes on to write, 'no one ever says that an Untouchable pollutes the land he tills'. The Untouchable is thus not simply impure: he is also inferior, reduced to a state of near servitude; and this rank needs to be recalled and maintained by various rules.

The actors themselves do not seem to be conscious of the religious reasons for a good many ritual taboos. A sociologist friend told me one day that it was not until he went to university that he discovered the religious origins of many everyday practices. It is also interesting to note that not one of Good's informants had ever taken a ritual bath after contact with an Untouchable,[127] whereas they were very strict when it came to contact with death. The large Hindu temples, too, have come round to the presence of untouchable pilgrims within their walls. Some ritual prohibitions strongly resemble a posteriori rationalizations: for example, Gujaratis are hard put to explain why Djed weavers are considered to be untouchable. Some told Pocock that it was because the fabrics were finished with a substance made from bone.[128]

Writing about the danger of pollution, Herrenschmidt rightly remarked that 'Indians have a markedly "Jesuitical" approach, "See no evil, hear no evil, etc. " Whatever happens to you in private has only the importance you give it. It is your own affair.'[129] Yet I have noticed that the higher castes punish the violation of various taboos with a violence that has nothing ritual about it. When an Untouchable breaks one of these rules, high-caste people think more in terms of burning his house or torturing him than taking a ritual bath. Repression is an essential element of the system - a fact that comes out clearly in the recent movements we have already touched on. But, although the concept of ritual pollution forms the ideological basis of the system, it does not explain everything. The barber exercises highly polluting duties, and he also performs many tasks in preparation for funerals; yet he is not untouchable.[130] Mosse is emphatic that the ideology of impurity cannot be separated from power and servitude.[131] Harijans' status is defined as much by their condition as agricultural labourers as by their role as funeral attendants. Elsewhere, Mosse rightly judges that the category cannot be defined without reference to the state of servitude (*atimai* in Tamil).[132] In Alapuram, no one mentions their function of gravedigger to account for the low status of Pallars; the high-castes say that Pallars are low people over whom they enjoy certain rights (*urimai*) within a relationship of servitude (*atimai*), and Pallars explain their own lowness in terms of servitude and poverty, not in ritual terms.[133] Furthermore, we have also had occasion to see that Untouchables usually present the caste system as a human institution, in no way sanctioned by the gods.[134]

In short, the opposition between pure and impure does indeed underpin the caste

126. M. L. Reiniche, *Les Dieux et les hommes,* p. 13.

127. A. Good, *The Female Bridegroom,* pp. 14-15: see also J. Den Ouden, *De Onaanraakbaren van Konkunad* (1975), p. 158.

128. D. Pocock, *Kanbi and Patidar,* p. 39.

129. O. Herrenschmidt, 'Entretien avec O. Herrenschmidt par M. et F. Montrelay'. *Cahiers Confrontations,* 13 (1985), p. 12.

130. Cf. e.g. J. Parry, *Caste and Kinship in Kangra,* p. 72; A. Mayer, *Caste and Kinship in Central India,* p. 37; and D. Pocock, *Kanbi and Patidar,* p. 34.

131. D. Mosse, 'Caste, Christianity and Hinduism', p. 247.

132. Ibid., p. 183.

133. Ibid., p. 237.

system; but it establishes a relative scale of purity that leaves Untouchables indistinguishable from the rest of the population. I have nevertheless attempted to show, in this chapter, that Untouchables are different, and that they form a separate class of society. What sets them apart are the numerous discriminations and disabilities imposed on them. Untouchables, then, are that social category that lives *both* in a state of ritual impurity *and* in social servitude.

This stigma does not mean that Untouchables constitute a homogeneous category, though. We have already seen, and will see again and again, the many factors that divide them. In an interesting work, Den Ouden emphasized precisely the many differences between the various untouchable castes he studied in Irupatur village, not far from Coimbatore. He mentions, for instance, that the Pallars stand out sharply from the other untouchable groups. They are militant and aggressive,[135] they play a crucial role in the festival of the goddess, in which the other untouchable castes have no part,[136] and the higher castes do not place them on the same footing as the other three untouchable castes;[137] thus they are sometimes allowed on to the verandah of a Kavuntar's house,[138] and in the fields, Pallars and Kavuntars eat together, while the Sakkiliyars are segregated.[139] But it is also true that the highest of the untouchable castes are not all that different from the lowest 'touchables'.

This absence of homogeneity has led some to challenge the existence of a specific untouchable category. For instance, Parry notes that untouchability is ultimately relative, a matter of degree rather than nature.[140] The distinction between touchable and untouchable castes seems to him a loose one. This is a position I cannot accept. First of all, some castes have changed status to such an extent over the last century that they are no longer truly representative. This is clearly the case of militant castes like Chamars, Mahars or Pallars. These castes are numerically large, and have managed to better their economic situation appreciably. The Pallars' present position is, in good measure, the outcome of these recent changes and of this improvement in their socio-economic situation.[141] The Pallars in Den Ouden's study acknowledge that they owe their position to their numerical and economic strength, whereas the Paraiyars' situation remains weak.[142] Therefore the fact that they do not constitute a homogeneous category does not mean that they are not distinguishable from the rest of the population. It is because he poses the problem strictly in terms of relative purity that Parry refuses to consider them as a distinct class.

In reality, Untouchables are still subjected to certain disabilities and discriminations. In Irupatur,[143] none of the four low classes is allowed to take water from the Kavuntar well, and none of the high castes accepts food cooked by these four castes.[144] Even though the intensity and the form of these discriminations may vary, they are no less

134. R. Deliège, 'Les Mythes d'origine chez les Paraiyar'. *L'Homme,* 109 (1989), p. 112.
135. J. Den Ouden, *De Onaanraakbaren van Konkunad* (1975), p. 49.
136. Ibid., p. 112.
137. Ibid., p. 154.
138. Ibid., p. 162.
139. Ibid., p. 149.
140. J. Parry, *Caste and Kinship in Kangra,* p. 115.
141. D. Mosse, 'Caste, Christianity and Hinduism', p. 189.
142. J. Den Ouden, *De Onaanraakbaren van Konkunad* (1975), p. 118.
143. Ibid., p. 85.

universal, and serve above all to segregate the Untouchables from the rest of the population.

144. Ibid., p. 137.

-6-

Untouchable Occupations

Chapter 5 may have given the reader the impression of a clear separation between Untouchables and the rest of Indian society. Yet the disabilities, discrimination, taboos and segregation affecting Untouchables are only one aspect of their condition; for, as we have said, they cannot be completely marginalized, they cannot be absolutely excluded from society. In fact, it is a hallmark of their condition to be at once rejected and indispensable, to be an integral part of society and constantly banished to the margins. The paradox of their exclusion is also that, without them, society would be unable to function: whether in the ritual or the strictly economic spheres, the tasks they perform are absolutely essential. In the course of this chapter, I shall attempt to rectify the impression of exclusion that may have been left by the preceding section, as here we shall be dealing with the great importance of the untouchable castes.

At the beginning of the nineteenth century, Abbé Dubois eloquently expressed the paradoxical position that Untouchables occupy in Indian society. Writing on the 'Paria caste', he had this to say: 'It is painful to think that its members, though so degraded, are yet the most useful of all.'[1]

It is this 'usefulness' that we shall be discussing in the present chapter. Untouchable occupations fall into two categories: ritual functions, on the one hand, and more strictly economic activities, on the other. Of course, this division itself is somewhat of a problem, since the two kinds of activities are not always clearly separated. For example, agricultural work, a secular occupation if ever there was one, also has some clearly ritualized features; what goes on on the threshing floor, as Reiniche points out for example, gives the onlooker the feeling of 'having attended a sort of rite'.[2] Likewise, many economic tasks, such as rendering carcasses, collecting night-soil or sweeping the streets, can be traced directly to the ritual impurity of the untouchable castes. In spite of these relatively fluid boundaries, however, it is possible to distinguish purely ritual activities, like beating the drum at funerals, from those that are materially necessary for making a living, for example, agricultural work, or brick- or salt-making. This chapter will focus primarily on the second category, for these are the tasks that enable Untouchables to subsist and that occupy the better part of their time.

1. J. Dubois, *Hindu Manners, Customs and Ceremonies* (Oxford: Oxford University Press, 1906), p. 49.
2. M. L. Reiniche, 'La Notion de *jajmâni:* qualification abusive ou principe d'intégration?'. *Purusârtha,* 3 (1976), p. 72.

Characteristic Features

It is not my intention to write an economic history of untouchability; but it is clear that one cannot discuss the material life of Untouchables without a diachronic overview, for their material conditions of existence have undergone many changes in the last few decades. Since Indian independence, in particular, more activities have opened up to Untouchables; they have gained access to professions that were formerly forbidden, and they have spared no effort to improve their lives. As a result, it is now not unusual to come across untouchable university professors, airline cabin attendants or, more frequently, primary school teachers, lawyers and even medical doctors. We will have to account for this diversification; yet, however great it has been, the fact remains that the huge majority of Untouchables today are still relegated to traditional activities, and in any event, to menial tasks.

In spite of the emergence of a small elite, then, life, for most of today's Untouchables, is not basically different from what it was in precolonial times. Gough, for instance, believes that the living conditions of Untouchables in Tanjore district did not improve perceptibly between 1952 and 1976.[3] Elsewhere, it seems that the standard of living has risen slightly, especially since independence; but it is still precarious. We will look at a few of these features in the following sections.

Poverty

Although some anthropologists tend to underrate this aspect of the untouchable condition, poverty, and even abject poverty, is a basic feature of their economic life. An opulently rich Untouchable would no longer be altogether an Untouchable, whatever anyone says. Their material destitution is the first thing that strikes the traveller, or at any rate it is what struck the first foreign observers of Indian society; nor did they fail to underscore the extreme poverty of these lowest classes. Although accustomed to the poverty of eighteenth-century French society, Abbé Dubois describes his visit to dying Untouchables in the following evocative terms:

"I could only partially avoid the sickening smell by holding to my nose a handkerchief soaked in the strongest vinegar. I would find there a mere skeleton, perhaps lying on the bare ground, though more often crouching on a rotten piece of matting, with a stone or a block of wood as a pillow. The miserable creature would have for clothing a rag tied around the loins, and for covering a coarse and tatted blanket that left half the body naked. I would seat myself on the ground by his side, and the first words I heard would be: 'Father, I am dying of cold and hunger.' ... The only thing that really afflicted me was having to stand face to face with such a

3. K. Gough, *Rural Change in Southeast India: 1950s to 1980s* (Delhi: Oxford University Press, 1989).

spectacle of utter misery and all its attendant horrors, and possessing no means of affording any save the most inadequate remedies."[4]

Some anthropologists, such as Srinivas and Leach, attempt to minimize this side of untouchability by arguing that there are 'mystical' sanctions for all those that mistreat their untouchable servants. According to the eminent Indian anthropologist, untouchability cannot be viewed in terms of exploitation because there are rules that guarantee that untouchable labourers receive 'fair' treatment.[5] Srinivas thus legitimizes the system by shifting the emphasis to the economic security it provides for the most disadvantaged. This is, I must say, a rather odd idea, and one I find totally unacceptable. For it goes without saying that landowners were obliged to ensure their workers a minimum level of subsistence or run the risk of not finding any! More remarkable, however, is the extremely low standard of living they were guaranteed. We will even see that the Untouchables' economic life was essentially in the red. Their income was never sufficient to make ends meet, for that would have meant giving them the means to end the dependency that kept them tied to the higher castes and enabled the system to go on. It would also have meant allowing them to attain a dignity that, as we have seen, was denied them. This is clearly the reason that Untouchables did not traditionally have the right to own the basic means of production, foremost of which is land.

Today poverty is still one of the fundamental features of the Untouchables' life, and they themselves usually conceptualize untouchability in terms of material destitution. It should be clear, then, that untouchability cannot be reduced to a mere economic problem - we have already said that the problem of poverty in India is not identical with that of untouchability; but, at the same time, material deprivation is inherent to untouchable status. Moreover, the higher castes are always prompt to stress that, if Untouchables are too well paid, they become arrogant and unwilling to work. A good number of the prohibitions affecting Untouchables were meant precisely to symbolize this poverty - for instance the ban on wearing clothing above the waist and below the knees. The many social consequences of poverty are also found among Untouchables: malnutrition, infant mortality, illiteracy, alcoholism and prostitution all are rife.

Dependency

While the mountain tribes also lived in precarious material conditions, they nevertheless enjoyed a certain degree of freedom and placed a high value on their political and economic independence. They were frequently accountable only to themselves, and demonstrated their ability to defend their rights. They tilled their own land and hunted in their own forests. Therefore poverty can rhyme with liberty, even in India; but not in the case of the Untouchables, whose second characteristic is economic dependence on higher castes. Deprived of landownership, Untouchables

4. J. Dubois, *Hindu Manners, Customs and Ceremonies,* p. 59.
5. M. N. Srinivas, 'Some Reflections on the Nature of Caste Hierarchy'. *Contributions to Indian Sociology* (NS), 18 (1984), pp. 151-67, p. 166.

depended for the most part on their own labour to make a living. In some cases they were not even free labourers, but lived in a state of semi-slavery. This was the case in Kerala, where they could be sold by their master, who also had the right to put them to death.[6] Nor were they allowed to work for themselves. The dominant castes owned not only the farmland, but the pastures, the places of worship, the land where the houses stood, and so forth. The labourers were therefore totally dependent.

Modern society has largely perpetuated this system of dependence, to which has been added indebtedness. Even the free labourers who no longer depend on the upper castes for survival can still be bound to them by debts they have contracted. All the inhabitants of Valghira Manickam village are Paraiyars; nevertheless, the Kallars of neighbouring Kanda Devi village consider themselves to be the owners of the land. It frequently happens that Paraiyars are obliged to buy the land they have been living on for decades from Kallars, even though the Kallars do not hold an official deed. The Paraiyars do not dare put in irrigation for fear of upsetting the Kallars. The Kallars often allow the Paraiyars to cultivate certain fields under a system of landholding called *varam*, which sets the rent at one-third of the harvest. As the bulk of the economy is now monetarized, this dependence is obviously most often perpetuated in the form of debt. Throughout India, various forms of 'serfdom' tie a labourer to a master for a longer or shorter period of time (sometimes indefinitely) in repayment of a debt.

The Untouchables' dependent status was and still is reflected in many obsequious practices and attitudes. They are supposed to appear humble and to show respect. They greet a high-caste person by touching his feet with both hands, which they then bring to their forehead, as though their own head was no better than their masters' feet. They always sit on a lower level than their masters, and step off the path to let them pass, and so forth. The Untouchable never exists of and for himself. He is by definition Untouchable with respect to non-Untouchables, to whom he is always subordinate.

Debt

Poverty and dependence are maintained and reinforced by the chronic deficit that characterizes the untouchable budget. In other words, and contrary once again to what Srinivas claims, an Untouchable's income is never sufficient to meet even his most basic needs. Traditionally Untouchables were paid in kind with a set quantity of grain at harvest time. This was much less than the amount received by other social categories. Craftsmen, for example, were guaranteed a more or less decent income; but this was not the case for Untouchables, who had to be kept in a state of dependence and abjection. In Tamil Nadu, the salary of the well-known 'bonded labourer' varied with his caste: Untouchables were called *pannaiyal*, and received less grain than their

6. K. Saradamoni, *Emergence of a Slave Caste: Pulayas of Kerala* (Delhi: People's Publishing House, 1980), p. 53.

non-untouchable counterparts, known as *velaikarrar*[7] In general, the Untouchables received just enough to eat, and, for the rest of their needs, like clothing, were dependent on 'gifts' from their master at important times of the year. Sometimes, too, they were forced to beg. This is what Reiniche means when she emphasizes that the traditional economy barely ensures agricultural labourers a subsistence living, so that for other expenditures they must turn to their employer, who lends them the money, with the result that the debt is passed from one generation to the next. Reiniche concludes: 'this undying debt is, in our opinion, part of the system.'[8]

This chronic deficit has come down to modern times, where agricultural labourers are more than ever in need of cash. As they are insolvent, the only thing Untouchables can do is sell their labour; and that is why, in exchange for an advance, they are willing to tie themselves for an unspecified period of time to their creditors. Let us take, for example, the brick-makers of Valghira Manickam: each year a large portion of the local labour force consents to migrate to Madras for six months to work in the brick factories in order to pay back the money advanced them by their landlord. The widespread system of bonded labour is another consequence of this chronic deficit.

An Indispensable Function

Although they are poor, dependent and indebted, Untouchables are nonetheless indispensable to both the ritual and the economic spheres. The usefulness of their labour, which is essential to society, stands in obvious contrast to their exclusion from the same society. The paradox of Indian untouchability lies in this combination of a beggar-like status with an indispensable economic function: those who do the bulk of the agricultural work are at the same time regarded as marginals of a sort. This economic aspect of the fundamental ambiguity of untouchability stems to a large extent from their ritual functions. To put it simply: Untouchables are those who are charged with ridding society of its organic wastes, with keeping the demons away from worship, and with absorbing a good part of the pollution connected with death. These essential tasks make them permanently impure, and require their exclusion from society. From the ritual standpoint, then, the Untouchables' impurity is clearly the basic corollary of the Brahmins' purity. Untouchables protect the world from inauspicious influences.

But their social importance does not end there. Untouchables are also, and from a certain viewpoint above all, agricultural workers. It is not uncommon in India to come across small landowners who practically never touch the soil with their own hands. The Brahmins who own land do not even have the right to till their own fields. Throughout India, much of the agricultural work is therefore done by 'landless peasants', who come largely from the untouchable castes. Some of them are regarded

7. K. Gough, *Rural Change in Southeast India,* p. 431, or Den Ouden, *De Onaanraakbaren van Konkunad: De Economische, Politieke en Educatieve Positie der Scheduled Castes* (*1966-1976*) (Wageningen: Vakgroep Agrarische Sociologie van de Niet-Westerse Gebieden, 1977), p. 86.

8. M. L. Reiniche, 'La Notion de jajmâni', p. 78.

primarily as tillers of the soil: this is the case of the Pallars, who, as we saw, stress the particularly auspicious nature of their economic role and see themselves as 'providers of agricultural bounty': they even claim that a farm will not prosper unless there is a Pallar to till it.[9] They are the only ones who know how to harvest the fields and thresh the grain.[10]

Working as night-soil removers, sweepers and renderers, Untouchables fulfil other similarly vital functions. This second aspect of their work obviously contributes to their segregation from other fringe groups who carry out secondary tasks of no great social necessity. By contrast, Untouchables are perfectly and absolutely a part of the economy. Their economic integration appears as an extension of their ritual role, which, as Hocart writes, is essential to the smooth running of the sacrifice.

A Ritual Function

The foregoing remarks underscore the fact that almost all untouchable castes fulfil some ritual functions. In Chapter 2, we saw how Hocart highlighted the sacrificial basis of the caste system and, consequently, of untouchability. Let us recall Hocart's famous formula: 'every caste is a priesthood.' From this viewpoint, Untouchables are primarily 'priests of the demons'; it is they who keep the *asura* under control and thus ensure that both the sacrifice and society as a whole run smoothly. Throughout India, the untouchable castes can be seen taking part in religious ceremonies; roughly speaking, their ritual role consists of protecting society from harmful influences, from pollution associated with death, from demons and from organic wastes. In the course of the ritual proper, they may, for instance, beat drums to keep the demons away. Certain castes, like the North Indian Doms, have specialized in the preparation of funeral pyres. All over India, Untouchables take an active part in life-cycle rituals by absorbing bad omens and pollution: the Bhanji women of Uttar Pradesh[11] receive salt, flour or seed for ridding the family of the dangers of pollution and death. In central India, midwives come from the untouchable castes.[12] Untouchables are also gravediggers, messengers (conveying bad news), tanners and, of course, sweepers.

Yet, as Fuller, among others, has shown, Untouchables do not participate in the various rituals on an equal footing with other castes.[13] Contrary to what Moffatt has written, calling them 'last among equals',[14] Fuller stresses that their position in the

9. As a reminder, see K. Kapadia, 'Gender, Caste nd Class in Rural South India'. (Doctoral dissertation, London School of Economics, Department of Anthropology, 1990), p. 118.

10. M. L. Reiniche, 'La Notion de jajmâni', p. 85.

11. G. Raheja, *The Poison in the Gift: Ritual Prestation and the Dominant Caste in a North Indian Village* (Chicago: Univeristy of Chicago Press, 1988), p. 117.

12. L. Babb, *The Divine Hierarchy: Popular Hinduism in Central India* (New York: Columbia University Press, 1975), p. 73.

13. C. Fuller, *The Camphor Flame: Popular Hinduism and Society in India* (Princeton, NJ: Princeton University Press, 1992), p. 138.

14. M. Moffatt, *An Untouchable Community in South India: Structure and Consensus* (Princeton, NJ Princeton University Press, 1979), p. 222.

ritual is always ambiguous: though they consume part of the offerings, they do not eat with the others; they are not allowed to enter temples - a deeply rooted prohibition even today, except for the large city temples, which are more anonymous; and they never participate as true partners or co-worshippers, Fuller concludes. Around Coorg (Karnataka), the harvest festival opens with a ceremony in which the village headman calls out the different caste names, and the Pulayas are called 'those who stay outside'.[15] This is a typical expression of the Untouchables' ambiguity: invited to participate while remaining outside.

A whole series of occupations derives from the Untouchables' inherent impurity. All tasks involving cleaning or removal of refuse naturally fall to them; thus we find castes of streetsweepers, night-soil collectors, renderers, scavengers and so forth. Similarly, tanners and drummers, who use leather to make their instruments, exercise what are seen as ignominious occupations. Ritual logic is nevertheless not absolutely consistent: washermen, who wash the clothing polluted by menstruation or death, along with barbers, carry out important mortuary tasks; but they are not regarded as truly untouchable, nor are they excluded from society.

Manual Labour

Above all, Untouchables are those who do the physical work, and throughout India they are, *par excellence*, those who perform the menial tasks. On many farms they are the ones who work the soil with their hands. When they are not employed as farm labour, or during the dry season, they can be seen swarming over construction sites like ants, carrying heavy loads on their heads. In India, anything a man or a woman wants to transport is carried on the head, from a stem of bananas to a load of cement, and it is not unusual to see someone carrying a trunk, a wardrobe, a load of stones or even a bed. For some, this technique has become a trade: these are the legendary 'coolies', many of whom come from untouchable castes.

The distinction between intellectual work and manual (it would be tempting to say 'physical') labour is clearly marked in India: Brahmins are a sort of 'scholarly' class, the only ones able to study the sacred texts; in contrast, the heads of the lowly are only good for carrying heavy loads. The dirty clothing that used to be worn by Untouchables, as we have seen, reflected their disgrace, and even today the upper castes do not appreciate their 'putting on airs', in other words, dressing decently. Likewise, a Harijan who goes to school is seen as one less worker.[16] Indians think of the different castes (*jati*) as different species, each of which is good at a particular job: Brahmins are regarded as mediocre farmers, for example.[17] In the same vein, the

15. M. N. Srinivas, *Religion and Society among the Coorgs of South India* (Bombay: Asia Publishing House, 1962), p. 202.

16. Sachchidananda, *Social Change in Village India* (Delhi: Concept, 1988), p. 15.

17. M. N. Srinivas, 'Le Système social d'un village du Mysore', in R. Lardinois (ed.), Miroir de l'Inde: études indiennes en sciences sociales (Paris: Editions de la Maison des Sciences de l'Homme, 1988, pp. 49-90), p. 50.

function of Untouchables is to serve society by removing its impurities. 'Why did God create carpenters, grain parchers, potters, barbers, cattlemen and the like?', one of Wiser's (high-caste) informants asked him. 'Did God not intend that each should perform his own work? And certainly it was not necessary for a Banghi to read when his work was to clean cesspools.'[18]

We have now seen the main characteristics of the Untouchables' economic position, which have probably marked their life for many centuries. The question that immediately springs to mind is whether this picture is still valid for modern-day India. In so far as we are talking about 'general characteristics', the answer is, yes. The vast majority of today's Harijans are still poor, dependent and manual labourers. The coolies, farm workers and sweepers often come from the Scheduled Castes.

Nevertheless, the situation has become much more diversified, and Harijans, too, have begun to lead modern lives; the literacy rate, although still low, is an indicator of their desire for upward mobility and economic advancement. An elite has emerged from the untouchable castes that has taken advantage of the legislation to move up the social ladder, becoming doctors, engineers, college professors or, more frequently, office workers and schoolteachers. In some cases, Untouchables have even managed to use their professional skills to improve their condition. More generally, today we see a certain diversification of occupations among both Untouchables and the population as a whole, and we shall be looking at these transformations, which, however limited, are of undeniable importance. In all events, it is inaccurate to depict Untouchables as passively enduring their sad fate. That being said, I shall nevertheless begin with the more traditional features of their economic life.

Traditional Rural Society

The divisions I have chosen are of more an analytical than a historical nature. When I talk about rural life and the traditional division of labour, I am not referring to some remote, bygone past. Although untouchable economic activities began diversifying rapidly towards the end of the nineteenth century, the majority still exercise the same economic activities as they have from time immemorial. In a study of Tanjore district, in Tamil Nadu, Kathleen Gough says that the number of farm workers has even risen in the last decades: in 1951, landless peasants represented 40 per cent of the agricultural labour force, whereas by 1976 this proportion had risen to 59 per cent.[19] Of course, the landless peasant at the end of the twentieth century is very different from the semi-slave of the late nineteenth century, but he is still at the bottom of the social ladder, and his living conditions are still precarious.

18. W. Wiser, *The Hindu Jajmani System: A Socio-Economic System Interrelating Members of a Hindu Village Community in Services* (Lucknow: Lucknow Publishing House, 1936), p. 121.

19. K. Gough, *Rural Change in Southeast India,* p. 138.

Agricultural Workers

Until the nineteenth century, most Untouchables were farm workers. Today many still work in agriculture, but not in the overwhelming proportions they once did. The ban on owning land, as I have said, was a basic feature of untouchability. As land was the primary means of production, this prohibition forced Untouchables into the precarious situation of dependency outlined above. In the past, agricultural workers lived in semi-slavery. In Kerala, for example, Pulayas were the absolute property of their master; they could be sold or transferred like cattle.[20] It seems that India experienced a scarcity of labour in the 1840s, so that the British and indigenous laws abolishing 'slavery' were well received, and many Untouchables were emancipated: some Chamars acquired land, and a number of Paraiyars began working plots as tenant farmers.[21]

Nowadays, following Gough, we can identify three types of agricultural workers: bonded labourers, regular or contractual workers, and day-labourers. Gough, and others after her, believe that the gradual shift from the first category towards the third signals the transition from a semi-feudal system to capitalist agriculture. In effect, the ties between agricultural workers and their masters can no longer be described as traditional obligations, having become purely commercial; but it seems that this proletarization of sorts has aggravated the precariousness of the Untouchables' economic situation.[22] Gough's first two categories can thus be merged into a single one encompassing all traditional forms of agricultural work - in other words all those in which master and servant were linked by non-commercial ties. We will examine these first, before going on to day-labour, which is now virtually generalized.

The various forms of traditional agricultural work can be classified according to the degree of freedom enjoyed by the worker: for instance, throughout India slavery has given way to various forms of bonded labour, though in some places the worker haskept his formal freedom. In practice, however, the line between these various types of labour was a thin one, for even where he was not legally a slave, the agricultural worker was still bound to his master by customary, moral and even hereditary ties. His freedom and mobility were therefore still limited, if not exactly determined. In Karnataka, for example, a runaway had few places to hide; the members of his own family were reluctant to take him in, because an escape could bring down repressive measures on the fugitive's family. The distinction between true slaves, who could be bought and sold, and other workers was therefore tenuous.[23] We will begin by examining the most radical forms of attachment, which culminate in the various forms of bonded labour.

20. K. Saradamoni, *Emergence of a Slave Caste,* p. 52.

21. C. Bayly, *Indian Society and the Making of the British Empire* (Cambridge: Cambridge University Press, 1988), p. 146.

22. See also E. Epstein, *South India Yesterday, Today and Tomorrow* (London: Macmillan, 1973), p. 164.

23. E. Harper, 'Social Consequences of an Unsuccessful Low Caste Movement', in J. Silverberg (ed.), *Social Mobility in the Caste System* (The Hague: Mouton, 1968, pp. 35-65), pp. 44 and 48.

Bonded labourers: as we have just seen, it appears that, in some parts of India at least, the scarcity of manual work made bonded labour particularly attractive, and Gough goes as far as to class the *pannaiyal* 'among the more fortunate workers in Kirippur village',[24] something that Den Ouden confirms for Konkunad too. The life of bonded labourers in Tamil Nadu was probably not as hard as it was for their counterparts in other areas of India; but it seems that even where their condition was merciless, they still considered themselves somewhat 'privileged'. This is what Breman tells us, and claims that it was true in the past as well: 'For lack of continuous employment in the traditional agricultural economy, those who had managed to find someone to provide for them had every reason to consider themselves lucky ... It followed that servitude was in fact preferred to free labour by landowners and agricultural labourers alike ...'[25]

In a later passage[26] the same author concludes that today: 'For the Dublas, servitude still offers the best guarantee of a living.' This no doubt explains why, on New Year's Day in 1976, Gough saw workers lined up outside the masters' houses in the hope of being taken on as *pannaiyal:* now this was during Mrs Gandhi's state of emergency, and she had taken strict measures to end bonded labour, making the *pannaiyal* system illegal, purportedly in the interests of the worker! The distinction between free and unfree workers is therefore still not always clear-cut. This conceptual fluidity is not without serious practical consequences, since, as we have seen, the government wanted to ban practices that the 'victims' wished continued. This was true not only of the *pannaiyal* in Tamil Nadu, as similar difficulties can be found in other parts of India: in Bihar, for example, the local government does not recognize the existence of bonded labourers in its territory, and claims that the workers 'attached' to a farm prefer this solution, which brings it into conflict with the organs responsible for applying the 1976 Bonded Labour Act.[27]

Attachment to a master ensured these workers a minimum level of subsistence; this explains their interest in such a restrictive solution, which requires them to forgo their freedom. For let there be no mistake, the life of 'bonded workers' was - and is - far from idyllic! So be sure, the system we are talking about rests, to a certain extent, on the consent of the actors; if they are to comply, they must see some interest in it, which seems to be the case; and yet, if they were 'privileged' in any way, it is because they were offered slavery in place of starvation and perhaps death. In agreeing to this arrangement, they put themselves virtually at the 'beck and call' of a master, day and night, with little hope that their debt would be forgiven. If they chose, and continue to choose, this solution, it is because they were forced to do so by material conditions; it is of course the fundamental insufficiency of their income that puts them at the mercy of the landowners. In some cases the duration of the agreement tying them to their master was fixed: in Tamil Nadu, *pannaiyal* worked one year for their master. But in other parts of India, it was an altogether different story, and a man might be tied to another for the rest of his life for having borrowed a trifling sum.

24. K. Gough, *Rural Change in Southeast India,* p. 430.

25. J. Breman, *Patronage and Exploitation: Changing Agrarian Relations in South Gujarat* (Delhi: Manohar, 1974), pp. 43-4.

26. Ibid., p. 191.

27. I. Bharti, 'Bihar's Most Wretched'. *Economic and Political Weekly,* September 22 (1990).

It is possible that this system may have replaced simple slavery, and that throughout India emancipated Untouchables soon fell into this new form of dependence and servitude. Nowadays, lawsuits brought by the government have added to the massive increase in the labour force, making this form of bonded labour less common than before; but it is far from having disappeared. As in the past, it can still be found throughout India, even though each region has a different name for it: in North India, people speak of *beggar*; in Madhya Pradesh, it is *mahidari*; in Tamil Nadu, *pannaiyal*; in Orissa, *gothi*; in Rajasthan, *sagri*; *hali* in Gujarat, and so on.[28]

All these systems rest on the following general principle: a worker in need of money borrows a sum from his master and agrees to work for him until the debt has been repaid. In the best of cases, as in the *pannaiyal* system in Tamil Nadu, the length of the agreement is stipulated. Elsewhere, no duration is set for repayment of the debt, and a man can thus be deprived of his freedom for the rest of his life, and his sons sometimes go on to inherit the debt. In the *hali* system found in Gujarat, as Breman points out,[29] the idea that the debt could ever be repaid is something that is not even seriously considered. This system can be seen as an attempt to maintain 'semi-feudal' relationships in a society where individuals are theoretically free.

The system prevailing in southern Gujarat has been studied in depth by Breman, and is worth pausing over. The main caste concerned was originally a tribe; but the Dublas are now tribals in name only, and can today be assimilated to the untouchable castes, whose functions they fulfil in this region.[30] The two villages studied by Breman exhibit a few variations, especially concerning the duration of the bond. The traditional system of bonded labour is somewhat less stringent here; first of all, many agricultural workers have become day-labourers, and only some Dublas still work as farm servants. They are in debt to their master, and therefore cannot leave whenever they please. To be sure, they could always run away to some other part of India; but that would be an act of desperation, for their prospects are no better elsewhere. Moreover, as we have said, they consider their condition to be relatively privileged because of the job security afforded by their status. By contrast with what happened under the traditional system, the *hali* worker is no longer tied to his master for life, and his debt can no longer be passed on to his descendants. In addition, the working conditions are more or less agreed upon, so that the *hali* is no longer at the mercy of his master. Nevertheless, Breman emphasizes that these servants are always given the most degrading tasks, and that girls are reluctant to marry such men.[31] The master - servant relationship has also become much more impersonal; the servant is no longer proud of his master, and the master no longer feels morally responsible for the well-being of his man.[32]

Farm servants earn an even lower daily wage than day-labourers. The latter receive 12 *annas* a day plus two meals, while servants receive the equivalent of 8 *annas*. Today wages tend to be paid in cash, which, in Breman's opinion, is to the workers'

28. See Indian School of Social Sciences, *Bonded Labour in India: A Shocking Tale of Slave Labour in Rural India* (Calcutta: Indian School of Social Sciences, 1975).

29. J. Breman, *Patronage and Exploitation,* p. 59.

30. See P. Shah, *The Dublas of Gujarat* (Delhi: Bharatiya Adimjati Sevak Sangh, 1958), p. 35.

31. J. Breman, *Patronage and Exploitation,* p. 143.

32. Ibid., p. 184.

disadvantage. *Hali* workers also receive items of clothing and gifts at festival times; but what differentiates day-labourers above all is the availability of regular work. Agricultural workers go long months without employment, and are often obliged to migrate to the dockyards of Bombay or to the brickworks.[33]

In Gujarat, farm servants bear less and less resemblance to the slaves of the nineteenth century. On the contrary, they are becoming more like the 'regular workers' that we shall be discussing later. Of course this transformation entails more freedom, but unfortunately more unemployment as well; as Breman emphasizes, the guarantee of two meals a day has the same appeal whatever the century; by contrast, with the monetarization of wages, inflation reduces some wage-labourers to poverty.[34]

Thanks to such authors as Gough and Den Ouden, we also have important details about the present-day situation of *pannaiyal* in the state of Tamil Nadu. These data largely confirm Breman's remarks about the 'breakdown' of the system. Here, too, only a small portion of the workforce is still involved in this traditional relationship. Their number fell further still between 1952 and 1976, the period covered by Gough's study. In another part of the same state, Den Ouden observed, in 1976, that the *pannaiyal* he had recorded in 1966 had disappeared.[35]

Pannaiyal in Konkunad were tied for a year. The contracts were usually made on the first day of the months of *mali* (15 February) and *cittirai* (14 April). The sum depended on the worker's age and the nature of the contract; workers preferred to be paid in kind, because money tended to burn a hole in their pockets. It is also striking that 'touchable' *pannaiyal* earned more than untouchable *pannaiyal*.[36] Today it seems that certain untouchable castes have lost interest in *pannaiyal* work; this is the true of Pallars, in particular, the cream of the agricultural workforce. Pallars are regarded as true specialists; here, too, people say that a farm will not prosper unless there is a Pallar to till it; they are hard-working, determined and stalwart. Owing to these qualities and to a certain militancy, Pallars have gradually broken into modern sectors of economic life and are now engaged in more lucrative and prestigious professions, as we shall see later. They have turned away from agricultural work, and now only Sakkiliyars present themselves for work as *pannaiyal*. But, like Paraiyars, Sakkiliyars are considered to be poor farmers; they are reputed to drink, and to be lazy and incompetent, so that their services are hardly in demand. They themselves recognize that Pallars are more productive and better qualified.

The same shift can be seen in the rice-growing district of Tanjore. In Kumbapettai village, for example, *pannaiyal* workers have dropped from 37 per cent of the agricultural labour force, in 1952, to 9 per cent in 1976; and in the village of Kirippur the figure has gone from 62 per cent to 14 per cent in the same period. 'Non-untouchable' *pannaiyal* used to be called *velaikkarar*; they fulfilled the various functions of untouchable workers. A number of specific tasks were reserved for them: they did garden work, drove ox-carts, supervised other workers or tended the cattle;

33. Ibid., p. 129.
34. Ibid., p. 40.
35. J. Den Ouden, *De Onaanraakbarren van Konkunad* (1977), p. 54.
36. Ibid., p. 86. See also B. Beck, *Peasant Society in Konku: A Study of Right and Left Subcastes in South India* (Vancouver: University of British Columbia Press, 1976), p. 284; and K. Gough, *Rural Change in Southeast India*, pp. 298 and 431.

their wives worked as servants in the masters' houses. At the same time, Untouchables, both men and women, did the bulk of the field work for a lower salary than the *velaikkarar*. Over the last few years, *pannaiyal* working conditions have improved slightly; Gough notes that it is now unusual for a master to beat one of his workers, whereas in the 1950s such an event was commonplace. Likewise, *pannaiyal* no longer work after dusk and cannot be called in the middle of the night. They are therefore asked to render fewer services. Lastly, the former practice of giving gifts and clothing has tended to disappear. In other words, the relationship has been emptied of its original substance and is gradually merging with the work of the 'regular coolie'.

Agricultural workers complain about the deterioration of their living conditions. These complaints are, of course, one of the *clichés* about the 'good old days'. Nevertheless, most of the authors I have consulted confirm this impression, and stress the increasing impoverishment of agricultural workers over the past few decades. Monetarization of salaries, the end of the patronage relationship and the greater supply of labour have all combined to make agricultural workers' lives more precarious. I also wonder whether anthropologists, too, have not had a tendency to stress the harmonious social relations of the past; even if agricultural workers earn less today - something that I am not at all sure of - it must be admitted that they have at the same time won more freedom, leisure time and dignity. This transformation has not been in vain, nor even futile, for in addition to having regained their status as humans, it also means that they now have the possibility of seeking new sources of income, which they have not failed to do, as we shall see.

Regular workers: farm workers, in certain cases, therefore enjoy a relative degree of freedom. And it has increased over the last few decades as the traditional forms of 'patronage' and 'clientelism' have waned. Nevertheless, in rural areas, one continues to find many agricultural workers still bound by the traditional ties to local peasants. The Chamars of Senapur, studied by Cohn in the early 1950s, seem to fit into this category, and we shall pause here briefly to describe their life in this village of Uttar Pradesh.

Thakurs are the dominant caste of Senapur in the sense that they consider themselves the owners of the land; moreover, no one disputes this claim, and all the castes that work the land pay rent, as tenant farmers (*praja*), to the Thakurs; if they were to fail to pay their rent, they could be evicted from their land. The Thakur is often addressed as 'grandfather', and he himself calls his tenant farmers 'my children'. He is responsible for their well-being, and they side with him in conflicts. Each Thakur family receives the services of a number of specialists, known as *parjuniya*: among them we find, for instance, water-carriers (Kahars), barbers (Nais), priests (Brahmins), blacksmiths (Lohars), washermen (Dhobis) and agricultural workers, who are also servants (Chamars). The relationship between *jajman* and *parjuniya* is a hereditary one, and a Thakur cannot change it arbitrarily. Most of the Senapur agricultural workers are Chamars. Because of the ritual prohibition forbidding Thakurs and Brahmins to till the land, Chamars perform this task. Each field they till gives them the right to a portion of the harvest, and so the Chamars share the fields among themselves; when the field has been ploughed, their wives sow the seed. Chamars do all the agricultural jobs, from sowing to threshing. By contrast, none of the Senapur Chamars works as a tanner, the traditional caste occupation. When a Thakur travels, it is a Chamar who must carry his baggage. In short, a Chamar has very little free time. When he has finished working in his master's fields, he must cultivate his own plot of land, for his wages do not suffice to make ends meet.

A Chamar never stops working, not even on holidays. Every day he is up before dawn, while the village is still asleep. He eats breakfast only if there is something left from the previous day, which is not often. By contrast, he must see to it that his master's animals are fed; then he goes into the fields, where he will work all morning. In the afternoon, he can look after his own land and, in the dry season, he will look for coolie work, building roads, for instance. The women work as hard as the men, without counting the household chores, which they must do as well. Chamars do not grow enough to produce their own seed, so they are forced to buy it from Thakurs, which puts them in debt to the latter. So paradoxically, those who have the fewest debts are also the poorest. Generally speaking, there is not enough agricultural work in the village for the Chamars to earn their living, and so they are obliged to seek part-time jobs outside. On the other hand, the new distribution of land that resulted from the government's agrarian reform had little effect on them, since only three became landowners.[37]

The position of Untouchables within traditional village economy has been the object of much debate in the context of the discussion of what is known as the '*jajmani* system'. The question was whether the '*jajmani* system' was basically integrative or exploitative. The radical diversity of the interpretations stemmed from the use of a single term to designate very different relationships.

Strictly speaking, the term *jajmani* applies to the ritualized relationships of economic life; these are most fully expressed in the relations between landowners and craftsmen. But as Fuller has so well put it, the traditional relations included under the term *jajmani* do not cover all of the socio-economic relations found in a village.[38] Fuller stresses, for example, that the (partial) monetarization of the economy largely predated British colonial rule, and Gough similarly recalls that village economy used to be based on the exchange of different types of services.[39] Likewise, some castes are not a part of the traditional exchange network,[40] and those that are often do not put in the whole of their production. In Malwa, for instance, only some of the vessels made by the potters are given to the *asami* (or *jajman*); the rest are sold.[41] The Mang Untouchables of Maharashtra provide the villagers with different types of rope; but the long, thick kind used in wells does not fall within the framework of the traditional relations known there as *balutedar*.[42] In Tirunelveli, a distinction must be made

37. For the above, B. Cohn, 'The Chamars of Senapur: A Study of the Changing Status of a Depressed Caste'. (Doctoral dissertation, Cornell University, 1954).

38. C. Fuller, 'Misconceiving the Grain Heap: A Critique of the Concept of the Indian Jajmani System', in J. Parry and M. Bloch (eds), *Money and the Morality of Exchange* (Cambridge: Cambridge University Press, 1989), p. 40.

39. K. Gough, 'Caste in a Tanjore Village', in E. Leach (ed.), *Aspects of Caste in South India, Ceylon and North-west Pakistan* (Cambridge: Cambridge University Press, 1960, pp. 11-60), p. 85.

40. J. Benson, 'A South Indian Jajmani System'. *Ethnology,* 15 (1976), p. 242.

41. D. Miller, 'Exchange and Alienation in the Jajmani System'. *Journal of Anthropological Research,* 42 (1986), p. 539.

42. H. Orenstein, 'Exploitation of Function in the Interpretation of Jajmani'. *Southwestern Journal of Anthropology,* 18 (1962), p. 304.

between work, in the Western sense of the term, which Tamils place under the heading of *velai*, and hereditary obligations, which they call *tozhil*. Agricultural work is essentially *velai* and not *tozhil*. At harvest time, an agricultural worker receives two different forms of payment: the *sampalam*, for the agricultural work, and the *sastiram*, in exchange for the traditional services he provides.[43]

If the very basis of *jajmani* relations indeed worked to integrate the different village castes into a system of reciprocity, as Wiser showed over a half century ago,[44] the fact remains that purely economic relations and relations of servitude existed side by side with the exchange system, and resulted in a profound social inequality between the principal elements of society. This intertwining of basically different socio-economic relations is perhaps what makes the originality of the traditional Indian economy, which was capable of integrating while exploiting; from the Untouchables' point of view, we again see the ambiguity of their position: at once rejected and indispensable, sometimes they were 'clients' and at other times servants.

Whatever their rights and prerogatives, they were never sure of more than a precarious income, normally insufficient to ensure their family a decent living; they were therefore forced to work outside agriculture, to resort to begging or, often, to go hungry and to live in filthy, uncomfortable quarters and in ignorance. It is rather remarkable that the discussion of the *jajmani* system almost never attempts to assess the relative well-being of the various social classes. The different proportions of the harvest received on the threshing floor tell us nothing about the global income of a category of workers, since certain specialists (for instance barbers or blacksmiths) serve many more *jajman* than others, in particular agricultural workers. But it is certain that the system ultimately operated in such a way that it provided the castes of craftsmen, such as carpenters or blacksmiths, with a much more decent income than it did agricultural workers. Whatever 'reciprocity' it may have ensured, then, the system also perpetuated social inequalities.

With the evanescence of traditional social relations, agricultural workers in general, and Untouchables in particular, have lost some of their advantages, their income and their job security. Epstein noted that, between 1954 and 1970, the peasants of Dalena village (Karnataka) ended the traditional working relations, thus depriving agricultural workers of a guaranteed minimum livelihood.[45] Not only were the Adi-Karnataka (the local untouchable caste) not allowed the benefit of the newly expanded irrigation system; they also saw their lives become more precarious.[46] Epstein suggests that the increased supply of labour resulted in a decreased number of work-days per individual; some workers, she writes, work no more than ten days a month, and the growing productivity of agriculture has therefore increased social inequalities by being of benefit only to the landowners.

The conclusions of this comparison between two Karnataka village economies in the 1950s and the 1970s are confirmed by a similar study of two villages in Tanjore

43. A. Good, 'The Actor and the Act. Categories of Prestation in South India'. *Man (NS)*, 17 (1982), pp. 23-41, p. 28.

44. W. Wiser, *The Hindu Jajmani System;* see also H. Gould, 'A Jajmani System of North India: Its Structure, Magnitude and Meaning'. *Ethnology,* 3 (1964), pp. 12-41.

45. S. Epstein, *South India Yesterday, Today and Tomorrow,* p. 46.

46. Ibid., pp. 82 and 163.

district (Tamil Nadu) carried out by another well-known anthropologist, Kathleen Gough. Here too, traditional relations between masters and agricultural workers have grown weaker and gradually given way to purely economic relations; at the same time, agricultural workers have seen their job security disappear, and have turned to day-labour. In Kumbapettai village, for example, day-labourers represented 48 per cent of the agricultural labour force in 1952, and 79 per cent in 1976. At the same time, the number of *pannaiyal* and 'contractual workers' shrank over the years until it represented only a small percentage of the agricultural labour force at the end of the 1970s:

"The sharp rise in day-labour is of course the consequence of the oversupply of workers. This results from the population growth, from the eviction of tenant farmers and, to a certain extent, from the decline of certain trades such as pottery or toddy tapping. The rise in day-labour, in turn, has meant a rise in worker exploitation, in Marx's sense of the term. In 1952, when the majority of workers were *pannaiyal* or regular coolies, the master looked after their needs, their food and family lodging all year long, whether they were actually working or not. In 1976, this was no longer true for 79 per cent of the workers who were employed on a day-to-day basis as coolies. They were paid only for the days worked and had to forage, look for odd jobs in other villages, steal or go hungry, in the slack season."[47]

While *pannaiyal* worked day and night for up to 300 days a year, day-labourers had work for only a limited number of days. Gough calculates that, in Kirippur village, for example, the younger men worked between 130 and 160 days a year, while the oldest often could not find more than 120 days of work.[48] Their income fell accordingly. Gough stresses the desolation reigning in the villages at the end of the 1970s; with the climate of 'cheerfulness, hospitality and reciprocity' she contrasts the 'terrible poverty' that plagued 'at least half of the population' in 1976; a stroll through the village became a painful experience, full of sadness at the sight of people living in such 'bitter distress'.[49]

Gough's impression of desolation and the picture she paints of the deterioration in living conditions may seem rather bleak, and perhaps slightly 'impressionistic'. One might even be tempted to think it dictated by the author's Marxist presuppositions, according to which the deterioration of living conditions under the capitalist system is inevitable. And yet we have seen that this interpretation is shared by other authors, who stress that the more vulnerable portions of the population have not benefited from the general improvement in living standards. This is of course true for the agricultural workers, whose situation has probably even deteriorated somewhat. The same conclusions can be found for example in Wadley and Derr's study of Karimpur, a village in Uttar Pradesh, well known to anthropologists since the 1920s, when a couple of American missionaries carried out a study that gave rise to several important works:[50]

"There is no doubt that the standard of living in Karimpur is better now than in 1925

47. J. Den Ouden, *De Onaanraakbarren van Konkunad* (1977), p. 302.

48. K. Gough, *Rural Change in Southeast India,* p. 434.

49. Ibid., p. 440.

50. For example, W. Wiser and C. Wiser, *Behind Mud Walls:* 1930-1960. Berkeley, CA: University of California Press, 1969).

and also better than in 1968. If we look at health care or mortality rates, quality of housing, source of water, quality of clothing, educational levels, or consumer goods (watches, radios, cycles, etc.), the village has prospered. Yet there are many whose families have seen none of this increased prosperity. Their standard of living is comparable to that of their grandfathers in the 1920s, and some may even be hungrier."[51]

Yet the village studies we have concentrated on until now mask some essential aspects of reality and, more particularly, certain social processes;[52] in effect, while agricultural workers are still an underprivileged group, their number has remained relatively stable, and in the last few decades there has been a clear shift towards new occupations. A substantial portion of the agricultural labour force has turned to other sectors of economic life, leaving agriculture altogether. This is particularly the case of the Harijans, whose occupations are today far more diversified than in the past. Furthermore, over the same period, the agricultural lands have apparently not become massively concentrated in a few hands. On the contrary, small landowners continue to proliferate. According to Harriss, small farmers have not undergone a true process of proletarization,[53] nor is it certain that agricultural workers have seen their wages fall in real terms since independence. Comparing today's monetary income with former income in kind remains an extremely delicate if not perilous undertaking. Any assessment of recent socio-economic changes must take into account the diversification of economic activities and the overall improvement in living and working conditions (reduction of working hours, etc.). In the villages I studied, many Harijans had left agricultural work and held all kinds of jobs, as we shall see.[54]

Day-labourers: those who have stayed on in agriculture find themselves in an unenviable situation, having lost their traditional advantages, in particular the certainty of finding work every day. We now know that this century has seen the gradual erosion of the 'patron - client' relationship, and that, little by little, agricultural workers have become day-labourers, paid primarily in cash and showing very little loyalty to any one master. It is to this category of agricultural workers, by far the most widespread today, that we shall now turn.

Many agricultural workers are no longer tied to a single master, but are paid by the day; they have no social obligations to their employers, and constitute a veritable rural proletariat whose only possession is their labour. The coolie's salary is usually paid in cash. It varies with the region, and with the gender as well, since women invariably earn less than men; generally speaking, one can calculate that women's salaries are no more than 50 or 60 per cent of those of men. This difference seems to be motivated

51. S. Wadley and B. Derr, 'Karimpur 1925-1984: Understanding Rural India through Restudies', in P. Bardhan (ed.), *Conversations between Economists and Anthropologists: Methodological Issues in Measuring Economic Change in Rural India* (Oxford: Oxford University Press, 1989), p. 113.

52. J. Breman, 'Extension of Scale in Fieldwork: From Village to Region in Southern Gujarat', in P. Bardhan (ed.), *Conversations between Economists and Anthropologists: Methodological Issues in Measuring Economic Change in Rural India* (Oxford: Oxford University Press, 1989), p. 128.

53. J. Harriss, 'Knowing about Rural Economic Change: Problems Arising from a Comparison of the Results of "Macro" and "Micro" Research in Tamil Nadu', in P. Bardhan (ed.), *Conversations between Economists and Anthropologists: Methodological Issues in Measuring Economic Change in Rural India* (Oxford: Oxford University Press, 1989), p. 159.

54. See also R. Deliège, 'Job Mobility among the Brickmakers of South India'. *Man in India,* 69 (1989).

more by social reasons than by purely economic reckoning, for women have a fairly high rate of productivity.

According to Gough, demographic pressure and the introduction of new technologies like the electric irrigation pump have led to a problem of under-employment among agricultural workers, who are no longer able to find work every day, and therefore suffer an appreciable drop in income. The alleged deterioration in their standard of living invites some scepticism, however, for it has always been very low; and furthermore, any attempts to quantify the phenomenon invariably encounter a number of obstacles. However, it is nonetheless true that agricultural workers lead very precarious lives and, in many regions, the agricultural sector is no longer capable of absorbing the bulk of local labour. In the dry regions particularly, agricultural work is only one activity among others, and workers have switched to other sectors, often construction-related, which sometimes ensure the better part of their income. These will be discussed later. For the moment, let us return to Valghira Manickam village, which is itself located in an arid region very different from the well-irrigated rice fields of Tanjore that retained Gough's attention.

In Valghira Manickam, agriculture has become a relatively secondary activity, limited to the months of September to January. The rest of the year, most of the villagers work manufacturing bricks. During the rainy season, which is also the farming season, this activity is no longer possible, because the rains would ruin the bricks before they were baked. So the villagers turn to fieldwork. Some till their own plot of land or one they rent from a Kallar in the next village. But the majority have no land, and therefore work for the local farmers. This is the hardest time of year for the villagers, because the arid land of Ramnad does not produce enough to maintain a class of workers or even to guarantee them a decent income for the whole season. Monetary income is scarce during this period, and the villagers are not able to feed their families.

The difficulties one encounters in evaluating the living standard of agricultural workers are not without cause. For example, the number of working days varies considerably, and salaries are far from uniform. This is why I followed the activities of four couples of agricultural workers every day for the entire month of September 1981, although I did not tell them that they were being observed. The number of working days varied from four (a pregnant woman) to twenty-three. The men worked more days than the women, 19.7 on average as compared to 11.5. The average amount earned per couple for the month was 209 rupees, in other words less than 105 rupees per person. As each couple had several young children, it is evident that the income of these families was precarious indeed, no doubt well below the poverty line so assiduously determined by economists. The price of rice at the time was around three rupees per kilo. So the average salary enabled a family to buy rice and no doubt a few vegetables now and then, since the most common and cheapest vegetable, eggplant, cost around one rupee per kilo.

In addition to these basic needs, there are obviously other expenses that must be met, such as clothes, house repairs, medical bills, and so on. Moreover, Paraiyars are not necessarily the most rational economic agents: they have in common with the rest of the Indian population a taste for the cinema, the men like a glass of tea, and the children clamour for a treat when the ice-cream vendor comes down the street. To make matters worse, when the men are out of work, they tend to play cards with the money that is in such short supply; and finally, many men drink.

Lack of money does not necessarily lessen the need to dream and escape, although the women show more self-discipline on this point: Gough calculates that women spend 99 per cent of their income on the family, while for men, the proportion falls to 77 per cent. These figures no doubt reflect the reality described above. When they have a little money, Paraiyars often spend it in an irrational way; this is the case of several men who had obtained a loan of 200 rupees to buy a cow: they spent several days scouring the countryside for the 'right' cow, and spent a good deal of money in the process, so that, in the end, all they could afford was a mediocre milker. But the month of September is relatively favourable compared with the period from October to December, which confronts Paraiyars with even more serious problems.

The case of this small village in Tamil Nadu no doubt provides us with a fairly good idea of conditions elsewhere, and this brief analysis of the Paraiyar budget gives us a glimpse of its basically adverse nature. Their income is not enough to make ends meet; even if the money were managed more rationally, there would still be a chronic deficit. Paraiyars therefore are always short of money, and that is why they accept the advances on salary offered them by the owners of the brickworks in Madras. These advances carry them through the rainy season, after which they migrate to Madras, where they work off their debt in the factories.

Brick-making and Other Activities

When they cannot make a living from agricultural work and they have neither a skill nor capital, Untouchables try various jobs, originally to make up the shortfall, but that today tend to become their main activity. This is the case of brick-making in Valghira Manickam; thanks to this occupation, Untouchables manage to meet their basic needs for the better part of the year. Elsewhere, salt-making or road-construction fulfil a similar function. Harijans are the major source of labour in the salt marshes. But there, too, the work is seasonal. According to Djurfeldt and Lindberg, salt-making is quite a profitable undertaking from which the workers do not benefit, since, at the time of the study, they earned only two rupees a day,[55] hardly enough to live on.

Road-construction can be more profitable for the worker. Of course in many cases he is only paid as a day-labourer, but sometimes he can obtain a contract, in other words he receives a certain amount for doing a specific job. His profits will depend on the number of workers he hires or the time it takes to do the work. The Paraiyars of Valghira Manickam found this formula particularly attractive because it procured them a little money.

Brick-making, too, has its advantages, since it is piece-work, that is, the worker is paid for the number of bricks he makes. So exceptionally hard workers can expect to earn more than the average, and that is what makes this such a popular job among the

55. G. Djurfeldt and S. Lindberg, *Behind Poverty: The Social Formation in a Tamil Village* (London: Curzon Press, 1975), p. 185.

Valghira Manickam villagers. Of course they never make a fortune, or even an appreciable income; but they always earn more than they would doing agricultural work. With a little capital, a man can even go to work for himself and set up his own brick-making business, which will add a little more to the family's well-being. Brick-making is done in two's, often by a husband-and-wife team. After having mixed the earth and water, they can proceed to making the bricks proper; for this they use a form. The bricks are then laid out on the ground to dry and then baked in the large rudimentary ovens that are so much a part of the Indian landscape. The bricks will not be tallied until they are baked; if a downpour ruins the bricks beforehand, the worker must take the loss. In 1981, workers received 14 rupees per thousand bricks. A couple can produce up to two thousand bricks a day, but this is a maximum rarely achieved; and workers cannot make bricks every day: they must prepare the clay, build the oven, and so forth. So, although brick-making remains relatively more lucrative than agricultural work, it still does not allow a radically different lifestyle.

Some workers manage to set up their own brick production, but for this they need capital; the baking is the most costly factor, because significant quantities of wood must be bought. Usually an oven can accommodate between 25,000 and 50,000 bricks. The sale price depends on the season: in the rainy season it is much higher, because supply is scarce; during the dry season, the price remains fairly low, but still ensures the owner a good income, part of which must be reinvested in the next lot. Small businessmen or self-employed entrepreneurs thus tend to spring up among the untouchable community and try to dig themselves out of the hole they have been living in for centuries. It is the start-up capital that is most often lacking; nevertheless, today many Untouchables have managed to buy a pair of oxen and a cart. With these they can transport goods, which enables them to live a little more comfortably. The same is true for bricklayers, who earn substantially more than coolies (15 rupees a day in 1981) because of the greater demand for their work. The higher standard of living enjoyed by bricklayers and carters can be seen in the fact that their wives often no longer work outside the home. As soon as the family has a decent income, by local standards, the wife often stops working.

New Occupations

The above few lines are ample indication that the image of the Untouchable passively awaiting a better life has seen its day. For more than a century now, throughout India and with varying degrees of success, Untouchables have been striving to improve their lot and to find more dignified and above all better-paying jobs. If they had more resources and capital, these efforts would no doubt be more numerous and better rewarded.

There is one sector, however, where Untouchables have been able to put their traditional skills to good use and improve their condition. As we have said, in addition to providing agricultural labour, they are the ones who keep the village clean: sweeping, collecting excrement and removing dead animals and other refuse. These jobs were so degrading that no other Indian would have accepted them. But the disgust they inspired turned out to be a windfall for the Untouchables, as it virtually guaranteed them a monopoly on certain kinds of work in the modern world, and thereby access to relatively enviable salaried jobs.

Clearly it was the changes that came with colonization that gave Untouchables access to modern professions and enabled them to escape the wretched conditions in which they had been maintained. At the same time, the British and the Christian missionaries introduced India to an egalitarian ideology, to which Untouchables did not hesitate to refer in support of their claim to a higher status in society. Many social movements grew up, as a consequence, and these will receive special attention in the following chapters. For the moment, however, we can turn to the professional mobility and diversification of occupations that have marked the lives of Untouchables for over a century.

Servants and Soldiers

British rule in India, Marx wrote, destroyed the small 'semi-barbarian communities' and produced the 'only social revolution ever to have occurred in Asia …'.[56] While it seems difficult to speak of a 'social revolution', colonial rule did enable the lower castes to rise, at least in part, above their former condition. Untouchables were not slow to take up new occupations and professions and, soon, they had their own elite. Many new possibilities were available; we shall review only a few of the principal opportunities.

Submission, loyalty and endurance were among the qualities that made Untouchables attractive to the European families living in India, though they cannot have had much competition from the other castes, for no one was eager to become a servant. But the Untouchables saw this as a means to escape their frightful condition, and a certain number seized upon this windfall. Many Jaisvaras, a Chamar subcaste, thus became servants, known as 'grooms'.[57] Traditionally, many Untouchables were village watchmen, which allowed them to find jobs as guards or policemen.[58] This was particularly true of the Mahars, many of whom went to work for the British. Numerous subordinate positions in the police force were thus quickly filled by Untouchables.[59] Finally, many emigrated to other countries, like Burma, Malaysia and Sri Lanka (then Ceylon), where the growing numbers of plantations required a massive supply of labour. In the Punjab, Chamars formed the principal emigrant community,[60] after Jats. None of their new jobs made Untouchables truly wealthy, but they did enable them to

56. K. Marx and F. Engels, *Textes sur le colonialisme* (Moscow: Éditions en langues étrangères, n.d.), p. 41.

57. B. Cohn, 'The Chamars of Senapur', p. 78.

58. R. Miller, '"They Will Not Die Hindus"; the Buddhist Conversion of Mahar Ex-Untouchables'. *Asian Survey,* 3 (1967), p. 639.

59. F.Bailey, *Caste and the Economic Frontier* (Manchester: Manchester University Press, 1957), p. 149.

60. W. McLeod, *The Sikhs: History, Religion and Society* (New York: Columbia University Press, 1989), p. 104.

sever their ties with the village; some were able to set aside a little money to send their children to school, thus sowing the seeds of a social elite. For instance, in one Gujarati village studied by Van der Veen, the children of the servants of Parsi and European families went to school in Bombay, where they subsequently found good jobs.[61]

But the army was the best source of social promotion, because it rapidly offered Untouchables the possibility of a relatively well-paid job, sometimes complete with housing, and usually the obligation to learn to read and write. It is said that Mahars were already used by the Marathas and the Reshwas in defending their forts; but it was the British army that recruited them systematically.[62] Military jobs became very popular among certain large untouchable castes, who signed up en masse; at one point, it is estimated that one-sixth of the Bombay army was composed of Mahars![63] Chamars began enlisting at the beginning of the nineteenth century; but after the 1857 uprising they were replaced by Mazbhis, Sikh Untouchables, who were recruited in massive quantities. As the upper castes opposed their integration into the army as such, the Mazbhis were formed into separate companies. Stimulated by the Sikh model, they had a strong tradition of violence and aggressiveness. The British had quickly understood that the Untouchables could act as a counterweight to the domination of the high castes within the army, and so the Mazbhis, grouped into the 'First Pioneer Sikh Regiment', came to play an important role in putting down the uprising. When it was over, two more regiments were created.

These valiant, highly disciplined untouchable units enjoyed a good reputation among senior officers. But this distinctly favourable sentiment was not strong enough to counteract the prevailing racial theories of the time, which led the British to prefer to recruit 'martial races': Lord Roberts, commander-in-chief of the Indian army from 1885 to 1893, judged, for example, that by birth and by *varna* Untouchables were fundamentally 'unmilitary': 'What good would a battalion of dhobi be against the formidable Pathans?', he wrote, not without a suggestion of contempt.[64] In times of major conflict, though, this turned out to be a disastrous policy, and the army was forced to recruit massively among Untouchables; this was the case in both world wars. In 1914, the '111th Mahar' was created. And during the Second World War, 10,000 Mahars and 33,000 Mazbhis were enlisted in combat units. The 'Chamar Regiment', for its part, served in Assam and Burma. And many other untouchable castes were recruited as well.[65]

Within the army, Untouchables held the lowest jobs, and there were almost no officers in their ranks. They preferred to be grouped into Untouchable units rather than to mix with the other castes and thus be made to feel inferior. Only a few were members of the elite corps or the specialized branches, such as the air force. But, as

61. Cited by M. Holmström, *Industry and Inequality: The Social Anthropology of Indian Labour* (Cambridge: Cambridge University Press, 1984), p. 200.

62. E. Zelliot, 'Learning the Use of Political Means. The Mahars of Maharashtra', in R. Kothari (ed.), *Caste in Indian Politics* (Poonz: Orient Longman, 1970, pp. 29-69), p. 32.

63. S. Patwardhan, *Change among India's Harijans: Maharashtra - A Case Study* (New Delhi: Orient Longman, 1973), p. 21.

64. S. Cohen, 'The Untouchable Soldier: Caste, Politics and the Indian Army'. *Journal of Asian Studies,* 29 (1969), p. 457.

65. Ibid., p. 458.

we have just seen, what matters here is that tens of thousands of Untouchables were able, thanks to the armed forces, to achieve an honourable rank in society, to learn to read and write, and to give their children some schooling. It was into such a context, into a Mahar family of soldiers, that the great untouchable leader, Ambedkar, was born. More generally, in his study of the Bangalore factories, Holmström reports that 45 per cent of the workers came from the Scheduled Castes and had a father who had been in the police force or in the army; and he concludes: 'This confirmed my strong impression, from earlier work, that these have been the chief paths of upward mobility for Harijans in the past, and that the present generation of Harijans able to take advantage of government educational concessions and job reservation come from an army or police background.'[66]

Sweepers and Refuse-collectors

The Untouchables' traditional function, namely evacuating wastes, was to give them a near monopoly on certain salaried jobs. It was for instance, unthinkable for any other caste to take work as sweepers or scavengers, so that tens of thousands of Untouchables thus had a chance to find salaried work in what is commonly called the 'organized sector' of the economy, in other words, jobs that provided social protection. In the village of Kapileswar, not far from Bubaneshwar, the Hadis, a caste of sweepers, are traditionally the lowest and the most despised; but as the capital has expanded, members of this caste have been engaged in massive numbers as government employees, that is, as sweepers, with a monthly salary, social benefits and, of course, job security. This is, Freeman writes, a remarkable case of upward socio-economic mobility, whereas other higher castes have gained very little from modern society.[67]

In Valghira Manickam, many Paraiyars also work in the nearby town of Devakottai as municipal sweepers. They are far better off than coolies in general. They have a relatively high, steady salary, interest-free loans, retirement benefits, social protection, and so forth. Their relative well-being is a source of envy, and their job is almost hereditary: when one of these workers dies, a member of his family is hired in his place. In saying that they are well off, I do not mean that they earn fabulous sums, far from it; they remain poor, and still experience material hardship; but their lot is infinitely preferable to that of the coolies, who indeed regard them as privileged. Their lifestyle is not radically different from that of other workers; but at least they manage to eat every day and to clothe themselves decently. Often, too, they are able to ensure that their children have a minimum amount of schooling and to harbour a few ambitions for them. It is interesting to note that the strong ritual impurity traditionally attaching to the various occupations having to do with waste removal does not really apply to municipal sweepers. Their economic status seems to have completely

66. M. Holmström, *South Indian Factory Workers: Their Life and Their World* (Cambridge: Cambridge University Press, 1976), p. 34.

67. J. Freeman, *Scarcity and Opportunity in an Indian Village* (Menlo Park, CA: Cummings, 1977), pp. 100 and 110.

obliterated the disgrace formerly associated with this work, and in Valghira Manickam the municipal sweepers are therefore rather proud of their job.

Similarly, in Benares, great numbers of Mehtars, both men and women, are employed by the city. It was among this population that Searle-Chatterjee conducted her field study, which contains a variety of examples.[68] Her analysis largely confirms what I have just said. Benares sweepers consider their work to be unpleasant and dirty, but they are unconcerned about the ritual pollution it is supposed to engender. Moreover, they associate their occupation with a certain difficulty, of which they are proud.[69] They are fond of alcohol, meat and sex, and place a great deal of importance on their honour, which they are prompt to defend with violence and passion. They are physically sturdy, and can be arrogant at times. When their work takes them into the courtyard of a high-caste house, they often behave in a proud, almost insolent manner.[70] In the narrow streets of the city, they warn of their approach so that no one will be defiled, and they avoid the riverbanks early in the morning when pilgrims are bathing; for similar reasons, they carry their broom over their shoulder; but otherwise they show little sign of servility.

"In broad streets, however, sweepers walk boldly, and confidently, even contemptuously, knowing how people fear their touch. Similarly, in their dealings with municipal officials at the Health Office, they are forthright and unabashed. They deal, after all, only with low-level officials, themselves not of much higher castes, and they have the strength of numbers."[71]

Out of a concern for hygiene and dignity, they now refuse to carry baskets of refuse on their heads, and they know that any threat of strike action is taken seriously, so great is the fear of an epidemic that might result from any work stoppage. This is why their salaries tend to be relatively high and why, in Kanpur or Delhi, sweepers and scavengers have obtained important job benefits. They behave with a certain degree of self-confidence, and, for instance, can be seen making fun of high-caste people who venture into their quarter; a few years ago a group of women bloodied a taxi driver for having dared to touch the breasts of a sweeper.

At the time of Searle-Chatterjee's study, the basic salary of a sweeper was 103 rupees a month. In addition to their official duties, municipal sweepers also cleaned the houses of a number of private individuals, which procured them various financial and other advantages. According to Searle-Chatterjee, at the time, a family of sweepers could generate an income comparable to that of a university lecturer.[72] Furthermore, they enjoyed a variety of other benefits, such as two weeks of vacation, interest-free loans, sick leave, low-cost housing, and so forth.[73]

The positive discrimination system, which we shall examine later, has encouraged the recruitment of Untouchables for jobs in the administration, usually in low-level

68. M. Searle-Chatterjee, 'The Polluted Identity of Work: A Study of Benares Sweepers', in S. Wallman (ed.), *The Anthropology of Work* (London: Academic Books, 1979); and *Reversible Sex Roles: The Special Case of Benares Sweepers* (Oxford: Pergamon Press, 1981).

69. M. Searle-Chatterjee, 'The Polluted Identity of Work', p. 284.

70. Ibid., p. 278.

71. Ibid., p. 276.

72. Ibid., p. 276; see also *Reversible Sex Roles,* p. 38, for examples of family budgets.

73. M. Searle-Chatterjee, 'The Polluted Identity of Work', p. 274.

posts. In effect, for the most part they have filled the least prestigious occupations. Between 1953 and 1975, the percentage of Untouchables in grade-1 jobs (the highest level), went from 0.35 per cent to 3.4 per cent. Over the same period, the percentage of grade-4 jobs occupied by Untouchables rose from 4.5 per cent to 10.7 per cent.[74] It could obviously be said that, overall, social inequalities are reproduced within the administration, with Untouchables under-represented at the highest levels of the hierarchy. But this is a rather simplistic view of reality. How could one even imagine that such a disadvantaged group could compete with the upper castes in highly skilled areas from which they have been excluded for thousands of years? From the standpoint of village Untouchables, however, a job as a sweeper represents an appreciable improvement in socio-economic status.

Doctors and Workers

If official government jobs represented a certain advancement for Untouchables, they have not stopped there, and some have even gone on to achieve much more enviable positions in society. In relative terms, these represent a very small proportion of the untouchable population; but even so, their number is far from negligible, and this elite can play an important role within the community. We are talking about those who have managed to obtain highly visible jobs, primarily in the organized sector of the economy or in prestigious professions like medicine. These elites are often ashamed of their origins, and do not always play a leadership role within their community; but even in this case their importance should not be under-rated, for they provide a role model: they are proof that it is possible for Untouchables to improve their lot, to fill important occupations and to perform them as well as anyone. Psychologically speaking, the effect of this is invaluable: in Valghira Manickam, people liked to cite the case of the Pallar doctors in Devakottai; this gave them a sense of pride, even if they themselves were Paraiyars and claimed not to associate with Pallars.

Although it may seem surprising at first glance, it appeared to me that factory workers were in a way the first rung of this elite. Such work in itself is not highly prestigious; but it is nevertheless much sought after, and belongs to what Holmström calls 'the citadel'. The image of factory work, he comments,[75] is not one of exhausting labour in 'satanic mills', but one of educated workers who have acquired new skills in modern factories. Furthermore, while factory work demands, at the outset, a solid secondary education, this is not an exorbitant requirement, and a factory job is therefore an immediately accessible goal for many educated Untouchables in the villages. It is therefore a true elite job. Moreover, many people are ready to make considerable sacrifices in order to get one of these jobs: they pay large bribes, sometimes in vain; often, too, they agree to work for years on end for two or three rupees a day (less than a coolie) in the hope of eventually being officially taken on. I

74. M. Galanter, *Competing Equalities: Law and the Backward Classes in India* (Berkeley, CA: University of California Press, 1984), p. 88.

75. M. Holström, *Industry and Inequality,* p. 63.

met many young men who had spent several years working, virtually without pay, in factories where they were never hired. This is a deliberate policy on the part of employers, in order to avoid paying payroll taxes, and it is thought that only 50 per cent of the people working in industry have fully fledged worker status.[76]

If one regards factory work as a highly desirable goal, a citadel 'into which everyone outside is trying to get in',[77] it must be said that the Untouchables' efforts have been crowned with success, since they represent 15 per cent of all factory workers in Bangalore, the same proportion as in the general Indian population,[78] whereas, according to Holmström, at the start of industrialization there was a tendency to exclude them from factories.[79] Remarkably, in the city of Kanpur, Kori Untouchables are the principal caste among factory workers, just ahead of Brahmins, though all the upper castes are represented there as well.[80] In terms of values and lifestyle, the Indian working class closely resembles the middle class; we are far from Dickens here. Factory workers live in brick houses with electricity; they have a radio, a few chairs, a gas cooking ring; their children go to school and aspire to an even better life. Yet this relative gentrification does not mean that there has been any blurring of caste barriers nor that Untouchable workers have totally merged with the other castes.

In the city of Kanpur, Kori Untouchables work massively in local industry. It seems that the social standing of workers here is somewhat different from that of Bangalore workers, for Kanpur underwent its industrial development much earlier. Koris have been employed as factory workers for several generations, and, as a consequence, are less conscious of their privileges than village agricultural workers, with whom they no longer have much contact. This is also no doubt why they have a tradition of struggle within the Communist Party, whereas, Holmström tells us, Bangalore workers are terrified at the thought of losing their jobs.[81] Unlike Holmström and Heuzé, Molund therefore maintains that factory workers are radically different from middle-class Indians.[82] To be sure, they earn as much and often more than white-collar workers; but their lifestyle is very different.[83] Yet the emergence of a working-class identity is hampered by the caste divisions that subsist among the workers: Kanpur Koris regard the other castes as *parjat*, 'those from the other side', 'outsiders'.[84] The lower castes are still kept at a distance, and Koris refuse to eat in public with Jatavs, another untouchable caste, even though their attitude towards the latter has changed in recent times.[85] Bhangis (sweepers), on the other hand, are still the object of ritual aversion. One can clearly see here the limits to the development of a class consciousness; Koris themselves are still driven out of the tea-shops, or their tea is served them in

76. Ibid., p. 149; see also G. Heuzé, 'Unité et pluralité du monde ouvrier indien', in J. Pouchepadass (ed.), *Caste et classe en Asie du Sud* (Paris: Éditions de l'École des Hautes Études en Sciences Sociales, 1982), p. 197 or S. Molund, *First We Are People ... The Koris of Kanpur between Caste and Class* (Stockholm: Stockholm Studies in Social Anthropology, 1988), p. 56.
77. M. Holström, *Industry and Inequality,* p. 6.
78. M. Holmström, *South Indian Factory Workers,* p. 25.
79. M. Holström, *Industry and Inequality,* p. 55.
80. S. Molund, *First We Are People,* p. 15.
81. M. Holström, *Industry and Inequality,* p. 258.
82. S. Molund, *First We Are People,* p. 51.
83. Ibid., pp. 52 and 80.
84. Ibid., p. 112.
85. Ibid., p. 130.

earthenware pots.[86] It does them no good to argue that the fundamental division in society is not that between *barejat* (high castes) and *chote*jat (low castes), but that between *barelog* (rich people) and *chotelog* (poor people); and they too have founded an organization to defend their own caste interests: the Koli-Rajput Welfare Society.

Koris are a good example of Untouchables' upward mobility and the persistence of their identity in the urban context. They also show that untouchability does not vanish when socio-economic status improves. These elements are also found among the Jatavs of Agra, on whom Lynch has written a remarkable study. The Jatav case illustrates the full ambiguity of the upward mobility of Harijans, who remain, relatively speaking, an object of contempt in spite of a certain socio-economic advancement. The Jatavs are a Chamar subcaste who took advantage of the development of Agra's shoe industry to improve their lives. Here again is a case of Untouchables using their traditional skills to find a place in the modern world. Traditionally, Jatavs were cobblers, and when the modern shoe industry began to develop, they encountered little competition from other castes; as a consequence, 85 per cent of the labour force in these industries is Jatav.[87] The city has three big shoe plants, forty-eight small-scale factories, and hundreds of workshops. The jobs in this industry are located in both the organized and the unorganized sectors. The wages for a worker in the organized sector are three times those of workers in the unorganized sector, who, in addition, have to contend with seasonal variations.[88]

Like the sweepers, Jatavs and Chamars have often used their leather-working skills to better their social condition.[89] The shoe industry in the city of Karnal (Haryana) underwent an expansion similar to that in Agra, and this time it was the Chamars who drove the development.[90] The Chamars behind the Ad Dharm movement, which will be discussed in the next chapter, came for the most part from families who owed their prosperity to the hide trade.[91] In Lucknow, Chamars even managed to make tanning an estimable activity and leather-working an altogether respectable occupation.[92] A study of the village of Garupur (Meerut district, Uttar Pradesh) shows that the Jatavs of this agglomeration (16 per cent of the population) underwent a remarkable socio-economic development. Of the active male Jatav population, 58 per cent found work outside the village community, whereas the proportion does not exceed 23 per cent for the other castes.[93] The rate of change picked up rapidly between 1970 and 1980, and the subsequent rise in income enabled the Garupur Jatavs to open their own elementary school in the village and to pay the teachers out of their own funds. The progress made by this caste is not only astounding in itself, but also exceeds that of the other, higher

86. Ibid., p. 142.

87. O. Lynch, *The Politics of Untouchability: Social Mobility and Social Change in a City of India* (New York: Columbia University Press, 1969), p. 35.

88. Ibid., p. 50.

89. G. Sharma, *Legislation and Cases on Untouchability and Scheduled Castes in India* (Delhi: Indian Council of Social Sciences Research, 1986), p. 32.

90. Ibid., p. 40.

91. M. Juergensmeyer, *Religion as Social Vision: The Movement against Untouchability in 20th Century Punjab* (Berkeley, CA: University of California Press, 1982), pp. 17, 36 and 115.

92. R. S. Khare, *The Untouchable As Himself: Ideology, Identity and Pragmatism among the Lucknow Chamars* (Cambridge: Cambridge University Press, 1987), p. 73.

93. E. Lapoint and D. Lapoint, 'Socio-Economic Mobility among Village Harijans'. *The Eastern Anthropologist,* 38 (1985), p. 6.

castes: for instance, in 1980, 27 per cent of the male Jatavs in the village had gone to secondary school, compared with 21 per cent of non-Jatavs.[94]

This could be an exception; as I have said, literacy among Untouchables is considerably lower than among the upper castes;[95] nevertheless, such exceptions were inconceivable thirty or forty years ago, and therefore attest to very real progress on the part of Untouchables. Nor is this an isolated case; at the other end of India, the Pallars have distinguished themselves in the same way: for instance, in Coimbatore district Pallars are over-represented in the textile mills.[96] When it comes to schooling, Paraiyar and Pallar children rank sixth and eighth out of a total of eighteen castes.[97]

The cases of social mobility analysed here show surprising analogies. First of all, they are collective phenomena - in other words, in each case communities as a whole improve their lot; and second, they rest largely on traditional Untouchable functions. This means that the upward social mobility did not come about because of any radical changes in society, nor did it result from protective measures taken by the government. Last of all, these changes are not due to a prior improvement in the educational level of Untouchables. Learning to read and write generally came after the changes, not before. Furthermore, Untouchables had very little help in attaining these posts. At best there was an absence of serious competition; but in some cases they even encountered resistance.

The cases of individual mobility we are now going to see are quite different. These, on the contrary, are often the result of the government's policy of positive discrimination in favour of the most disadvantaged sections of society. Without these measures, there would be few untouchable doctors, engineers, deputies or lawyers. Wherever there are competitive examinations demanding a high level of technical skill, Untouchables have little chance of success. To attain important functions they therefore needed discriminatory measures. Likewise, without parliamentary seats reserved for Untouchables, few people would vote for them. Even such a well-known personality as Jagjivan Ram has never been elected in a general constituency. The economic success stories we have just seen are therefore relative: to be sure, they represent an undeniable improvement over traditional living conditions; but they are far from having resolved all problems confronting Untouchables, and they have not raised them to the socio-cultural level of the upper castes.

Most of those who have attained to socially prestigious positions owe their success to state protection. As we have said, they serve as fundamental role models for the rest of the untouchable population; but it is not certain that their importance for the community goes much beyond this psychological function. Indeed, some observers have underscored the split between this skilled elite and the mass of Untouchables. Sachchidananda, for example, has written, in a study devoted to this group: 'By and large, however, large numbers of the elite both in towns and villages have taken little interest in bettering the lot of their less fortunate brethren. They feel alienated from

94. Ibid., p. 9.

95. See, for example, D. Venkateswarlu, 'Socio-Economic Differences between Harijans, Middle-Castes and Upper-Castes: A Comparative Study of Six Villages in Andhra Pradesh'. *The Eastern Anthropologist,* 39 (1986), p. 214.

96. J. Den Ouden, *De Onaanraakbarren van Konkunad* (1977), p. 58.

97. Ibid., p. 237.

their own base … Their major preoccupation is to satisfy the needs of their immediate family and kin.'[98]

The diagnosis is severe; but it is in no way contrary to reality. Yet it must not be forgotten that, in all parts of India, there are leaders who have launched major social movements. The high-paid jobs obtained by Untouchables tend to be clustered in the civil-service sector, since that is where the privileges are. This results in a loss of esteem from their colleagues, since everyone knows that they did not obtain their jobs on their own merits.[99] And they sometimes have difficulty getting a promotion, because these higher positions are not eligible for protective measures.[100] When they live in the anonymity of a city, many members of untouchable elites prefer to conceal their background and to pass as members of a respectable caste.[101] As we shall see below, the system of political representation operates in such a way that untouchable representatives are rarely among the most militant, because they are designated by the mainstream political parties and elected by a cross-section of voters.

It is hard to evaluate the numerical importance of the modern elites. There is no doubt, however, that they represent no more than a tiny portion of the mass of Untouchables, although in absolute numbers they are far from negligible. It is not uncommon to encounter such elites, even in rural areas. Yet observers have often noted that they are recruited from the most favoured sections of the caste, and therefore do not create a truly dynamic movement.

Change and Continuity

The position of Untouchables within the economic life of India is a combination of change and continuity. There is continuity in that their present-day situation is the direct continuation of past conditions; the general features outlined at the start of this chapter still apply to the majority of the untouchable population. They are still poor, oppressed, and relegated to manual labour, menial tasks and agricultural work. The immense majority still live by their wits, with pitiful salaries and inadequate resources. With respect to the past, some have even lost the security that went with the traditional economy. This is the case with the tens of millions of agricultural workers who are no longer sure of finding a bit of rice in their bowl every day. Independent India has succeeded in preventing large-scale famines; but it has done little more for the millions of men and women toiling away at the bottom of the social ladder.

But we have also seen that, in spite of everything, Untouchables have fought to improve their lives and to attain more enviable positions. It is reassuring to see that some have even proved to be more dynamic than the members of some of the higher castes. Although they are far from only exceptional cases, it must nevertheless be said

98. Sachchidananda, *Social Change in Village India,* p. 24.

99. Ibid., p. 21.

100. See S. Molund, *First We Are People,* p. 148.

101. L. Vincentnathan, 'Harijan Subculture and Self-Esteem Management in a South Indian Community'. (Doctoral dissertation, University of Wisconsin, Madison, 1987), p. 197.

that, for historical reasons, only certain castes have succeeded: for example Chamars, Jatavs, Mahars, Koris, various castes of sweepers and Pallars. Others have not made similar progress: in Tamil Nadu, for example, Sakkiliyars are still extremely disadvantaged. The changes discussed have taken place within a continuity, without any veritable revolution; the most meaningful remain rooted in traditional caste functions: this is the case of the Mahar soldiers, the Mehtar sweepers of Benares, or the Jatav shoemakers of Agra. All these groups have substantially improved their lot thanks to their traditional skills; but often, too, it must be said, because of the lack of competition.

More radical changes, on the other hand, occur only in individual cases. These are not uncommon, but they do not give rise to any radical transformation in the caste. There is even some tendency, among those who enjoy such a rise in the world, to conceal their caste identity or to sever ties with the rest of their group. Nevertheless, these relatively isolated cases prove to Untouchables in general that, under favourable circumstances, they are capable of exercising prestigious professions.

Has the Untouchables' lot improved since Indian independence? We have seen what a thorny question this is, and that the answers diverge considerably. Some emphasize that the lives of agricultural workers have become more precarious owing to demographic pressure and the end of the client system that existed until recently. But more and more Untouchables have left the land and taken up new occupations. Today one sees a great variety of jobs in the villages that I have studied: for example, Paraiyars and Pallars now only marginally earn their livelihood in agriculture. In Valghira Manickam, brick-making has become the primary occupation, while in Alangkulam now only women work exclusively in agriculture. But the improvement in living conditions resulting from this diversification is only relative; the immense majority of Untouchables still live in highly precarious conditions, even when they can be sure of a daily meal.

-7-

Emancipation Movements

While poverty and social exclusion seem to be an integral part of untouchability, we have every reason to think that Untouchables have never accustomed themselves to this oppression. It is, if not probable, then at least quite possible, that in the past some of them rebelled; but we have almost no information on any movements that may have occurred. Whatever possibilities of revolt they had were highly limited. Untouchables were divided, starving, illiterate; they had neither the means nor the weapons nor the power to make their grievances known or to express their anger. No doubt the only thing to do in these circumstances was to make the best of the situation and try to endure it as best they could. It was probably for this reason that their mobilization has been essentially vertical;[1] in other words, they have traditionally espoused the quarrels of their masters.

Although upward social mobility was not totally impossible in precolonial India, it was nevertheless relatively restricted, especially for the very lowest castes. It is even likely that these had scant opportunity to improve their actual caste status to any degree, and that any mobility was primarily an individual matter: a few individuals, for various reasons, sometimes succeeded in improving their lot, but their caste as a whole was never able to raise its status significantly. Furthermore, precolonial India was a relatively closed society; contact with the outside, though not entirely absent, was limited and superficial. Such insularity was hardly conducive to the exchange of ideas or to change.

The arrival of the British brought about a number of modifications. In Chapter 6, we saw that Untouchables have begun pursuing a greater variety of occupations and that some have proved capable of bettering their condition. This diversification has of course been accompanied by ideological changes; Western society and values struck a blow to the local concept of natural law, and over the years, the Untouchables' subjection began to seem less and less a part of the natural order. From this time on, caste movements began to appear, and it is this process that we shall be examining in the present chapter.

1. L. Rudolph and S. Hoeber Rudolph, *The Modernity of Tradition: Political Development in India* (Chicago: University of Chicago Press, 1967), p. 153.

The importance of these social movements is visible in their magnitude, their number and their impact. To be sure, all Untouchables have not been affected to the same degree, and it is even possible that the majority were not even actively involved; yet even those who did not actively participate have been influenced by their ideology, and today there is hardly a single Untouchable who believes that his social position is the result of some permanent pollution; all decry the injustice of their state and aspire to a better life for their children.

At the root of these movements is the Western ideology of equality. Yet it is striking that these values never led to a questioning of the Indian social structure as a whole. That is to say, these movements never carried a truly revolutionary message nor, as we shall see, did they ever challenge the strictly non-egalitarian foundations of Indian society. As a consequence, they almost never had a universal impact, but ultimately always turned into an instrument for the defence of a single caste, without ever opposing the caste system as such. While they were often based on egalitarian ideologies, they proved incapable of putting their ideas into practice, and unfailingly ended up as caste organizations. This ambiguity is particularly well illustrated by the Irava movement. The philosophy of its founder, Sri Narayana Guru, can be summed up as: 'One religion, one God, one caste.' The Iravas never attempted to involve other castes, and quickly rejected all contact with Pulayas, an untouchable caste. Nor was Ambedkar, who will be the subject of the next chapter, able to rally the untouchable castes of Maharashtra to himself. In fact, not a single movement succeeded in attracting a significant proportion of the untouchable population, and every one of them sooner or later became the affair of one caste. None actually shook the system.

Precolonial Movements

We have little information on social movements before the colonial era. In fact, we know very little about the life of Untouchables during this period. Social history hardly excited the pandits' imagination, and only a few religious texts mention *Chandalas*, primarily for the purpose of enumerating the social disabilities inflicted on them. Nevertheless, there is every reason to believe that the possibilities of upward mobility were very few for these lower castes. Religion was the sole avenue, but it was a limited one.

It seems, for instance, that various religious movements were accepting of 'Untouchables'. The first movement with social overtones that comes to mind is of course Buddhism. The Buddha taught that wisdom is within the reach of everyone and that, by leading an ascetic life, anyone can free himself from the cycle of reincarnations.[2] He did not hesitate to include among his disciples a few from 'lower' castes. But in spite of such egalitarian premisses, Buddhism never questioned the social inequalities; it never challenged the caste system, preferring instead to transcend it.[3]

2. M. Carrithers, *The Buddha* (Oxford: Oxford University Press, 1983), p. 20.

3. D. Forrester, *Caste and Christianity: Attitudes and Policies on Caste of Anglo-Protestant Missions in India* (London: Curzon Press, 1980), p. 11; or A. Béteille, *The Backward Classes in Contemporary India* (Delhi: Oxford University Press, 1992), p. 42.

Several centuries later, a number of religious movements, known generically as *bhakti*, appeared within Hinduism. Some researchers have delighted in pointing out their quasi-revolutionary bent. The historian Mukherjee, for example, argues that the *bhakti* movement is opposed to the caste system.[4] But the reality is not that simple. Although it indeed seems that some of the prominent figures came from very low castes - I am thinking for example of Tiruvalluvar - these movements never really challenged the caste order or even the concept of untouchability.

The case of Chokhamela is significant in this light.[5] This holy man (*sant*) was one of the important figures of the *bhakti* tradition; as a member of the Mahar caste of Maharashtra, he came from an untouchable background. In fact he and his family never ceased performing the menial tasks incumbent on their caste. There are even poems that describe him removing the earthly remains of a cow. Most of these compositions are typical of the poems depicting other *bhakti* holy men; they are devotional songs about divine love. A few, however, mention their author's caste and reveal the distress his condition caused him:

Why did you give me life
If it was only to give me this kind of life?
In your cruelty, you have rejected me by giving me life.

Or

Oh God! My caste is so low,
How can I serve you?
Everyone rejects me,
How can I see you?

Generally speaking, however, holy men do not denounce the caste system. Although Chockhamela was proof that even a Mahar could be the recipient of God's grace, this did not affect the social position of the other members of his caste. When Mahars became more radical, in the twentieth century under the leadership of Ambedkar, they rejected Chockhamela's legacy.

Fuller has shown that the *bhakti* movements did not contest the caste system; if the Kannada poets of the tenth and twelfth centuries seem slightly more radical, their Tamil predecessors carefully refrained from criticizing the supremacy of the Brahmins. The *bhakti* current never advocated equality, then; on the contrary, it always made the best of the existing inequalities.[6] Observation of modern-day practices substantiates this point of view: the devotional chanting sessions (*bhajan*) in Mylapore, near Madras, reinforce the middle-class Brahmin status of the participants.[7] In fact, Untouchables are not allowed to enter temples of the Ramanandi and Swaminarayan orders.[8]

On the whole, then, the devotional movements did not unsettle the caste system, and

4. R. Mukherjee, *The Rise and Fall of the East India Company* (New York: Monthly Review Press, 1974), p. 140.

5. See E. Zelliot, *From Untouchable to Dalit: Essays on Ambedkar Movement* (Delhi: Manohar, 1992), pp. 5-32.

6. C. Fuller, *The Camphor Flame: Popular Hinduism and Society in India* (Princeton, NJ: Princeton University Pres,s 1992), pp. 157-8.

7. Ibid., p. 162.

8. Ibid., pp. 168 and 173.

even less untouchability itself. They were in no way an avenue of upward social mobility for Untouchables. Likewise, renunciation as a way of stepping outside the caste system was a limited solution, open to only a few individuals; it never enabled a whole caste to raise its social status. Whatever may be said, in India's past there seems never to have been any process of social mobility open to the lower castes; and it is probable that, at the start of the nineteenth century, Untouchables were in the position in which they had been from time immemorial.

Early Movements

It was not until the nineteenth century that events got under way. The abjection of Untouchables at the time held them at a certain distance from the first movements; but the success of these early protests meant that better conditions in society were not only possible, but ethically desirable, at least if one referred to the new values introduced by the British. Thus the Chamars of Senapur were struck by the Yadavas' efforts to win a better place in society: this was the first time a low caste had been bold enough to challenge Thakur supremacy, and their daring, which was crowned with a measure of success, encouraged the Chamars to rise up against the destitution in which they had been vegetating for centuries.[9] At the same time, those who managed to move up in society provided proof that Untouchables, too, were capable of learning to read and write, to handle a gun or to do jobs that had, until then, been closed to them. In the next chapter we shall see the Mahars' pride when, in 1930, one of their own, B. R. Ambedkar, was invited to sit down with government ministers at the Round Table Conference. Such examples refute Hindu natural law or the *Dharmashastra*, which taught that Untouchables are an inferior category, barely human, incapable of rising to the level of the higher castes. From then on, Untouchables had living proof of their capacity to rise above the destitution in which they had been kept for thousands of years.

The nineteenth-century social movements made a few inroads on Indian society and shook the traditional caste order. Untouchables were still relatively uninvolved in these movements, but they were very impressed; as the first breaches in the old order were opened, new hopes were born.

Anti-Brahmin Movements

Is it an accident that the state that saw the first untouchable movements and the birth of their greatest leader also saw the development, in the nineteenth century, of a movement in protest of the Brahmins' dominant position? Even to ask the question is

9. B. Cohn, 'The Chamars of Senapur: A Study of the Changing Status of a Depressed Caste'. (Doctoral dissertation, Cornell Univeristy, 1954), p. 138.

already an answer, and it is legitimate to think that a climate developed in Maharashtra that was particularly conducive to the questioning of social inequalities. Although Untouchables were not the main actors of the anti-Brahmin movements, not always being concerned by the issues involved and even being excluded at times, they would nevertheless take over their themes to substantiate their own claims.

The first anti-Brahmin movement grew up in Maharashtra, then, where there was a long-standing rivalry between Brahmins and the peasant castes with which the Marathas were associated. This was the caste of Shivaji, a seventeenth-century warrior who nearly succeeded in routing the Moghul rulers. The authority of Shivaji, and of the Marathas as a whole, was based on the competence of the Chitpavan Brahmins, who occupied the post of Peshwa and, little by little, imposed themselves as rulers. The opposition that rapidly arose between Peshwas and Marathas lasted until the nineteenth century. In 1818, Bajirao Peshwa was ousted by the Marathas, and Elphinstone's government installed Pratap Singh, a descendant of Shivaji, on the throne. This sounded the death knell of Brahmin political power and heralded the start of upward mobility for the peasant castes. More and more Kunbis began calling themselves Marathas, and, by the time of the 1901 census, practically no one listed himself as a Kunbi. This social ascension of the Kunbi-Marathas should be understood primarily as a power struggle. The middle castes feared that Brahmins might take advantage of British rule to entrench further their dominant position in local society. Education was becoming a key factor in social mobility, and Brahmins were a scholarly caste, and therefore the best equipped to respond to the demands of the newly emerging professions. It was in this context that a powerful movement of non-Brahmin castes developed into what was also and above all an anti-Brahmin movement.

The most memorable figure of this Maharashtra movement was indisputably Jotirao Phule; he was a Mali, from a caste of horticulturalists, and held a respectable position in the local hierarchy. As a social reformer, Phule first targeted the evils besetting Indian society, and quickly came to hold Brahmins entirely responsible for the social and intellectual decline. Society, he argued, was split into two clans: on the one side, Brahmins and, on the other side, Shudras, whom he regarded as the 'community of the oppressed'. But we must not let this whiff of populism obscure the fact that the debate revolved above all around the interests of the dominant classes; Untouchables drifted along with the current, but the debate did not really interest them. True, Phule multiplied the initiatives on their behalf, for example by urging education for Untouchables. But they were also an alibi that he used to illustrate the oppression in which were mired, he argued, all those whom he lumped together under the term 'Shudra'. For instance, he led a struggle against the Brahmin monopoly of priestly functions. He denounced Shudras' dependence on these priests, who were called in at every important stage of the life-cycle, and he urged Shudras to do without their services in the various ceremonies. This injunction had little to do with Untouchables, whom Brahmins have always refused to serve anyway.[10]

10. For the foregoing, see principally R. O'Hanlon, *Caste, Conflict and Ideology: Mahatma Jotirao Phule and Low Caste Protest in Nineteenth-Century Western India* (Cambridge: Cambridge University Press, 1985).

Yet the impact of this movement on the most disadvantaged groups was not felt any the less for that. Even though in practice he was addressing primarily the landowning middle castes, in terms of values he was attacking the entire Hindu social order and arguing for the equality of all men. There was, then, a current of new ideas in nineteenth-century Marathi society that was regularly fuelled by missionaries' attacks on the social inequalities inherent in Hinduism. And as they shook the traditional values, these movements also paved the way for Untouchables' demands.

The province of Madras was to be the site of another anti-Brahmin movement. This one differed in a few respects from its counterpart in Maharashtra; it had strong 'Dravidian' overtones, for example, contrasting the indigenous (non-Brahmin) inhabitants with the invaders from the north (the Brahmins); opposition to Brahmins here took the form of an anti-clericalism with strong rationalist connotations; and finally, the Tamil movement quickly found a political expression that is still deeply alive today. But with regard to the position of the lower castes within the movement, we find the same features as in Maharashtra. Tamil society is divided into three categories: Brahmins, non-Brahmin middle castes and Untouchables.[11] As in Maharashtra, it was the second group that would lead the anti-Brahmin movement. Here, too, the issues of education and access to modern professions were central to the birth of the movement and led to the formation of the Justice Party, in 1917.[12] As in Maharashtra, too, the nationalist movement and the Congress Party were perceived as being dominated by Brahmins, and it was for this reason that the non-Brahmin castes of Madras set up a form of political representation for themselves. Once again Untouchables were not involved in the struggle. And they had virtually no representation in the Justice Party.[13] By contrast, the Vellalars, one of the most powerful and wealthiest castes of Tamil Nadu, seem to have been the *fer de lance* of the Dravidian movement.[14] Nadars, on the other hand, one of the most dynamic lower castes, played only a very marginal role.

On the whole, Untouchables kept their distance from this power struggle, then. The castes at the head of the movement were also those that dominated and exploited Untouchables in rural areas. Nevertheless, as I have said, it had finally become possible to contest institutions that had thousands of years of immutable existence behind them, and certain low castes did not fail to assert their rights with virulence. Such was the case of two South Indian castes, the Nadars and the Iravas, who appreciably improved their position in local society. These two castes were not wholly identical with the most deprived sectors of society; rather, they occupied an intermediate position: although they were not allowed to enter temples, their members could not wear decent clothes and they had to bear other kinds of discrimination as well, they could be called semi-Untouchables, for they were clearly distinct from such low castes as Pulayars or Paraiyars. The struggle of the Nadars and the Iravas was exemplary on all accounts. It enabled two clearly lower classes to achieve a relatively

11. A. Béteille, 'Caste and Political Group Formation in Tamil Nad', in R. Kothari (ed.), *Caste in Indian Politics* (Poona: Orient and Longmanm, 1970), p. 263.

12. Ibid., p. 269.

13. Ibid., p. 284.

14. G. S. Ghurye, *Caste and Race in India* (Bombay: Popular Prakashan, 1969), p. 373.

enviable social standing, and this success became a model for other oppressed classes. That is why it interests us here.

The Nadar Movement

If Shanars, as they were then called, were distinct from untouchable castes properly speaking, it is probably because, in some areas, they were allowed to own land and even enjoyed some political power. Unlike Pallars and Paraiyars, Shanars were allowed to enter the *agraharam*, or Brahmin quarter, and their own quarter was not completely segregated from the village.[15] The majority of this caste of toddy-tappers was particularly deprived, but contrary to the usual pattern, their emerging elite did not sever their caste ties; instead, they used their numerical strength to demand their rights. The Shanars never mounted a challenge to the caste system, though; what interested them was the prosperity and the social standing of their own caste. Therefore they never sought the support of the other low castes; quite the contrary, in fact, for in 1899 Pallar Untouchables sided with the Maravars to repress the Shanars of Sivaksi.[16]

Shanars responded *en masse* to the missionaries' invitation to conversion. Significant portions of the caste had already gone over to Catholicism; but in the nineteenth century, they literally flocked to the various Protestant denominations. In the 1840s,[17] some 60,000 Shanars swelled the ranks of the Church Missionary Society. In the same period, the London Missionary Society also recruited massively.[18] We will be taking a closer look at the phenomenon of conversion later in this chapter, so we will simply note here that the missionaries supported the Nadars in their struggle for social promotion. It was due to the efforts of Colonel Munro, the British Resident in the Principality of Travancore, that its Christian women won the right, in 1814, to cover their breasts after the fashion of the Syrian Christians.[19]

High-caste Hindus reacted sharply to this decree, and there were periodical outbreaks of violence over the following decades. Historians call this battle the Breast Cloth Controversy. In 1858, Nayars were still assaulting Nadar women in the market place. The following year, the town of Nagercoil was shaken by twenty days of rioting over the same issue; houses were plundered and burned; in July 1859, in an attempt to settle the question, the Maharaja of Travancore finally authorized Nadar women of Hindu religion to cover their breasts.[20] The missionaries opened schools and urged their congregations to send their children. Thousands of Nadars, as they were

15. R. Hardgrave, *The Nadars of Tamilnad. The Political Culture of a Community in Change* (Bombay: Oxford University Press, 1969), p. 23.

16. G. S. Ghurye, *Caste and Race in India,* p. 385.

17. R. Hardgrave, *The Nadars of Tamilnad,* p. 47.

18. D. Kooiman, *Conversion and Social Equality in India: The London Missionary Society in South Travancore in the 19th Century* (Delhi: Manohar, 1989), p. 70.

19. R. Yesudas, *A People's Revolt in Travancore: A Backward Class Movement for Social Freedom* (Trivandrum: Kerala Historical Society, 1975), p. 115.

20. R. Jeffrey, *The Decline of Nayar Dominance: Society and Politics in Travancore, 1847-1908* (Brighton: Sussex University Press, 1976), p. 66.

beginning to call themselves, thus learned to read and write; they were also taught the rudiments of arithmetic and English, so that they found themselves in a good position for jobs as foremen (*kanganies*) on the new tea and coffee plantations of Ceylon. An impressive number of Nadars emigrated, returning a few years later to invest their money at home.[21]

At the same time, the Nadars of Ramnad district, in the state of Madras, gained control of the commercialization of palm products and became a particularly industrious community.[22] They began to 'Sanskritize' their social practices: in other words, many became vegetarian; they cremated their dead instead of burying them; they dressed after the fashion of the higher castes; and so forth. These changes drew an angry reaction from the higher castes: in 1890, a group of Vellalars managed to prevent Nadars wearing sandals; five years later, the Zamindar of Ettaiyappuram refused to let them enter the temple, triggering a wave of conversions to Catholicism. The most serious incidents occurred in 1899, when the Nadars of Sivakasi attacked the Maravars, who reacted with the help of Brahmins, Vellalars, Kallars and ... Pallars. Some one hundred and fifty Nadar villages were attacked, and thousands of houses destroyed.

But this did not stop the Nadars' remarkable ascent. They set up a caste organization to defend their interests. One of their number, K. Kamaraj, rose to the highest positions: he was appointed Chief Minister of Tamil Nadu in 1954, and became national president of the Congress Party in 1963. The Nadars never threw in their lot with the lower castes: and Christian Nadars refused to be assimilated to Untouchables within the Church. The Hindu Nadars waged a victorious struggle to obtain entry to the temples, but refused to join forces with Untouchables; and, in 1939, the Sivakasi temple was opened to Nadars three days before Harijans were allowed to enter, so that the two causes might be clearly dissociated.[23] Today Nadars have finally gained a respectable position in Tamil society.

The Iravas of Kerala

In Malayalam-speaking areas, the toddy-tappers belong to the Irava caste, whose position in the social structure is very similar to that of the Nadars in Madras. Likewise, the Iravas engaged in a struggle very similar to that waged by the Nadars, although the two movements were not directly connected. The Iravas succeeded in obtaining a considerably better position within local society, and today they are one of the most influential communities in Kerala. In 1951, C. Keshavan became Chief Minister of Travancore-Cochin, and in 1962 R. Shankar won the post in the state of Kerala. The 1965 elections resulted in a legislative assembly in which 40 per cent of the members were Iravas. Between 20 and 30 per cent of the students accepted for

21. D. Kooiman, *Conversion and Social Equality in India,* p. 132.
22. R. Hardgrave, *The Nadars of Tamilnad,* p. 97.
23. Ibid., p. 190.

medical school are from this caste, which also controls several newspapers, among them the daily *Kerala Kaumudi*.[24]

To achieve this, the Iravas were obliged to wage a courageous struggle. In the nineteenth century, they occupied a highly disadvantaged position in Malayali society, although they were clearly separate from Pulayas and Paraiyars. Unlike the Nadars, Iravas never went over to Christianity. As Syrian Christians occupied a privileged position in Malayali society and avoided any contact with the lower-caste 'Latin' Christians, it may be supposed that this example did not encourage Iravas to convert; this disinclination may also have been exacerbated by the fact that their movement was started by a Hindu reformer, Sri Narayana Guru, born in 1854 in Chempazanthi, not far from Trivandrum.

In many ways, Sri Narayana Guru resembles the numerous philosophical gurus found throughout the history of Hinduism. He differs, however, by his modest background as well as by his role as social reformer. The study of Sanskrit, to which he was led by his intellectual capacities, acquainted him with that great religious tradition. Rapidly he renounced the world and his family, and took up a wandering life, practising yoga and meditation. But this monastic discipline did not fully satisfy him, for in his mind a social-religious doctrine was developing, which he burned to put into practice. In 1888, at Aruvipuram, near Trivandrum, he defied Brahmin tradition and consecrated a temple to Shiva. By this act, he wanted to make God accessible to the members of his own community and to castes that were forbidden to enter temples. He founded an organization, the Sree Narayana Dharma Paripalana (SNDP) Yogam, or 'Society for the propagation of the dharma of Sri Narayana", and took up residence in a monastery at Varkala, where he lived until his death in 1928.

The action led by Sri Narayana Guru is typical of low-caste movements. His philosophy was not intended for any one caste, but had a universal vocation, which can be summed up in the famous phrase: 'One religion, one God, one caste'. This is a fundamentally egalitarian message that transcends social differences in the encounter with a single God. But at the same time, it addresses primarily low castes with a view to freeing them from their oppression. Yet his philosophy caught on only among Iravas, who made Sri Narayana Guru a veritable caste hero and the symbol of their struggle. Like most religious reformers, he urged Iravas to 'Sanskritize' their lifestyle, in other words to adopt high-caste customs and ways in order to appear more respectable. He forbade alcohol and sexual licence; he preached vegetarianism and stressed the importance of bodily hygiene.[25]

In spite of the respect he commanded, Sri Narayana's authority did not really go beyond Irava caste boundaries; but for them he became a caste symbol. All Irava institutions use his name and, to take just one example, today countless schools in Kerala are called 'Sri Narayana College'. Yet the guru's influence on the caste movement itself was limited. When, for instance, he implored Iravas to remember the even lower castes, reminding them that the social equality they were demanding

24. See C. Pullapilly, 'The Izhavas of Kerala and the Historic Struggle for Acceptance in Hindu Society'. *Journal of Asian and African Studies*, 11 (1976).

25. For the above, see V. T. Samuel, *One Caste, One Religion, One God: A Study of Sree Narayana Guru* (Delhi: Sterling, 1977).

should extend to these as well, his appeals went unheard. In effect, the Irava movement never even pretended to reach out to the untouchable castes; on the contrary, they were kept at a distance. The Irava movement was one of a caste endowed with a brilliant elite that successfully allied itself with a relatively deprived majority in order to use their numerical strength to gain an important position in Kerala society. Their primary goal was to compete with other groups such as Nayars or Syrian Christians; but overthrowing the existing social order had never been on their agenda. The principal founders of the Irava movement, like Doctor Palpoo or the poet, Asan, never encouraged the least ambiguity as to the exclusively Irava character of their struggle. At certain points, the Iravas tolerated the presence of lower castes, as in the *satyagraha* at Vaikom; but these were purely momentary associations that in no way implied a community of interests.

The case of the poet, Kumaran Asan (1873-1924), is typical. A disciple of Sri Narayana Guru, he was appointed to Travancore's legislative assembly, the Sri Mulam Popular Assembly, in 1905. He backed the election of Ayyankali, a Pulaya leader, to the assembly; but his activities as a member were entirely devoted to improving the Iravas' lot, as is attested by his many assembly speeches,[26] which made little mention of the lower castes in general. Moreover, the SNDP Yogam evolved into a veritable caste organization, of which all Irava leaders were members. At the beginning of the twentieth century, the demands of the SNDP Yogam centred on basic rights for Iravas: admission to government schools, temple entry, political representation and so forth. The most enlightened members argued that Iravas and Pulayas should eat together;[27] but S. Aiyappan was assaulted by the SNDP Yogam leaders when he attempted to organize such a meal.[28] Thus caste barriers were never truly called into question,[29] and, on the contrary, the SNDP Yogam helped weld the Iravas into a veritable 'ethnic bloc'.

Nevertheless, one of the Iravas' major struggles was of particular consequence for Untouchables all over India. With an educated, dynamic and skilled elite at their head, the Iravas fought for the right to enter Hindu temples, whose doors had always been closed to them. Westernized families like that of Doctor Palpoo, an important Irava figure, had always been treated as though they had the plague. Iravas were therefore torn between action and conversion. Indeed, one wonders whether they may not have used the threat of conversion to blackmail the Hindu authorities, since they do not seem to have made a move in that direction, despite the solicitude lavished on them. In fact, Sri Narayana even spoke out against conversion. By contrast, they did not stint their efforts to gain access to the streets leading to the temples and the temple courtyards. The most spectacular action was undertaken in Vaikom on 30 March 1934. The Iravas organized a *satyagraha*, a non-violent occupation of the streets leading to the temples, with the aim of 'opening' them to lower castes. At this time, these streets

26. T. Ravindran, *Asan and Social Revolution in Kerala: A Study of His Assembly Speeches* (Trivandrum: Kerala History Society, 1972).

27. M. S. Rao, *Social Movements and Social Transformations: A Study of Two Backward Classes Movements in India* (Delhi: Macmillan, 1979), p. 57.

28. K. Saradamoni, *Emergence of a Slave Caste. Pulayas of Kerala* (Delhi: People's Publishing House, 1980), p. 146.

29. M. S. Rao, *Social Movements and Social Transformations,* p. 120.

were closed to lower castes, including Iravas; in fact, the upper castes of Travancore and Cochin had put up signs formally indicating the forbidden zones.[30]

Although the Vaikom *satyagraha* was dominated by Iravas, other castes, including Pulayas, joined the movement. On 30 March, a Nayar, an Irava and a Pulaya symbolically led a march of some 1,000 persons to the Vaikom temple. The Irava leader, T. K. Madhavan (1885-1930), was himself close to the Congress Party, which would also become involved in the movement, primarily through the figure of Gandhi, who travelled to Kerala, where he immediately called on Sri Narayana Guru. In the course of their discussion, it seems that the two men expressed conflicting views on the use of violence.[31] On the first day, the three leaders of the march were arrested, but they were immediately replaced by others, who were arrested in turn. The action continued for 20 months: in November 1925, the Maharani opened most of the streets leading to the temples to all classes of society. Although the temple itself remained inaccessible, this decree was a partial victory; for the first time, a breach had been opened in religious orthodoxy, and it had been forced to yield some ground; temple-entry movements broke out all over India, and particularly in Maharashtra. At this time, Iravas were solidly behind the Congress Party, which defended the idea of 'communal representation' at political meetings.

The first leaders of the Irava movement were generally from well-to-do, middle-class backgrounds. Doctor Palpoo was the first Irava doctor, and Asan was a poet and journalist; C. V. Kunhuraman, too, was a journalist. T. K. Madhavan came from a well-off family of merchants; his classmates were Nayar children whose parents worked for his own parents; and yet Nayars were allowed to walk on the road, while he was obliged to use the gutter. Since official jobs were closed to them, many Iravas went into trade, set up small businesses, and did well; they became the principal supporters of the SNDP Yogam. This class was particularly sensitive to the issue of temple-entry, because they aspired to a social life that reflected their economic success.

In the early 1930s, the temple-entry struggle therefore occupied an essential place in local political life. After the Guruvayur *satyagraha*, the threat of conversion surfaced again. At this time, Ambedkar had been forced to sign a pact with Gandhi that left him so bitter that in 1935 he swore that he would not die a Hindu. A year earlier, the SNDP Yogam had beat him to the punch by formally declaring that Iravas were not Hindus. In 1935, C. Krishnan had a Buddhist temple built in Calicut. The same year, the Irava leaders met with Ambedkar and invited him to preside over a meeting in which a Buddhist monk who had travelled from Ceylon was to take part. A few people also converted to Sikhism and to Islam, so that confusion was rife.[32]

It was in this context that the Dewan, or Chief Minister, of Travancore, a particularly distinguished Tamil Brahmin by the name of C. P. Ramaswami Iyer, sensed an impending cataclysm for Hinduism and urged the Maharaja to open the temples of his principality to the lower castes. On 11 November 1936, the prince proclaimed that no restriction could prevent all Hindus entering the temples of the principality and

30. A. Aiyappan, *Social Revolution in a Kerala Village: A Study in Culture Change* (Bombay: Asia Publishing House, 1965), p. 132.

31. R. Jeffrey, 'Temple-Entry Movements in Travancore, 1860-1940'. *Social Scientist,* 4 (1976), pp. 3-27, p. 18.

32. M. S. Rao, *Social Movements and Social Transformations,* p. 75.

praying there. The text of this proclamation more or less paraphrased Queen Victoria's 1858 proclamation to the Indian population.[33] This was an event of capital importance in the history of Hinduism, for it satisfied a major demand of the low-caste movement and thus prevented a veritable haemorrhage from the faith. In Kerala, the Irava response was instantaneous, and all threats of conversion became immediately anachronistic. The Travancore proclamation was followed by many others throughout India, and little by little, temples opened their doors to the lower castes. The Minakshi temple in Madurai was the first in Madras province to admit Nadars and Harijans, on 8 July 1939. On this occasion, a bitter conflict split the temple's Brahmin priests and the temple trustees. Over the month of July, many Tamil temples began admitting Untouchables, and on 5 August the Madras legislative assembly passed the Temple Entry Authorization and Indemnity Act.[34]

These laws were an important victory for Untouchables all over India. One symbol of social exclusion had fallen. The Nadar, Irava and anti-Brahmin movements had created a favourable climate for Untouchable emancipation and had popularized values that ran counter to the traditional caste system. The Iravas subsequently redirected their efforts to more political demands. They thronged to Kerala's powerful Communist Party, and by and large proceeded with their social ascent.[35]

Religious Conversions

The missions acted in parallel with the movements just described; but their appeal was addressed more directly to Untouchables. However, it would be untrue to think that the missionaries who arrived in India were fired by sentiments of social justice and equality. On the contrary, they quickly realized that, if they were to show too much interest in the lower castes, they were liable to be assimilated to these groups and find themselves totally cut off from the majority of the population. The first missionaries therefore concentrated on the upper castes. But high-caste people were particularly resistant and reticent; in the end, the missionaries encountered a more favourable reception among the low castes, and throughout India an impressive number of Untouchables swelled the Christian ranks.

Catholicism

The Catholic missions were the first to spread across the Indian subcontinent. As early as the sixteenth century, Catholic priests began accompanying the Portuguese expeditions with the aim of evangelizing India. The best-known of these pioneers is no doubt Saint Francis-Xavier, who succeeded in converting whole sections of the

33. D. Forrester, *Caste and Christianity,* p. 85.
34. C. Fuller, *Servants of the Goddess: The Priests of a South Indian Temple* (Cambridge: Cambridge University Press, 1984, pp. 116-21.
35. G. Rajendran, *The Ezhava Community and Kerala Politics* (Trivandrum: The Kerala Academy of Political Sciences, 1974), p. 46.

castes of fishermen on the southern peninsula. He landed in India in 1542, and soon left Goa for the Malabar coast, where he met with success among the fishermen. Thousands of Mukkuvars and Arayars were converted in a matter of months, thus laying the foundations of a Latin Catholic Church composed of the lower castes; this Church continues to exist alongside the Syrian Church, which enjoys an appreciably higher social standing. Another caste of fishermen had already converted to Catholicism: in 1532, the Tamil Paravars, feeling threatened by the Muslims, sent a delegation of 72 of their members to Cochin to ask the Portuguese for their help. Within the space of a few months, 20,000 Paravars thus underwent conversion,[36] and virtually the entire caste followed.

In Kerala, the Latin and Syrian Churches remained separate, a division that was ratified by the Vatican in 1923.[37] The Tamil Church, for its part, reproduced the divisions of Hindu society. As we saw, Tamil Paravars converted as a caste, with the aim of allying themselves with the Portuguese; in effect, at the time, Christianity was strongly associated with *parangi* (or *ferangi*, foreigners).[38] The question missionaries put to the potential converts left no doubt: 'Do you want to become a member of the family of foreigners (*parangi kulam*)?'[39] The methods of the Italian Jesuit, Roberto De Nobili (1577-1656) completely transformed this mentality.

This Tuscan aristocrat decided to settle in Madurai, a centre of Tamil and South Indian religious culture, and then set about building bridges between the local culture and Christianity. De Nobili took up residence in one of the town's Brahmin quarters, dressed like a *sanniyasi*, and adopted the Brahmin way of living. He refused to associate with the Portuguese invaders, and maintained that he 'was not a *parangi*'; he would present himself as a Kshatriya from Rome, where his family was of a rank comparable to that of the local *raja*. He undertook an intensive study of Sanskrit and Tamil literature, and translated the Catholic religious concepts into the Tamil language, in which he also wrote poetry. He rapidly acquired a reputation as a holy man, and was credited with a number of miracles. He is said to have made as many as 100,000 converts among the upper castes. De Nobili did not set out to eliminate caste differences; he argued instead that caste was an essentially secular institution. Therefore two churches were built in Madurai: one for De Nobili's converts and the other for low-caste worshippers. Subsequent delegations of missionaries were divided into *sanniyasi*, in charge of the upper castes, and *pandaraswami,* who worked among the lower castes.[40] The latter were particularly active in the 'Maravar area', in other words, the present-day region of Ramnad and Tirunelveli. Father De Britto (1647-1693, canonized in 1947), the martyr of the South Indian Church, made every effort to convert the local princely families; but the *pandaraswami* realized their greatest success by converting great numbers of Shanars and Paraiyars.

Later missionaries tended to stress caste differences within the Church, and raised

36. S. Bayly, *Saints, Goddesses and Kings: Muslims and Christians in South Indian Society, 1700-1900* (Cambridge: Cambridge University Press, 1989), p. 325.

37. G. Koilparampil, *Caste in the Catholic Community in Kerala: A Study of Caste Elements in the Inter-Rite Relationships of Syrians and Latins* (Cochin: St Theresa's College, 1982), p. 91.

38. D. Forrester, *Caste and Christianity,* p. 15.

39. S. Bayly, Saints, *Goddesses and Kings,* p. 388.

40. J. Auguste, *Le Maduré: l'ancienne et la nouvelle mission* (Brussels: Desclée de Brouwer, 1894), p. 59.

Vellalars to the rank of a veritable priestly caste within Catholicism.[41] Caste barriers were thus reinforced, and the Untouchables who had joined the Church found themselves marginalized: the Nadars of Vadakankulam, for example, would not allow Paraiyars in their chapel.[42] Churches were built with two naves, called 'trouser-churches', so that the high-caste parishioners would not be defiled by contact with Untouchables; and the issue of untouchability poisoned the life of many parishes.[43]

The Catholic Church in Tamil Nadu fell under the domination of high castes like the Vellalars and the Udayars, while Untouchables were relegated to an extremely low position. The Church failed to provide them with means of achieving a modicum of social respectability, nor did it offer them the comfort of a welcoming community.[44] One may even wonder if, by becoming Catholic, Untouchables had not taken a step backwards, particularly since their conversion automatically caused them to be removed from the list of Scheduled Castes, thus forfeiting the rights reserved for these groups.[45] Harijan Catholics live, for the most part, on the fringes of parish life; in Valghira Manickam, the priest never visits them, and they only rarely attend religious services. They receive no comfort from the Church; the Catholic schools do not encourage their enrolment, and the various Catholic institutions do not hire them except for jobs that no one else would take.

When questioned about this, Catholic Untouchables are very bitter. They stress the contempt shown by most religious authorities, and invariably say that it was no use becoming Christian. Their knowledge of the religion is very limited as well. It is therefore not surprising that some do not hesitate to re-convert to Hinduism in order to be put back on the Scheduled Castes lists. The faith of the majority, however, is too deeply rooted for them to change religions. In addition, they make it clear that it is vain to try to better their socio-economic status by converting, and that today they do not look to religion to raise their standard of living.

Protestantism

Disillusionment is not a new phenomenon. At the end of the nineteenth century, the idea was already prevalent that it was no use expecting the Catholic Church to break the chains of untouchability. The Protestant and Anglican Churches were thus the beneficiaries of the growing Untouchable resentment towards Hinduism. The Reformed Churches came to India much later. The first missionaries arrived at the end of the eighteenth century, but it was not until the nineteenth century that they spread

41. S. Bayly, *Saints, Goddesses and Kings,* pp. 412 and 414.

42. Ibid., p. 435.

43. P. Wiebe and S. John-Peter, 'The Catholic Church and Caste in Rural Tamil Nadu', in H. Singh (ed.), *Caste among the Non-Hindus in India* (Delhi: National Publishing House, 1977), p. 45.

44. My book, *The World of the Untouchables: Paraiyars of Tamil Nadu,* contains an extensive description of Paraiyar marginalization within the Catholic Church.

45. See R. Deliège, 'A Comparison between Hindu and Christian Paraiyars of South India'. *Indian Missiological Review,* 12, (1990).

over the subcontinent. They had a particularly difficult time in the beginning; and for decades, entire missions managed to make a mere handful of converts. They received no support from the British authorities,[46] who were often agnostic and, in any case, had little desire to alienate the local population. Colonel Munro, the British Resident in Travancore, was a notable exception to this generally suspicious attitude. Conversely, the missionaries did not share the military ambitions of the East Indies Company functionaries;[47] the working-class background of the first missionaries of the London Missionary Society hardly drew them to strongly hierarchical social structures, and the Company saw them as 'revolutionaries', whose excesses were to be feared if not contained.[48] The missionaries in turn did not hesitate to accuse the 'Honourable Company' of encouraging Hinduism and the evils of idolatry; they expressed indignation at the funding of temples when they were not railing against the participation of British officials in Hindu religious festivals.[49] The first missionaries did not hide their disgust at the caste system, which they found to be an infamous institution and deeply ingrained in Hinduism. They therefore did not aim at converting whole castes, but concentrated instead on individuals. Furthermore, they were aware of the danger of focusing exclusively on the lower castes, for, like the Catholics, they did not want to be assimilated to this one section of society. The conversion of too many Untouchables thus threatened to cancel out all their efforts.[50] The Presbyterians from the Punjab mission quickly became convinced of the necessity of first converting members of the upper castes, who would in turn be sure to attract the lower castes.[51] In 1857, the conversion of one Chuhra Untouchable filled the Presbyterian Church with consternation; might this not alienate the rest of the population? The missionaries therefore decided to concentrate their attention on the higher classes, and opened schools to attract and evangelize them.

But this was not how the upper castes understood it; they let themselves be drawn in by the schooling, but, except for a few, showed no sign of changing religions. In the first three quarters of the nineteenth century, the Protestant Churches shone by their stagnation: famines brought in a few orphans, whom they duly converted;[52] but aside from that, they had to make do with precious little. Between 1855 and 1872, the Punjab Presbyterian Mission converted forty-three adults.[53] The second half of the nineteenth century was already well advanced when the Protestant Churches were obliged to alter their strategy.[54] In effect, the Untouchables' social aspirations drove them into the arms of the missionaries, and the movement was exacerbated by the fact

46. S. Manickam, *The Social Setting of Christian Conversion in South India: The Impact of the Wesleyan Methodist Missionaries on the Trichy-Tanjore Diocese to the Harijan Communities of the Mass Movement Area, 1820-1947* (Wiesbaden: Franz Steiner Verlag, 1977), p. 131.

47. D. Kooiman, *Conversion and Social Equality in India,* p. 27.

48. D. Forrester, *Caste and Christianity,* p. 25.

49. Ibid., p. 56.

50. D. Kooiman, *Conversion and Social Equality in India,* p. 78.

51. F. Stock and M. Stock, *People Movements in the Punjab* (Bombay: Gospel Literature Society, 1978), p. 20.

52. S. Manickam, *The Social Setting of Christian Conversion,* p. 60.

53. F. Stock and M. Stock, *People Movements in the Punjab* (Bombay: Gospel Literature Society, 1978), p. 23.

54. G. Oddie, *Social Protest in India: British Protestant Missionaries and Social Reforms, 1850-1900* (Delhi: Manohar, 1979), p. 131.

that, during the famine, the missions had, through their various aid programmes, demonstrated their compassion for the most needy. Throughout India, as if by magic, Protestant Churches of every denomination saw tens of thousands of Untouchables join their ranks, whereas for 75 years they had been unable to attract more than a handful. This was the beginning of what was called the 'mass movements', which continued far into the twentieth century. Untouchables, no longer drawn to the Catholic Church, placed their hopes of socio-economic promotion in the Reformed Churches. The latter dropped their individual-conversion strategy in favour of mass conversions.[55] We shall review a few of these movements.

The Nadars of South Kerala and Tamil Nadu were the first mass conversions to Protestantism. Having failed in their attempt to convert the Syrian Christians, Protestant missionaries quickly resolved to focus on the lower castes. The majority of the converts in the London Missionary Society and the Church Missionary Society were Paraiyars, Pulayars and, above all, Nadars.[56] Their number rose sharply between 1868 and 1900.[57] The missionaries actively defended the Nadars' cause, and converts from this caste met with real economic success; however, it must be remembered that those who remained Hindu also rose in society.

In the province of Madras, 'Parias' converted to Protestantism after the great famine of 1876-7.[58] But it was in the twentieth century that the Madras Methodist Mission enjoyed its greatest success, its membership jumping from 2,500 in 1913 to 52,273 in 1947. The converts of the 1930s were primarily Paraiyars and Madharis (Sakkiliyars).[59] Relations between these two castes remained quite distant, and the Madharis felt somewhat neglected by the Church; in 1970, nearly three thousand of them left, and did not return until 1973.[60] Methodist missionaries and their newly baptized converts had to confront the virulent opposition of Hindus; riots broke out in Mannagudi, in 1909,[61] and farmers refused to hire Christian workers, forcing the missionaries to encourage their members to take up new occupations. In spite of these efforts, however, numerous Harijans remained poor.

In the Telugu region (present-day Andhra Pradesh), the Methodists had focused their efforts on the high castes; but their few converts went back to Hinduism when they realized that lower castes were also converting: in effect, following the 1899-1900 famine, Malas began converting in massive numbers. And they in turn objected to members of the other large untouchable caste of Andhra, the Madigas, joining their ranks. The Madigas thus became Christian in the villages where the Malas had remained Hindu.[62] Today high-caste Telugus regard Protestantism as a religion for Untouchables, and it therefore holds no interest for them; moreover, no other caste has converted since the mass movement.[63] Converts seem to have benefited very little

55. D. Forrester, *Caste and Christianity,* p. 73.
56. S. Bayly, Saints, *Goddesses and Kings,* p. 292.
57. D. Kooiman, *Conversion and Social Equality in India,* p. 70.
58. G. Oddie, *Social Protest in India,* p. 130.
59. S. Manickam, *The Social Setting of Christian Conversion,* p. 95.
60. Ibid., p. 192.
61. Ibid., p. 152.
62. P. Luke and J. Carman, *Village Christians and Hindu Culture: Study of a Rural Church in Andhra Pradesh,* South India (London: Lutterworth Press, 1960), p. 64.

from their change of religion. Their knowledge of the basic tenets of Christianity is extremely limited: most have never heard of the Resurrection, the Ascension, Pentecost or the Virgin Mary. Instead, they continue to sacrifice to the goddess and the demons, whose anger they fear.[64] They are largely unconcerned about the Church's injunctions: most girls are married before the age of 15, and their marriages are performed by non-Christian priests.[65] Adultery, alcoholism, fighting and 'immorality' are just as frequent as among Hindus.[66] One Hindu observer remarked ironically on the monetary as well as other efforts that the missionaries had expended for more than a century to obtain such paltry results.

In Gujarat and the Punjab, the Meghs showed some inclination to join Christianity, but there were only a few dozen conversions a year. When the Churhas, another untouchable caste, showed an interest in Christianity, the Meghs turned to the Arya Samaj, a Hindu organization specializing in the reconversion of low castes. Ten thousand Chudras went over to the United Presbyterian Church of Punjab between 1881 and 1891. In 1881, there were a total of 35,000 Christian Churhas; they numbered 462,681 in 1931. Ultimately one-third of the caste converted to Christianity.[67] The movement was so massive that missionaries did not have time to deal with every request.

It seems, though, that these conversions did not fundamentally affect the material life and social status of Untouchables.[68] Christians generally expressed their resentment, and many went back to Hinduism in order to benefit from the advantages offered by the government. Christian Untouchables often felt they had been deceived, or even betrayed. Today their marginalization is twofold: they are still Untouchables, and are now Christians in a largely Hindu country. Paradoxically, then, their situation is perhaps now even more difficult.[69] Their Hindu brothers have often improved their social position tangibly, and this success can only exacerbate the bitterness of Christian Untouchables. In these circumstances, it is not surprising to find Protestant Untouchables among the converts to Islam in the early 1980s.

Many other deprived Christians found some comfort in fundamentalist sects, a phenomenon that has been well analysed by Caplan. In Madras, for example, a number of these sects provided disappointed Christians with a convincing explanation for the origin of evil.[70] Numbers of 'prophets' defied the authority of the Church of South India (CSI) and drew ever greater crowds. They took on the causes of evil, using popular ideas about affliction.[71] New Churches also sprang up among Kerala's Christian Paraiyars and Pulayas. Some members of these castes had joined the small

63. Ibid., p. 157.

64. Ibid., p. 170.

65. Ibid., p. 193.

66. Ibid., p. 198.

67. F. Stock and M. Stock, *People Movements in the Punjab,* p. 116.

68. P. Wiebe, 'Protestant Missions in India: A Sociological Review'. *Journal of Asian and African Studies,* 5 (1970), p. 298.

69. L. Caplan, *Class and Culture in Urban India: Fundamentalism in a Christian Community* (Oxford: Oxford University Press, 1987), p. 92.

70. L. Caplan, 'The Popular Culture of Evil in Urban South India', in D. Parkin (ed.), *The Anthropology of Evil* (Oxford, Blackwell, 1985), p. 120; see also his 'Popular Christianity in Urban South India'. *Religion and Society,* 30 (1975).

71. L. Caplan, *Religion and Power: Essays on the Christian Community in Madras* (Madras: The Christian Literature Society, 1989), p. 98.

Syrian Mar Thomas Church; but they were quickly disappointed by the way they were treated by this high-status community; and, in 1907, Poykayil Johannan, a Mar Thomite Paraiyar, founded the Divine Church of Visible Salvation (Prathyaksha Raksha Daiva Sabha). The thousands of sect members considered their founder to be an incarnation of God, come down to earth to emancipate the slaves.[72] After Johannan's death in 1938, his wife attempted to carry on, but the sect declined and eventually died out. It seems that many of its members, including the founder's widow, subsequently returned to Hinduism.[73]

One Pulaya, named Solomon Morkose, left the CSI to found the Cheramar Daiva Sabha (Church of the Pulayas). In the 1960s, a bishop by the name of Stephen lured a large number of Pulayas away from the CSI to form an independent Church.[74] These movements within Christianity are symptomatic of an uneasiness or even a failure. Apparently conversion to Christianity did not always produce an improvement in the lives of Untouchables, either in economic or in social terms. Sometimes conversion even created as many problems as it solved: in some instances Untouchables had to contend with angry employers,[75] and in all cases they lost the legal advantages reserved for Untouchables. Today Hindu Untouchables are no poorer and no more oppressed than their Christian brothers.

Islam

It could therefore be considered that conversion is no longer an attractive option for Untouchables and that, in reality, the Hindu religion is no longer under threat. Yet in the last few decades, there have been two more cases of mass conversion: first of all the Mahars' massive conversion to Buddhism, which will be discussed in the next chapter; and, secondly, the conversion of a few thousands of Tamil Pallars to Islam. The latter case, although limited, is still revealing of a certain uneasiness, and we can examine it more closely.

The first conversions took place in Ramnad and Tirunelveli districts, in Tamil Nadu. The area around the town of Ramnad is dominated by Thevars (or Kallars), a farming caste prone to violence. Pallars, the main Untouchable caste in the vicinity, are not known for their resignation either, and the caste members are among the strongest militants. In addition, in the early 1980s, the region was troubled by various clashes between Thevars and Pallars.[76] In April 1981, the police fired on protesters in the town of Ramnad. In the months that followed, the Untouchables of several local villages

72. K. C. Alexander, 'The Neo-Christians of Kerala', in J. M. Mahar (ed.), *The Untouchables in Contemporary India* (Tucson: University of Arizona Press, 1972), pp. 153-64, p. 156.

73. S. Fuchs, *Rebellious Prophets: A Study of Messianic Movements in Indian Religions* (Bombay: Asia Publishing House, 1965), p. 282.

74. K. C. Alexander, 'The Problem of Caste in the Christian Churches of Kerala', in H. Singh (ed.), *Caste among the Non-Hindus in India* (Delhi: National Publishing House, 1977), p. 58.

75. S. Manickam, *The Social Setting of Christian Conversion.*

76. M. Kalam, 'Why the Harijan Convert to Islam Views Reservations with Reservation'. *South Asia Research,* 4 (1984).

converted to Islam. Meenakshipuram was one of the principal sites of conversion. There are many Muslims in the region, and they seem to have assured the Harijans of total equality in their community. Several hundreds of families took the step, and some observers quote the figure of 10,000 conversions in a matter of a few months. The totality of the Athiyuthu Harijan community converted at this time, and many of the men had themselves circumcised, even though this was not an obligation. Muslims from the area flocked to encourage the converts. Every day the bus from Madurai brought Muslims to the village; upon arriving, they would hurry over to the converts and embrace them, a gesture that went straight to their hearts.[77] It is interesting to note that some Protestant Harijans took part in this movement and converted to Islam.[78]

The Pallar converts to Islam were not the most deprived Harijans in the area.[79] No doubt they were not victims of the harshest discrimination, and the converted villages had not been directly affected by the recent outbreaks of violence. These relatively favourable circumstances make the conversions all the more striking. They indeed appear as an expression of the Harijans' bitterness towards Indian Society as a whole. The conversions to Islam provoked a veritable outcry among Hindus: government ministers, gurus, figures from all walks of life were sent in to staunch the haemorrhage and, if possible, to bring the stray sheep back to the fold. The Muslims were accused of having bought the converts with large sums of money from the Persian Gulf. Intercaste meals were organized by Hindu personalities, and the whole nation was rocked with emotion.

The Muslim community seems to have accepted the converts, but it is too early to assess the true impact of conversion on the Pallars' lives. Will they stop being Pallars? Will they marry Muslim women? Even if time answers these questions in the affirmative, India's political context makes it highly unlikely that there will be any more massive movements of Untouchables to Islam. As we have already said, conversion no longer seems the order of the day, and in all probability, Meenakshipuram will remain a relatively isolated case.

Religious Movements Within Hinduism

Traditionally, religion has always been the privileged area for expressing social discontent or other forms of protest. Hinduism is particularly tolerant of new religious currents, which hardly cause a tremor; on the contrary, they merely add to the extraordinary diversity of Hindu 'sects' and traditions. With the case of Sri Narayana Guru, we saw a few striking examples of a new line within Hinduism itself, and there have been others as well. We shall now look at a few of these.

77. A. Wingate, 'A Study of Conversion from Christianity to Islam in Two Tamil Villages'. *Religion and Society,* 27 (1981), p. 9.

78. Ibid., p. 4.

79. M. A. Kahn, 'A Brief Summary of the Study of "Mass Conversions" of Meenakshipuram'. *Religion and Society*, 28 (1981), p. 42.

The Satnamis of Chhattisgarh

Chhattisgarh district, in Madhya Pradesh, was the site of a fairly typical religious movement. Its instigator, Ghasi Das, was in all likelihood a Chamar.[80] Sometime in the 1820s, Ghasi Das, at that time a village servant in Girod, not far from Raipur, set out on a pilgrimage to Puri. He was never to reach that town, but returned prematurely to his village joyfully shouting '*Sat nam, Sat nam*' (One true God). He took up an ascetic life, spending his days in the forest in prayer and meditation. A short time later, he began performing miracles; the news went out that he cured snakebite, and his reputation quickly spread among the local Chamars, who formed the habit of coming to consult him. Visitors would return home with a little of the water he had used to wash his feet.[81] But Ghasi Das was not content with this cult; he decided to found a new doctrine and withdrew into the forest for six months. At daybreak on the prescribed day, he came down from his hill and entered the village where, like the Buddha, he revealed the message he had received from heaven. He proclaimed the equality of all men and declared himself the 'high priest' of the new sect, adding that the office was to remain in his family for ever. The seven precepts revealed by Ghasi Das were in the tradition of all Hindu religious reformers: abstinence from alcoholic beverages, vegetarianism, abolition of idol worship and the prohibition on using the cow as a plough animal all belong to the Brahminic tradition; the prohibition on eating red lentils, tomatoes and red peppers was probably motivated by their colour, which is that of blood. The abolition of caste was without consequence, as Chamars were the only ones who joined the sect.

Ghasi Das died in 1850, and his son Balak Das succeeded him. He adopted the sacred thread of the Brahmins and aroused the animosity of the upper castes, particularly the Rajputs, who finally assassinated him in 1860. His murder sparked the anger of the sect members, and riots and scenes of violence erupted throughout the region. Balak Das' descendants split the movement over the question of whether or not tobacco-smoking was allowed.[82] Although the current did not spread far beyond Chhattisgarh, today it is estimated that around 50 per cent of the Chamars of the region identify with the movement, which manifests itself in the form of a certain militant aggressiveness. It is reported that Satnamis would touch high-caste people in order to embarrass them by their purported pollution; they also made a show of wearing ornaments reserved for the upper castes, and in various ways demonstrated their contempt for Hindu customs. Many incidents brought them into conflict with the upper castes. Satnamis have enjoyed a certain measure of economic success, and today many are landowners.[83]

In spite of this opposition, the Satnamis' religion does not seem all that different from that of the Hindu majority.[84] The sect has its own temples, and its members go on

80. K. Jones, *Socio-Religious Reform Movements in British India* (Cambridge: Cambridge University Press, 1989), p. 128.

81. S. Fuchs, *Rebellious Prophets,* p. 100.

82. K. Jones, *Socio-Religious Reform Movements in British India,* p. 130.

83. S. Fuchs, *Rebellious Prophets,* p. 104.

pilgrimage to Girod, the founder's home town; however, the sect has been beset by constant infighting since the death of Balak Das.

The Ad-Dharms of Punjab

A similar movement grew up in the Punjab at the start of the 1920s. It is noteworthy that, as in Madhya Pradesh, these movements were not launched by the most deprived sections of the population, but by fairly privileged groups. Another striking feature is the mixture of modernity and tradition that characterizes their members: they preach a novel message of social equality and demand better living conditions, but their movement is rooted essentially in tradition, and in most cases is accompanied by a 'Sanskritization' of values and customs.

The social and political consciousness of Untouchables was most certainly stirred by the national liberation movement. In the beginning, the Congress Party had little concern for the fate of the most deprived. Their goal was to open the highest posts to Indians. For a long time the movement was dominated by strongly Westernized, high-caste figures, and it was only under Gandhi's leadership that the Congress became a truly popular movement. Through its claim to speak for all Indians in its dealings with the British, the Congress showed its solidarity with the poorest groups and could not disregard the lot of the low castes. Untouchables organized in an attempt to take advantage of this windfall, and, from the turn of the century, various associations for the defence of Untouchables began appearing, like the All-India Depressed Classes Association and the All-India Depressed Classes Federation, both founded in 1910. Their aim was to pressure the Congress Party into making the lot of Untouchables part of their programme: in 1917, the Congress Party, meeting in Calcutta, included the abolition of untouchability in their platform.[85]

Untouchables were courted from all sides. Arya Samaj began accepting the lower castes and created a ceremony, called *shuddhi*, which enabled Untouchables to purify themselves, and thus to rise to the level of the other castes.[86] The Punjab was a particular worry for the Arya Samaj, for, since Hindus were not a majority in this Sikh region, they feared their numbers would fall even lower owing to the Churhas' massive conversion to Christianity. In 1910, Arya Samaj purified some 36,000 Meghs, an untouchable caste and rival of the Churhas. Arya Samaj opened many schools for Untouchables, and thus enabled an elite to emerge within these groups. At the same time, the rise of the hide trade helped a great number of Chamars to improve their lives. Arya Samaj schools became very popular with this Chamar elite. In fact, one Chamar, Sant Ram B.A., created within the Arya Samaj movement an association for

84. L. Babb, 'The Satnamis: Political Involvement of a Religious Movement', in J. M. Mahar (ed.), *The Untouchables in Contemporary India* (Tucson: University of Arizona Press, 1972), p. 146.

85. M. Juergensmeyer, *Religion as Social Vision : The Movement against Untouchability in 20th Century Punjab* (Berkeley, CA: University of California Press, 1982), p. 23.

86. F. Stock and M. Stock, *People Movements in the Punjab*, p. 63; and K. Jones, *Socio-Religious Reform Movements in British India,* p. 101.

the promotion of social equality, called Jat Path Thorak Mandal (The Society for the Abolition of Caste).

But conflict soon broke out between this radical elite and the Hindu organization. In 1924, Sant Ram left Arya Samaj, and the following year, another Chamar, Swami Shudaranand, began making inflamed speeches denouncing the manoeuvres of this organization that was enticing Untouchables to join purely as a means of increasing their political force. This denunciation sowed discord among the Chamars, and particularly troubled Mangoo Ram, an Arya Samaj schoolteacher. This young man, from a family of leather merchants, had gone to university. In 1909, he left for the United States to work as a foreman, where he stayed until 1925. Upon returning to the Punjab, he immediately called attention to himself by opening a school for Untouchables, and soon won great popularity among the members of his own caste.

His encounters with Swami Shudraranand and other Untouchable leaders disappointed by Arya Samaj led him to believe that the creation of a new religion should be a primary goal of the emancipation movement. They called this new religion Ad-Dharm, the original religion. It was based on a sort of natural pantheism, with heavy emphasis on the equality of all men.[87] They chose the colour red as their symbol, and adopted a new form of greeting, *Jai Guru Dev*. Eight men, termed *updeshak* (missionaries), were sent out to preach the good news in the villages; they were aided by fifty-five *pracharak* (preachers). The movement met with rapid success, not only among Chamars, but also, it seems, among Churhas. In 1929, a few leaders, including Swami Shudraranand, left Ad-Dharm and went back to Arya Samaj; but the haemorrhage did not spread beyond these few personalities, who were later accused of having sold out. At the time of the 1931 census, the leaders asked their members to give their religion as Ad-Dharm. The Hindu reaction was violent; houses were torched, and two Ad-Dharmi were killed. In spite of this pressure, 418,798 people officially declared themselves Ad-Dharm. In Jullundur district, 80 per cent of Untouchables were listed as Ad-Dharm.

The movement played a particularly important role in raising the consciousness of Untouchables in the Punjab. Mangoo Ram clashed violently with Gandhi, and threw his support behind Ambedkar at the Round Table Conferences. When Gandhi began a hunger strike to show his opposition to the system of separate electorates, Mangoo Ram too began a fast, but in defence of the system. At this time, some even advanced the idea of an Achutistan (a country for Untouchables). Wary of the high-caste Congress Party leaders, Ad-Dharmis backed the British. When Gandhi led his Salt March, in 1930, Ad-Dharmis even organized demonstrations in support of British rule. When, in 1928, the Congress Party decided to boycott the Simon Commission, 150 Ad-Dharmis appeared before it, in Lahore, to explain the Untouchables' demands. In the 1936 elections, the movement ran candidates against the Congress, and managed to win seven of the eight seats reserved for Untouchables. Later the movement leaders joined forces with the Muslims, with the same idea of opposing the high-caste Congress membership. By the time of Independence, though, the Ad-Dharm

87. For this section, see M. Juergensmeyer, *Religion as Social Vision*.

88. R. S. Khare, *The Untouchable as Himself: Ideology, Identity and Pragmatism among the Lucknow Chamars* (Cambridge: Cambridge University Press, 1984).

movement had fallen apart, and no longer represented much of anything.

Other Movements

Similar movements of various sizes sprang up all over India. The cult of Ravi Das, a *bhakti* holy man of Chamar origin, spread through this caste.[88] The Madigas of Andhra Pradesh popularized the worship of a god called Yogi Pothuluri Virabramham. Members of this cult called themselves Rajayogi; but in 1909 the god's image was solemnly handed over to Monsignor Elmore, a Protestant bishop, and most of the Rajayogis converted to Christianity.[89]

Untouchable demands did not always take a religious form, but in almost every part of India, Untouchables formed associations and rose up against the servitude in which they had been languishing for centuries. In Kerala, Ayyankali (1863-1941) seized upon the Irava movement to mobilize the Pulayas. He organized agricultural-worker strikes to obtain the right to attend school. In 1900, for the first time the Pulayas stood up to the Nayars, who wanted to prevent them walking on the roads. Thanks to the movement launched by Ayyankali, they won this right at the start of the twentieth century. Ayyankali was present on every battlefront, and met with opposition from all castes, including Iravas and Muslims, who objected to his efforts to gain access to the markets. In 1905, Ayyankali founded the Sadhu Jana Paripalana Sangham (Association for the Welfare of the Poor), which succeeded in obtaining a six-day week for agricultural workers. Although this association won some spectacular victories, it never managed to unite the poor, and, as its name indicates, it was dominated by Pulayas.[90] Ayyankali was subsequently appointed to the Travancore legislative assembly, the Sri Mulam Popular Assembly, as the Pulaya representative.[91] In 1915-16, Nayars and Pulayas clashed violently over women's right to cover their breasts.

The question of religion was of little concern to Pulayas; but they seem to have been strong supporters of the powerful Kerala communist movement.[92] One of the leaders of Cochin's Pulaya Mahajana Sabha, P. K. Chathan, became a minister in the 1957-9 communist cabinet. Nevertheless, this political engagement did not rule out feelings of caste membership, and Pulayas did not form ties with the other heavily communist castes like Iravas or Paraiyars.

So it was that most untouchable groups succumbed to the pitfall of caste. Their egalitarian ideology was confined to their own group, and the emancipation movements invariably turned into caste movements. This was the case of the Bhangis in North India. It was a Brahmin close to Arya Samaj circles, Shankar Lal, who led the first Bhangi association, in Jodhpur. Later an organization called Marwar Mehtar

89. S. Fuchs, *Rebellious Prophets,* pp. 260-3.
90. See K. Saradamoni, *Emergence of a Slave Caste,* pp. 146-58.
91. T. Ravindran, *Asan and Social Revolution in Kerala,* p. xxvii.
92. For example, K. Gough, 'Village Politics in Kerala', in A. R. Desai (ed.), *Rural Sociology in India* (Bombay: Popular Prakashan, 1978), p. 753.

Sudhar Sabha was created in Marwar province. In 1946, this association instigated a sweepers' strike aimed at obtaining better working conditions. Two years later, the association was found throughout the state, under the name of Rajputana Mehtar Sudhar Sabha.[93] Before that, the local Banghis had been involved in a socio-religious movement inspired by Naval Sahib, who, because of his miraculous powers and spiritual elevation, was recognized as a holy man.[94] He, too, denounced idol worship, the eating of meat, alcohol, violence and extravagant spending. In Karnataka, the Holerus refused to remove dead cows and to gather wood for high-caste funeral pyres, which they judged to be degrading tasks.[95] And the same scenario was repeated all over India. Taking advantage of the egalitarian accents of the nationalist ideology, Untouchables everywhere began asserting their dignity in movements more or less strongly coloured by religious overtones.

Recent Movements

The movements discussed above have not completely ceased their activities. But I would like to look at a few more recent movements. Now, at the end of the twentieth century, there are many movements for the defence of Harijans. Most are not much different from their predecessors. When they launch a universal appeal, they have trouble finding an audience; so they usually limit themselves to one caste. For instance, in the last decades, there has appeared a caste organization among the Pallars called the Devandrakula Vellala Mahasabha, which was involved notably in the incidents at Bodinayakanur, near Madurai, in 1989, in which thirty people were killed and many more wounded.[96] Today Harijans appear much less fearful than in the past. They do not hesitate to retaliate with violence when they feel wronged or when they are victims of 'atrocities'. Recent movements therefore tend to be more determined and radical.

The Dalit Panthers

Maharashtra was the birthplace of one of the most radical, though short-lived, movements. The very name of the movement is typical of the increased aggressiveness of Untouchables, who no longer go by euphemisms, but are proud to be called *dalit*, or 'the downtrodden', the 'exploited', while the term 'panther', which is itself significant, is obviously an echo of the American Black Panthers, with whom the young *dalits* sometimes identify.[97] The Dalit Panthers were born on 9 July 1972, in

93. Shyamlal, *The Banghis in Transition* (New Delhi: Inter-India Publications, 1984), p. 50.

94. Ibid., p. 57.

95. E. Harper, 'Social Consequences of an Unsuccessful Low Caste Movement', in J. Silverberg (ed.), Social Mobility in the Caste System (The Hague: Mouton, 1968), pp. 35-65, p. 63.

96. S. Ganeshram, 'Communalism in Tamil Nadu: A Study of Bodi Riots'. *Economic and Political Weekly,* 2 December (1989).

Siddhartha Nagar, a quarter of Bombay. Its founders, among them J. V. Pawar and Dhasal, emphasized the need to fight for their basic rights, and held that every 'atrocity' must be avenged. The movement caught on quickly; in 1974, there were an estimated 25,000 members, in the majority Neo-Buddhist Mahars (see above, this chapter). Although its manifesto contained a certain number of radical positions,[98] the movement soon began to suffer from its weak ideological foundations and from the absence of efforts to strengthen it. It finally broke up in 1974, under the strain of rivalry between two of its leaders, Dhale and Dhasal. By 1977, nothing remained of this organization, which had never tried to reach out to rural areas.[99]

However short-lived it may have been, this movement is nonetheless interesting. It was indisputably symptomatic of a state of mind, especially among young urban Untouchables. And it is therefore not surprising to see it spring up now and again in various forms and places. The term *dalit* has also passed to posterity, and is now used by all sorts of radical organizations. Among these, for example, we find the Karnataka Dalit Sangharsh Samiti (KDSS), a movement devoted to the defence of *dalit* rights and the propagation of new values; popular theatre and journalism are two of their favourite vehicles. The Delhi State Dalit Panthers is another movement dominated by young intellectual activists, and one that seems to privilege ideological weapons. Nevertheless, it was also heavily involved in supporting a movement of brick-factory labourers.[100] Finally, in Gujarat, there is another organization that also calls itself the 'Dalit Panthers'; in the early 1980s it attracted attention by its involvement in the defence of victims of high-caste agitation against the Untouchables of this state.[101] Today, indeed, there are hundreds of *dalit* organizations all over India.

The Maharashtra Literary Movement

Several writers in the Dalit Panther current were the first of a veritable Marathi literary movement known as Dalit Sahitya ('literature of the downtrodden'). Once again Neo-Buddhist Mahars dominate this remarkable movement. Their ideology is openly militant and often aggressive: the wretched Untouchable becomes a proud *dalit*, sure of his rights and his strength. Like the Dalit Panthers, these authors have no intention of hiding; rather, they proclaim their revolt loud and clear. Their weapon is the pen, and many of their poems express these sentiments. The principal figures of this movement are intellectuals, of course; but it would be unfair to say they were totally cut off from the masses. Daya Pawar's excellent autobiography is ample proof of this.[102]

Without ever playing on the reader's pity, and often with humour and sensitivity, Pawar tells of his childhood in a deprived family, with a father who stole, drank and

97. See for example, V. Rajshekar Shetty, *Dalit: The Black Untouchables of India* (Atlanta, GA: Clarity Press, 1987).

98. See B. Joshi (ed.), *Untouchables! Voices of the Dalit Liberation Movement* (London: Zed Books, 1986), pp. 141-7.

99. See L. Murugkar, *Dalit Panther Movement in Maharashtra: A Sociological Appraisal* (Bombay: Popular Prakashan, 1991).

100. B. Joshi, 'Recent Developments in Inter-Regional Mobilization of Dalit Protest in India'. *South Asia Bulletin,* 7 (1987), p. 89.

101. A. Yagnik and A. Bhatt, 'The Anti-Dalit Agitation in Gujarat'. *South Asia Bulletin,* 4 (1984), p. 54.

102. D. Pawar, *Ma vie d'intouchable* (Paris: La Découverte, 1990).

frequented brothels. Nevertheless, he draws a picture full of tenderness for this *dada* (daddy), who always said he would leave the world as naked as he came into it; of his grandmother, Pawar tells us that 'she never knew a whit of happiness in her whole life'. Because of his intellectual capacities and his mother's determination, the young Pawar went to school, and was torn between two worlds: 'On the one hand, I was taught in school to tell the truth, and on the other hand, I would go to the flea market to sell whatever Dada had stolen. The schoolroom seemed to me unreal compared to the real world, like a picture in a lovely frame.'[103]

The people among whom he was born were filthy, sordid, liars and thieves, and were loathsome to him. The girls from his caste frightened him, with their hair sticking out all over and their disgusting rags, and he dreamed of the Marathi girls, whom he knew he could never approach:[104] 'People in the marârvâdâ lived like cattle. They had their own, rugged philosophy. I began to detest them, but those whose lives were my ideal wanted nothing to do with me. I found myself in a strangely awkward situation.'[105]

The Mahars in Pawar's writings are proud, caustic, sometimes even arrogant:

"'The Mahars of the time did not take insults lying down. They had black skin, were big and strong and addressed Marathis as equals. The farmers would try to give them the top of the stack, but the Mahars wanted their share from the bottom, where the best ears were.[106]

One day the villagers blocked the way to our well because, they said, the Mahar women's shadow would fall on the god Maruti and defile him. To get to the well by another route, you had to go through more than half a mile of mud. The Mahars had a fight with the villagers over opening the way. We went to court. The Mahars argued heatedly: 'We are not going to give up our customary passage. If you want, all you have to do is put Maruti somewhere else.'"[107]

Other writers seem, on the whole, to have a more militant, even aggressive style. Recent translations of many *dalit* poems give us a much more detailed idea of this movement, which is sometimes surprisingly radical and aggressive.[108]

Limitations

The assessment one can make of more than a century of social movements is mixed. Harper, detailing the Holerus' efforts, concludes that their movement was a failure because it did not put an end to social inequalities. His judgement may be a bit harsh, but above all it seems to miss the real point of the social movements we have just

103. Ibid., p. 34.
104. Ibid., p. 79.
105. Ibid., p. 47.
106. Ibid., p. 64.
107. Ibid., pp. 67-8.
108. See, for example, J. Gokhale-Turner, 'Bhakti or Vidroha: Continuity and Change in *Dalit Sahitya'*. *Journal of Asian and African Studies,* 15 (1980), pp. 29-42; G. Omvedt, 'Dalit Literature in Maharashtra: Literature of Social Protest and Revolt in Western India'. *South Asia Bulletin,* 7 (1987); or E. Zelliot, *From Untouchable to Dalit.*

looked at. In effect, it can be said that none of them claimed to struggle for a society that was egalitarian and fair. To be sure, all, without exception, made reference to a democratic ideology and the ideal of equality, and even fraternity, but none made any true effort to implement this vague programme. The Irava case is paradigmatic. Although at the outset the Iravas were inspired by the egalitarian philosophy of a guru, they soon focused all their efforts on their own struggle, to the extent that they constituted one of the major obstacles to the emancipation of the Pulayas. From a certain point of view, it could be said that the Irava movement failed because it was incapable of producing any change in the hierarchical structure of society. But that would be assigning it a role it never set out to play.

One initial general remark needs to be made here: none of the movements studied was able to rise above caste differences; none even managed to unite two or three castes in the same state. In other words, in the recent history of India there has been no true movement to unite Untouchables against the system that oppresses them. Ambedkar was no doubt the man who tried the hardest; but we shall see, in the next chapter, that his efforts were relatively futile and that, in his lifetime, he was sometimes reduced to the role of Mahar leader. For the rest, untouchable movements inevitably became caste movements, working within the system for the promotion of a single caste, sometimes at the expense of the others. When one untouchable caste would convert to Christianity, the others would prefer Arya Samaj. When one caste would refuse to remove dead cows, this sad privilege would often fall to the other local untouchable castes. Seeking the lowest common denominator is not a viable strategy for upward mobility, and therefore the social movements did not succeed in either eliminating or weakening the caste system. It is even possible that caste organizations tended to reinforce the institution.

Yet these movements had an effect on society that was far from negligible. They had much to do with popularizing the ideas of equality and democracy, to such an extent, in fact, that today the ideology of hierarchy is no longer acceptable. There is hardly a social force in India today that dares openly advocate an elitism and social ranking. Now, when Brahmins protest, it is for social justice, stressing, for instance, the unfairness of the positive discrimination system to the poorest members of their caste. Social equality has thus become an almost natural value, and it is inequality that now seems aberrant. In other words, it is true that the social movements turned into caste movements; but at the same time they shook the ideology of hierarchy on which the system was founded. The caste system has by no means disappeared, though; all one has to do is talk with a high-caste farmer or read the newspaper accounts of the many 'atrocities' to be convinced of this. But it is no longer an official ideology, it is losing ground; for instance, it is not uncommon to hear a high-caste person voice his nostalgia by saying that after Moghul rule, India came under British rule, only to throw itself into 'Chamar rule'. Untouchables had to deal with a particularly strong and often violent resistance that is barely attenuated even today. But it must also be acknowledged that the majority of Untouchables were heavily influenced by these movements, and that today hardly anyone among them believes their deprivation to be justified.

The contemporary decline in religious movements has not been compensated by a politicization of other movements. In spite of a few attempts, Untouchables have not succeeded in developing a true political expression of their own. Ambedkar's Republican Party was the most convincing effort; but it never really managed to put down roots. It must be said that Gandhi's electoral system hardly favoured untouchable militancy either, since, in order to be elected, an Untouchable had to have high-caste votes. It is not surprising, in these conditions, to witness the Republican Party's 'pathetic defeat'.[109]

This defeat stemmed in part from the fact that the boundaries between the different castes were never really questioned. Today they still stand, as strong and as insurmountable as ever. Endogamy, for example, has never been seriously contested, and this is the main problem with the Untouchables' struggle; while they were able to bring off a partial success here and there, their lack of unity made them wholly incapable of using their numerical strength to exert group pressure or as a political force. It is even striking to see that we have no example of fusion or even of a significant *rapprochement* between two untouchable castes. An even more serious problem is the incapacity of two untouchable castes to unite in any significant way against higher castes. A few organizations bring together two or even several castes from one state, but their impact is minimal, and none of the large-scale movements discussed here has managed such a feat.

All these movements seem to waver between two attitudes towards Indian society and the Hindu religion: rejection, or, on the contrary, integration. In the next chapter, we shall see that Ambedkar formulated the question in almost identical terms, and the debate that opposed him to Gandhi reflects this dilemma. Should Untouchables be integrated into the political system or, on the contrary, should they be regarded as a separate community and given their own representatives? The Iravas hesitated a long time between the two attitudes, all the while brandishing the spectre of conversion. And at each violation of their rights, a few thousand Nadars would go over to Christianity. These hesitations reflect the ambiguousness of the Untouchables' position in society, which we have stressed on many occasions. Are they a *part of* society or, on the contrary, *apart from* society? If they themselves do not quite know where they stand, and if they give different and constantly changing answers to this question, it is precisely because of this ambiguity. We shall see how inconsistent Ambedkar seems on this point: was it the same man who agreed to preside the Constituent Assembly and then, a few years later, solemnly repudiated Hinduism and converted to Buddhism? These apparently contradictory acts stem from this ambiguity and reflect it.

Nevertheless, even if we see groups throughout India attempting to set themselves apart from Hinduism and Indian society, the huge majority of Untouchables have opted for integration. The centripetal forces have indeed prevailed over the centrifugal pull. Nothing says that the latter will not surface at some later time, as in the case of the recent wave of conversions to Islam; but at these moments the Hindu majority calls Untouchables to order, stressing that they are an integral part of 'Hindu society', if I may use the expression: this is notably and notoriously the role played by Gandhi in the 1930s; it is also one of the essential functions of Arya Samaj, which 'purifies'

109. V. Rajshekar Shetty, *Dalit Movement in Karnataka* (Madras: The Christian Literature Society, 1978), p. 98.

Untouchables; it is also the role perspicaciously played by the Maharaja of Travancore and his Chief Minister; and finally, it is what we see in Ramnad district, when gurus of all castes take part in intercaste meals.

If the majority has opted for integration, they have not necessarily done so for their own pleasure, but because they had no choice. 'Only Hindu gods are available', was the symbolic comment of one man; for Untouchables, there is no salvation outside Indian society. There is something desperate or provocative about the opposition movements we have observed or those we see emerging today: this is particularly true of the conversions to Islam and the dalit movements. Moreover, nothing says that these reactions will not gather strength.

-8-

B. R. Ambedkar

Leader of the Untouchables

Over the twentieth century, the condition of Untouchables has undergone unprecedented transformations, some of which we saw in the preceding chapter. Untouchables began increasingly to look to the egalitarian ideas introduced by the British. Their contact with Christian missionaries, democratic political parties, socialist ideology, the national liberation movement and the general modernity of the twentieth century gradually convinced them that there was nothing legitimate or inevitable about their lot in life; they grew less and less inclined to accept being treated as outcastes, and soon refused to perform what they saw as humiliating or degrading tasks. It was then they realized that, wherever the opportunity presented itself, they could successfully occupy more esteemed social positions. The first low-caste movements finally persuaded them that they, too, could demand formal equality and a more respectable place in society.

But their destitution was hardly conducive to the affirmation and defence of their rights. How could a person demand respect on an empty stomach, when he was unable to read or write and clothed in rags? They clearly needed someone capable of presenting their case. Gandhi took this task upon himself; but he was not an Untouchable and the ideas he put forward did not always express their deepest aspirations. Several leaders emerged from their own ranks: Ayyankali, M. C. Rajah, Jagjivan Ram and a few others. Yet none equalled renown of Bhimrao Ramji Ambedkar, a charismatic figure born into the Mahar caste of Maharashtra, who hotly contested Gandhi's right to speak for Untouchables.

Ambedkar is by far the greatest figure ever born to the untouchable community; it would unfortunately be tempting to say that he was the only real leader they ever produced. As such, he stands out in the history of modern-day India. The personality of Dr Ambedkar is fascinating in more than one respect. His running conflict with Gandhi constitutes one of the most significant episodes of decolonization; this was not a drawing-room disagreement, or even a power struggle between two great men; it was a crucial debate, the outcome of which was to affect millions of lives, even today. Ambedkar was also a true statesman, in the noblest sense of the term. While it was his desire to speak for Untouchables, he also had a sense of the nation and the state, even though he was sometimes led to regret his loyalty. It is therefore a paradox that this great man did not always succeed in exercising a radical influence outside his own caste. He who strove to 'do away with' the caste system often found himself a prisoner of the role of simple caste leader. This paradox can be seen in Ambedkar's own life and work, a paradox in which all Untouchables are caught up. Ultimately, not only was Ambedkar unable to surmount the divisions between the different untouchable castes, but, by certain of its aspects, his radical stance stigmatized Untouchables as different from the rest of society, as a separate category - a position he at other times rejected.

One wonders if Ambedkar's conversion to Buddhism, after twenty years of equivocating, might not express a certain distress, a disenchantment with the ideal of a casteless society. Nevertheless, in spite of his contradictions, or perhaps because of them, the man still works his spell, and today is recognized as a great figure of modern-day India.

His life

The Mahars are an important caste in Maharashtra. They are also a numerically dominant untouchable caste in this region, accounting for more than 9 per cent of the state's overall population and over one third of its Untouchables. Mahars look on the other untouchable castes as rivals: especially the Mang rope-makers, and the Chambhars, who are leather-workers. Traditionally, Mahars were village watchmen, and performed numerous services for the higher castes. Because of their traditional occupation, as we have seen, they were used as soldiers by the Marathas and the Peshwas; but it was the British who systematically recruited Mahars for the army. As soldiers were required to know how to read and write, the British set up classes for these men and their families. Ambedkar was born into one such family.

Compared with the rest of his caste, his background must have been a fairly privileged one. He recalls that even the women of the family could read, which was extremely rare at the time. Already by the end of the nineteenth century, then, an intellectual and social elite was beginning to emerge among the Mahars. It was into this same caste, at the end of the tirthteenth century, that the *bhakti* holy man (*sant*) Chokhamela was born; but, still, it was not until the nineteenth century that a veritable[1] elite would begin to develop. In 1888, a retired soldier, Gopal Baba Walangkar, founded a newspaper, called *Vital Vidhansak*, aimed at Untouchables, retracing their glorious past and disparaging the upper castes. Walangkar, too, threatened to convert to a different religion; he also started a petition to create a Mahar regiment. Other social reformers, like Kamble and Bansode, were also Mahars.

It was in this favourable context that, in 1891, in the village of Mahu (in the present-day state of Madhya Pradesh), the child was born who one day would be given the name Ambedkar by a Brahmin, in memory of his grandfather's home village of Ambadave (Ratnagiri district). The grandfather had enlisted in the British army, and

1. E. Zelliot, 'Dr. Ambedkar and the Mahar Movement'. (Doctoral dissertation, University of Pennsylvania, 1969), p. 57.

was emulated by his three sons, the youngest of whom, Ramji Sakpal, would become Ambedkar's father. Ramji Sakpal was assigned to the 106th Sappers and Miners; he married Bhimabai Murbadkar, the daughter of a major, the highest rank an Indian could attain in the British army. Ramji Sakpal must have had considerable intellectual baggage, since he was made headmaster of the army's teachers' college in Mahu, where Ambedkar was born. Shortly after the birth of this, their fourteenth, child, Ramji Sakpal retired, and the family moved into a Mahar pensioned soldiers' colony, in the heart of Ratnagiri district.

In 1900, young Ambedkar was admitted to the English school in Satara, where he was segregated from the others in the classroom. In 1904, the family moved to Bombay, in part, it seems, to continue the boy's education. In 1907, he was accepted to Bombay university; a few Mahars, including his father, had reached a comparable educational level in the army, but Ambedkar seems to have been the first or the second to go to University. Whichever the case, this performance was something to celebrate, and the family threw a party for the graduate. S. K. Bole, who was subsequently elected to the legislative assembly, attended, and gave Ambedkar a book on the life of the Buddha. This present has become part of the Ambedkar legend, because Mahars regard it as a prophecy.

Shortly before that, Ambedkar had been married to Ramabai Walangkar, a girl of nine or ten at the time, from a modest family, although she was related to Gopal Baba Walangkar. Ambedkar's wife seems to have stayed in the background. The couple had four children. After the death of his first wife, Ambedkar married a young Brahmin, Savitabai, who also converted to Buddhism.[2]

Convinced of the young man's intellectual capacities, the Gaikwad, Maharaja of Baroda, provided him with a monthly stipend of 25 rupees to attend Elphinstone College (Bombay University). Ambedkar easily obtained his Bachelor of Arts degree. His stipend obliged him to enter the service of the Maharaja of Baroda, which proved to be a distressing experience; and years later Ambedkar could not keep the tears from his eyes when he thought about it. His colleagues made life difficult for him: the carpets were removed from wherever he was to be, files were tossed on to his desk in order to avoid having any contact with him, and no one was willing to lodge him. He was soon called back to Bombay to the bedside of his dying father. During his stay there, he met the Maharaja, and asked for permission to continue his studies. As the Maharaja's son was a student at Harvard at the time, it was decided to send Ambedkar to the United States. There he spent three years, from 1913 to 1916, at New York's Columbia University, where he studied mainly economics, but also took courses in sociology, history and even anthropology, the latter from Goldenweiser. He wrote a paper for Goldenweiser on the caste system, which was published in 1917 in *Indian Antiquary.* The article did not address the issue of untouchability directly, but the author developed the important theme of the original homogeneity of the Indian people.[3]

2. W. Vijayakumar, 'A Historical Survey of Buddhism in India: A Neo-Buddhist Interpretation', in T. Wilkinson and M. Thomas (eds), *Ambedkar and the Neo-Buddhist Movement* (Madras: The Christian Literature Society, 1972), p. 31.

3. E. Zelliot, 'Dr. Ambedkar and the Mahar Movement', p. 81. 4. E. Zelliot, *From Untouchable to Dalit: Essays on Ambedkar Movement* (Delhi: Manohar, 1922), pp. 58-9.

He earned his Master of Arts degree in 1915, but his doctorate was awarded him only much later, in 1927, after the publication of his thesis on *The Evolution of Provincial Finances in British India.* The years in America seem to have made a great impression on the young man. Several professors, whom he regarded as friends, influenced him profoundly: John Dewey, Edwin Seligman and James Robinson, in particular. Ambedkar was one of the few Indian politicians to have studied in the United States. It is probable that his life and career bore deep traces of this stay, and he never contemplated any other political system for the new India than parliamentary democracy. One thing that made him a relatively rare figure among popular leaders in the colonies of that time, was that Marxism and communism never seemed to him a suitable solution for his country. He also lived like a Westerner, and never affected a return to Indian traditions. To the Mahars, he seemed a model of modernity, of the benefits of civilization. Already one can see the first signs of his radical opposition to Gandhi, the apostle of tradition.

After the United States, he obtained a fellowship to study in England, where he spent a year; he attended classes at the London School of Economics and was admitted to Grey's Inn, where he prepared his bar examinations. But he finished his studies only after a brief return to India. When he finally moved back to that country, he made a brilliant career as a barrister; but he also taught law at Bombay's Government Law College, was vice president of the textile union in the same city, a member of the upper house, a member of the viceroy's executive council, later chairman of the committee charged with framing India's Constitution, and finally Law Minister in the first cabinet of the newly independent country. He converted to Buddhism a few months before his death, in 1956.

This remarkable career alone made a strong impression on his fellow Untouchables. One Mahar song of praise, for instance, enumerates his university degrees in a sort of litany: BA, MA, Ph.D., M.Sc., D.Sc., Barrister at Law … Zelliot notes with insight that the pictures of Ambedkar gracing every Mahar home and the statues found on public display throughout Maharashtra always show him in Western dress, with suit and tie, holding a book (the Constitution).[4] Unlike other leaders of decolonization, this man, from one of the lowest castes, never troubled to dress in Indian fashion, but, on the contrary, took pains to project an image of a Westernized man, cultured and superior. This image earned him enormous prestige among Mahars. In effect, they had the reputation of being repulsive, dirty, dull and foolish. Contemporary accounts describe Mahars as vermin. Closer to us, Pawar clearly recalls how the women of his caste used to disgust him with their hair crawling with lice and their filthy clothes.[5] And here was one of their own, capable of rising to the top of society and widely acknowledged as someone of importance.

When Ambedkar was asked to represent the Depressed Classes at the 1930 session of the Round Table Conference, the news hit Mahars like a bomb, even in the remotest villages: the whole caste was incredibly proud to see one of their own seated at the same table with ministers and princes! A new myth was born among Mahars; and it made the old claims to prestigious origins a thing of the past. By his very example,

4. E. Zelliot, *From Untouchable to Dalit,* pp. 58-9.
5. D. Pawar, *Ma vie d'intouchable,* (Paris: La Decouverte, 1990), p. 79.

Ambedkar became at once a model and a symbol. For a long time Gandhi himself thought that he was just another Brahmin taking an interest in the cause of the most deprived, and one of his British professors described him as a sort of Scottish-American. Pawar remembers that his death had all Mahars in tears, and he told the chief officer: 'Sir, he was a member of our family. How could you understand the depths from which he raised us?'[6] Whereas upper-caste nationalist leaders were anxious to show their Indian roots (sometimes very fragile ones), Ambedkar demonstrated his own dignity and that of his fellow Untouchables by conducting himself like a Westerner. Gentlemanly bearing, cultivated speech, distinguished dress were all handicaps for upper-caste leaders; for Ambedkar, they were assets that personified the ambitions of an entire segment of the population.

His ideas

The foregoing does not mean that Ambedkar was some sort of chubby dandy of no real stature. His university studies are proof enough of his intellectual capacities; but it was more in his political life and his writings that Ambedkar revealed his true nature and originality. Depending on the circumstances, he was capable of being both radical and moderate; he was unstinting in the defence of his fellow Untouchables, without losing sight of national interests; he preached firmness, but rejected violence. While he may occasionally have changed his mind over the course of his long political career, he was by and large consistent.

Ambedkar began his public life in 1919, when, as an untouchable university graduate, he was called to testify before the election commission responsible for finalizing the modalities of the new Bombay provincial government. He was not speaking on behalf of an organization, for he had no mandate; he was speaking as an Untouchable, unconnected with any group. This young Columbia graduate was confident that the government would be able to end the most flagrant forms of social injustice. He had faith in democratic institutions, he believed in the future and, to members of the commission, he looked like a moderate, self-confident and optimistic fellow. This was the beginning of his political career and of the organization of many Depressed Classes Conferences. Young Ambedkar was not inspired by the issue of religion so present in the earlier untouchable campaigns. At the outset, he thought that education, political power and dignity, instead, would enable Untouchables to improve their lives, and it was on these that he intended to concentrate his efforts. That is no doubt why he was not unduly enthusiastic about the many temple-entry movements. To his mind, it was poverty that needed to be eliminated, and it was democratically held elections that would enable Untouchables to express their strength. Ambedkar appears as a legalist: he had no liking for violence, nor did he care to take part in dangerous protests; and did not encourage Mahars to do so either. On the contrary, he warned them of the dangers of violence and himself preferred legal action. But his legalism did not bear the fruits he had hoped; Ambedkar's aspirations were

6. Ibid., p. 192.

disappointed, but he did not give up; he continued to eschew violence. In the 1920s, he even advocated using the Gandhian *satyagraha* in the struggle to gain entry to the temples of Poona, Nasik and Amraoti.

These protests proved a bitter failure. Hindus continued to exclude Untouchables from their temples, and Ambedkar began to nurture the idea that it was useless to attempt to participate in Hindu society. In the early 1930s, he seems to have begun stressing the irreversible nature of untouchability and the senselessness of fighting for integration; he therefore considered that the temple-entry movements should stop, since Untouchables would never become members of Hindu society anyway, or worship what he began calling Hindu 'idols'. It was at this point that he conceived the idea of two nations, an idea that was also gaining ground among India's Muslim population, and led to the outcome we know. In 1930, he told an audience at Nasik: 'Our problems will not be solved by temple-entry ... Today's *satyagraha* is a challenge to the Hindu way of thinking. Are the Hindus ready to consider us men or not? We will discover this today.' The repeated failure of these movements eventually convinced him that the god sitting in the temple was made of stone. He began to regret having put his faith in the government, which had not raised a finger to improve Untouchables' lives, and he advised the latter to take their destiny into their own hands. The change is clear, and it was profound. It is paradoxical that the man who had paid so little attention to religious struggles would come to regard them as so important once they had failed.

The turning-point came in a radical manner in 1935, when Ambedkar solemnly announced: 'I will not die a Hindu.' The threat of conversion had been brandished by Untouchables from the nineteenth century onwards, but Ambedkar was not using it as blackmail; the man who uttered these words was full of resentment, and convinced that Hinduism no longer held out any hope for Untouchables. It is nevertheless surprising that this prophecy was not fulfilled until 21 years later, when Ambedkar led Mahars in a massive conversion to Buddhism. We shall explore this particularly important episode in a later section, for the moment returning to Ambedkar's ideas and how they clashed with those of Gandhi.

The Conflict between Gandhi and Ambedkar

The conflict between Gandhi and Ambedkar is an important chapter in the history of India's nationalist movement. It was a personality clash, to be sure, but also a confrontation between fundamentally divergent ideas about the defence of Untouchables. One wonders whether Ambedkar's conversion might not also have been a reaction to Gandhi's Hinduism. Ambedkar was no doubt one of the few prominent leaders of the national liberation movement to have openly opposed Gandhi, and it is only a slight exaggeration to say that he hated the man. His book, *What Congress and Gandhi Have Done to the Untouchables,* reflects the virulence of his feelings; but it is also a brilliant political analysis; with remarkable foresight, Ambedkar already perceived the price Untouchables would have to pay for Gandhi's concessions.

Gandhi's biographers are manifestly uncomfortable with these events. As a rule they depict Gandhi as a champion of the untouchable cause, and they have some difficulty understanding, or acknowledging, his quarrel with Ambedkar. Nanda, who easily runs to hagiography, even manages not to mention Ambedkar in connection with the Round Table Conference negotiations. Sinha and Ray follow suit,[7] and, in their 600-page history of India, contrive superbly to ignore the name of Ambedkar. Nanda makes a furtive reference to him when discussing Gandhi's fast, and accuses him of having gone back on his signed agreements and of vilifying Gandhi.[8] Fisher has little more praise, and depicts Ambedkar as a man filled with hatred, who prefers the English to Indians, and Muslims to Hindus, and is basically indifferent to the possibility that Gandhi might die.[9] Their Manichaeism prevents these authors seeing complex issues that were at stake in this quarrel and that deserve a more serene discussion.

In the 1920s, Ambedkar did not yet know Gandhi personally; but the latter's non-violent methods suited the pacific nature of Ambedkar, who made use of Gandhi's *satyagraha*. Or rather, he was drawn into several demonstrations of this type, for, as we have seen, he was not himself inclined to mass action. It should also be noted that Ambedkar seems never to have envisaged joining the Congress Party, a remarkable fact in itself, since at that time the Congress was *the* political platform for the Young Turks of the nationalist movement. But on these points, Ambedkar seems to have been closer to the ideas of such leaders as Nehru. And he remains circumspect as to the willingness of Congress Party members really to put an end to the discriminations inflicted on Untouchables. Commenting on Gandhi's actions, on the occasion of the *satyagraha* at Vaikom (Kerala), he criticizes him for not defending Untouchables vigorously enough:

"If one looks more closely one finds that there is a slight disharmony between Mahatma Gandhi and untouchability … For he does not insist on the removal of untouchability as much as he insists on the propagation of Khaddar on Hindu-Muslim unity. If he had, he would have made the removal of untouchability a precondition for membership of the Congress as he made yarn spinning a precondition of voting in the party."[10]

It was during the Round Table Conference that relations between the two men broke down irretrievably. The Congress refused to take part in the first session of the conference, held in London in 1930, because it was in the midst of waging a disobedience campaign. The Muslim delegation went to London, where Ambedkar and Rao Bahadur Srinivasan were representing the Depressed Classes. This trip produced a memorable effect on the Maharashtra Mahars, who, from this moment on, began literally to worship their leader. Ambedkar and Srinivasan came across as moderates; they did not demand the provision of separate electorates. At this time, the most radical untouchable leaders generally admitted to preferring the British Raj to an eventual Hindu Raj, and they were not in favour of independence. But this was not

7. N. Sinha and N. Ray, *A History of India* (Calcutta: Orient Longman, 1986).

8. S. B. Nanda, *Gandhi: sa vie, ses idées, son action politique en Afrique du Sud et en Inde* (Verviers: Marabout, 1968), p. 248.

9. L. Fisher, *La Vie du Mahatma Gandhi* (Paris: Belfond, 1983), p. 291.

10. Quoted by E. Zelliot, 'Dr. Ambedkar and the Mahar Movement', p. 99.

quite Ambedkar's position, for he wanted to make the liberation of Untouchables part of a broader programme. Unlike other leaders, he was thus in favour of 'autonomy', *swaraj.* Upon arriving in London, he made a speech in which he asked that India have 'a government by the people and for the people'.

At the first session, the Muslim delegation found themselves sitting with the Untouchable representatives on the 'minorities' commission, where they advanced several radical positions. Among other things, they demanded 'communal' representation in the executive councils. It seems that Ambedkar and Srinivasan let themselves be somewhat carried away by this militant enthusiasm, and began demanding a separate electorate for Untouchables and representation in the provincial governments. It is hard to know exactly what caused Ambedkar to change his mind, but it is important to look at what this change involved. At the start of the negotiations, the two untouchable representatives agreed to call for 'reserved seats' for Untouchables in the legislative assemblies. In other words, they wanted a certain number of places set aside for Untouchables. But soon this position was not radical enough to suit them; following the Muslim delegation, or inspired by their boldness, they began to demand separate electorates, that is to say a system by which Untouchables would elect their own representatives separately from the Hindu majority; clearly the 'two nations' theory lurked behind this stand. In effect, this theory viewed Untouchables as forming a separate community, with few if any ties to the rest of the nation.

The defection of the Congress Party rendered the first session insignificant for the most part. In 1931, the Gandhi-Irwin pact put an end to the civil disobedience campaign; Congress Party leaders, whom Gandhi had not gone to the trouble of consulting, were stupefied and furious upon hearing the news. Nevertheless they agreed to send a delegation to the second session of the Round Table Conference, to be held in London from 7 September to 1 December 1931. Gandhi represented the Congress, and sat with Ambedkar on the minorities commission. As the two men did not know each other, it was arranged that they meet in Bombay, before their departure for Europe. Their relations were ill fated from the outset. Ambedkar complained that Gandhi had been rude to him, and Gandhi admitted later that he did not have much faith in Ambedkar, and that he did not even know that he was an Untouchable; this was something he realized only after the London conference! In reality, Gandhi seems to have known nothing about the activities of the Depressed Classes, and this ignorance, if it was not indeed contempt, was to set off the conflict between the two men.

The work of the minorities commission was brought to a standstill in the early days of the conference by Gandhi's stubborn refusal to recognize any minorities other than Sikhs and Muslims. In reality both men were vying for recognition as the Untouchables' legitimate representative. Gandhi maintained that he personally represented the great mass of Untouchables, and he rejected the idea that they should be considered as a 'separate class' of the Indian population. He was willing to grant this right to Muslims, to whom he conceded the principle of separate electorates; but he turned a deaf ear to the Untouchables' demands, because for him this was tantamount to dividing Hinduism. Gandhi was driven above all by the religious aspect of the problem. The debate was immediately reported in India; and back in London, Ambedkar received various telegrams of support from untouchable associations that were against Gandhi.[11] Upon returning to Bombay, on 28 December 1931, Gandhi was met at the dockside by a demonstration of Untouchables. But they were not unanimous in their protests, and some of their leaders, such as M. C. Rajah, from Madras, were opposed to the idea of separate electorates.

A short time later, Gandhi was once more arrested by the British authorities and imprisoned at Yeravda, near Poona. On 17 August 1932, the British government announced that Untouchables would be given two votes, one for their own representatives and one for the general electorate. Gandhi was furious, and immediately wrote to the Prime Minister, Ramsay McDonald, asking him to abandon the idea. The Prime Minister wrote back saying that he could not decide anything for the Untouchables, and that it was up to their representatives to change this decision if they wanted to. On 13 December 1932, Gandhi decided to undertake a 'fast unto death'. It was an almost Machiavellian move, a veritable piece of blackmail, making Ambedkar directly responsible for Gandhi's life. This position was not without piquancy, since the press and the Congress Party leaders, who had until then refused to recognize him as the spokesman for the Untouchables, were now investing him with that very role. Ambedkar felt trapped, and he was infuriated. He had very little room for manœuvre. All eyes were fixed on him. One of Gandhi's sons tearfully begged him, in public, to spare his father's life, as he was deteriorating daily. 'All eyes were turned to me as the man of the hour, or rather as the villain of the piece', he wrote later. Gandhi tempered his intransigence somewhat by declaring his willingness to accept the idea of seats reserved for Untouchables. Ambedkar was then able to negotiate without losing too much face. He travelled to Poona where, on 24 September, the two men signed an agreement that would be known as the 'Poona Pact', the 'Yeravda Pact' or even the 'Gandhi-Ambedkar Pact'. In reality the document was signed by other untouchable leaders as well: A. Solanki, Rajbhoj, P. Balu, M. C. Rajah, R. B. Srinivasan and so on. The demand for separate electorates had been withdrawn; but 148 seats in the provincial assemblies and 18 per cent of the seats in the central parliament were reserved for Untouchables. This was an unhoped-for proportion. As was often the case, Gandhi alone signed for the Congress; he had committed the party without consulting the membership, and this pact was not to the liking of all.

Sensing the opposition, throughout the 1930s Gandhi spared no effort on behalf of Untouchables. On 7 November 1933, he undertook a trip of 20,000 kilometres to preach the eradication of untouchability. One wonders whether the opening of the temples to Untouchables in Travancore, in 1936, and elsewhere in the years that followed, may not have been triggered by Gandhi's action, and by the fear of seeing the lower classes leave Hinduism in droves. For, in 1935, a disillusioned Ambedkar announced that, although he had been born a Hindu, he would not die one. The Iravas of Kerala assured him that they would follow if he changed religions. Ambedkar hit Gandhi where it hurt most, for he knew how concerned he was about the religious problem. From that time on, Ambedkar, too, gave increasing importance to religion, his preoccupation culminating in 1956 with his conversion to Buddhism.

Ambedkar's bitterness comes out most strongly in his book, *What Congress and*

11. M. Juergensmeyer, *Religion as Social Vision: Social Mobility and Social Change in a City of India* (New York: Columbia University Press, 1969), p. 127; and O. Lynch, *The Politics of Untouchability*, p. 81.

Gandhi Have Done to the Untouchables. This was an angry pamphlet showing astonishing insight, for Ambedkar's premonitions have unfortunately come true: the electoral system instituted by the Poona Pact does not provide Untouchables with adequate representation. The designation of Gandhi as the Congress Party representative to the Round Table Conference is commented on by Ambedkar in the following terms: 'Unfortunately, the Congress chose Mr. Gandhi as its representative. A worse person could not have been chosen to guide India's destiny. He treated the non-Congress delegation with contempt, even insulted them.'[12] Gandhi, he goes on, looked down on the other representatives and did not hesitate to insult them. 'Everyone felt that Mr. Gandhi was the most determined enemy of the Untouchables.'[13] Some even felt that he had gone to the conference for the sole purpose of opposing untouchable demands. His hunger strike confronted Ambedkar with 'the most difficult dilemma a man has ever had to face'. In spite of the concessions he managed to wring from Gandhi, Ambedkar regarded the Poona Pact as a Hindu tool for controlling the Untouchable representatives. The same was true of the organization Gandhi created to defend the Untouchables' cause, the Harijan Sevak Sangh. This organization was entirely in the hands of the Congress Party. There was not a single Untouchable on its board of directors; speaking to this point, Gandhi maintained that the struggle for the welfare of Untouchables was a penance to be borne by Hindus. Furthermore, as the organization was funded by these same Hindus, Untouchables had no right to demand a seat on the board.[14] Gandhi's philosophy, Ambedkar concluded, was an insult to Untouchables: Gandhi was seeking the end of domination by a foreign power, but he did not question the social system that allowed one caste to dominate another.[15]

One consequence of the reservation of seats for Untouchables was that the candidate had to be elected by all voters, in other words by a majority of non-Untouchables. The elected member therefore represents not only Untouchables but all who voted for him. At the time he was writing this book, in 1945, Ambedkar seems to have been bitterly disappointed. He had lost the 1942 elections in a lamentable fashion, and was aware of the growing influence of the Congress Party. He therefore adopted a more circumspect approach to India's independence, and joined those who feared that a Hindu Raj might replace British rule.[16] It is hard to believe that, two years later, he would be Law Minister in the first cabinet of independent India.

The real debate, he ultimately concluded, was whether or not Untouchables were a separate part of Indian national life. The Congress Party maintained that Untouchables were no different from the rest of the population; but Untouchables argued that, on the contrary, they could not marry Hindus, could not eat with them, could not touch them and could even less associate with them. Therefore Untouchables could not be considered a part of the Indian nation.

That was what the disagreement between the two men was really about. Reading

12. B. R. Ambedkar, *What Congress and Gandhi Have Done to the Untouchables* (Bombay: Thacker & Co., 1945), p. 55.
13. Ibid., p. 70.
14. Ibid., p. 142.
15. Ibid., p. 302.
16. Ibid., p. 167.

these lines, one gains a sense of just how much Ambedkar changed over the years. In the 1920s, he believed, somewhat naively, that untouchability would disappear without a struggle. Twenty years later he was no longer so sure. He continued to reject the use of violence, but now advocated difference, separation, *chacun chez soi*. He felt it was useless to fight for temple entry; the Hindu gods belonged to the Hindus, and Untouchables were not part of that community.

The majority of Untouchables did not follow Ambedkar in his radical evolution. Even the Mahar leaders were not particularly in favour of converting. They did not dare go against their historical leader, but practically no other castes joined them. In a sense, history has proved Gandhi right. It was probably suicidal to demand separate electorates; in cutting up the nation into a number of blocs, there was a danger of ultimately splitting or fragmenting the country. But why, then, did Gandhi accept the principle of separate electorates for Muslims? Blinded by religious considerations, perhaps he did not realize that the dramatic consequences of separate electorates threatened to exacerbate the Muslim problem. Jinnah, however, had understood just that, for he saw separate electorates as the premisses of a separate nation. To my mind, Ambedkar was wrong in following Jinnah's perilous lead. But it is equally true that the system of reserved seats did not provide Untouchables with the political representation they deserved. Ambedkar was confronted with the fundamental dilemma of Untouchables; sometimes he claimed they were part of the nation and sometimes he maintained they were apart from the nation. These hesitations are not due to the leader's versatility, however; rather, they too reflect the ambiguity of Untouchables' position in society.

The Religious Problem

The quarrel between Gandhi and Ambedkar must have marked the latter deeply. It was probably no accident that the rejection of Hinduism was to become one of his main themes following the events of the early 1930s. Before that, as I have said, Ambedkar seems to have had little enthusiasm for religious questions. In his eyes, the temple-entry campaign was not an essential priority of the Untouchable emancipation movement. In contrast, the motives behind Gandhi's rejection of separate electorates were primarily religious: he wanted to preserve the unity of the 'Hindu nation' by eliminating all centrifugal tendencies. The defeat was a particularly painful one for Ambedkar, and he therefore set about putting Gandhi in the wrong by claiming that Untouchables were not Hindus. This change of perspective could also be seen in his attitude towards Hindu mythology. In effect, the early untouchable leaders had fashioned origin myths that recounted the Untouchables' past *grandeur* and assimilated them to Kshatriyas or other prestigious sections of Indian society. Ambedkar's goal in the 1920s was altogether different. It was no use, he said, trying to rewrite the past; what mattered were the present and the future. Yet in 1948, Ambedkar, too, tried his hand at a history of Untouchables, and published a book entitled *The Untouchables: Who Were They? And Why They Became Untouchables.* In many ways, this pseudo-history looks much like a myth, for it was meant to legitimize

Ambedkar's attraction to Buddhism: in it he defends the idea that Brahmins hated Untouchables and held them in contempt because they were Buddhists.[17]

This transformation became public at Yeola, near Nasik, in 1935, when Ambedkar solemnly announced that he would not die a Hindu. Gandhi took immediate offence at this declaration and riposted that one could not change religions as one changed shirts. But Ambedkar persisted and, on 13 October 1935, he declared:

"Because we have the misfortune of calling ourselves Hindus, we are treated thus. If we were members of another Faith, none would dare treat us so. Choose any religion which gives you equality of status and treatment. We shall repair our mistake now. I had the misfortune of being born with the stigma of an Untouchable. However, it is not my fault: but I will not die a Hindu, for this is in my power."[18]

The prophecy took some twenty years to be fulfilled, since the conversion to Buddhism finally took place on 14 and 15 October 1956, less than two months before he died. The period between 1935 and 1956 was one of a long religious quest, of questioning and probably some hesitations, but also of many contacts with a variety of religious authorities always eager to welcome the masses of Untouchables. Ambedkar does not seem to have been tempted by Christianity or Islam. He considered these to be alien religions with no ties to the ancient tradition of India. Nor was he convinced that they would lead to the emancipation of Untouchables; in fact the example of the South Indian Catholics led him to believe just the opposite. By contrast, he took Sikhism more seriously, and advanced contacts were made with religious authorities in the Punjab. The Sikhs' militant tradition was no doubt an attraction, but Untouchables did not seem to be placed on an equal footing with the main communities of this religion. At the end of the nineteenth century, a few hundred Untouchables, led by Pandit Ayoti Das, had already converted to Buddhism in South India; but this was not a true mass movement.[19]

In the end, Ambedkar chose Buddhism as the best solution. It was a religion born on the Indian continent, no doubt as a reaction against the sacrificial ritualism of the Brahmins, whose authority and legitimacy the Buddha contested. Furthermore, the Buddha had a number of very low-caste individuals among his disciples. As a philosophical and religious system, the goal of Buddhism, too, was liberation and the end of suffering. These features most certainly influenced Ambedkar, and in his small book, *Buddha and Marx*, he argued that Asia was going to have to choose between the two models, and he personally saw Buddhism as a replacement for Marxism. Buddhism did not constitute a total break with Hinduism, either; and for many centuries Indians had been divided between the two. Lastly, Buddhism was in many ways a sort of religious reform movement that preached against 'superstitions', ritualism and the multiplicity of gods. It was also based on a highly developed philosophy.

The desire to detract from Hinduism, to vent his anger and his resentment towards

17. B. R. Ambedkar, *The Untouchables: Who Were They? And Why They Became Untouchables* (New Delhi: Amrit Books, 1948), p. 76.

18. Quoted by E. Zelliot, *From Untouchable to Dalit*, p. 206.

19. A. Fiske, 'Scheduled Castes Buddhist Organizations', in J. M. Mahar (ed.), *The Untouchables in Contemporary India* (Tucson: University of Arizona Press, 1972), p. 116.

this religion, were also probably among the factors motivating Ambedkar. The long oath that officializes the conversion begins with a negation and an abjuration of Hinduism, the promise no longer to worship Brahma, Shiva and Vishnu and not to consider them as gods. Rejection of Hinduism[20] was moreover the primary reason given by the Buddhist converts interviewed by Fiske; they said they were 'fed up with the rotten life of Hinduism'.[21]

On the day chosen by Ambedkar, hundreds of thousands of Mahars, probably half a million, made their way to Nagpur and followed their master into Buddhism. Forty-five booths were set up to welcome and enrol the converts. A few weeks later, the day Ambedkar's body was cremated, a hundred thousand more went over to Buddhism; the 1961 census lists three million followers, whereas there were a mere 2,500 in 1951. The Mahars' conversion was thus a religious event of exceptional magnitude, no doubt one of the most remarkable in the twentieth century.

The Political Struggle

The impact of this movement was not felt beyond the boundaries of Maharashtra state, nor did it transcend the one caste. While Ambedkar was a leader of national stature, a true statesman, he had difficulty extending his influence to more than his own Mahar caste. His immense prestige, for instance, left the Mangs unmoved; this second-ranking untouchable caste of Maharashtra kept its distance and refused to join Ambedkar's campaigns. Ambedkar should not be reduced to the simple rank of caste leader, though. However limited his influence may have been, it nevertheless affected several castes in the Punjab, Uttar Pradesh and Madhya Pradesh. Moreover, if the mass of Untouchables remained impervious to his action, this was not true of intellectuals and the more militant untouchable groups. In statistical terms, this may have been an insignificant minority; but politically speaking, it was very important, because it could be considered as a sort of vanguard. And Ambedkar's prestige has scarcely diminished over the last decades. Today he is a model for all Untouchable organizations in India; in the last few years he has even received increasing attention from the Indian leadership.[22] If in many ways Ambedkar remained a mere Mahar leader, it was in spite of his efforts to associate other Untouchables in his actions and his desire to speak on behalf of all of India's Untouchables.

The Mangs and the Chambhars stayed on the fringes of Ambedkar's movement. P. N. Rajbhoj, one of his principal assistants, was a Chambhar; but he was a relatively isolated case. S. N. Shivtarkar, another Chambhar colleague, was even ostracized by his caste for having eaten with Mahars, whom they regarded as lower![23] Ambedkar himself did not underrate the divisions between the various untouchable castes; when,

20. A. Fiske, 'The Understanding of "Religion" and "Buddhism" among India's New Buddhists', in T. Wilkinson and M. Thomas (eds), *Ambedkar and the Neo-Buddhist Movement* (Madras: The Christian Literature Society, 1972), p. 104.

21. Ibid., p. 107.

22. See P. Radhakrishnan, 'Ambedkar's Legacy'. *The Hindu*, 20 January, 1991, p. 19.

23. E. Zelliot, *From Untouchable to Dalit*, p. 133.

at Nagpur in 1920, he urged the different Mahar subcastes to eat together, he was careful not to extend the idea to the other castes taking part in the meeting.[24] What counted for the young Ambedkar was the political struggle. One wonders whether his interest in the religious question may not be a corollary of his political disappointments when all his efforts in this arena proved to be in vain. After Independence, the Mangs continued to back the Congress Party, against the Mahar-dominated Republican Party.[25]

Yet, in his purely political campaigns, Ambedkar had made a promising start. After years of presiding over the conferences of the Bahishkrit Hitakarini Sabha (Association of Depressed Classes), he founded, in 1936, the Independent Labour Party to safeguard the interests of the labouring classes in the 1937 elections. The name of the party is revealing of the Western influence on the life of its founder. It was a classic labour party with, in principle, no hint of the caste party or Untouchable party about it. But in fact it was dominated by Mahars, and most of the 'tickets' would go to members of this caste. One Mang was elected to the legislative assembly; but the party list had no Chambhar candidates, and one member of this caste, the famous cricketer, P. Bahu, even ran as a Congress Party candidate against Ambedkar in the Parel-Byculla constituency of Bombay. The 1937 elections handed the Independent Labour Party a remarkable victory. In the province of Bombay, it took eleven of the fifteen seats reserved for Untouchables, the other four going to the Congress. It even became the second-ranking opposition party after the Muslim League. It also won several seats in the Central Provinces. But its electoral success was short-lived.

In addition, Ambedkar was faced with the dilemma of whether or not to seek non-Untouchable voices. He was divided and no doubt had few illusions: he knew how hard it was to break down old barriers. While he was theoretically in favor of unions, he also criticized the preponderance of the upper castes in their leadership; likewise, his distrust of Marxism was reinforced by the fact that he felt the Communist Party to be dominated by 'a bunch of Brahman boys'. This circumspection led him to create, in 1942, a new party with the more explicit and significant name of the Scheduled Castes Federation (SCF). The new party no doubt signalled the end of his illusions about the possibility of uniting the labouring masses. One of its platform planks was the creation of separate villages for the Scheduled Castes; and observers ironized that what the Untouchables were really looking for was a 'Maharstan' (an allusion to Pakistan).

The 1946 elections produced a humiliating defeat. The Congress Party was riding high, and swept all the seats. Not a single SCF candidate was elected in Bombay. But the bitter taste of defeat was soon sweetened by Ambedkar's appointment to the post of Law Minister in independent India's first cabinet. He was also made president of the committee charged with framing the Constitution. It is hard to tell how much Ambedkar really influenced this document. Article 17, officially abolishing untouchability, was of course associated with his name; but it is probable that the Congress Party, too, was determined to banish the institution. Kulke and Rothermund

24. E. Zelliot, 'Learning the Use of Political Means': The Mahars of Maharashtra', in R. Kothari (ed), *Caste in Indian Politics* (Poona: Orient Longman, 1970), pp. 29-69, p. 42.

25. S. Patwardhan, *Change among India's Harijans: Maharashtra - A Case Study* (New Delhi: Orient Longman, 1973), p. 48.

think that Ambedkar did not carry enough political weight really to orient the Constitution. For these German historians, it was Sadar Patel, Minister of Home Affairs and number two in the Congress Party, who was the real architect.[26] Moreover, it was Patel who opposed amendment of the Hindu Law filed by Ambedkar; sickened by this move, and in worrying health, the latter submitted his resignation.

Between 1947 and 1951, Ambedkar rose to the highest offices in the state. But this prestige did not prevent another bitter defeat for him and his party in the 1951-2 elections. Only one SCF candidate, P. N. Rajbohj, won a seat, whereas another Chambhar, running under Congress Party colours, beat Ambedkar in Bombay. Independent India was in need of unity, and the Congress Party reaped the massive rewards of this need in new India's first general elections. Ambedkar was beaten again in the 1954 partial elections; but because of his moral authority, he was finally appointed to the Rajya Sabha, the upper house. His death, on 6 December 1956, prevented him from being present at the formation of his third political party, the Republican Party. This party won a few seats in 1962 and 1967; but paradoxically, it performed better in the general constituencies than in those reserved for Untouchables.[27]

Ambedkar's successive election failures stemmed above all from the voting system established by the Poona Pact. In those constituencies reserved for Untouchables, all candidates are Untouchables, but they are presented by different parties and elected by the entire population of voters: in other words, in the majority by non-Untouchables.[28] And of course, it is not in the interest of high-caste people to vote for a militant Untouchable! It is even highly unlikely that one would be selected by a mainstream party like the Congress. Once elected, the candidate must keep in mind that he owes his seat to the whole electorate and that he does not represent Untouchables alone. Ambedkar himself had foreseen the problem: 'A candidate whose majority is due to the votes of persons other than Untouchables has no right to say that he is a representative of the Untouchables, and the Congress cannot claim to represent the Untouchables through him because he belongs to the Untouchables and stood on the Congress ticket.'[29]

Such a system tends to favour the major parties, and their candidates tend to win the reserved seats; in 1967, the Congress Party alone took 47 out of the 77 reserved seats in the Lok Sabha. In short, this system led to the election of candidates who are from untouchable castes, but who are not truly representative of them.

The Myth and its Impact

Today Dr Ambedkar has lost nothing of his aura for Mahars and a few other communities. Babasaheb, as he has come to be known, is a demi-god, and his photo is present in every Mahar home. However, there is nothing very extraordinary about

26. H. Kulke and D. Rothermund, *A History of India* (London: Routledge, 1990), p. 315.
27. L. Dushkin, 'Scheduled Castes Politics', in J. M. Mahar (ed.), *The Untouchables in Contemporary India* (Tucson: University of Arizona Press, 1972), p. 200.
28. Ibid., p. 204.
29. B. R. Ambedkar, *What Congress and Gandhi Have Done to the Untouchables*, p. 157.

the deification of living people in India, where the world of the gods is never totally separate from that of men.[30] Two portraits have become indispensable for any Neo-Buddhist ceremony: the Buddha and Babasaheb. Agra's Jatavs greet each other using his first name, *Jai Bhim*, and commemorate his words and deeds in numerous stories and songs.[31] Mahars today are familiar with many episodes from the untouchable movement and Ambedkar's life. In support of their reticence about the Congress Party, for instance, they still cite the example of Tilak, who, in March 1918, had proudly announced his aversion to any god who favored untouchability, but at the end of the meeting had refused to sign a resolution condemning the institution.[32]

Today Buddhist Mahars are notable for their dignity and sobriety. They have banished alcohol and meat from their way of life, and their weddings are simpler and less costly affairs.[33] The principal rite in their wedding ceremony consists of placing flowers around the portraits of the Buddha and Ambedkar and then pronouncing their vows: the young man promises to respect his wife, not to insult her, not to drink alcohol, and not to commit adultery, and to ensure his wife's moral and material well-being. The young woman in turn promises to keep their house clean and to lead a life worthy of her husband.[34] If I were not wary of paradoxes, I would say that Buddhist Mahars have become a 'Sanskritized' caste. They place great importance on education, hygiene and dignity.

The Jatavs of Agra are one of the few other castes to have followed Ambedkar into Buddhism. They are an economically dynamic community, and were one of the first to join the untouchable struggle for emancipation. In the 1930s, they supported Ambedkar in his quarrel with Gandhi by sending him a telegram in London, and their loyalty has never flagged. The Jatavs regard Ambedkar as a true hero, the 'Martin Luther of Buddhism'. Part of his ashes are placed in the Bodh Vihara Buddhist stupa in Agra.[35] Jatav Buddhism remains largely a formal religion. They are concerned above all with demarcating themselves from Hindus, with whom they have in fact few differences. The same holds true, no doubt, for Mahars, who are even accused by Mangs of being Buddhists in name only.[36]

The Mangs' resentment of Mahars can be explained by the latter's relatively privileged position in Marathi society. When their traditional role as village servants became obsolete, Mahars were forced to find other ways of earning a livelihood; many emigrated to the cities and took up new occupations.[37] Their social conscience told them to persevere, and today they have carved out a relatively enviable place in Maharashtra's social structure. The Mahar literacy rate is also considerably higher

30. C. Fuller, *The Camphor Flame: Popular Hinduism and Society in India* (Princeton, NJ: Princeton University Press, 1992), p. 1.

31. O. Lynch, 'Dr B. R. Ambedkar: Myth and Charisma', in J. M. Mahar (ed.), *The Untouchables in Contemporary India* (Tucson: University of Arizona Press, 1972), p. 98.

32. E. Zelliot, 'Dr Ambedkar and the Mahar Movement', p. 147.

33. R. Taylor, 'The Ambedkarite Buddhists', in T. Wilkinson and M. Thomas (eds), *Ambedkar and the Neo-Buddhist Movement* (Madras: The Christian Literature Society, 1972), p. 133.

34. T. Wilkinson, 'Buddhism and Social Change among the Mahars', in T. Wilkinson and M. Thomas (eds), *Ambedkar and the Neo-Buddhist Movement* (Madras: The Christian Literature Society, 1972), p. 96.

35. O. Lynch, *The Politics of Untouchability*, p. 145.

36. S. Patwardhan, *Change among India's Harijans*, p. 48.

37. Ibid., p. 72.

than the Mangs'. At the start of the 1960s, 85 per cent of the college scholarships reserved for the Scheduled Castes went to Mahars, while Chambhars took 8 per cent and the Mangs a mere 2 per cent.[38] This figure seems to have remained relatively constant, and today Mahars continue to be over-represented among the students from untouchable castes.[39]

Ambedkar's charisma and his action are not alien to this success. In assessing his work, one may regret the small impact he had on Untouchables as a whole; in reality, all his prestige and skill were not enough to bridge the differences between Scheduled Castes. It would be difficult, however, to hold Ambedkar personally responsible for this relative failure. Instead, the finger should be pointed at the pernicious character of untouchability, whose victims become its perpetrators. Babasaheb has become a model for many militant Untouchables all over India. In the end, his impact on millions of Mahars and on a few other castes is proof that some degree of emancipation was indeed possible.

38. Ibid., p. 84.

39. J. Aikara, *Scheduled Castes and Higher Education: A Study of College Students in Bombay* (Poona: Dastane Ramachandre, 1980), p. 34.

-9-

Positive Discrimination

In the time that has elapsed since India's independence, the socio-religious movements have lost some of their importance, and for the most part Untouchables have shifted their attention to other issues, a prime target among which has been the positive discrimination system. One might even wonder whether this system has not become the main battleground for Untouchables today. 'Positive discrimination' designates the set of measures adopted by the Indian government in favour of certain disadvantaged social categories, the purpose of which is to rectify the inequalities and discriminations that afflict them. Other groups in the world enjoy similar privileges: for instance, Blacks in America, women in Scandinavia, German-speaking groups in the Upper Adige. But in no other country has the system become as widespread as it is in India. In some parts of the country, the category 'Backward Classes' takes in 80 per cent of the population. The Backward Classes movement seems in fact to be a perversion of the system; but I will not dwell on this point.[1] Instead, I will focus on the untouchable groups, now called Scheduled Castes, who, together with the Scheduled Tribes, constitute an entirely separate category.

The Basis of the System

Article 15 of the Indian constitution prohibits any discrimination on the basis of creed, race or caste. The equality of all citizens is confirmed by Article 16, paragraph 3, which stipulates that the state nevertheless has the right to adopt various measures in favour of 'backward classes'. While it formally abolishes untouchability (Article 17), the Constitution nevertheless provides that Untouchables shall benefit from various measures taken to promote their economic interests.[2] And that is not the least of the

1. See R. Deliège, *Le Système des castes* (Paris: Presses Universitaires de France: 1993), pp. 117-22.
2. G. Sharma, *Legislation and Cases on Untouchability and Scheduled Castes in India* (Delhi: Indian Council of Social Sciences Research, 1975), p. 15.

ambiguities contained in this founding text, which thus acknowledges precisely the existence of that which it has just abolished.

The Constitution recognizes three population categories as 'backward classes'. Untouchables, representing some 15 per cent of the population, are classified as Scheduled Castes. Hill and forest tribes represent a mere 7 per cent of the population, but, unlike Untouchables, they are strongly concentrated in certain regions; these are grouped under the heading Scheduled Tribes. The third category is ill-defined, because each state is free to decide which castes or social categories are covered; its size varies with the region and with varying sensibilities; these 'backward social categories' which are neither tribes nor Untouchables are called the 'Backward Classes', or the 'Other Backward Classes' (O.B.C.). Although the issue of O.B.C. has become a major political problem today, we shall restrict our discussion to the first category.

The advantages granted to the Scheduled Castes can also be grouped into three categories.[3] First, the Constitution provides for 'reservations' in the case of socially important jobs or resources: for example, reserved seats in various legislative bodies, civil-service posts and places in universities that are subject to a *numerus clausus.* In other words, Untouchables are entitled to a certain number of representatives in government, a certain number of civil servants or, for instance, a certain number of places in medical school. The second set of measures concerns state expenditures reserved for Untouchables: scholarships, loans, land grants, medical care all come under this heading. Third, the state has taken a number of special measures, for instance campaigns against untouchability, special steps to free bonded labourers, and so forth. Let us take a closer look at the first two sets of measures.

- In the legislative assemblies, the number of reserved seats is proportional to the percentage of Untouchables in the overall population. Thus, in 1976, 78 seats in the lower house (Lokh Sabha) were occupied by Untouchables; this figure represents 14.4 per cent of the total number of members. In the state legislative assemblies, 540 seats are reserved for Untouchables out of a total of 3,997. Of course, Untouchables may also run in so-called 'general' constituencies, but in reality very few are elected in this way; in 1977, only three members of the Lokh Sabha managed this feat. Even as well-known a politician as Jagjivan Ram has never ventured to try. This is a rather special system, then, and it looks as though the fears expressed by Ambedkar in *What Congress and Gandhi Have Done to the Untouchables* have been realized. In effect, the idea of separate electorates was withdrawn at the time of the Poona Pact, and since then untouchable candidates have run in 'reserved constituencies'. In other words, in these reserved constituencies, only candidates from the Scheduled Castes may seek election. Each political party therefore presents a candidate who satisfies this requirement, and the candidates are elected by the population as a whole, that is by a majority of non-Untouchables.

These 'reserved' constituencies were designated on the basis of the relatively high proportion of Untouchables living there; but Untouchables do not constitute the majority of the population, and their vote does not determine the outcome of the elections. Under such conditions it is easy to understand why untouchable political

3. M. Galanter, *Competing Equalities: Law and the Backward Classes in India* (Berkeley, CA: University of California Press, 1984, p. 43.

formations meet with failure: the mainstream national parties clearly have the greatest chance of taking these seats, since the majority of voters in these precincts are not Untouchables. Moreover, the vast majority of Untouchables do not vote in reserved constituencies, and therefore have little occasion to show their preference for untouchable candidates.

The electoral system thus presents a certain paradox: on the one hand, untouchable candidates in reserved constituencies are elected by a majority of non-Untouchables and, on the other hand, most Untouchables do not have the opportunity to vote for an untouchable candidate because they are not registered in a reserved constituency. We shall return to this problem later. The local assemblies, known as *panchayats* must also have a certain number of untouchable representatives; but the states are free to set the number, and some states, like Bengal and Gujarat, have not taken steps in this direction; in the case of Gujarat, Untouchables are therefore under-represented in the *panchayats.*

• In the area of education, a variety of measures have also been adopted in favour of Untouchables, but the effort has been concentrated for the most part on higher education. The number of university scholarships, for example, has gone from 731 in 1948 to 37,372 in 1958, 156,834 in 1968 and 350,000 in 1975. In spite of these measures, however, untouchable students are concentrated primarily in the least prestigious departments. Few are enrolled in medicine or applied sciences, the most reputed faculties. It also seems that the Untouchables are among the most mediocre students. In Maharashtra, for instance, it is estimated that 85 per cent of them leave the university without a diploma. Since elementary education is free and open to all, few special efforts have been made in favour of Untouchables there. Between 1961 and 1981, the percentage of Untouchables able to read and write went from 10.2 to a mere 21.3 per cent

• The last facet of these measures concerns jobs in the civil service. The state is an important source of material security for Untouchables, who attach great importance to government jobs. The central and federal administrations therefore reserve part of their job allocation for the Scheduled Castes and Scheduled Tribes. The effect of these measures can be felt down to the smallest villages. In central administration, 15 per cent of the recruitment by examination and 16 per cent of the recruitment without examination are allotted to Untouchables. In the federal administration, these percentages vary with the job category, and can be as high as 80 per cent in the case of certain menial jobs. Since Independence, the percentage of Untouchables employed in the public sector has increased considerably at all levels of the hierarchy. Between 1953 and 1975, grade-1 civil servants went from 0.35 per cent to 3.4 per cent, grade-2 from 1.3 per cent to 5 per cent and grade-3 from 4.5 per cent to 10.7 per cent. By contrast, the representation of Untouchables in grade-4 jobs has been much more impressive from the outset, hovering at around 17 per cent since the 1960s. Positions at this level are virtually an untouchable monopoly: for instance, sweepers, scavengers and servants.

These few figures show a clear under-representation of Untouchables in the higher-level jobs; nevertheless, over the last few years there has been some improvement: in 1984 6.4 per cent of grade-1 jobs, 10.4 per cent of grade-2 jobs, 14.0 per cent of grade-3 jobs and 20.2 per cent of grade-4 jobs were held by Untouchables, who at the time represented 15.8 per cent of the overall Indian population.[4] But these statistics also show that reservation reproduces the basic social inequalities, since Untouchables are over-represented in the menial jobs, while they are unable even to fill the quotas for the more prestigious posts. Still, a grade-4 civil-service job is a decided improvement for an agricultural worker or a coolie.

The Limitations of a System

Today the positive discrimination system is a primary battleground for Untouchables. One of the first criteria for evaluating this system should be the Untouchables' deep attachment to these measures. Although they were originally established for thirty years, they were extended after this period expired, and today one must agree with Béteille when he says that quotas have become inevitable[5] and that it would be inconceivable to end them in the foreseeable future. Any move in this direction would probably not only be a political disaster, but would almost certainly trigger a veritable uprising.

Over the last years, the extension of 'reservations' to the Backward Classes has caused much ink to flow. Yet the conclusions of the Mandal Report do not concern the reservations for Scheduled Castes properly speaking, which do not seem to be in dispute in contemporary India. In any case, it is important not to confuse the two issues - a pitfall that analysts do not always manage to avoid. The Backward Classes often use the poverty and oppression of some sections of the population as an alibi to entrench their political domination further. The demand for extension of quotas in their favour is not motivated by a concern for justice in compensation for centuries of oppression; it is part of a power struggle. As far as the Scheduled Castes are concerned, the problem is altogether different: in this case, reservations are a means of alleviating the poverty and oppression that have plagued this social category for centuries. The problem is that once such a 'social policy' has been adopted, it tends to become an 'entitlement'; and it is virtually impossible to end it without giving rise to incomparable frustration in the population. Untouchables today are so attached to these measures that they have come to view them as a right. Yet it is by no means sure that the system has always borne the fruits that had been hoped. In discussing this problem, Galanter speaks of 'expensive successes'. One sometimes wonders whether it has truly been an overall success.

Evaluating the system is not an easy job, as any assessment is obviously bound up with political and philosophical choices. When one looks at the concrete results, it is hard to know what is actually due to reservations. Even if the system had not existed, the grade-4 civil-service jobs, for instance, would have gone to Untouchables. In effect, few Indians covet a job as a street sweeper or scavenger. On the other hand, it

4. P. Radhakrishnan, 'Ambedkar's Legacy to Dalits: Has the Nation Reneged on Its Promises?'. *Economic and Political Weekly*, 17 August (1991), p. 1920.

5. A. Béteille, *The Backward Classes in Contemporary India* (Delhi: Oxford University Press, 1992), p. 106.

is likely that the presence of Untouchables in grade-1 positions is, to a large extent, due to the system of reservations. Without these, there would be only a handful of Untouchables in these posts; and even under the present conditions, it is impossible to find candidates for all the reserved jobs. As a rule, interviews are a formidable ordeal for untouchable candidates: a recent study shows that, in Madhya Pradesh, 21 per cent of the untouchable candidates who had made it past the first selection performed well in the interview, whereas the rate for other social categories is 41 per cent.[6]

In spite of its merits, then, the system poses a number of problems.

1. The reservation system has largely contributed to 'stigmatizing' Untouchables by placing them in a category that is clearly separate from the rest of society. Until then, the boundaries of untouchability were fairly fluid, and one might have seen a progressive gravitation of certain social categories towards the middle castes, as in the case of the Iravas and the Nadars. Today, the Scheduled Castes are clearly segregated from the rest of society, and so the system helps, in a manner of speaking, to reinforce untouchability. This is all the more striking because, unlike the case of Black Americans, no outward signs distinguish Untouchables from the rest of the population. Putting them into a separate social category gives them a distinctive character, and when the population decides to vent its resentment, members of the Scheduled Castes become easy scapegoats. It is hard to see any other reason for the Vanniyars of Tamil Nadu to have initially directed their anger at Harijans when demanding more recognition from the government. Béteille has convincingly shown that the British, with their strategy of divide and rule, were the ones who pushed the quota system.[7] In sum, the system helps reinforce a category that it had been specifically created to eliminate.

Furthermore, it is often rumoured that the Untouchables in a high-level job or who have obtained admission to medical school owe their success less to their own abilities than to the fact that they belong to a low caste. This criticism is a bit unfair, for an Untouchable doctor has also had to prove his ability before being accepted for medical school and to pass the examinations at the end; but in reality it is often considered that these people occupy posts they do not deserve. As a consequence, their authority in administrative jobs is more fragile, and they are regarded as second-class civil servants. This contempt makes itself felt particularly in the case of promotions, which Untouchables have difficulty obtaining.

2. In the case of India, the positive discrimination system is a direct legacy of socialist conceptions, which look principally to the state to emancipate the masses. In Nehru's mixed economy, the state therefore occupies a large place,[8] and the local population is very conscious of its importance. The efforts made in the framework of the reservation system also go in this direction: the state becomes the main employer, the focus of all ambitions. Individual initiative is therefore not taken into account. The Pallars of Alangkulam village have gained very little from the reservation system. Like many other Untouchables in the region, though, they have worked hard to

6. M. Galanter, *Competing Equalities*, p. 99.

7. A. Béteille, *The Backward Classes in Contemporary India*, p. 103.

8. L. Rudolph and S. Hoeber-Rudolph, *In Pursuit of Laskhmi: The Political Economy of the Indian State* (Chicago: University of Chicago Press, 1987), p. 23.

improve their lives. Many, for instance, have bought a cart or invested in a brick kiln. But these efforts receive no form of encouragement from the government.[9] The positive discrimination system thus tends to encourage a 'welfare' mentality, in which people rely on the state to provide for them. The many private-sector initiatives, on the other hand, receive scant encouragement; yet it is these that create wealth and drive the Indian economy.

3. Similarly, the system of scholarships has tended to focus on high-level educational programmes. To be sure, it has enabled many Untouchables to obtain important jobs, and without it, very few, for example, would become doctors. Yet at the same time, tens of millions of Untouchables remain illiterate. In other words, the government has concentrated its efforts on higher education and has tended to neglect elementary schooling, with the result that millions of children, and not only Untouchables, will never have the opportunity to learn to read and write.

4. It is perhaps in the area of politics that the system seems most perverse. We have seen how the reservation of constituencies deprives Untouchables of effective representation. The majority never get the chance to vote for an untouchable candidate, and those who are elected owe their victory to a non-Untouchable majority. Gandhi was no doubt right in thinking that the system worked to integrate Untouchables into the nation; that is its good side. But in so doing, it also prevents Untouchables obtaining effective political representation or having their desires taken into account.

5. At the socio-economic level, one may wonder just who benefits from the advantages reserved for Untouchables. In effect, an elite has grown up within the Untouchable groups that tends to reproduce itself and thus to monopolize the advantages provided by the government. This is known as the 'creamy layer'. Galanter cites a study on Haryana, which finds that one out of eight families in this state benefits from reservations in one form or another.[10] But he considers the impact to be modest. On the contrary, it seems rather remarkable to me; but it must be remembered that there are a good number of municipal street-sweepers among the beneficiaries who would have got the jobs even if reservations had not existed. Higher-level jobs such as grade-1 posts, though, tend to be monopolized by an elite that can no longer be regarded as exploited. Furthermore, in each state, certain castes corner a maximum number of advantages at the expense of the other untouchable castes. For instance, in Maharashtra, Mahars represent 35 per cent of the Untouchables in the state, but they hold up to 60 per cent of the reserved jobs. The same phenomenon exists in other states, so that it could be said that the positive discrimination system also contributes to exacerbating the inequalities between the different untouchable castes. However, we have insufficient data on the extent of the problem.

The system thus seems to pose as many problems as it solves. Yet it is hard to see how India could backtrack. In many cases the social categories that are opposed to reservations have not considered the question of social justice.

9. See R. Deliège, 'At the Threshold of Untouchability: Pallars and Valaiyars in a Tamil Village', in C. Fuller (ed.), *Caste Today* (Oxford: Oxford University Press, 1996).

10. M. Galanter, *Competing Equalities*, p. 108.

Anti-reservation Agitation

Over the last few years, various voices have spoken out against the positive discrimination system. One of the most notable movements came out of Gujarat at the start of the 1980s. This almost spontaneous reaction was symptomatic of a certain frame of mind, as is the continuation of strong anti-Untouchable feelings among Westernized urban-dwellers. At the root of this particularly aggressive protest were the medical students of Ahmedabad, a modern, industrial city. The primary issue was a reduction in the number of reserved admissions to medical school; but the protesters seized upon the occasion to vent their hatred of Untouchables in general. Furthermore, the Brahmin and Banya instigators were quickly replaced by Patidars, a powerful peasant caste. Students, university professors, bank employees, civil servants and medical doctors figured among the leaders of the movement, which rapidly took a violent turn. Yet the aggressions were not directed against the Backward Castes, even though they were the principal beneficiaries of the reserved admissions, but against Untouchables, and particularly Vankars and Garodas. Throughout the month of February 1981, the entire state experienced a wave of murders, lootings, house-burnings and destruction of every kind. Dozens of Untouchables were killed, either by high-caste gangs or by the police.[11]

These manifestations bring us back to a sad reality. After having watched the Untouchables struggle for over a century to gain a modicum of respectability and well-being in Indian society, it is disheartening to see that the most modern and Westernized, and perhaps the most intelligent, segments of the population do not seem willing to acknowledge their right to dignity, but instead continue to exhibit an age-old and undiminished hatred for these groups.

11. See A. Yagnik and A. Bhatt, 'The Anti-Dalit Agitation in Gujarat'. *South Asia Bulletin,* 4 (1984).

Conclusion

Reading the foregoing chapters, one might be tempted to think that untouchability is a thing of the past. We saw Untouchables seize new economic 'opportunities' to improve their lives and diversify their professional activities. Movements of a socio-religious nature have sprouted in most parts of India, starting in the nineteenth century when Untouchables began to reject the position that had been allotted them in Indian society for thousands of years. Later, under the banner of their remarkable leader, the Mahars of Maharashtra no doubt carried the struggle for emancipation to its most extreme point yet; but socio-religious movements as a whole touched the lives of millions of individuals all over India. It is hard to know what the Untouchables of some two or three hundred years ago thought, for, aside from their myths, we have very few reliable sources. What is clear, at the end of the twentieth century, is that the huge majority of Untouchables do not regard themselves as impure, nor do they consider their condition to result from misconduct in some previous life. Instead, they believe that their children deserve a better life than they have had; all aspire to more comfortable material circumstances; all demand more dignity.

This might indicate that a radical change had occurred if untouchability concerned Untouchables alone. But untouchability is above all the expression of a set of social relations, of the relationship between different social actors. And that is where the shoe pinches. Although one of the partners in the relationship seems to have changed, this is not true of the rest; among the higher castes, in effect, little in their basic conception of untouchability seems to have changed. To be sure, most peasants have had to make the best of Untouchables' refusal to perform certain menial tasks; they have sometimes reluctantly had to remove the occasional dead cow themselves, or pay someone else to do it. Modern public life has erected a series of obstacles to the ancestral practice of untouchability. These changes only make the persistence of untouchability all the more striking. In the past, a clearly structured ideology based on the opposition between pure and impure was adduced to legitimize the practice. Today this ideology is outdated and has been supplanted by the democratic and egalitarian ideas of modern India. Nevertheless, there remains a large discrepancy between ideology and social practice. Untouchability persists, and one might even say that, from a certain point of view, it is thriving in spite of modern ideologies.

All one has to do to be convinced of this is to talk with a high-caste peasant. One day a Udayar farmer in Tamil Nadu told me a story about a love affair similar to the one carried by *Time* magazine that I cited at the outset. There, too, the young people had been killed by the girl's father, and the farmer calmly explained that it was the only thing to do; he too would kill his children if they eloped with a Harijan. All present were in agreement; and since then I have heard the same story repeatedly. Some will say that peasants are not as a rule noted for their modernity, and that the more evolved social classes are less radical. But to this objection, I must reply that the man I spoke with belongs to a social class that is by far the largest and most representative, and that India is, and will be for a long time, a rural society. This farmer's sons and daughters had gone to school, and some of them held modern jobs. I am not entirely convinced that the feelings connected with untouchability have changed all that much in the most forward-looking classes either. A few days after this conversation, I was visiting a large Catholic seminary in Tamil Nadu. Untouchables were vastly under-represented; when they learned that I was working in a Paraiyar village at the time, a few of the young seminarians, thoroughly nice young men, held forth in terms that, although courteous, were not basically any different from what our farmer had said.

The anti-reservation agitation that occurred in Gujarat is also highly symptomatic. Ahmedabad is a town with a strong industrial tradition that goes back to the nineteenth century. Contrary to what one might think, the agitation did not emanate from jobless workers, not from an urban *lumpenproletariat* easily stirred to violence, but from the very flower of the Indian intelligentsia, the medical students. It is stupefying to see these young people, most of whom come from the modern classes of a modern city and who, moreover, are studying to be doctors, at the head of one of the most radical attacks on Untouchables, who are not even the main beneficiaries of the system of 'reservations' in medical schools.

Since Independence, the reservation system has certainly been one of the factors contributing to the accentuation of caste differences, notably by turning caste into a political force.[1] Recent changes in the caste system and the relative weakening of the ideology of pure and impure have not managed to put an end to untouchability or even to attenuate it significantly. Moreover, although Untouchables have won some very real victories, these remain limited and relative. There is indeed an Untouchable elite, but the influence they have on the mass of their fellow-Untouchables is relative; in addition, they tend to sever their ties with the rest of the caste and to reproduce their own group. And finally, the emergence and development of this elite has lagged behind the growth of the overall Untouchable population. So that, even though new untouchable doctors, lawyers and civil servants appear every day, many many more children are being born who will become agricultural labourers, coolies or sweepers. Likewise the considerable rise in the literacy rate is insufficient to stem the growing tide of illiterates.

In sum, it is apparent that the problem of untouchability has not been resolved by its constitutional abolition or by recent changes in Indian society; its ghost will continue to haunt the country for many years to come, and the recent political trends do not encourage optimism on this point. Among today's politicians, one would be hard put to find figures of the stature of Gandhi, Nehru and Ambedkar, capable of awakening the conscience of the nation. Instead, what we see is a new grass-roots political class, entangled in often petty and sometimes violent conflicts. The weakness of the central

1. A. Béteille, *The Backward Classes in Contemporary India* (Delhi: Oxford University Press, 1991), pp. 113 and 117.

government, the growing importance of the states, the Backward Classes movement, the rise of a Hindu nationalism with strongly fundamentalist overtones hold out little hope of a rosy future for Untouchables, and I see no reason to be particularly optimistic. To be sure, the results of the recent liberalization of the Indian economy will have a decisive impact. But whatever the outcome, it cannot, in the short or medium terms, solve the problems of such a large segment of the population, especially since poverty is not restricted to the untouchable castes.

I have been struck by the dignity, maturity and relative absence of violence with which the Untouchables have waged their struggle. It is true that, today, they are less reluctant to answer violence with violence; but by and large, they have refrained from bloodshed. If they have not affronted Indian society, it is because they are seeking to be a part of it, because they feel both Indian and Hindu. Their marginality has always been relative, if not paradoxical: they were excluded from a society in which they played an important role; they were both rejected and indispensable. This is the originality of India's Untouchables; they are not like other fringe categories, not like Max Weber's 'pariah people'. Untouchables have always felt close to this society that rejects them. They have never had a separate culture or religion, and their sporadic attempts to set themselves apart from the rest of society have always ended in failure; one has only to look at the conversion movements. The majority of Untouchables know that their only salvation lies in integration. Yet this does not mean that the future years will be free of uprisings, that we will not see a resurgence of messianic movements, or that no radical political party will appear on the horizon. Untouchability will be a political, economic, social and moral problem for a long time to come.

Bibliography

Abbasayulu, Y. B. 'Scheduled Caste Elite: A Study of Scheduled Caste Elite in Andhra Pradesh'. Hyderabad: Osmania University, 1978.

Aikara, J. *Scheduled Castes and Higher Education: A Study of College Students in Bombay.* Poona: Dastane Ramachandre, 1980.

Aiyappan, A. *Social and Physical Anthropology of the Nayadis of Malabar.* Madras: Bulletin of the Madras Government Museum, 1937.

— *Iravas and Culture Change.* Madras: Bulletin of the Madras Government Museum, 1945.

— *Social Revolution in a Kerala Village: A Study in Culture Change.* Bombay: Asia Publishing House, 1965.

Alexander, K. C. 'The Neo-Christians of Kerala', in J. M. Mahar (ed.), *The Untouchables in Contemporary India.* Tucson: University of Arizona Press, 1972, pp. 153-64.

— 'The Problem of Caste in the Christian Churches of Kerala', in H. Singh (ed.), *Caste among the Non-Hindus in India.* Delhi: National Publishing House, 1977.

— 'Caste Mobilization and Class Consciousness: The Emergence of Agrarian Movements in Kerala and Tamil Nadu', in F. Frankel and M. S. Rao (eds), *Dominance and State Power in Modern India: Decline of a Social Order.* Delhi: Oxford University Press, 1989, pp. 361-413.

Ambedkar, B. R. *What Congress and Gandhi Have Done to the Untouchables.* Bombay: Thacker & Co., 1945.

— *The Untouchables: Who Were They?* And *Why They Became Untouchables.* New Delhi: Amrit Books, 1948.

Amnesty International. *Inde: torture, viols et morts en détention.* London: Éditions Francophones d'Amnesty International, 1992.

Auguste, Jean. *Le Maduré: l'ancienne et la nouvelle mission.* Brussels: Desclée de Brouwer, 1894.

Augustin, P. 'Conversion as Social Process'. *Religion and Society,* 28 (1981), pp. 31-57.

Aron, R. *Les Étapes de la pensée sociologique.* Paris: Gallimard, 1967.

Aurora, G. S. *Tribe, Caste, Class Encounters.* Hyderabad: Administrative Staff College of India, 1972.

Babb, L. 'The Satnamis: Political Involvement of a Religious Movement', in J. M. Mahar (ed.), *The Untouchables in Contemporary India.* Tucson: University of Arizona Press, 1972, pp. 143-52.

— *The Divine Hierarchy: Popular Hinduism in Central India*. New York: Columbia University Press, 1975.

Baboo, B. 'Cognition and Structure: Explaining the "Exploitation" of an Untouchable Caste in Orissa'. *The Eastern Anthropologist*, 39(1986), pp. 187-93.

Baechler, J. *La Solution indienne: essai sur l'origine du régime des castes.* Paris: Presses Universitaires de France, 1988.

Bailey, F. *Caste and the Economic Frontier*. Manchester: Manchester University Press, 1957.

— 'For a sociology of India?'. *Contributions to Indian Sociology*, 2 (1959), pp. 88-101.

— *Tribe, Caste and Nation*. Manchester: Manchester University Press, 1960.

— 'Tribe and Caste in India'. *Contributions to Indian Sociology,* 5 (1961), pp. 7-19.

— 'Closed Social Stratification in India'. *Archives européennes de sociologie,* 4 (1963), 107-24.

Balagopal, K. 'The Anti-Mandal Mania'. *Economic and Political Weekly,* 16 Oct. 1990, pp. 2231-4.

Barbosa, D. *A Description of the Coast of East Africa and Malabar in the Beginning of the 16th Century.* London: Hakluyt Society, 1970.

Barnett, S. 'Urban Is As Urban Does: Two Incidents on One Street in Madras City, South India'. *Urban Anthropology,* 2 (1973), pp. 129-60.

— 'Identity Choice and Caste Ideology in Contemporary South India', in K. David (ed.), *The New Wind: Changing Identities in South Asia.* Paris and The Hague: Mouton, 1977.

Barnett, S., L. Fruzzetti and A. Ostor. 'A Hierarchy Purified: Notes on Dumont and His Critics'. *Journal of Asian Studies*, 35 (1976), pp. 627-50.

Barth, F. *Indus and Swat Kohiythan: An Ethnographic Survey*. Oslo: Studies of the Etnografiske Museum, 1956.

— *Political Leadership among the Swat Pathans.* London: The Athlone Press, 1959.

— 'The System of Social Stratification in Swat, North Pakistan', in E. Leach (ed.), *Aspects of Caste in South India, Ceylon and North-West Pakistan.* Cambridge: Cambridge University Press, 1960, pp. 113-46.

— *Models of Social Organisation.* London: Occasional Paper No. 23 of the Royal Anthropological Institute of Great-Britain and Ireland, 1966.

Basham, A. L. *The Wonder that Was India: A Survey of the History and Culture of the Indian Sub-Continent before the Coming of the Muslims.* London: Fontana-Collins, 1967.

Bayly, C. *Indian Society and the Making of the British Empire.* Cambridge: Cambridge University Press, 1988.

Bayly, *S. Saints, Goddesses and Kings: Muslims and Christians in South Indian Society,* 1700-1900. Cambridge: Cambridge University Press, 1989.

Beaglehole, J. 'The Indian Christians: A Study of a Minority'. *Modern Asian Studies,* 1 (1967), pp. 59-80.

Beck, B. *Peasant Society in Konku: A Study of Right and Left Subcastes in South India.* Vancouver: University of British Columbia Press, 1972.

Benson, J. 'A South Indian Jajmani System'. *Ethnology*, 15 (1976), pp. 239-50.

Berreman, G. *Hindus of the Himalayas: Ethnography and Change.* Berkeley, CA: University of California Press, 1963.

— 'Structure and Function of Caste Systems', in G. De Vos and H. Wagatsuma (eds), *Japan's Invisible Race: Caste in Culture and Personality.* Berkeley, CA: University of California Press, 1967, pp. 277-307.

— 'Concomitants of Caste Organization', in G. De Vos and H. Wagatsuma (eds), *Japan's Invisible Race: Caste in Culture and Personality.* Berkeley, CA: University of California Press, 1967, pp. 308-26.

— 'Caste: The Concept of Caste', in E. Sills (ed.), *International Encyclopedia of the Social Sciences.* New-York: Macmillan Free Press, 1968, vol. II, pp. 333-9.

— 'Race, Caste and Other Invidious Distinctions in Social Stratification'. *Race*, 13 (1972), pp. 378-414.

— *Caste and Other Inequities: Essays on Inequality.* Meerut: Folklore Institute, 1979.

Béteille, A. 'A Note on the Referents of Caste'. *Archives européennes de sociologie*, 5 (1964), pp. 130-4.

— 'The Future of the Backward Classes: The Competing Demand for Status and Power'. *Perspectives, Supplement to the Indian Journal of Public Administration*, 11 (1965), pp. 1-39.

— 'Closed and Open Social Stratification'. *Archives européennes de sociologie*, 7 (1966), pp. 224-46.

— *Caste, Class and Power: Changing Patterns of Stratification in a Tanjore Village*. Bombay: Oxford University Press, 1966.

— 'The Decline of Inequality?', in A. Béteille (ed.), *Social Inequality*. Harmondsworth: Penguin, 1969, pp. 362-80.

— *Castes: Old and New. Essays in Social Structure and Social Stratification.* Bombay: Asia Publishing House, 1969.

— 'Caste and Political Group Formation in Tamil Nad', in R. Kothari (ed.), *Caste in Indian Politics*. Poona: Orient and Longman, 1970.

— 'Peasant Association and the Agrarian Class Structure'. *Contributions to Indian Sociology (NS)*, 4 (1970), pp. 126-38.

— 'Pollution and Poverty', in J. M. Mahar (ed.), *The Untouchables in Contemporary India.* Tucson: University of Arizona Press, 1972, pp. 412-20.

— *Studies in Agrarian Social Structure*. Delhi: Oxford University Press, 1974.

— 'The Concept of Tribe with Special Reference to India'. *Archives européennes de sociologie*, 27 (1986), pp. 297-318.

— *Essays in Comparative Sociology.* Delhi: Oxford University Press, 1987.

— *The Backward Classes in Contemporary India*. Delhi: Oxford University Press, 1992.

— 'Caste and Family in Representations of Indian Society'. *Anthropology Today,* 8 (1992), pp. 13-18.

Bhai, N. *Harijan Women in Independent India.* Delhi: B. R. Publishing Corporation, 1986.

Bharti, I. 'Bihar's Most Wretched'. *Economic and Political Weekly,* 22 Sept. 1990, pp. 2124-5.

Bhatt, G. S. 'The Chamars of Lucknow'. *The Eastern Anthropologist*, 8 (1954), pp. 27-42.

— 'Trends and Measures of Status Mobility among the Chamars of Dehradun'. *The Eastern Anthropologist*, 14 (1961), pp. 229-42.

Bhoite, M. and A. Bhoite. 'The Dalit Sahitya Movement in Maharashtra: A Sociological Analysis'. *Sociological Bulletin,* 26 (1977), p. 60-75.

Bliss, C. and N. Stern. *Palanpur: The Economy of an Indian Village*. Oxford: Clarendon Press, 1982.

Blunt, E. *The Caste System of Northern India with Special Reference to the United Provinces of Agra and Oudh.* Delhi: S. Chand & Co., 1969 (first edition1931).

Bose, A. and N. Jodha. 'The Jajmani System in a Desert Village'. *Man in India*, 45 (1965), pp. 1-22.

Bose, A. and S. Malhotra. 'Studies in Group Dynamics: Factionalism in a Desert Village'. *Man in India*, 44 (1964), pp. 311-28.

Bose, N. K. 'Who Are the Backward Classes?'. *Man in India*, 34 (1954), pp. 89-101.

Bouglé, C. *Essai sur le système de castes*. Paris: Presses Universitaires de France, 1969 (first edition 1935).

Breman, J. *Patronage and Exploitation: Changing Agrarian Relations in South Gujarat.* Delhi: Manohar, 1974.

— 'Extension of Scale in Fieldwork: From Village to Region in Southern Gujarat', in P. Bardhan (ed.), *Conversations Between Economists and Anthropologists: Methodological Issues in Measuring Economic Change in Rural India.* Oxford: Oxford University Press, 1989, pp. 126-36.

Briggs, G. *The Chamars*. Delhi: B. R. Publishing Corporation, 1920.

— *The Doms and Their Near Relations.* Mysore: Wesley Press, 1953.

Caplan, L. 'Popular Christianity in Urban South India'. *Religion and Society*, 30 (1975), pp. 28-44.

— 'Caste and Castelessness among South Indian Christians'. *Contributions to Indian Sociology* (NS), 14 (1980), pp. 213-38.

— 'The Popular Culture of Evil in Urban South India', in D. Parkin (ed.), *The Anthropology of Evil*. Oxford: Blackwell, 1985, pp. 110-27.

— *Class and Culture in Urban India: Fundamentalism in a Christian Community.* Oxford: Oxford University Press, 1987.

— *Religion and Power: Essays on the Christian Community in Madras*. Madras: The Christian Literature Society, 1989.

Capwell, C. 'The Esoteric Beliefs of the Bauls of Bengal'. *Journal of Asian Studies*, 33 (1974), pp. 255-64.

Carrithers, M. *The Buddha*. Oxford: Oxford University Press, 1983.

Census of India, 1971. *Scheduled Castes and Scheduled Tribes* (Table C-VIII, Parts A & B). Delhi: Government of India Press, 1975.

Charsley, S. '"Untouchable": What Is in a Name?'. *The Journal of the Royal Anthropological Institute,* 2 (1996), pp. 1-24.

Cohen, S. 'The Untouchable Soldier: Caste, Politics and the Indian Army'. *Journal of Asian Studies,* 29 (1969), pp. 453-68.

Cohn, B. 'The Chamars of Senapur: A Study of the Changing Status of a Depressed Caste'. Doctoral dissertation, Cornell University, 1954.

— 'Some Notes on Law and Change in North India'. *Economic Development and Cultural Change,* 8 (1959), pp. 79-93.

— 'The Changing Status of a Depressed Caste', in A. Desai (ed.), *Rural Sociology in India.* Bombay: Popular Prakashan, 1969, pp. 354-63.

Cornell, J. 'Buraku Relations and Attitudes in a Progressive Farming Community', in G. De Vos and H. Wagatsuma (eds), *Japan's Invisible Race: Caste in Culture and Personality.* Berkeley, CA: University of California Press, 1967, pp. 153-85.

Crooke, W. *The Tribes and Castes of Northern India.* Delhi: Cosmos, 1974 (first edition 1896).

Dalton, D. 'The Gandhian View of Caste and Caste after Gandhi', in P. Mason (ed.), *India and Ceylon: Unity and Diversity*. Oxford: Oxford University Press, 1967.

Daniel, V. *Fluid Signs: Being a Person the Tamil Way.* Berkeley, CA: University of California Press, 1984.

Das, B. 'Untouchability, Scheduled Castes and Nation Building'. *Social Action*, 32 (1982), pp. 269-82.

Delfendahl, B. *Le Clair et l'obscur*. Paris: Anthropos, 1973.

Deliège, R. 'Souffrance et échange: quelques croyances religieuses des intouchables catholiques de l'Inde du Sud'. *Anthropos*, 82 (1987), pp. 415-26.

— 'Patrilateral Cross-Cousin Marriage among the Paraiyars of South India'. *Journal of the Anthropological Society of Oxford*, 18 (1987), pp. 223-36

— *Les Paraiyars du Tamil Nadu*. Nettetal: Steyler Verlag, 1988.

— 'Les Mythes d'origine chez les Paraiyar'. *L'Homme*, 109 (1989), pp. 107-16.

— 'Job Mobility among the Brickmakers of South India'. *Man in India*, 69, 1989, pp. 42-63.

— 'A Comparison between Hindu and Christian Paraiyars of South India". *Indian Missiological Review*, 12 (1990), pp. 53-64.

— 'Replication and Consensus: Untouchability, Caste and Ideology in India'. *Man (NS)*, 27 (1992), pp. 155-73.

— *Le Système des castes*. Paris: Presses Universitaires de France, 1993.

— 'The Myths of Origin of the Indian Untouchables'. *Man (NS)*, 28 (1993), pp. 533-49.

— 'Les Chrétiens de Saint Thomas du Kérala (Inde du Sud)'. *Dictionnaire d'Histoire et de Géographie religieuses*. Paris: Letouzey & Ané, 1994. — — 'Caste without a System: A Study of South Indian Harijans', in M. Searle-Chatterjee and U. Sharma (eds), *Contextualising Caste: Post-Dumontian Approaches*. Oxford: Blackwell, 1994, pp. 122-46.

— 'At the Threshold of Untouchability: Pallars and Valaiyars in a Tamil Village', in C. Fuller (ed.), *Caste Today*. Oxford: Oxford University Press, 1996, 65-92.

— 'In the Skin of an Untouchable?'. *Anthropology Today,* 14 (1998), pp. 14-16.

— *The World of the Untouchables: Paraiyars of Tamil Nadu*. Delhi: Oxford University Press, 1998.

Den Ouden, J. *De Onaanraakbaren van Konkunad: een Onderzoek naar de Positie-verandering van de Scheduled Castes in een Dorp van het District Coimbatore, India.*

Wageningen: Mededelingen Landbouwhogeschool, 1975.

— *De Onaanraakbaren van Konkunad: De Economische, Politieke en Educatieve Positie der Scheduled Castes (1966-1976)*. Wageningen: Vakgroep Agrarische Sociologie van de Niet-Westerse Gebieden, 1977.

— 'Social Stratification as Expressed through Language: A Case Study of a South Indian Village'. *Contributions to Indian Sociology (NS),* 13 (1979), pp. 33-59.

Desai, I. P. 'Anti-Reservation Agitation and Structure of Gujarat Society', in Centre For Social Studies (ed.), *Caste, Caste Conflict and Reservation.* Surat-Delhi: Ajanta Publications, 1985, pp. 124-36.

De Vos, G. and H. Wagatsuma (eds). *Japan's Invisible Race: Caste in Culture and Personality.* Berkeley, CA: University of California Press, 1967.

De Vos, G. and H. Wagatsuma. 'Socialization, Self-Perception and Burakumin Status', in G. De Vos and H. Wagatsuma (eds), *Japan's Invisible Race: Caste in Culture and Personality,* Berkeley. University of California Press, 1967, pp. 229-41.

— 'Group Solidarity and Individual Mobility', in G. De Vos and H. Wagatsuma (eds), *Japan's Invisible Race: Caste in Culture and Personality.* Berkeley, CA: University of California Press, 1967, pp. 242-58.

— 'Minority Status and Attitude towards Authority', in G. De Vos and H. Wagatsuma (eds), *Japan's Invisible Race: Caste in Culture and Personality.* Berkeley, CA: University of California Press, 1967, pp. 259-73.

Djurfeldt, G. and S. Lindberg. *Behind Poverty: The Social Formation in a Tamil Village*. London: Curzon Press, 1975.

D. N. 'Dominant Castes, Ruling Classes and the State'. *Economic and Political Weekly,* 10 Nov. 1990, pp. 2467-70.

Donoghue, J. 'The Social Persistence of an Outcaste Group', in G. De Vos and H. Wagatsuma (eds), *Japan's Invisible Race: Caste in Culture and Personality.* Berkeley, CA: University of California Press, 1967, pp.137-52.

D'Souza, V. 'Does Urbanism Desegregate Scheduled Castes? Evidence from a District in Punjab'. *Contributions to Indian Sociology, (NS),* 11 (1977), pp. 219-39.

— 'The Religious Factor and The Scheduled Castes'. *Social Action*, 32 (1982), pp. 283-91.

Dube, S. *Indian Village.* London: Routledge & Kegan Paul, 1955.

Dubois, J. (L'abbé). *Hindu Manners, Customs and Ceremonies.* Oxford: Oxford University Press, 1906 (first edition 1806).

Dumézil, *G. Mythe et épopée.* Paris: Gallimard, 1968, 3 vols.

Dumont, L. *Une Sous-caste de l'Inde du Sud*: *organisation sociale et religion des Pramalai Kallar.* Paris: Mouton, 1957.

— 'Caste, racisme et "stratification": réflexions d'un anthropologue'. *Cahiers internationaux de sociologie,* 39 (1960), pp. 91-112.

— 'Les Mariages nayar comme faits indiens'. *L'Homme,* 1 (1961), pp. 11-36.

— 'Tribe and Caste in India'. *Contributions to Indian Sociology,* 6 (1962), pp. 120-2.

— *Homo Hierarchicus: essai sur le système des castes.* Paris: Gallimard, 1966. English translation: *Homo Hierarchicus. The Caste System and Its Implications,* trans. Mark Sainsbury, Louis Dumont and Basia Gulati. Chicago and London: University of

Chicago Press, 1980 (complete revised edition).

— *La Civilisation indienne et nous*. Paris: A. Colin, 1975.

— *Dravidien et Kariera: l'alliance de mariage dans l'Inde du sud et en Australie.* Paris: Mouton, 1975.

— *Essais sur l'individualisme: une perspective anthropologique sur l'idéologie moderne*. Paris: Le Seuil, 1983.

Dupuis, J. *L'Inde et ses populations*. Bruxelles: Éditions Complexe, 1982.

Dushkin, L. 'Scheduled Caste Policy in India: History, Problems, Prospects'. *Asian Survey*, 3 (1967), pp. 626-36.

— 'Scheduled Castes Politics', in J. M. Mahar (ed.), *The Untouchables in Contemporary India.* Tucson: University of Arizona Press, 1972, pp. 165-227.

Dutt, R. *The Economic History of India in the Victorian Age*. London: Kegan Paul, Trench, Trubner & Co., 1903.

Eck, D. *Banaras*: *City of Light.* London: Routledge & Kegan Paul, 1983.

Eichinger Ferro-Luzzi, G. 'Women's Pollution Periods in Tamilnad (India)'. *Anthropos*, 69 (1974), pp. 113-61.

Enthoven, R. *The Tribes and Castes of Bombay.* Bombay: Government Central Press, 1922, 2 vols.

Epstein, S. 'Productive Efficiency and Customary Systems of Rewards in Rural South India', in R. Firth (ed.), *Themes in Economic Anthropology.* London: Tavistock, 1967, pp. 229-52.

— *South India Yesterday, Today and Tomorrow*. London: Macmillan, 1973.

Fernandes, W. 'Caste and Conversion Movements in India'. *Social Action*, 31 (1981), pp. 261-90.

Fisher, L. *La Vie du Mahatma Gandhi*. Paris: Belfond, 1983 (first edition 1950).

Fiske, A. 'Scheduled Castes Buddhist Organizations', in J. M. Mahar (ed.), *The Untouchables in Contemporary India.* Tucson: University of Arizona Press, 1972, pp. 113-42.

— 'The Understanding of "Religion" and "Buddhism" among India's New Buddhists', in T. Wilkinson and M. Thomas (eds), *Ambedkar and the Neo-Buddhist Movement.* Madras: The Christian Literature Society, 1972, pp. 101-28.

Forrester, D. *Caste and Christianity: Attitudes and Policies on Caste of Anglo-Protestant Missions in India.* London: Curzon Press, 1980.

Franke, R. *Life Is a Little Better: Redistribution as a Development Strategy in Nadur Village, Kerala.* Boulder, CO: Westview Press, 1993.

Freeman, J. *Scarcity and Opportunity in an Indian Village.* Menlo Park, CA: Cummings, 1977.

— *Untouchable: An Indian Life History.* Stanford, CA: Stanford University Press, 1979.

Freund, J. *Sociologie de Max Weber*. Paris: Presses Universitaires de France, 1961.

Fuchs, S. *The Children of Hari: A Study of the Nimar Balahis in the Central*

Provinces of India. Vienna: Verlag Herold, 1950.

— *Rebellious Prophets: A Study of Messianic Movements in Indian Religions*. Bombay: Asia Publishing House, 1965.

— *At the Bottom of Indian Society: The Harijan and Other Low Castes*. Delhi: Munshiram Manoharlal, 1980.

Fuller, C. *The Nayars Today*. Cambridge: Cambridge University Press, 1976.

— *Servants of the Goddess: The Priests of a South Indian Temple*. Cambridge: Cambridge University Press, 1984.

— 'Sacrifice (Bali) in the South Indian Temple', in V. Sudarsen, G. Reddy and M. Suryanarayana (eds), *Religion and Society in South India: A Volume in Honour of Prof. N. Subba Reddy*. Delhi: B. R. Publishing Corporation, 1987, pp. 21-35.

— 'The Hindu Pantheon and the Legitimation of Hierarchy'. *Man (NS)*, 23 (1988), pp. 19-39.

— 'Misconceiving the Grain Heap: a Critique of the Concept of the Indian Jajmani System', in J. Parry and M. Bloch (eds), *Money and the Morality of Exchange*. Cambridge: Cambridge University Press, 1989, p. 33-63.

— *The Camphor Flame: Popular Hinduism and Society in India*. Princeton, NJ: Princeton University Press, 1992.

Fussman, G. 'Pour une problématique nouvelle des religions indiennes anciennes'. *Journal asiatique*, 265 (1977), pp. 21-70.

Fustel de Coulanges, N. *La Cité antique: étude sur le culte, le droit et les institutions de la Grèce et de Rome*. Paris: Hachette, 1912.

Galanter, M. 'Law and Caste in Modern India'. *Asian Survey*, 3 (1963), pp. 544-59.

— 'Group Membership and Group Preferences in India'. *Journal of Asian and African Studies*, 2 (1967), pp. 91-124.

— "The Abolition of Disabilities: Untouchability and the Law", in J. M. Mahar (ed.), *The Untouchables in Contemporary India*. Tucson: University of Arizona Press, 1971, pp. 228-316.

— *Competing Equalities: Law and the Backward Classes in India*. Berkeley, CA: University of California Press, 1984.

Gandhi, M. *The Removal of Untouchability*. Allahabad: Navajivan Publishing House, 1954.

— A*n Autobiography or the Story of My Experiments with Truth*. Harmondsworth: Penguin, 1982 (first edition 1929).

Ganeshram, S. 'Communalism in Tamil Nadu: A Study of Bodi Riots'. *Economic and Political Weekly*, 2 Dec. 1989, pp. 2640-2.

Geertz, C. 'Religion as a Cultural System', in M. Banton (ed.), *Anthropological Approaches to the Study of Religion*. London: Tavistock, 1966, pp. 1-46.

Ghurye, G. S. *The Scheduled Tribes*. Bombay: Popular Prakashan, 1963.

— *Caste and Race in India*. Bombay: Popular Prakashan, 1969 (first edition 1932).

Goffman, E. *Stigmates: les usages sociaux des handicaps*. Paris: Éditions de Minuit, 1975.

Gokhale, B. J. 'Dr. Bhimrao Ramji Ambedkar: Rebel against Hindu Tradition'.

Journal of Asian and African Studies, 11 (1976), 13-23.

Gokhale-Turner, J. 'Bhakti or Vidroha: Continuity and Change in Dalit Sahitya'. *Journal of Asian and African Studies,* 15 (1980), pp. 29-42.

Gold, A. *Fruitful Journeys*: *The Ways of Rajasthani Pilgrims.* Berkeley, CA: University of California Press, 1988.

Good, A. 'Elder Sister's Daughter Marriage in South Asia'. *Journal of Anthropological Research,* 36 (1980), pp. 474-500.

— 'Prescription, Preference and Practice: Marriage Patterns among the Kondaiyankottai Maravar of South India'. *Man (NS)*, 16 (1981), pp. 108-29.

— "The Actor and the Act: Categories of Prestation in South India". *Man (NS),* 17, 1982, pp. 23-41.

— *The Female Bridegroom: A Comparative Study of Life-Crisis Rituals in South India and Sri Lanka.* Oxford: Clarendon Press, 1990.

Gough, K. 'The Social Structure of a Tanjore Village', in McKim Marriott (ed.), *Village India: Studies in the Little Community.* Chicago: University of Chicago Press, 1955, pp. 36-52.

— 'Caste in a Tanjore Village', in E. Leach (ed.), *Aspects of Caste in South India, Ceylon and North-West Pakistan.* Cambridge: Cambridge University Press, 1960, pp. 11-60.

— 'Harijans in Thanjavur', in K. Gough and H. Sharma (eds), *Imperialism and Revolution in South Asia.* New York: Monthly Review Press, 1973, pp. 222-45.

— 'Village Politics in Kerala', in A. R. Desai (ed.), *Rural Sociology in India.* Bombay: Popular Prakashan, 1978, pp. 736-67.

— *Rural Society in Southeast India.* Cambridge: Cambridge University Press, 1981.

— *Rural Change in Southeast India: 1950s to 1980s*. Delhi: Oxford University Press, 1989.

Gould, H. 'The Hindu Jajmani System: A Case of Economic Particularism'. *Southwestern Journal of Anthropology,* 14 (1958), pp. 428-37.

— 'Castes, Outcastes and the Sociology of Stratification'. *International Journal of Comparative Sociology,* 1 (1960), pp. 220-38.

— 'A Jajmani System of North India: Its Structure, Magnitude and Meaning'. *Ethnology*, 3 (1964), pp. 12-41.

Guha, A. 'Reservations in Myth and Reality'. *Economic and Political Weekly,* 15 Dec. 1990, pp. 2716-18.

Gumperz, J. 'Dialect Differences and Social Stratification in a North Indian Village'. *American Anthropologist*, 60 (1958), pp. 668-82.

Hardgrave, R. *The Nadars of Tamilnad: The Political Culture of a Community in Change.* Bombay: Oxford University Press, 1969.

— 'Political Participation and Primordial Solidarity: The Nadars of Tamil Nad', in Rajni Kothari (ed), *Caste in Indian Politics.* Poona: Orient Longman, 1970, pp. 102-128.

Harjinder Singh (ed.). *Caste among the Non-Hindus in India.* Delhi: National Publishing House, 1977.

Harper, E. 'Two Systems of Economic Exchange in Village India'. *American Anthropologist*, 61 (1959), pp. 760-78.

— 'Ritual Pollution as Integrator of Caste and Religion'. *Journal of Asian Studies*, 23 (1964), pp. 151-97.

— 'Social Consequences of an Unsuccessful Low Caste Movement', in J. Silverberg (ed.), *Social Mobility in the Caste System*. The Hague: Mouton, 1968, pp. 35-65.

Harriss, J. 'Knowing about Rural Economic Change: Problems Arising from a Comparison of the Results of "Macro" and "Micro" Research in Tamil Nadu', in P. Bardhan (ed.), *Conversations between Economists and Anthropologists: Methodological Issues in Measuring Economic Change in Rural India*. Oxford: Oxford University Press, 1989, pp. 137-73.

Hazari. *Untouchable: The Autobiography of an Indian Outcaste*. London: Pall Mall Press, 1951.

Herrenschmidt, O. 'Entretien avec O. Herrenschmidt par M. et F. Montrelay'. *Cahiers Confrontations*, 13 (1985), pp. 9-23.

— *Les Meilleurs Dieux sont hindous*. Lausanne: L'Age d'Homme, 1989.

Heuzé, G. 'Unité et pluralité du monde ouvrier indien', in J. Pouchepadass (ed.), *Caste et classe en Asie du Sud*. Paris: Éditions de l'École des Hautes Études en Sciences Sociales, 1982, pp. 189-222.

— 'Troubled Anthropologists: The Controversy over Quotas in India'. *Anthropology Today*, 7 (1991), pp. 5-7

Hirschon, R. *Heirs of the Greek Catastrophe: The Social Life of Asia Minor Refugees in Piraeus*. Oxford: Clarendon Press, 1989.

Hocart, A. *Les Castes*. Paris: Librairie orientaliste Paul Geuthner, 1938.

— *Kings and Councillors: An Essay in the Comparative Anatomy of Human Society*. Chicago: University of Chicago Press, 1970 (first edition 1936).

Holmström, M. *South Indian Factory Workers: Their Life and their World*. Cambridge: Cambridge University Press, 1976.

— *Industry and Inequality: the Social Anthropology of Indian Labour*. Cambridge: Cambridge University Press, 1984.

Houska, W. 'Religious Belief and Practice in an Urban Scheduled Caste Community'. Doctoral dissertation, Syracuse University, 1981.

Hutton, J. *Caste in India: Its Nature, Functions, and Origins*. Delhi: Oxford University Press, 1973 (first edition 1946).

Indian School of Social Sciences. *Bonded Labour in India: A Shocking Tale of Slave Labour in Rural India*. Calcutta: Indian School of Social Sciences, 1975.

Isaacs, H. *India's Ex-Untouchables*. New York: Harper Torchbooks, 1964.

Iyer, A. K. *The Tribes and Castes of Cochin*. New Delhi: Cosmos, 1981 (first edition 1909), 3 vols.

Jaffrelot, C. *Les Nationalistes hindous: idéologie, implantation et mobilisation des années 1920 aux années 1990*. Paris: Presses de la Fondation Nationale des Sciences

Politiques, 1993.

Jeffrey, R. *The Decline of Nayar Dominance: Society and Politics in Travancore, 1847-1908*. Brighton, Sussex University Press, 1976.

— 'Temple-Entry Movements in Travancore, 1860-1940'. *Social Scientist,* 4 (1976), pp. 3-27.

Jones, D. and R. Jones. 'The Scholar's Rebellion: Educational Interests and Agitation Politics in Gujarat'. *Journal of Asian Studies,* 36 (1977), pp. 457-76.

Jones, K. *Socio-Religious Reform Movements in British India.* Cambridge: Cambridge University Press, 1989.

Joshi, B. (ed.) *Untouchables! Voices of the Dalit Liberation Movement.* London: Zed Books, 1986.

Joshi, B. 'Recent Developments in Inter-Regional Mobilization of Dalit Protest in India'. *South Asia Bulletin*, 7 (1987), pp. 86-96.

Juergensmeyer, M. *Religion as Social Vision: The Movement against Untouchability in 20th-Century Punjab.* Berkeley, CA: University of California Press, 1982.

Kahn, M. A. *Seven Years of Change: A Study of Some Scheduled Castes in Bangalore District.* Madras: Christian Literature Society, 1979.

— 'A Brief Summary of the Study on "Mass Conversions" of Meenakshipuram: a Sociological Enquiry'. *Religion and Society,* 28 (1981), pp. 37-50.

Kalam, M. 'Why the Harijan Convert to Islam Views Reservations with Reservation'. *South Asia Research*, 4 (1984).

Kananaikil, J. 'Marginalisation of the Scheduled Castes: A Sociological Interpretation'. *Social Action*, 32 (1982), pp. 247-68.

Kapadia, K. 'Gender, Caste and Class in Rural South India'. London School of Economics, Department of Anthropology. Doctoral dissertation, 1990.

Karve, I. *Maharashtra Land and Its People*. Bombay: Maharashtra State Gazetteers General Series, 1968.

Khare, R. S. *The Untouchable as Himself: Ideology, Identity and Pragmatism among the Lucknow Chamars*. Cambridge: Cambridge University Press, 1984.

Kohli, A. *The State and Poverty in India: The Politics of Reform.* Cambridge: Cambridge University Press, 1987.

— *Democracy and Discontent: India's Growing Crisis of Governability.* Cambridge: Cambridge University Press, 1990.

Koilparampil, G. *Caste in the Catholic Community in Kerala: A Study of Caste Elements in the Inter-Rite Relationships of Syrians and Latins.* Cochin: St Theresa's College, 1982.

Kolenda, P. 'Religious Anxiety and Hindu Fate', in E. Harper (ed.), *Religion in South Asia.* Berkeley, CA: University of California Press, 1964, pp. 71-81.

— 'Untouchable Chuhras through their Humor: "Equalizing" Marital Kin through Teasing, Pretence, and Farce', in O. Lynch (ed.), *Divine Passions: the Social Construction of Emotion in India.* Berkeley, CA: University of California Press, 1990, pp. 116-53.

Kooiman, D. *Conversion and Social Equality in India: The London Missionary*

Society in South Travancore in the 19th Century. Delhi: Manohar, 1989.

Kosambi, D. 'Early Stages of the Caste System in Northern India'. *Journal of the Bombay Branch of the Royal Asiatic Society*, 13 (1946), pp. 33-48.

Kroeber, A. 'Caste', in E. Seligman and A. Johnson (eds), *Encyclopedia of the Social Sciences*. New York: Macmillan, 1930, pp. 254-6.

Kulkarni, S. D. 'Human Sacrifice and its Caste Context in the Eighteenth Century Maharashtra: A Case Study'. Poona: Gokhale Institute of Politics and Economics (mimeo), 1976.

Kulke, H. and D. Rothermund. *A History of India.* London: Routledge, 1990.

Landy, F. *Paysans de l'Inde du Sud: le choix et la contrainte.* Paris: Karthala, 1994.

Lapoint E. and D. Lapoint. 'Socio-Economic Mobility among Village Harijans'. *The Eastern Anthropologist,* 38 (1985), pp. 1-18.

Leach, E. R. 'What Should We Mean by Caste?', in E. Leach (ed.), *Aspects of Caste in South India, Ceylon and North Western Pakistan.* Cambridge: Cambridge University Press, 1960, pp. 1-10.

Lévi-Strauss, C. *Anthropologie structurale deux.* Paris: Plon, 1973.

Lewis, O. 'The Culture of Poverty'. *Scientific American*, 215 (1966), pp. 19-25.

Lipton, M. and J. Toye. *Does Aid Work in India? A Country Study of the Impact of Official Development Assistance.* London: Routledge, 1990.

Logan, W. *Malabar*. Madras: Government Press, 1906 (first edition 1887).

Loiseleur Deslongchamps, A. (ed.). *Lois de Manou, comprenant les institutions religieuses et civiles des Indiens.* Paris: De Crapelet, 1833.

Luke, P. and J. Carman. *Village Christians and Hindu Culture: Study of a Rural Church in Andhra Pradesh, South India.* London: Lutterworth Press, 1968.

Lynch, O. *The Politics of Untouchability: Social Mobility and Social Change in a City of India.* New York: Columbia University Press, 1969.

—— 'Dr B. R. Ambedkar: Myth and Charisma', in J. M. Mahar (ed.), *The Untouchables in Contemporary India.* Tucson: University of Arizona Press, 1972, pp. 97-112.

—— 'Political Mobilization and Ethnicity among the Adi-Dravidas in a Bombay Slum'. *Economic and Political Weekly,* 9, 39 (1974), pp. 1657-68.

McCormack, W. 'Caste and the British Administration of Hindu Law'. *Journal of Asian and African Studies,* 1 (1966), pp. 27-34.

McCurdy, D. 'The Changing Economy of an Indian Village', in J. Spardley and D. McCurdy (eds), *Conformity and Conflict: Readings in Cultural Anthropology*. Boston: Little, Brown & Co., 1971, pp. 219-28.

Macdonnell, A. *A History of Sanskrit Literature.* Delhi: Motilal Banarsidass, 1971.

McGilvray, D. 'Paraiyar Drummers of Sri Lanka: Consensus and Constraint in an Untouchable Caste'. *American Ethnologist*, 10 (1983), pp. 97-114.

McLeod, W. *The Sikhs: History, Religion and Society.* New York: Columbia

University Press, 1989.

Madan, G. *Western Sociologists on Indian Society*. London: Routledge & Kegan Paul, 1979.

Mahar, J. M. 'Agents of Dharma in a North Indian Village', in J. M. Mahar (ed.), *The Untouchables in Contemporary India.* Tucson: University of Arizona Press, 1972, pp. 17-37.

Mahar, J. M. (ed.) *The Untouchables in Contemporary India*. Tucson: University of Arizona Press, 1972.

Malcolm, J. A *Memoir of Central India*. Calcutta: Thacker, Spink & Co., 1880 (first edition 1823).

Mallik, B. K. 'Ambedkar: His Movement for Social Equality and Buddhism'. *The Great Concern,* 2 (1992), pp. 6-9.

Maloney, C. 'Religious Beliefs and Social Hierarchy in Tamil Nadu, India'. *American Ethnologist*, 2 (1975), pp. 169-92.

Mandelbaum, D. *Society in India.* Berkeley, CA: University of California Press, 1970, 2 vols.

Manickam, S. *The Social Setting of Christian Conversion in South India: The Impact of the Wesleyan Methodist Missionaries on the Trichy-Tanjore Diocese to the Harijan Communities of the Mass Movement Area, 1820-1947*. Wiesbaden: Franz Steiner Verlag, 1977.

Marcus, G. and M. Fisher. *Anthropology as Cultural Critique: An Experimental Moment in the Human Sciences.* Chicago: University of Chicago Press, 1986.

Mariott, McKim. 'Hindu Transactions: Diversity without Dualism', in B. Kapferer (ed.), *Transactions and Meaning: Directions in the Anthropology of Exchange and Symbolic Behavior.* Philadelphia: Institute for the Study of Human Issues, 1976, pp. 109-42.

Marx, K. and F. Engels. *Textes sur le colonialisme*. Moscow: Éditions en langues étrangères, n.d.

Mathew, T. 'Mandal and After'. *The Great Concern,* 2 (1992), pp. 21-4.

Mayer, A. *Caste and Kinship in Central India: A Village and Its Region.* Berkeley, CA: University of California Press, 1960.

— 'Caste: The Indian Caste System', in D. Sills (ed.), *International Encyclopedia of the Social Sciences.* New York: Macmillan Free Press, 1968, vol.II, pp. 339-44.

Meillassoux, C. 'Y a-t-il des castes aux Indes?'. *Cahiers internationaux de sociologie*, 44 (1973), pp. 5-23.

— *Femmes, greniers et capitaux*. Paris: Maspero, 1975.

Mencher, J. 'Kerala and Madras: a Comparative Study of Ecology and Social Structure'. *Ethnology,* 5 (1966), pp. 135-79.

— 'Continuity and Change in an Ex-Community of South India', in J. M. Mahar (ed.), *The Untouchables in Contemporary India.* Tucson: University of Arizona Press, 1972, pp. 33-58.

— 'The Caste System Upside Down, or the Not-so-Mysterious East'. *Current Anthropology,* 15 (1974), pp. 469-93.

— 'Land Reform and Socialism', in S. Devadas Pillai (ed.), *Aspects of Changing*

India. Bombay: Popular Prakashan, 1976.

— *Agriculture and Social Structure in Tamil Nadu: Past Origins, Present Transformations and Future Prospects*. Bombay: Allied Publishers, 1978.

Mendelsohn, O. and M. Vicziany. *The Untouchables: Subordination, Poverty and the State in Modern India*. Cambridge: Cambridge University Press, 1998.

Menon, A. *S. Social and Cultural History of Kerala*. Delhi: Sterling Publishers, 1979.

Miller, B. 'The Man Inside', in J. M. Mahar (ed.), *The Untouchables in Contemporary India*. Tucson: University of Arizona Press, 1972, pp. 363-411.

Miller, D. 'Exchange and Alienation in the Jajmani System'. *Journal of Anthropological Research*, 42 (1986), pp. 535-56.

Miller, D. B. *From Hierarchy to Stratification: Changing Patterns of Social Inequality in a North Indian Village*. Delhi: Oxford University Press, 1975.

Miller, R. 'Button, Button ... Great Tradition, Little Tradition, Whose Tradition?'. *Anthropological Quarterly*, 39 (1966), pp. 26-42.

— '"They Will Not Die Hindus": The Buddhist Conversion of Mahar Ex-Untouchables'. *Asian Survey*, 3 (1967), pp. 637-44.

Miller, R. and P. Kale. 'The Burden on the Head is Always There', in J. M. Mahar (ed.), *The Untouchables of Contemporary India*. Tucson: University of Arizona Press, 1972, pp. 317-62.

Mines, M. *The Warrior Merchants: Textiles, Trade and Territory in South India*. Cambridge: Cambridge University Press, 1984.

Moffatt, M. *An Untouchable Community in South India: Structure and Consensus*. Princeton, NJ: Princeton University Press, 1979.

Molund, S. *First We Are People ... The Koris of Kanpur between Caste and Class*. Stockholm: Stockholm Studies in Social Anthropology, 1988.

Morrison, W. 'Family Types in Badlapur: an Analysis of a Changing Institution in a Maharashtrian Village'. *Sociological Bulletin*, 8 (1959), pp. 45-67.

Mosse, D. 'Caste, Christianity and Hinduism: A Study of Social Organization and Religion in Rural Ramnad'. D.Phil. Thesis, Oxford University, Institute of Social Anthropology, 1985.

— 'Idioms of Subordination and Styles of Protest among Christian and Hindu Harijan Castes in Tamil Nadu'. *Contributions to Indian Sociology* (NS), 28 (1994), pp. 67-106.

Muhlmann, W. 'Max Weber and the Concept of Pariah-Communities', in O. Stammer (ed.), *Max Weber and Sociology Today*. New York: Harper & Row, 1971, pp. 251-6.

Mukherjee, R. *The Rise and Fall of the East India Company*. New York: Monthly Review Press, 1974.

Murugkar, L. *Dalit Panther Movement in Maharashtra: A Sociological Appraisal*. Bombay: Popular Prakashan, 1991.

Myrdal, G. *Asian Drama: An Inquiry into the Poverty of Nations*. New York: Pantheon, 1968, 3 vols.

Namboodiripad, E. 'Economic Backwardness of Harijans in Kerala'. *Social*

Scientist, 4 (1976), pp. 62-8.

Nanda, S. B. *Gandhi: sa vie, ses idées, son action politique en Afrique du sud et en Inde.* Verviers: Marabout, 1968.

Needham, R. *Exemplars*. Berkeley, CA: University of California Press, 1985.

Newell, W. 'Inter-Caste Marriage in Kugti Village, Upper Budl Nadl, Brahmaur Tahsil, Chamba District, Himachal Pradesh, India'. *Man,* 59 (1963), pp. 55-7.

Nigam, A. 'Mandal Commission and the Left'. *Economic and Political Weekly,* 18 Dec. 1990, pp. 2652-3.

Oddie, G. *Social Protest in India: British Protestant Missionaries and Social Reforms, 1850-1900*. Delhi: Manohar, 1979.

O'Hanlon, R. Caste, *Conflict and Ideology: Mahatma Jotirao Phule and Low Caste Protest in Nineteenth Century Western India.* Cambridge: Cambridge University Press, 1985.

Olcott, M. 'The Caste System in India'. *The American Sociological Review*, 9 (1944), pp. 648-57.

Omvedt, G. 'Dalit Literature in Maharashtra: Literature of Social Protest and Revolt in Western India'. *South Asia Bulletin*, 7 (1987), pp. 78-85.

Oommen, T. 'Sources of Deprivation and Styles of Protest: The Case of the Dalits in India'. *Contributions to Indian Sociology (NS)*, 18, 1984, pp. 45-61.

Opler, M. 'North Indian Themes: Caste and Untouchability', in J. M. Mahar (ed.), *The Untouchables in Contemporary India.* Tucson: University of Arizona Press, 1972, pp. 4-16.

Orans, M. 'Maximizing in Jajmaniland: A Model of Caste Relations'. *American Anthropologist,* 70 (1968), pp. 875-97.

Orenstein, H. 'Exploitation or Function in the Interpretation of Jajmani'. *Southwestern Journal of Anthropology,* 18 (1962), pp. 302-16.

Paradkar, B. 'The Religious Quest of Ambedkar', in T. Wilkinson and M. Thomas (eds), *Ambedkar and the Neo-Buddhist Movement*. Madras: The Christian Literature Society, 1972, pp. 33-70.

Patil, S. 'Should "Class" Be the Basis for Recognizing Backwardness'. *Economic and Political Weekly,* 15 Dec. 1990, pp. 2733-44.

Parry, J. 'The Koli Dilemma'. *Contributions to Indian Sociology (NS),* 4 (1970), pp. 84-104.

— 'Egalitarian Values in a Hierarchical Society'. *South Asian Review*, 7 (1974), pp. 95-124.

— *Caste and Kinship in Kangra*. London: Routledge & Kegan Paul, 1979.

— 'Ghosts, Greed and Sin: the Occupational Identity of the Benares Funeral Priests". *Man (NS)*, 21 (1980), pp. 453-73.

— '*The Gift*, the Indian Gift and the "Indian Gift"'. Man (NS), 21 (1986), pp. 453-73.

Passin, H. 'Untouchability in the Far East'. *Monumenta Nipponica*, 2 (1955), pp. 27-47.

Patwardhan, S. *Change among India's Harijans: Maharashtra - A Case Study*. New Delhi: Orient Longman, 1973.

Pawar, D. *Ma vie d'intouchable.* Paris: La Découverte, 1990.

Peter of Greece and Denmark, H. R. H. Prince. *A Study of Polyandry*. The Hague: Mouton, 1963.

Pfaffenberger, B. 'Social Communication in Dravidian Ritual'. *Journal of Anthropological Research,* 36 (1980), pp. 196-219.

Philip, P. 'The Harijan Movement in India in Relation to Christianity'. *International Review of Mission*, 24 (1935), pp. 162-177.

Pocock, D. 'Notes on Jajmâni Relationships'. *Contributions to Indian Sociology*, 6 (1962), pp. 78-95.

— *Kanbi and Patidar:A Study of the Patidar Community of Gujarat.* Oxford: Oxford University Press, 1972.

Poitevin, G. 'Préface' to D. Pawar, *Ma vie d'intouchable.* Paris: La Découverte, 1990, pp. 5-15.

Pradhan, G. *Untouchable Workers of Bombay City*. Bombay: Karnatak Publishing House, 1938.

Prakash, G. (ed.). *The World of the Rural Labourer in Colonial India.* Delhi: Oxford University Press, 1992.

Prasad, P. 'Rise of Kulak Power and Caste Struggle in North India'. *Economic and Political Weekly*, 17 Aug. 1991, pp. 1923-6.

Pratap, A. 'Till Death Do Us Part: The Caste System Is Virulently Alive in India'. *Time*, 15 April 1991, p. 61.

Price, J. 'A History of the Outcastes: Untouchability in Japan', in G. De Vos and H. Wagatsuma (eds), *Japan's Invisible Race: Caste in Culture and Personality.* Berkeley, CA: University of California Press, 1967, pp. 6-32.

Pullapilly, C. 'The Izhavas of Kerala and the Historic Struggle for Acceptance in Hindu Society'. *Journal of Asian and African Studies*, 11 (1976), pp. 24-5.

Quigley, D. 'Le Brahmane pur et le prêtre impur'. *Recherches sociologiques*, 23 (1992), pp. 69-89.

— *The Interpretation of Caste*. Oxford: Clarendon Press, 1993.

Radhakrishnan, P. 'Backward Classes in Tamil Nadu, 1872-1988'. *Economic and Political Weekly,* 10 March, 1990, pp. 509-17.

— 'Ambedkar's Legacy'. *The Hindu*, 20 January 1991, pp. 19-20.

— 'Ambedkar's Legacy to Dalits: Has the Nation Reneged on its Promises?'. *Economic and Political Weekly,* 17 Aug. 1991, pp. 1911-22.

Raheja, G. *The Poison in the Gift: Ritual, Prestation, and the Dominant Caste in a North Indian Village*. Chicago: University of Chicago Press, 1988.

Raj, S. 'Mass Religious Conversion as Protest Movement: A Framework'. *Religion and Society,* 28 (1981), pp. 58-66.

Rajendran, G. *The Ezhava Community and Kerala Politics*. Trivandrum: The Kerala Academy of Political Sciences, 1974.

Rajshekar Shetty, V. *Dalit Movement in Karnataka*. Madras: The Christian Literature Society, 1978.

— *Brahmanism: The Curse of India*. Bangalore: Dalit Sahitya Akademy, 1981.

— *Dalit: the Black Untouchables of India*. Atlanta, GA: Clarity Press, 1987.

Randeria, S. 'Carrion and Corpses: Conflict in Categorizing Untouchability in Gujarat'. *Archives européennes de sociologie,* 30 (1989), pp. 171-91.

Rao, M. S. *Social Change in Malabar*. Bombay: Popular Book Depot, 1957.

— *Social Movements and Social Transformations*: *A Study of Two Backward Classes Movements in India.* Delhi: Macmillan, 1979.

Ravindran, T. *Asan and Social Revolution in Kerala: A Study of His Assembly Speeches.* Trivandrum: Kerala History Society, 1972.

Reiniche, M. L. 'Les "démons" et leur culte dans la structure du panthéon d'un village du Tirunelveli'. *Purusârtha*, 2 (1975), pp. 173-203.

— 'La Notion de *jajmâni*: qualification abusive ou principe d'intégration?'. *Purusârtha*, 3 (1976), pp. 71-107.

— 'Statut, fonction et droit: relations agraires au Tamilnad'. *L'Homme*, 18 (1978), pp. 135-66.

— *Les Dieux et les hommes: étude des cultes d'un village du Tirunelveli (Inde du Sud)*. Paris: Mouton, 1979.

— 'La Maison du Tirunelveli (Inde du Sud)'. *Bulletin de l'École Française d'Extrême-Orient,* 70 (1981), pp. 21-57.

Rothermund, D. *Mahatma Gandhi: An Essay in Political Biography*. Delhi: Manohar, 1991.

Rudolph, L. and S. Hoeber Rudolph. *The Modernity of Tradition: Political Development in India.* Chicago: University of Chicago Press, 1967.

— *In Pursuit of Lakshmi: The Political Economy of the Indian State*. Chicago: University of Chicago Press, 1987.

Russel, R. and H. Lal. *Tribes and Castes of the Central Provinces of India.* Delhi: Cosmos, 1975 (first edition 1916).

Sachchidananda. *The Harijan Elite: A Study of the Status, Networks, Mobility and Role in Social Transformation.* Delhi: Thomson Press, 1976.

— *Social Change in Village India*. Delhi: Concept, 1988.

Samuel, V. T. *One Caste, One Religion, One God: A Study of Sree Narayana Guru.* Delhi: Sterling, 1977.

Santhakumari, R. *Scheduled Castes and Welfare Measures*. New Delhi: Classical Publishing Company, n.d.

Saradamoni, K. *Emergence of a Slave Caste: Pulayas of Kerala*. Delhi: People's Publishing House, 1980.

Saxena, P. K. *The Scheduled Caste Vote*r. New Delhi: Radha Publications, 1990.

Schwartzberg, J. 'The Distribution of Selected Castes in the North Indian Plain'. *Geographical Review*, 55 (1965), pp. 477-95.

Searle-Chatterjee, M. 'Kinship in an Urban Low Caste Locality'. *The Eastern Anthropologist*, 27, pp. 337-50.

— 'The Polluted Identity of Work: A Study of Benares Sweepers', in S. Wallman (ed.), *The Anthropology of Work*. London: Academic Books, 1979, pp. 269-86.

— *Reversible Sex Roles: The Special Case of Benares Sweepers*. Oxford:

Pergamon Press, 1981.

Sekine, Y. 'Pollution Theory and Harijan Strategies among South Indian Tamils'. Doctoral dissertation, University of London School of Oriental and African Studies, 1993.

Senart, E. *Caste in India: The Facts and the System.* Delhi: E.S.S., 1975.

Shah, G. 'Anti-Untouchability Movements', in Centre For Social Studies (ed.), *Caste, Caste Conflict and Reservation.* Surat-Delhi: Ajanta Publications, 1985, pp. 102-23.

Shah, P. *The Dublas of Gujarat.* Delhi: Bharatiya Adimjati Sevak Sangh, 1958.

Sharma, G. *Legislation and Cases on Untouchability and Scheduled Castes in India.* Delhi: Indian Council of Social Sciences Research, 1975.

Sharma, S. *The Chamars Artisans: Industrialisation, Skills and Social Mobility.* Delhi: B. R. Publications, 1986.

Sharma, U. 'Berreman Revisited: Caste and the Comparative Method', in M. Searle-Chatterjee and U. Sharma (eds), *Contextualising Caste: Post-Dumontian Approaches.* Oxford: Blackwell, 1994, pp. 72-91.

Shyamlal. *Caste and Political Mobilization: The Bhangis.* Jaipur: Panchsheel Prakashan, 1981.

— *The Bhangis in Transition.* New Delhi: Inter-India Publications, 1984.

Sigrist, C. 'The Problem of Pariahs', in O. Stammer (ed.), *Max Weber and Sociology Today.* New York, Harper & Row, 1971, pp. 240-50.

Sinha, N. and N. Ray. *A History of India.* Calcutta: Orient Longman, 1986.

Singh, D. R. *Rural Leadership among Scheduled Castes.* Allahabad: Publications, 1985.

Sivanandan, P. 'Economic Backwardness of Harijans in Kerala'. *Social Scientist,* 4 (1976), pp. 3-28.

Srinivas, M. N. 'The Social Structure of a Mysore Village', in M. N. Srinivas (ed.), *India's Villages.* London: Asia Publishing House, 1955, pp.15-32.

— *Caste in Modern India and other Essays.* Bombay: Asia Publishing House, 1962.

— *Religion and Society among the Coorgs of South India.* Bombay: Asia Publishing House, 1965 (first edition 1952).

— 'The Cohesive Role of Sanskritization', in P. Mason (ed.), India and Ceylon: *Unity and Diversity.* Oxford: Oxford University Press, 1967.

— *Social Change in Modern India.* Berkeley, CA: University of California Press, 1971.

— *The Remembered Village.* Berkeley, CA: University of California Press, 1976.

— 'Some Reflections on the Nature of Caste Hierarchy'. *Contributions to Indian Sociology (NS),* 18 (1984), pp. 151-67.

— 'Le Système social d'un village du Mysore', in R. Lardinois (ed.), *Miroir de l'Inde: études indiennes en sciences sociales.* Paris: Éditions de la Maison des Sciences de l'Homme, 1988, pp. 49-90.

Srinivas, M. N. and A. Béteille. 'The "Untouchables" of India'. *Scientific American,* 213 (1965), pp. 13-17.

Srivastava, *S. Harijans in Indian Society: a Study of the Status of Harijans and*

Other Backward Classes from the Earliest Times to the Present Day. Lucknow: The Upper India Publishing House, 1980.

Stevenson, H. 'Status Evaluation in the Hindu Caste System'. *Journal of the Royal Anthropological Institute of Great Britain and Ireland,* 84 (1954), pp. 45-65.

Stock, F. and M. Stock. *People Movements in the Punjab.* Bombay: Gospel Literature Society, 1978.

Taylor, R. 'The Ambedkarite Buddhists', in T. Wilkinson and M. Thomas (eds), *Ambedkar and the Neo-Buddhist Movement.* Madras: The Christian Literature Society, 1972, pp. 129-63.

Thurston, E. *Castes and Tribes of Southern India.* Madras: Government Press, 1909, 7 vols.

Tod, J. *Annals and Antiquities of Rajasthan or the Central and Western Rajpoot States of India.* London: Routledge & Kegan Paul, 1972 (first edition 1829), 2 vols.

Totten, G. and H. Wagatsuma, 'Emancipation: Growth and Transformation of a Political Movement', in G. De Vos and H. Wagatsuma (eds), *Japan's Invisible Race: Caste in Culture and Personality.* Berkeley, CA: University of California Press, 1967, pp. 33-67.

Trawick, M. 'Spirits and Voices in Tamil Songs'. *American Ethnologist,* 14 (1987), pp. 193-215.

Vagiswari, A. *Income-Earning Trends and Social Status of the Harijan Community in Tamil Nadu.* Madras: Sangam Publishers, 1972.

Vansina, J. *Oral Tradition as History.* London: James Currey, 1985.

Venkateswarlu, D. 'Socio-Economic Differences between Harijans, Middle-Castes and Upper-Castes: a Comparative Study of Six Villages in Andhra Pradesh'. *The Eastern Anthropologist*, 39 (1986), pp. 210-23.

Vidhyarthi, L. and N. Mishra. *Harijans Today.* Delhi: Classical Publications, 1977.

Vijayakumar, W. 'A Historical Survey of Buddhism in India: A Neo-Buddhist Interpretation', in T. Wilkinson and M. Thomas (eds), *Ambedkar and the Neo-Buddhist Movement.* Madras: The Christian Literature Society, 1972, pp. 1-32.

Vincentnathan, L. 'Harijan Subculture and Self-Esteem Management in a South Indian Community'. Unpublished doctoral dissertation. University of Wisconsin, Madison, 1987.

Von Der Weid, D. and G. Poitevin. *Inde: les parias de l'espoir*. Paris: L'Harmattan, 1978.

Wadley, S. (ed.) *The Powers of Tamil Women.* Delhi: Manohar, 1991.

Wadley, S. and B. Derr. 'Karimpur 1925-1984: Understanding Rural India through Restudies', in P. Bardhan (ed.), *Conversations Between Economists and Anthropologists: Methodological Issues in Measuring Economic Change in Rural India.* Oxford: Oxford University Press, 1989, pp. 76-127.

Wagatsuma, H. 'Postwar Political Militance', in G. De Vos and H. Wagatsuma (eds.), *Japan's Invisible Race: Caste in Culture and Personality.* Berkeley, CA:

University of California Press, 1967, pp. 68-88.

—— 'Non-Political Approaches: the Influence of Religion and Education', in G. De Vos and H. Wagatsuma (eds), *Japan's Invisible Race: Caste in Culture and Personality.* Berkeley, CA: University of California Press, 1967, pp. 89-112.

Wagatsuma, H. and G. De Vos. 'The Ecology of Special Buraku', in G. De Vos and H. Wagatsuma (eds), *Japan's Invisible Race: Caste in Culture and Personality.* Berkeley, CA: University of California Press, 1967, pp. 113-36.

Weber, M. *The Religion of India: The Sociology of Hinduism and Buddhism.* New York: The Free Press, 1958.

Wiebe, P. 'Christianity and Social Change in South India'. *Practical Anthropology,* May-June, 1970, pp. 128-36.

—— 'Protestant Missions in India: A Sociological Review'. *Journal of Asian and African Studies*, 5 (1970), pp. 293-301.

Wiebe, P. and S. John-Peter. 'The Catholic Church and Caste in Rural Tamil Nadu', in H. Singh (ed), *Caste among the Non-Hindus in India.* Delhi: National Publishing House, 1977.

Wilkinson, T. 'Buddhism and Social Change Among the Mahars', in T. Wilkinson and M. Thomas (eds), *Ambedkar and the Neo-Buddhist Movement.* Madras: The Christian Literature Society, 1972, pp. 71-100.

Wilkinson, T. and M. Thomas (eds). *Ambedkar and the Neo-Buddhist Movement.* Madras: The Christian Literature Society, 1972.

Wingate, A. 'A Study of Conversion from Christianity to Islam in Two Tamil Villages'. *Religion and Society,* 27 (1981), pp. 3-36.

Wiser, W. *The Hindu Jajmani System: A Socio-Economic System Interrelating Members of a Hindu Village Community in Services.* Lucknow: Lucknow Publishing House, 1936.

Wiser, W. and C. Wiser. *Behind Mud Walls: 1930-1960.* Berkeley, CA: University of California Press, 1969.

Yagnik, A. and A. Bhatt. 'The Anti-Dalit Agitation in Gujarat'. *South Asia Bulletin,* 4 (1984), pp. 45-60.

Yalman, N. 'On the Purity of Women in the Castes of Ceylon and Malabar'. *Journal of the Royal Institute of Great Britain and Ireland,* 93 (1963), pp. 25-58.

Yesudas, R. *A People's Revolt in Travancore: A Backward Class Movement for Social Freedom.*Trivandrum: Kerala Historical Society, 1975.

Zelliot, E. 'Dr. Ambedkar and the Mahar Movement'. Doctoral dissertation, University of Pennsylvania,1969.

—— 'Learning the Use of Political Means: The Mahars of Maharashtra', in R. Kothari (ed.), *Caste in Indian Politics.* Poona: Orient Longman, 1970, pp. 29-69.

—— 'Gandhi and Ambedkar – A Study in Leadership', in J. M. Mahar (ed.), *The Untouchables in Contemporary India.* Tucson: University of Arizona Press, 1972.

—— *From Untouchable to Dalit: Essays on Ambedkar Movement.* Delhi: Manohar, 1992.

Index